Emotions and their Influence on our Personal, Interpersonal and Social Experiences

Research indicates that each emotion is associated with cognitive appraisals that influence our decision-making, our behavior, and our relationships. Positive emotions may enhance our point of view and affect our decision to execute what we meant to. Negative emotions are known to not only affect the manner in which we view the world, but our plans, our willingness to interact with others, and our choices, both behaviorally, and cognitively. Emotions are also known to affect us physically. Positive emotions support our immune system, are responsible for our health enhancing behavior, and allow us to be open to our social support network. Negative emotions are known to hamper our immune system and thus make us more prone to illnesses, sometimes life threatening ones, and interfere with successfully coping with them. This book focuses on the role of emotions in everyday life, and particularly, the destructive effects of negative emotions such as anger, anxiety, depression, and the fear of death that humans share.

The articles in this book were originally published in *The Journal of Psychology.*

Ami Rokach is a Clinical Psychologist, specializing in treating and researching loneliness, anxiety conditions, and traumatic experiences. He is the Executive Editor of *The Journal of Psychology*, and teaches in the Psychology Departments of York University, Canada; The Centre for Academic Studies, Israel; and Walden University, USA.

T0347516

Emotions and their Influence on our Personal, Interpersonal and Social Experiences

Edited by
Ami Rokach

Routledge
Taylor & Francis Group

LONDON AND NEW YORK

First published 2018 by Routledge

2 Park Square, Milton Park, Abingdon, Oxfordshire OX14 4RN
52 Vanderbilt Avenue, New York, NY 10017

Routledge is an imprint of the Taylor & Francis Group, an informa business

First issued in paperback 2019

British Library Cataloguing in Publication Data
A catalogue record for this book is available from the British Library

ISBN 13: 978-1-138-29601-5 (hbk)
ISBN 13: 978-0-367-89120-6 (pbk)

Typeset in Times New Roman
by RefineCatch Limited, Bungay, Suffolk

Publisher's Note
The publisher accepts responsibility for any inconsistencies that may have
arisen during the conversion of this book from journal articles to book chapters,
namely the possible inclusion of journal terminology.

Disclaimer
Every effort has been made to contact copyright holders for their permission to
reprint material in this book. The publishers would be grateful to hear from any
copyright holder who is not here acknowledged and will undertake to rectify
any errors or omissions in future editions of this book.

Contents

Citation Information

The following chapters were originally published in *The Journal of Psychology*. When citing this material, please use the original page numbering for each article, as follows:

Chapter 1
Emotion Regulation Strategies, Secondary Traumatic Stress, and Compassion Satisfaction in Healthcare Providers
Cornelia Măirean
The Journal of Psychology, volume 150, issue 8 (2016), pp. 961–975

Chapter 2
Facial Expressions of Emotions: Recognition Accuracy and Affective Reactions During Late Childhood
Giacomo Mancini, Sergio Agnoli, Bruno Baldaro, Pio E. Ricci Bitti and Paola Surcinelli
The Journal of Psychology, volume 147, issue 6 (2013), pp. 599–617

Chapter 3
The Effect of Death Anxiety and Age on Health-Promoting Behaviors: A Terror-Management Theory Perspective
Özlem Bozo, Ayça Tunca and Yelíz Şimşek
The Journal of Psychology, volume 143, issue 4 (2009), pp. 377–389

Chapter 4
The Effects of Material and Experiential Discretionary Purchases on Consumer Happiness: Moderators and Mediators
Rebecca Thomas and Murray Millar
The Journal of Psychology, volume 147, issue 4 (2013), pp. 345–356

Chapter 5
Aggression among Male Alcohol-Dependent Inpatients who Smoke Cigarettes
Omer Saatcioglu and Rahsan Erim
The Journal of Psychology, volume 143, issue 6 (2009), pp. 615–624

Chapter 6
Angry Versus Furious: A Comparison Between Valence and Arousal in Dimensional Models of Emotions
L.Y. Lo, N. L. Hung, and M. Lin
The Journal of Psychology, volume 150, issue 8 (2016), pp. 949–960

Chapter 7

Faces of Shame: Implications for Self-Esteem, Emotion Regulation, Aggression, and Well-Being
Patrizia Velotti, Carlo Garofalo, Federica Bottazzi, and Vincenzo Caretti
The Journal of Psychology, volume 151, issue 2 (2017), pp. 171–184

Chapter 8

The Myth of the Angry Atheist
Brian P. Meier, Adam K. Fetterman, Michael D. Robinson and Courtney M. Lappas
The Journal of Psychology, volume 149, issue 3 (2015), pp. 219–238

Chapter 9

Assessment of Anger Terms in Hebrew: A Gender Comparison
Orly Sarid
The Journal of Psychology, volume 149, issue 3 (2015), pp. 303–324

Chapter 10

The Effects of Dysphoria and Personality on Negative Self-Referent Attitudes and Perceptions of the Attitudes of Others
Shadi Beshai, Jennifer L. Prentice, Jennifer L. Swan and Keith S. Dobson
The Journal of Psychology, volume 149, issue 5 (2015), pp. 498–516

Chapter 11

Hope, Anger, and Depression as Mediators for Forgiveness and Social Behavior in Turkish Children
Ebru Taysi, Ferzan Curun and Fatih Orcan
The Journal of Psychology, volume 149, issue 4 (2015), pp. 378–393

Chapter 12

Hostility/Anger as a Mediator Between College Students' Emotion Regulation Abilities and Symptoms of Depression, Social Anxiety, and Generalized Anxiety
Kia Asberg
The Journal of Psychology, volume 147, issue 5 (2013), pp. 469–490

Chapter 13

Social Hierarchy and Depression: The Role of Emotion Suppression
Carrie A. Langner, Elissa S. Epel, Karen A. Matthews, Judith T. Moskowitz and Nancy E. Adler
The Journal of Psychology, volume 146, issue 4 (2012), pp. 417–436

Chapter 14

Negatively Biased Emotion Perception in Depression as a Contributing Factor to Psychological Aggression Perpetration: A Preliminary Study
Amy D. Marshall, Lauren M. Sippel and Emily L. Belleau
The Journal of Psychology, volume 145, issue 6 (2011), pp. 521–535

For any permission-related enquiries please
visit: http://www.tandfonline.com/page/help/permissions

Notes on Contributors

Nancy E. Adler is the Lisa and John Pritzker Professor of Psychology in the Departments of Psychiatry and Paediatrics at the University of California, San Francisco, USA. Her current research interests include socioeconomic influences on health, reproductive health, and population health.

Sergio Agnoli is a Postdoctoral Research Fellow at the Marconi Institute for Creativity, University of Bologna, Italy. His research interests include emotional intelligence, creativity, emotional development, and the psychophysiology of emotions.

Kia Asberg is Associate Professor at WCU, Cullowhee, NC, USA. She is the Director of the Stress, Violence, Emotions, and Adjustment (SVEA) laboratory and her research interest is in the general area of stress and resilience, with additional focus on emotion regulation and related processes.

Bruno Baldaro is Full Professor of Clinical Psychology at the Department of Psychology, University of Bologna, Italy. His research interests are emotional intelligence, psychosomatic, clinical evaluation, and clinical psychophysiology.

Emily L. Belleau is a Clinical and Research Postdoctoral Fellow at McLean Hospital, Harvard Medical School Affiliate, MA, USA. Her research focuses on examining neurobiological indicators of risk and resiliency to internalizing disorders that lie at the interface of cognition and emotion, through a number of psychophysiological techniques.

Shadi Beshai is Assistant Professor at the University of Regina, Saskatchewan, Canada. His research interests are major depression, adult Cognitive Behavioral Therapy, and psychotherapy.

Pio E. Ricci Bitti is Professor Emeritus of Psychology and a member of the Research Centre for Emotion and Health at the Department of Psychology, University of Bologna, Italy. His research interests are expression and recognition of emotions, interpersonal communication, nonverbal behavior, regulation of emotion and health.

Federica Bottazzi received her Master's degree in Psychology from the University of Genoa, Italy. She plans to pursue a PsyD in Clinical Psychology, with research interests in aggression and emotion.

Özlem Bozo is Associate Professor in the Psychology Department at METU, Ankara, Turkey. Her research interests are gerontological health, caregiver wellbeing, psycho-oncology, and the relations between death anxiety and health-promoting and health-compromising behaviors.

Vincenzo Caretti is Full Professor of Human Sciences at LUMSA University, Rome, Italy. His research interests focus on psychopathy and addictive behaviors. He has been scientific advisor to several academic and inter-institutional programs aimed at understanding, preventing, and treating violent behaviors.

Ferzan Curun is Professor at Yeni Yüzyıl University, Istanbul, Turkey. Her current research interests are close relationships, positive psychology, and self and identity.

Keith S. Dobson is Professor at the University of Calgary, Canada. His research interests include relapse prevention of chronic depression, stigma in mental health, and cognitive-behavioral therapy.

Elissa S. Epel is Associate Professor at the University of California, San Francisco, USA. She is the Director of the Aging, Metabolism, and Emotions Lab, and COAST, Associate Director of the Centre for Health and Community, and Associate Director of the NIH-funded UCSF Nutrition and Obesity Research Centre. Her research interests include social and psychobiological stress mechanisms, obesity, and premature aging at the cellular level.

Rahsan Erim is a Psychiatrist at the Balikesir State Hospital, Turkey. Her research interests are mood disorder, schizophrenia, forensic psychiatry, and substance use disorder.

Adam K. Fetterman is Assistant Professor in the Department of Psychology at the University of Texas at El Paso, USA. His research interests are metaphor, emotion, attitude change, rationality, religiosity, and motivation.

Carlo Garofalo is Assistant Professor in the Department of Developmental Psychology, Tilburg University, The Netherlands. His main research interests concern the role of emotion regulation in the development and manifestation of personality pathology and antisociality, with a specific focus on psychopathic traits.

N. L. Hung is a Counselling Psychologist working in Hong Kong.

Carrie A. Langner is Associate Professor at California Polytechnic State University, San Luis Obispo, USA. Her current research interests include social hierarchy, health disparities, and collective identity.

Courtney M. Lappas is Associate Professor of Biology at Lebanon Valley College, PA, USA. Her research interests are T lymphocyte biology, adenosine receptor signaling, and immunopharmacology.

M. Lin is a Clinical Psychologist and working at Hong Kong Shue Yan University as a Senior Lecturer. Her current research interest is the applications of cognitive behavioral therapy in different domains.

L. Y. Lo is Assistant Professor at Hong Kong Shue Yan University. His current research interests include emotion perception and comparative psychology.

Cornelia Măirean, PhD, is Assistant Professor of Psychology at the Alexandru Ioan Cuza University, Iaşi, Romania. Her principal research interests are traumatic stress, personal growth, emotional adjustment, and transportation research.

Giacomo Mancini is Assistant Professor at the Department of Education Studies, University of Bologna, Italy. His current research interests are emotional intelligence and well-being during childhood and preadolescence.

Amy D. Marshall is Associate Professor of Psychology at Pennsylvania State University, USA. Her research interests include the role of post-traumatic stress disorder, social information processing, and neurohormonal dysregulation in couples' communication behaviors and intimate partner violence.

Karen A. Matthews is Distinguished Professor of Psychiatry at the University of Pittsburgh, PA, USA. Her research interests include cardiovascular risk, socioeconomic status and health, and women's health.

Brian P. Meier is Professor of Psychology at Gettysburg College, PA, USA. His research interests are aggression, embodiment, emotion, mindfulness, pro-social behavior, and religion.

Murray Millar is an Associate Professor at the University of Nevada, Las Vegas, USA. His current research interests are consumer satisfaction and persuasive communications.

Judith T. Moskowitz is Professor at the University of California, San Francisco, USA. Her current research interests include emotion, coping, and chronic stress.

Fatih Orcan is Assistant Professor at Karadeniz Technical University, Trabzon, Turkey. His research interests are structural equation modelling, missing data, and item parcelling.

Jennifer L. Prentice is a doctoral student at the University of Calgary, Canada. Her research interests are cross-cultural psychopathology, specifically depression, and mental illness stigma.

Michael D. Robinson is Professor of Psychology at North Dakota State University, USA. His research interests are personality, cognition, emotion, embodiment, and well-being.

Ami Rokach is a Clinical Psychologist, specializing in treating and researching loneliness, anxiety conditions, and traumatic experiences. He is the Executive Editor of *The Journal of Psychology*, and teaches in the Psychology Departments of York University, Canada; The Centre for Academic Studies, Israel; and Walden University, USA.

Omer Saatcioglu is Professor of Psychiatry at Işik University, Istanbul, Turkey. His research interests are substance use disorder, mood disorder, schizophrenia, and psychiatric rehabilitation.

Orly Sarid is Associate Professor at Ben-Gurion University of the Negev, Israel. Her research interests are stress, mental health, emotions, and behaviors.

Yeliz Şimşek is a graduate of the Psychology Department at METU, Ankara, Turkey. Her research interests are personal factors in healthy lifestyles, the relation between death anxiety and health promoting behaviors, as well as illness prevention and health promotion.

Lauren M. Sippel is Assistant Professor of Psychiatry at the Geisel School of Medicine, Dartmouth College, New Hampshire, USA. Her research interests pertain to how cognitive-processing deficits confer risk for and maintain PTSD, particularly in the context of interpersonal relationships.

Paola Surcinelli is Assistant Professor of Clinical Psychology at the Department of Psychology, University of Bologna, Italy. Her research interests include emotional development, individual differences in emotion recognition and emotional responses, emotion regulation in normal subjects and in clinical groups.

Jennifer L. Swan is a doctoral student at the University of Calgary, Canada. Her current research interests include facilitating self-recovery among disordered gamblers through brief treatments.

Ebru Taysi is Associate Professor at Suleyman Demirel University, Isparta, Turkey. Her current research interests are forgiveness, close relationships, and life-satisfaction and well-being.

Rebecca Thomas is a Senior Predictive Modeler at the Pinnacol Assurance Company and a graduate of the University of Nevada, Las Vegas, USA. Her current research interests are predicting consumer behavior and satisfaction.

Ayça Tunca is a graduate of the Psychology Department at METU, Ankara, Turkey. Her research interests are gender differences in coping with stress, schizophrenic patients' health-promoting behaviors, and the relations among work, stress, and psychological well-being.

Patrizia Velotti is Associate Professor at the Department of Educational Sciences, University of Genoa, Italy. She studies the role of emotion regulation and other intersecting mechanisms linked with mental health and psychopathology. She is Head of the Emotion Regulation Interpersonal and Intergroup Relations Lab where she conducts research projects addressing these issues in laboratory, field, and clinical settings.

Dedication

Dedicated, with love, to Natalie who allows me, on a daily basis, to experience the wonders of positive emotions, and to Benny – who as he was growing up – has unfortunately been subjected to many servings of aggressive, angry, and damaging emotions and behaviors, and to Pnina and Max, my parents, who helped him deal with it and flourish.

Introduction: Emotions and their Effect in Everyday Life

Ami Rokach

McLeod (2007) highlighted the importance that emotions have in our lives, and the reasons that they are as prominent as they are. He stated that an emotion is an immediate physical response to a situation, and it has a direct implication for action. Most of us, he contended, live in complex, crowded urban environments in which we are constantly faced with many, and competing, rules and stimuli. A spontaneous emotional response, under such conditions may lead to trouble. We, thus, learn early on to now allow emotions to dictate our response, but that does not mean that we actually follow it. In contemporary society, especially in the western world, we commonly learn about other people and relationships through personal interactions, and then we gather information about their emotional state, so that we can know how to approach them, or even predict their reactions and plan our responses.

Achar et al (2016) observed that "Emotions are multidimensional feelings that reflect information about consumers' relationship to their social and physical surroundings as well as their interpretations regarding these relationships" (p. 166). These authors examined emotions in relation to consumers' decision making, and noted that it is common now that marketing efforts create an emotional experience in consumers, in hopes of influencing their choices, since a consumer's incidental emotional state affects the decisions she or he might make. Moreover, they added, that appraisals associated with the experience of a specific emotion can 'carry over' by predisposing individuals' view of other unrelated events in line with the preexisting appraisals. Thus, for instance, fear or anger may lead to pessimistic risk perceptions where the person feels that he has little control, and anger may lead to optimistic risk perceptions, proving the impression that the individual has high control. Emotional experiences, added Xie & Zhang (2016), modulate various cognitive and perceptual processes, and although most of the research to date has focused on the effect of negative emotions, it is positive emotions and their influences on human cognition and behavior that have started to attract the interest of researchers, given their major roles in promoting better social affective functioning, such as subjective well-being.

Hillebrandt & Barclay (2017) reviewed research that highlighted the interpersonal effects of emotions. They asserted that emotions serve an important social function by communicating to those around, information about the person's state of mind and possible behavior, allowing prediction and planning of a response, such as when one is angry, and that may signal a readiness to harm others or self. While McLeod (2007) declared that "On the whole, we live in a world where rationality is valued and emphasized over emotion" (p. 171), Zhang, Kong & Li (2017) pointed out that even moral judgment, which in the past was regarded as completely rational, is now being seen as heavily influenced by one's emotions, so that the final moral judgment is the product of the interaction of emotions and reason. Humphrey, Burch & Adams (2016) indicated a close association between leadership and emotions, and recommended that researchers from both areas combine them in their research. They further stated that leadership is inherently an emotional process, where charismatic leadership attributes an important role in the leader's ability to inspire followers and create a sense of community. Such leadership may be particularly critical at times of crisis, or in times of great opportunities, when emotions are likely to be highly engaged.

Subjective well-being has been considered as one of the core issues in the field of positive psychology (see Lucas & Diener, 2015 for review). It has been suggested that subjective well-being (SWB) has three components: positive affect, negative affect, and life satisfaction (cognitive evaluation of one's life as a whole). Emotions are clearly associated with one's SWB, satisfaction from life, and a sense of achievement or failure to achieve (McCrea & Costa, 1987; Park, Peterson & Seligman, 2004). Needless to say, the sample of sources cited above, clearly indicates the importance and even centrality of emotions in our perceptions, judgments, and behaviors. That was the incentive in bringing the present volume to print.

This volume is a compilation of fourteen articles that are divided into three sections: (1) Emotions and their effect (2) Anger and aggression, and (3) Sadness, depression and anxiety. Below I will, briefly, describe each article, and indicate its way of contributing to our review of the field of emotions.

Emotions and their effect

Măirean addressed emotional regulation strategies, and focused on cognitive reappraisal and expressive suppression, secondary traumatic stress, and compassion satisfaction as expressed by healthcare providers. Another aim of this study was to examine if the relations between emotion regulation strategies and traumatic stress symptoms are moderated by compassion satisfaction. Results indicated the presence of negative associations between cognitive reappraisal and secondary traumatic stress, while expressive suppression is positively associated with arousal. Additionally, it was found, that cognitive reappraisal is positively related to compassion satisfaction, while secondary traumatic stress symptoms are negatively correlated with compassion satisfaction.

Mancini, Agnoli, Baldaro, Bitti, and Surcinelli examined the development of recognition ability and affective reactions to emotional facial expressions. More specifically, they aimed at exploring whether changes in the emotion recognition ability and the affective reactions associated with the viewing of facial expressions occur during late childhood. Their results revealed an overall increase in emotional face recognition ability from 8 to 11 years of age, particularly for neutral and sad expressions. Their results also indicated a gender difference, and found different developmental trends in males and females regarding the recognition of disgust. Additionally they found developmental changes in affective reactions to emotional facial expressions. They observed that whereas recognition ability increased over the developmental time period studied, affective reactions elicited by facial expressions were characterized by a decrease in arousal over the course of late childhood.

Bozo, Tunca, and Şimşek examined the effect of death anxiety on the reports of health-promoting behaviors and wanted to determine the role of age in this relation using a terror-management theory perspective. Participants were 100 individuals from young adult (those who were 20–35 years of age) and older adult (those who were 60 years of age and older) groups, whom the authors assigned to the death anxiety or control conditions. Employing ANOVA to analyze the results, it did not yield a significant main effect for age, but the main effect for the conditions was significant, indicating that people in the death anxiety condition reported more health-promoting behaviors than did people in the control condition. The interaction of the age and conditions was also significant.

Thomas and Millar examined the association of emotions with purchases done by buyers. The focus was on two types: experiential purchases which serve the purpose of acquiring a life experience, and material purchases which serve the purpose of acquiring an object. Research, to date, has demonstrated that experiential purchases are associated with more happiness than material purchases. And so, the current study investigated how the purchase influenced the self and how the purchase influenced interpersonal relationships. It was found that Impacts on the Self mediated the relationship between purchase type and happiness and Socioeconomic Status moderated the relationship.

Anger and aggression

Saatcioglu and Erim explored the relation between nicotine dependence and the severity of aggression among Turkish male alcohol-dependent inpatients who smoked cigarettes, as well as the effect of aggression in these groups. They found differences between male alcohol-dependent inpatients with nicotine dependence and those with non-dependence. Their findings indicated that smoking cigarettes (an addiction frequently observed with alcoholism) was positively correlated with aggressive behaviors. The authors suggested that smoking cigarettes may cause aggression or aggression may cause smoking. They further noted that exploring aggression and smoking cigarettes in association with alcohol dependence may help relapse prevention and improve effectiveness of treatment interventions in alcoholism.

Lo, Hung, and Lin investigated the 'dimensional model of emotions', and compared the roles of valence and arousal in recognizing emotional expressions. Their results indicated that the dimension of valence, due to its functional significance, would be more salient in the recognition of emotional expressions than the dimension of arousal would be. They found that participants in all age groups were more accurate and quicker in recognizing an emotion when the expression was paired up with another emotional expression that was different in the polarity of the valence dimension than with this similar polarity difference in the arousal dimension.

Velotti, Garofalo, Bottazzi and Caretti in an attempt to confirm previous knowledge on shame in association with other aspects of psychological functioning and well-being investigated the nomological network of shame experiences in a community sample, adopting a multidimensional conceptualization of shame. Results indicated that females scored higher than males on shame (in particular, bodily and behavioral shame), guilt, psychological distress, emotional reappraisal, and hostility. Males, on the other hand, reported higher levels of self-esteem, emotional suppression, and physical aggression. Associations between characterological shame and emotional suppression, as well as between bodily shame and anger occurred only among females. Among females they found that emotional suppression mediated the influence of characterological shame on hostility and psychological distress.

Meier, Fetterman, Robinson, and Lappas observed that although atheists disagree with the pillar of many religions, namely the existence of a God, it may not necessarily be the case that they are the angry individuals they may often be portrayed as the media. Meier et al examined the prevalence and accuracy of angry-atheist perceptions in seven studies with 1,677 participants from multiple institutions and locations in the United States. In studies 1–3 they found that people believe atheists are angrier than believers, people in general, and other minority groups, both explicitly and implicitly. Studies 4–7 then examined the accuracy of these beliefs. Belief in God, state anger, and trait anger were assessed in multiple ways and contexts. None of these studies showed any support for the popular belief that atheists are particularly angry individuals.

Sarid, an Israeli researcher, observed that appraisal of anger terms is based on past experience recollections, social norms, and gender roles. She examined anger terms in Hebrew (the language spoken in Israel), in order to find combinations of emotional components presented by a new composite variable that will exhibit differences between genders. Participants were asked to rate eight anger terms in Hebrew on a number of features that comprised five emotional components:

subjective feelings states, body reactions, expressions, action tendencies, and cognitive evaluations. Sarid found that simplified multivariate composite (defined as subjective experience minus regulation) explained 10% of the gender difference, while another simplified composite (combining the additive effect of the subjective experience and the actions that accompany this emotional state) explained 14% of difference between the anger terms. The author then discussed her findings in light of appraisal theory and social constructivist conceptualization.

Sadness, depression and anxiety

Beshai, Prentice, Swan, and Dobson were interested in how depressed individuals perceive the attitudes and perceptions of others, a perception which will clearly affect their interactions and responses to those around them. They found that individuals higher on dysphoria and sociotropy scores, were less likely to perceive others as harboring negative attitudes about themselves in comparison to those with elevated dysphoria and lower levels of sociotropy. Additionally, they noted, individuals showing elevated dysphoria and higher scores on subdomains of autonomy were more likely to perceive others as exhibiting negative attitudes about themselves than those with low levels of the trait.

Taysi, Curun and Orcan investigated forgiveness and social behavior of fourth grade students in Turkey, and its interactions with hope, anger, and depression. Results showed that depression mediates the relationship between anger and antisocial behavior and between hope and antisocial behavior. Anger mediates the relationship between hope and depression and between hope and antisocial behavior. Forgiveness was related to anger and hope directly.

Asberg examined the implications of internalizing problems among college students. She found that although college students' emotion regulation abilities corresponded with all types of internalizing symptoms, hostility/anger mediated fully the relationship for symptoms of depression and social anxiety, but not generalized anxiety (GAD). They added that the stronger interpersonal aspect inherent in depression and social anxiety relative to GAD may in part explain their findings, and propose that interventions and programs aimed at reducing internalizing problems, be instituted.

Langner, Epel, Matthews, Moskowitz, and Adler focused on social hierarchy, as a major determinant of health outcomes. They examined the associations between aspects of social hierarchy and depression, specifically focusing on emotion suppression. Suppressing negative emotions has mental health costs, but individuals with low social power and low social status may use these strategies to avoid conflict. Their results indicated that low social power was related to greater depressive symptoms, and this relationship was partially mediated by emotion suppression. In their second study they found that low education levels were correlated with greater depressive symptoms, and this relationship was partially mediated by anger suppression. Further, their results showed that suppression mediated the relationship between low education and subsequent depression up to 15 years later.

Marshall, Sippel, and Belleau focused on intimate partner aggression, and examined biased perception of emotional expressions as a mechanism in the frequently observed relationship between depression and psychological aggression perpetration. Their results indicated that depressive symptoms were positively correlated with psychological aggression perpetration in one's current intimate relationship, and this relationship was mediated by ratings of negative emotional expressions. These findings suggest that negatively biased perception of emotional expressions in a depressed person, may be an early stage of information processing that leads to aggressive relationship behaviors.

I truly hope that you will find this volume a worthwhile reference to the myriad influences that emotions have on various aspects of our lives, and which it is incumbent on us to identify, and learn how to approach and harness to our benefit.

References

Achar, C., So, J., Agrawal, N., & Duhachek, A. (2016). What we feel and why we buy: the influence of emotions on consumer decision-making. *Current Opinion in Psychology*, 10, 166–170. doi:10.1016/j.copsyc.2016.01.009

Hillebrandt, A., & Barclay, L. J. (2017). Comparing integral and incidental emotions: Testing insights from emotions as social information theory and attribution theory. *Journal of Applied Psychology*. doi:10.1037/apl0000174

Humphrey, R. H., Burch, G. F., & Adams, L. L. (2016). The benefits of merging leadership research and emotions research. *Frontiers in Psychology*, 7. doi:10.3389/fpsyg.2016.01022

McCrae, R. R., & Costa, P. T. (1987). Validation of the five-factor model of personality across instruments and observers. *Journal of Personality and Social Psychology*, 52, 81–90.

McLeod, J. (2007). Counseling skill. Berkshire, England: Open University Press, McGraw-Hill Education.

Park, N., Peterson, C., & Seligman, M. E. P. (2004). Strengths of character and wellbeing. *Journal of Social and Clinical Psychology*, 23, 603–619. doi: 10.1521/jscp.23.5.603.50748

Xie, W., & Zhang, W. (2016). The influence of emotion on face processing. *Cognition and Emotion*, 30(2), 245–257. doi:10.1080/02699931.2014.994477

Zhang, L., Kong, M., & Li, Z. (2017). Emotion regulation difficulties and moral judgment in different domains: The mediation of emotional valence and arousal. *Personality and Individual Differences*, 109, 56–60. doi:10.1016/j.paid.2016.12.049

Emotion Regulation Strategies, Secondary Traumatic Stress, and Compassion Satisfaction in Healthcare Providers

Cornelia Măirean

ABSTRACT

The aim of the present study is to examine the relationships between two emotion regulation strategies (cognitive reappraisal and expressive suppression), secondary traumatic stress, and compassion satisfaction in a sample of 190 healthcare providers. Another aim of this study is to examine if the relations between emotion regulation strategies and traumatic stress symptoms are moderated by compassion satisfaction. The respondents volunteered to take part in the research and completed self-reporting measures describing the use of emotional regulation strategies, the symptoms of secondary traumatic stress, and the compassion satisfaction. The results revealed negative associations between cognitive reappraisal and secondary traumatic stress, while expressive suppression is positively associated with arousal. Moreover, cognitive reappraisal is positively related to compassion satisfaction, while secondary traumatic stress symptoms are negatively correlated with compassion satisfaction. Furthermore, the relationship between expressive suppression and intrusions is moderated by compassion satisfaction. The implications of these results for enhancing professional quality of life in the context of secondary exposure to traumatic life events are discussed.

Introduction

In the context of healthcare, stressful life events do not occur in isolation from each other. It is well-documented that continuous exposure to traumatic life events predicts maladjustment, emotional exhaustion, feelings of distress, dissatisfaction, and secondary traumatic stress (Jeon & Ha, 2012; Măirean, 2016; Van der Wath, van Wyk, & Janse van Rensburg, 2013). These manifestations have been documented in different samples, including nurses and physicians from various fields (Duffy, Avalos, & Dowling, 2015; Măirean, 2016; Măirean & Turliuc, 2013; Young, Derr, Cicchillo, & Bressler, 2011). Concerning the secondary traumatic stress, the percentage of nurses affected vary from 21.42% (Măirean, 2016) to 82% of the sample (Duffy et al., 2015). Among physicians, previous studies report that considerable percentage of the samples (e.g., 35.2%) are at extremely high risk for secondary traumatization (El-bar, Levy, Wald, & Biderman, 2013).

Since continuous exposure to human pain and trauma, overload and emergency situations lead to a variety of negative emotions, people often try to control the way they feel or express different emotional states (Tschan, Rochat, & Zapf, 2005). Emotion regulation is defined as a process through which a person modulates his/her emotions elicited by daily events, consciously and unconsciously, in order to reduce their intensity and to respond appropriately to different environmental demands (Campbell-Sills & Barlow, 2007; Gratz & Roemer, 2004; Rottenberg & Gross, 2003). There are different emotional regulation strategies, considered either adaptive or maladaptive, especially based on their relationships to psychopathology (see reviews in Aldao, Nolen-Hoeksema, & Schweizer, 2010; Nolen-Hoeksema & Watkins, 2011). However, despite important progress in this field, a minimal amount of research was conducted to identify the relationship between emotion regulation strategies and specific outcomes in the context of secondary exposure to trauma. This study seeks to advance a better understanding of the relationship among emotion regulation, secondary traumatic stress, and compassion satisfaction, defined as the pleasure derived from being able to do the work well, in a sample of healthcare providers. Moreover, the interaction between emotion regulation and compassion satisfaction in predicting secondary traumatic stress is addressed. Two emotion regulation strategies, cognitive reappraisal and expressive suppression, were examined.

Reappraisal, Suppression, and Secondary Traumatic Stress

Gross (1998) identified two types of emotion regulation strategies: antecedent-focused strategies (regulatory efforts to control the emotional response tendencies, before they have become fully activated) and response-focused strategies (regulatory efforts to control the emotional responses, after they have been generated). Cognitive Reappraisal (CR) is an antecedent-focused emotion regulation strategy that involves thinking differently about a situation in order to change its meaning and emotional impact (Gross, 1998). Expressive suppression (ES) is a response-focused emotion regulation strategy that involves efforts attempting to actively inhibit the observable ongoing expression of emotional experience (Gross & Thompson, 2007) as a way of reducing distress (Gross, 1998). There is empirical evidence supporting the assumption that there are relatively stable tendencies that determine an individual to systematically use a particular emotion regulation strategy in different emotion eliciting situations (e.g., John & Gross, 2004; Liu, Prati, Perrewe, & Brymer, 2010).

Cognitive reappraisal and expressive suppression are considered as coping mechanisms and have been studied in association with different psychological outcomes. Previous studies showed that reappraisal appears to be effective across a variety of contexts, being associated with low levels of psychopathology (Aldao et al., 2010), with reduced negative affectivity (e.g., Goldin, McRae, Ramel, & Gross, 2008), increased pain tolerance (Hayes et al., 1999), greater self-esteem (Gross & John, 2003), increased levels of psychological well-being (Matta, Erol-Korkmaz, Johnson, & Biçaksiz, 2014), and even diminished cardiac reactivity (e.g., Campbell-Sills, Barlow, Brown, & Hofmann, 2006). On the other hand, the use of suppression has been linked to reduced positive affect and life satisfaction, low quality of life (Ciuluvica, Amerio, & Fulcheri, 2014), higher depression (e.g., Langner, Epel, Matthews, Moskowitz, & Adler, 2012), anxiety (Lemaire, El-Hage & Frangou, 2014), eating disorders (e.g., Evers, Stok, & De Ridder, 2010), and borderline personality disorder (e.g., Dixon-Gordon, Chapman, Lovasz, & Walters, 2011).

Several studies suggest a relationship between emotion regulation and posttraumatic stress symptoms (Bardeen, Kumpula, & Orcutt, 2013; Bonn-Miller, Vujanovic, Boden, &

Gross, 2011; Vujanovic, Bonn-Miller, Potter, Marshall, & Zvolensky, 2011). Specifically, cognitive reappraisal is generally associated with a low level of traumatic stress, whereas expressive suppression is associated with a high level of traumatic stress symptoms (e.g. Boden et al., 2013; Ehring & Quack, 2010; Moore, Zoellner, & Mollenholt, 2008). Although the previous studies mainly analyzed the relationship between emotion regulation and posttraumatic stress symptoms in persons directly exposed to traumatic life events, similar relationships may be identified between emotion regulation and secondary traumatic stress symptoms, as these symptoms are the same as those of PTSD experienced in persons directly exposed to the traumatic event (Beck & Gable, 2012). Moreover, a recent study confirmed the negative association between thoughts suppression and intrusions, symptoms of secondary traumatic stress, in a sample of medical workers (Turliuc, Măirean, & Turliuc, 2015). Another study documented the relationship between emotional regulation difficulties and stress, for persons indirectly exposed to traumas (psychologists). In this study, stress is operationalized as symptoms of arousal, a specific component of secondary traumatic stress (Finlay-Jones, Rees, & Kane, 2015). However, additional empirical evidence is needed to clearly confirm these patterns of results, in the context of secondary trauma exposure. Therefore, the first aim of the present research is to assess the relationship between cognitive reappraisal, expressive suppression, and the symptoms of secondary traumatic stress, after secondary exposure to trauma.

Role of Compassion Satisfaction

Compassion satisfaction is a component of the healthcare providers' professional quality of life and describes the orientation that a person has towards his/her jobs, in the field of working with persons that are in a critical situation and need the others' help to survive (Duarte, Pinto-Gouveia, & Cruz, 2016; Sansó et al., 2015). Moreover, compassion satisfaction has been defined as the pleasure derived from being able to do the work well, the pleasure that an employee has by helping others through his/her work, by contributing to others' well-being or even to the greater good of society (Larsen & Stamm, 2008; Stamm, 2010). Therefore, compassion satisfaction includes the ability to receive joy, gratification, and sense of purpose derived from providing care (Mangoulia, Koukia, Alevizopoulos, Fildissis, & Katostaras, 2015).

In the context of emotions generated by the work environment, some studies attempted to link emotion regulation with different work outcomes. Some previous studies with mixed samples comprised from persons that work in service industry and frequently require interaction with bosses, co-workers, and customers, showed that the persons who use reappraisal frequently experience greater satisfaction from their job, because they are better at dealing with stressful work situations and are able to maintain a positive affective state in spite of aversive situations. In contrast, the persons who use suppression report a more negative affect, lower job satisfaction, and a higher intention to quit compared to individuals who rarely use this emotion regulation strategy (Cote & Morgan, 2002). These results can be explained by the fact that emotion suppression leads to an emotional dissonance described as a lack of authenticity and a discrepancy between public displays of emotions and internal experiences of emotions (Heuven, Bakker, Schaufeli, & Huisman, 2006; Morris & Feldman, 1997). This psychological state may give rise to negative emotional experiences and emotional exhaustion, which further lead to low satisfaction (Morris & Feldman, 1997). Suppressed, but not eliminated, displays of unpleasant emotions are unlikely to improve social interaction and emotional states (Cote & Morgan, 2002). On the other hand, in a sample of employees in a hospice, a study showed that suppression was not significantly linked to one's emotional state at work (Liu et al., 2010). Although few studies have analyzed the association between emotion regulation and satisfaction with the workplace demands, we can assume that there is a link between these variables based on the previous studies that largely supported the fact that reappraisal has generally more favorable implications for psychological wellbeing and life satisfaction than suppression (John & Gross, 2004). However, future studies are needed in order to understand the relationship between emotional regulation strategies and satisfaction delivered from a secondary exposure to human pain and suffering. Therefore, the second goal of the present study is to assess the relationship between cognitive reappraisal, expressive suppression, and compassion satisfaction, in persons indirectly exposed to traumatic life events.

Among the positive outcomes associated with compassion satisfaction is the fact that it can balance the negative effects of caring, buffering the effects of stressful emotional states (Hooper, Craig, Janvrin, Wetsel, & Reimels, 2010; Poulin, Brown, Dillard, & Smith, 2013). Previous studies showed that healthcare providers with higher levels of compassion satisfaction have healthy coping mechanisms and resources to process and prevent the development of secondary traumatic events (Makic, 2015). Consequently, these persons report lower levels of secondary trauma (Berger, Polivka, Ann Smoot, & Owens, 2015; Hinderer et al., 2014; Sodeke-Gregson, Holttum, & Billings, 2013). Studying the relationship between compassion satisfaction and secondary traumatic stress represents the third aim of the present study. Moreover, given the fact that compassion satisfaction can prevent the development of secondary traumatic stress, we can assume that the relationship between emotion regulation and secondary traumatic stress is moderated by compassion satisfaction. According to Dutton and Rubinstein's (1995) theoretical model, both strategies for coping with stressful situations and compassion satisfaction are predictive of the development of secondary traumatic stress among healthcare providers. However, it was not examined how emotion regulation strategies, as coping strategies, and compassion satisfaction work together in accounting for variations in secondary trauma; therefore, the fourth aim of the present study is to assess the interaction between emotional regulation strategies and compassion satisfaction in predicting secondary traumatic stress.

Based on previous studies and extending previous results in the field, we propose the following hypotheses: (a) cognitive reappraisal will be negatively associated with secondary traumatic stress, whereas expressive suppression will be positively associated with secondary traumatic stress; (b) cognitive reappraisal will be positively associated with compassion satisfaction, whereas expressive suppression will be negatively associated with compassion satisfaction; (c) compassion satisfaction will be negatively associated with traumatic stress symptoms; and (d) the relationship between emotion regulation and traumatic stress symptoms will be moderated by compassion satisfaction.

Method

Participants

A number of 207 questionnaires were distributed to nurses and physicians from several hospitals in Romania. Participants who provided incomplete data were not included in the analysis. In total, 190 employees (87.4% female) participated in this study (72.1% nurses). The

Table 1. Demographic and professional characteristics of participants.

	N	%	M	SD
Age			33.27	10.71
Experience (years)			9.81	8.18
Hours per week			33.99	8.49
Gender				
Female	166	87.4%		
Male	24	12.6%		
Profession				
Physicians	53	27.9%		
Nurses	137	72.1%		

Note. N = 190.

ages of the participants varied between 20 and 65 years ($M = 33.27$, $SD = 10.71$). The experience in the healthcare field ranges from 1 to 40 years ($M = 9.81$ years, $SD = 8.18$), and the participants work with patients between 15 and 50 hours per week ($M = 33.99$, $SD = 8.49$) (see Table 1). The participants were selected from different hospital sections, including intensive care, cardiology, oncology, neurology, surgery, and urology.

Measures

The instruments were translated into Romanian using the forward-backward translation design, taking into account the guidelines recommended for adapting scales (Hambleton, 2005). No major discrepancies between the originals and the back-translated versions were identified. In order to verify the factorial validity of the scale, we used confirmatory factor analysis (CFA). For the model fit we applied the maximum-likelihood estimation and reported the following fit indexes: Root Mean Square Error of Approximation (RMSEA), Comparative Fit Index (CFI), and Tucker-Lewis Index (TLI) (Hu & Bentler, 1999). The results are presented below, for each scale.

The *Emotion Regulation Questionnaire* (ERQ; Gross & John, 2003) is a 10-item self-reporting scale designed to measure an individual's tendency to use cognitive reappraisal (six items: e.g. *When I want to feel less negative emotions (such as sadness or anger), I change what I'm thinking about.*) and expressive suppression (four items: e.g. *I control my emotions by not expressing them.*) to regulate emotions. Each item consists of a seven-point Likert scale (1—strongly disagree; 7—strongly agree). In the present study, the Cronbach Alphas for both cognitive reappraisal (.71) and expressive suppression subscales (.72) were acceptable. Confirmatory factor analysis (CFA) revealed the fact that one item (*I keep my emotions to myself.*) measuring expressive suppression has a squared multiple correlation lower than the recommended threshold of .20 (.177). After removing it, the model fit results were: χ^2 (23) = 24.94, $p = .353$; RMSEA = .02, 90% CI: [.01, .07]; CFI = .99; GFI = .97; TLI = .98). Taking into account the recommended thresholds for these values, we consider this model to fit the data to a satisfactory degree. Previous studies showed that ERQ has good reliability in samples comprised of trauma-exposed participants (Moore et al., 2008) or employees secondary exposed to trauma (e.g. Liu et al., 2010).

The *Professional Quality of Life Scale* (ProQOL; Stamm, 2010) is a 30-item scale designed to measure one's professional quality of life on two dimensions: compassion satisfaction and compassion fatigue. For the purpose of this research only the compassion satisfaction scale (10 items: e.g. *I am pleased with how I am able to keep up with [helping] techniques and protocols.*) was used. The Cronbach Alpha for this current sample is 0.86. The model fit results were satisfactory: χ^2 (18) = 34.33, p = .011; RMSEA = .06, 90% CI: [.03, .10]; CFI = .97; GFI = .95; TLI = .92). The instrument has been tested extensively and found to be reliable and valid as a measure of the three separate concepts, in samples comprised of nurses (Berger et al., 2015; Hooper et al., 2010; Young et al., 2011) and therapists who work with adult trauma clients (Sodeke-Gregson et al., 2013).

The *Secondary Traumatic Stress Scale* (STSS; Bride, Robinson, Yegidis, & Figley, 2004) is a 17-item scale designed to measure secondary trauma on three dimensions: intrusion (e.g., *Reminders of my work with clients upset me*), avoidance (e.g., *I had little interest in being around others*), and arousal (e.g., *I had trouble sleeping*). On a 5-point Likert scale, the respondents indicated their agreement with items that reflect specific responses related to their work with victims of traumatic life events. A higher total score indicates a higher level of secondary traumatic stress. The Cronbach Alphas for this current sample were 0.70 (intrusion), 0.79 (avoidance), respectively 0.77 (arousal). The model fits the data well: χ^2 (96) = 149.17, p = .002; RMSEA = .05, 90% CI: [.03, .07]; CFI = .96; GFI = .91; TLI = .94). Many published studies using the STSS demonstrated evidence for the scale's internal consistency, as well as convergent and discriminant validity in different samples of persons indirectly exposed to trauma, like hospital social workers (Badger, Royse, & Craig, 2008), interviewers of abused children (Perron & Hiltz, 2006), nurses, and physicians (Dominguez-Gomez & Rutledge, 2009; Duffy et al., 2015; Turliuc et al., 2015).

Demographic variables were collected via a questionnaire that covered age, gender, hospital unit, hours of work per week as well as work experience in the field.

Procedure

The participants volunteered to take part in the research of their own accord. Informed consent was obtained from all the participants. The participants were informed that their participation was voluntary, that the information would be kept confidential and would not become part of their evaluation. They were not remunerated for the participation. Since the workload in the workplace is high, the participants had one week to complete the survey and to leave it in a box placed within each unit. The participants completed all measures anonymously to protect their confidentiality, in the following order: demographics, ERQ, PROQ, and STSS. The importance of giving truthful answers was emphasized.

Overview of the Statistical Analyses

A preliminary analysis was conducted in order to investigate whether the profession (physicians vs. nurses), the professional experience, and the hours of work per week were related to reappraisal, suppression, compassion satisfaction, and secondary traumatic stress. Next, the correlation among the main study variables is presented. Then, it was tested whether the relationship between cognitive reappraisal, expressive suppression and secondary traumatic stress symptoms is moderated by compassion satisfaction. Hierarchical regression models for secondary traumatic stress symptoms were conducted, with professional experience as a covariate in step one, cognitive reappraisal, expressive suppression, and compassion satisfaction in step two; interactions between emotional regulation strategies and compassion satisfaction were entered in the final step. The variables were centered to minimize multicollinearity.

Results

Preliminary Analyses

The independent samples t-tests indicated no significant differences between physicians and nurses on reappraisal, suppression, compassion satisfaction, and secondary traumatic stress symptoms (all $p > .05$). Moreover, the results showed that there were no significant correlations between professional experience and hours of work per week, on the one hand, and reappraisal, suppression, and compassion satisfaction, on the other hand (all $p > .05$). The number of years of professional experience is negatively related to intrusions ($r = -.20, p < .001$).

Association Among the Main Study Variables

Descriptive statistics and intercorrelations for all variables included in the study are presented in Table 2. The results revealed negative correlations between cognitive reappraisal and intrusions ($r = -.19; p < .001$), avoidance ($r = -.34; p < .001$), and arousal ($r = -.39; p < .001$). Expressive suppression is positively associated with arousal ($r = .16; p = .049$). Moreover, cognitive reappraisal is positively associated with compassion satisfaction ($r = .27; p < .001$), while expressive suppression is only marginally negatively associated with compassion satisfaction ($r = -.13; p = .073$). Compassion satisfaction was negatively correlated with intrusions ($r = -.17, p = .017$), avoidance ($r = -.36, p < .001$) and arousal ($r = -.33, p < .001$). Based on Cohen's (2013) criteria for magnitude of effect sizes, all the above relationships are small to medium. None of the correlation coefficients for the relationships between the variables exceeded .80, suggesting no problems with multicolinearity (Tabachnik & Fidell, 2007).

Testing for Moderation

Hierarchical regression analysis was used to assess if compassion satisfaction interact with emotion regulation strategies in predicting secondary traumatic stress symptoms.

Cognitive reappraisal is a negative predictor of intrusions ($\beta = -0.19, t = -2.36, p = .019$), avoidance ($\beta = -0.31, t = -4.15, p < .001$) and arousal ($\beta = -0.38, t = -5.06, p < .001$). Moreover, compassion satisfaction is a negative predictor of all three symptoms of secondary traumatic stress: intrusions ($\beta = -0.13, t = -1.59, p = .011$), avoidance ($\beta = -0.28,$

Table 2. Pearson correlations, means, and SDs of analysed variables.

	M	SD	1	2	3	4	5	6	7	8
1. Reappraisal	27.16	4.01	.71							
2. Suppression	14.03	4.05	.14	.72						
3. Intrusions	11.08	3.68	−.19**	.13†	.70					
4. Avoidance	14.74	5.01	−.34**	.12†	.68**	.79				
5. Arousal	10.40	4.07	−.39**	.16*	.69**	.79**	.77			
6. Compassion satisfaction	39.15	6.18	.27**	−.13†	−.17*	−.36**	−.33**	.86		
7. Prof. experience	7.81	8.18	−.01	−.04	−.20**	−.06	−.12	−.03		
8. Hours per week	33.99	8.49	.01	−.03	−.02	−.13	−.12	.07	.19**	

Note. Cronbach's alphas are reported in the diagonals for each respective scale.
**$p < .001$. *$p < .05$. $N = 190$; † = the relations are marginally significant.

Table 3. Hierarchical regression models of emotional regulation strategies and compassion satisfaction on secondary traumatic stress symptoms (intrusions, avoidance, and arousal).

	β	t	ΔR^2	ΔF
Intrusions				
Step 1			0.05***	9.61**
Professional experience	−0.25**	−3.10		
Step 2			0.12***	4.23**
Reappraisal	−0.19*	−2.36		
Suppression	0.12	1.45		
CS	−0.13*	−1.59		
Step 3			0.13***	1.40*
CRxCS	−0.49	−0.83		
ESxCS	0.72*	1.43		
Avoidance				
Step 1			0.01	0.70
Professional experience	−0.04	−0.35		
Step 2			0.22***	14.18***
Reappraisal	−0.31***	−4.15		
Suppression	0.11	1.50		
CS	−0.28***	−3.66		
Step 3			0.23***	1.28
CRxCS	−0.25	−0.42		
ESxCS	0.70	0.17		
Arousal				
Step 1			0.01	2.97
Professional experience	−0.08	−0.64		
Step 2			0.23***	14.63***
Reappraisal	−0.38***	−5.06		
Suppression	0.13	1.67		
CS	−0.20**	−2.63		
Step 3			0.23***	0.33
CRxCS	0.10	0.16		
ESxCS	0.31	0.62		

Note. CR = cognitive reappraisal; ES = expressive suppression; CS = compassion satisfaction; $N = 190$.
*$p < .05$. **$p < .01$. ***$p < .001$.

$t = −3.66, p < .001$), arousal ($\beta = −0.20, t = −2.63, p = .008$). Furthermore, the interaction between expressive suppression and compassion satisfaction was significant in predicting intrusions ($\beta = 0.72, t = 1.43, p = .043$). The results are shown in Table 3.

We explored the moderating role of compassion satisfaction by calculating mean intrusions values for low, medium and high levels of cognitive reappraisal and compassion satisfaction. Medium values are based on the mean and the low and high levels of the variable are one standard deviation below and above the mean, respectively (Aiken, West, & Reno, 1991). The results showed that for the participants with a high tendency to use expressive suppression, there are no significant differences in the level of intrusions, according to their level of compassion satisfaction. However, the participants with a low tendency to use suppression show a lower level of intrusions when they have a high level of compassion satisfaction. Figure 1 displays the plot of the moderation effect.

Discussion

The goal of this present study was to enhance our understanding of the relationship between emotion regulation strategies, compassion satisfaction, and secondary traumatic stress in the context of secondary trauma exposure. The results shed light on (a) the direct relationships

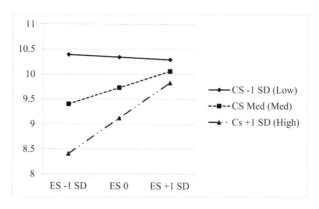

Figure 1. Presence of intrusions as a function of expressive suppression and compassion satisfaction. *Notes.* ES = expressive suppression, CS = compassion satisfaction. Simple effects were represented with expressive suppression and compassion satisfaction defined as at least +1 and −1 standard deviations from the mean, respectively.

between the above presented variables and (b) the interaction between emotional regulation strategies and compassion satisfaction in predicting secondary traumatic stress.

First, as expected, the results showed negative associations between cognitive reappraisal and all three symptoms of secondary traumatic stress—intrusions, avoidance, and arousal. Expressive suppression is positively associated with arousal and it is only marginally positively associated with intrusions and avoidance. Specifically, a high level of cognitive reappraisal is associated with a low level of intrusions, avoidance, and arousal, caused by secondary exposure to human pain, while a higher tendency to use expressive suppression is associated with a high level of arousal. This pattern of results offers an empirical support for the fact that the relationship among cognitive reappraisal, expressive suppression, and traumatic stress is highly similar in persons directly and indirectly exposed to traumatic life events (Boden et al., 2013; Moore et al., 2008).

Furthermore, we aimed to explore the associations between emotion regulation strategies and compassion satisfaction. The results showed that cognitive reappraisal was positively associated with compassion satisfaction. Therefore, these findings may suggest that the employees who use cognitive reappraisal of different situations may be more able to find meaning in their professional activities. These results are in line with previous studies, confirming the fact that cognitive reappraisal is a strategy that promotes increased levels of quality of life and psychological well-being (Gross & John, 2003; Matta et al., 2014). Moreover, it expands the previous results, by examining the relationship between cognitive reappraisal and compassion satisfaction, a less studied relation in the context of healthcare.

Quite unexpectedly, there were no significant correlations between expressive suppression and compassion satisfaction. Although we found a previous study that led to the same result (Liu et al., 2010), the relationship that we found between suppression of emotions generated by the work environment and work outcomes is different from what had been found in most of the previous research (e.g., Cote & Morgan, 2002; Gross & John, 2003). The expected negative relationship between expressive suppression of unpleasant emotions and compassion satisfaction was not supported by the current study. There are several possible reasons why the suppression of unpleasant emotions might not be associated with compassion satisfaction. One possible explanation may involve the context where this research took place. In the context of healthcare, especially in hospitals, daily situations that generate negative emotions are more frequent than in everyday life. As a consequence, the workers may use the expressive suppression of emotions more frequently and more intensely than other people, in order to deal with daily critical situations. Moreover, a person may prefer expressive suppression, in order to demonstrate to others the ability to deal with stressful situations, by not showing the negative emotions the person feels. Therefore, its negative consequences may be overshadowed. It is well-known that the rules that guide these professional experiences, in terms of emotional labour, are often substantially different from those governing emotions elicited by daily events, in other contexts. Specifically, the work environment that involves interactions with customers or patients implies displaying the required emotions, by controlling and not showing negative emotional states. According to previous research, emotional labor is required every day in different fields, like daycare workers, nursing, and healthcare, being documented in both nurses and physicians. It includes suppression of negative emotions, which are felt but not expressed (Hochschild, 2012). Therefore, it is possible that the habitual suppression of unwanted emotions does actually reduce the intensity with which these emotions are experienced. However, suppressed, but not eliminated, negative emotions, may not be consistently associated with compassion satisfaction, as it was expected.

Concerning the relationship between compassion satisfaction and secondary traumatic stress symptoms, as we expected, the results showed that a low level of compassion satisfaction is associated with high levels of intrusions, avoidance, and arousal. The results are in line with the results of previous studies that showed negative associations between compassion satisfaction and stress (Berger et al., 2015; Hinderer et al., 2014; Sodeke-Gregson et al., 2013). Moreover, the current results showed that compassion satisfaction moderates the relation between expressive suppression and intrusions. A lower level of intrusions is reported by the participants with a low tendency to use suppression and a high level of compassion satisfaction. These results may suggest that the relationship between expressive suppression and traumatic stress is not presented in all individuals, but may be dependent on other personal characteristics. Compassion satisfaction proved to be a variable that interacts with suppression in predicting intrusions. The fact that interaction appears only in connection with intrusions can be explained through previous studies that support the ironic character of suppression, that is, the suppressed emotions determine a higher level of intrusions following exposure to a trauma (Beck, Gudmundsdottir, Palyo, Miller, & Grant, 2006).

Several limitations of this study should be noted. Firstly, the current sample was predominantly comprised of Caucasian women. A replication of the current findings among men is needed, because previous work suggests that the relationship between emotion regulation strategies and symptoms of distress might be moderated by gender (Zlomke & Hahn, 2010). Secondly, medical workers are routinely exposed to trauma as part of their job and may use emotion regulation strategies more frequently, in order to cope with critical or emergency situations at work. The use of this sample may limit the generalization of the current findings to other secondary trauma populations. Thirdly, the sample was largely comprised of nurses, with a small proportion of physicians, from different specialties. This convenience sample was used given the fact that the number of medical staff from a single hospital department who agree to take part in a study is too low to form a sample. Thus, the data from all the participants who agreed to complete the scales were analyzed as a single group, after comparing nurses and physicians in terms of the study variables. The nonsignificant differences allowed the analysis of the data as a single group. However, future studies with more homogeneous samples in terms of daily activities are needed. Moreover, the present study is limited because the relationships among emotion regulation, secondary traumatic stress, and compassion satisfaction were analyzed at a single moment in time. Therefore, it is not possible to notice causal relationships. Future research needs to examine in more detail the nature of the relationship between these variables.

Despite the aforementioned limitations, the findings of this study add to the previous literature confirming specific relationships among emotion regulation, compassion satisfaction, and secondary traumatic stress. Moreover, it expands the previous findings by highlighting the interaction between emotion regulations and compassion satisfaction in predicting secondary traumatic stress, in a sample of Romanian healthcare workers. This work environment is of particular interest due to the fact that it is characterized by a high level of stress and overload (Spânu, Baban, Bria, & Dumitrascu, 2013). Intervention and training should focus on teaching cognitive reappraisal skills, in order to improve one's professional quality of life. Employees should learn to reappraise the unpleasant emotions rather that suppress them, because the reduction of negative emotions and the amplification of pleasant emotions can increase the employees' satisfaction and reduce traumatic stress.

Funding

This study was supported by the Sectoral Operational Programme Human Resources Development (SOP HRD), financed from the European Social Fund and by the Romanian Government under the contract number POSDRU/159/1.5/S/133675.

References

Aiken, L. S., West, S. G., & Reno, R. R. (1991). *Multiple regression: Testing and interpreting interactions*. Newbury Park, CA: Sage.

Aldao, A., Nolen-Hoeksema, S., & Schweizer, S. (2010). Emotion regulation strategies across psychopathology: A meta-analysis. *Clinical Psychology Review, 30*, 217–237. doi.org/10.1016/j.cpr.2009.11.004

Badger, K., Royse, D., & Craig, C. (2008). Hospital social workers and indirect trauma exposure: An exploratory study of contributing factors. *Health & Social Work, 33*, 63–71. doi.org/10.1093/hsw/33.1.63

Bardeen, J. R., Kumpula, M. J., & Orcutt, H. K. (2013). Emotion regulation difficulties as a prospective predictor of posttraumatic stress symptoms following a mass shooting. *Journal of Anxiety Disorders, 27*, 188–196. doi.org/10.1016/j.janxdis.2013.01.003

Beck, C. T., & Gable, R. K. (2012). A mixed methods study of secondary traumatic stress in labor and delivery nurses. *Journal of Obstetric, Gynecologic, and Neonatal Nursing, 41*, 747–760. doi.org/10.1111/j.1552-6909.2012.01386.x

Beck, J. G., Gudmundsdottir, B., Palyo, S. A., Miller, L. M., & Grant, D. M. (2006). Rebound effects following deliberate thought suppression: Does PTSD make a difference? *Behavior Therapy, 37*, 170–180. doi.org/10.1016/j.beth.2005.11.002

Berger, J., Polivka, B., Smoot, E. A., & Owens, H. (2015). Compassion fatigue in pediatric nurses. *Journal of Pediatric Nursing, 30*, e11–e17. doi.org/10.1016/j.pedn.2015.02.005

Boden, M. T., Westermann, S., McRae, K., Kuo, J., Alvarez, J., Kulkarni, M. R., … Bonn-Miller, M. O. (2013). Emotion regulation and posttraumatic stress disorder: A prospective investigation. *Journal of Social and Clinical Psychology, 32*, 296–314. doi.org/10.1521/jscp.2013.32.3.296

Bonn-Miller, M. O., Vujanovic, A. A., Boden, M. T., & Gross, J. J. (2011). Posttraumatic stress, difficulties in emotion regulation, and coping-oriented marijuana use. *Cognitive Behaviour Therapy, 40*, 34–44. doi.org/10.1080/16506073.2010.525253

Bride, B. E., Robinson, M. M., Yegidis, B., & Figley, C. R. (2004). Development and validation of the secondary traumatic stress scale. *Research on Social Work Practice, 14*, 27–35. doi.org/10.1177/1049731503254106

Campbell-Sills, L., & Barlow, D. H. (2007). Incorporating emotion regulation into conceptualizations and treatments of anxiety and mood disorders. In J. J. Gross (Ed.), *Handbook of emotion regulation* (pp. 542–560). New York, NY: Guilford.

Campbell-Sills, L., Barlow, D. H., Brown, T. A., & Hofmann, S. G. (2006). Effects of suppression and acceptance on emotional responses of individuals with anxiety and mood disorders. *Behaviour Research and Therapy, 44*, 1251–1263. doi.org/10.1016/j.brat.2005.10.001

Ciuluvica, C., Amerio, P., & Fulcheri, M. (2014). Emotion regulation strategies and quality of life in dermatologic patients. *Procedia-Social and Behavioral Sciences, 127*, 661–665. doi.org/10.1016/j.sbspro.2014.03.331

Cohen, J. (2013). *Statistical power analysis for the behavioral sciences*. New York, NY: Erlbaum.

Cote, S., & Morgan, L. M. (2002). A longitudinal analysis of the association between emotion regulation, job satisfaction, and intentions to quit. *Journal of Organizational Behavior, 23*, 947–962. doi.org/10.1002/job.174

Dixon-Gordon, K. L., Chapman, A. L., Lovasz, N., & Walters, K. (2011). Too upset to think: The interplay of borderline personality features, negative emotions, and social problem solving in the laboratory. *Personality Disorders: Theory, Research, and Treatment, 2*, 243–260. doi.org/10.1037/a0021799

Dominguez-Gomez, E., & Rutledge, D. N. (2009). Prevalence of secondary traumatic stress among emergency nurses. *Journal of Emergency Nursing, 35*, 199–204. doi.org/10.1016/j.jen.2008.05.003

Duarte, J., Pinto-Gouveia, J., & Cruz, B. (2016). Relationships between nurses' empathy, self-compassion and dimensions of professional quality of life: a cross-sectional study. *International Journal of Nursing Studies, 60*, 1–11. doi.org/10.1016/j.ijnurstu.2016.02.015

Duffy, E., Avalos, G., & Dowling, M. (2015). Secondary traumatic stress among emergency nurses: A cross-sectional study. *International Emergency Nursing, 23*, 53–58. doi.org/10.1016/j.ienj.2014.05.001

Dutton, M. A., & Rubinstein, F. L. (1995). Working with people with PTSD: Research implications. In C. R. Figley (Ed.), *Compassion fatigue: Coping with secondary traumatic stress disorder in those who treat the traumatized* (pp. 82–100). New York, NY: Brunner/ Mazel.

Ehring, T., & Quack, D. (2010). Emotion regulation difficulties in trauma survivors: The role of trauma type and PTSD symptom severity. *Behavior Therapy, 41*, 587–598. doi.org/10.1016/j.beth.2010.04.004

El-bar, N., Levy, A., Wald, H. S., & Biderman, A. (2013). Compassion fatigue, burnout and compassion satisfaction among family physicians in the Negev area—a cross-sectional study. *Israel Journal of Health Policy Research, 2*, 1–8. doi.org/10.1186/2045-4015-2-31

Evers, C., Stok, F. M., & De Ridder, D. T. D. (2010). Feeding your feelings: Emotion regulation strategies and emotional eating. *Personality and Social Psychology Bulletin, 36*, 792–804. doi.org/10.1177/0146167210371383

Finlay-Jones, A. L., Rees, C. S., & Kane, R. T. (2015). Self-compassion, emotion regulation and stress among Australian psychologists: Testing an emotion regulation model of self-compassion using structural equation modeling. *PloS One, 10*, e0133481. doi.org/10.1371/journal.pone.0133481

Goldin, P. R., McRae, K., Ramel, W., & Gross, J. J. (2008). The neural bases of emotion regulation: Reappraisal and suppression of negative emotion. *Biological Psychiatry, 63*, 577–586. doi.org/10.1016/j.biopsych.2007.05.031

Gratz, K. L., & Roemer, L. (2004). Multidimensional assessment of emotion regulation and dysregulation: Development, factor structure, and initial validation of the difficulties in emotion regulation scale. *Journal of Psychopathology and Behavioral Assessment, 26,* 41–54. doi.org/10.1007/s10862-008-9102-4

Gross, J. J. (1998). Antecedent- and response-focused emotion regulation: Divergent consequences for experience, expression, and physiology. *Journal of Personality and Social Psychology, 74,* 224–237. doi.org/10.1037//0022-3514.74.1.224

Gross, J. J., & John, O. (2003). Individual differences in two emotion regulation processes: Implications for affect, relationships, and wellbeing. *Journal of Personality and Social Psychology, 85,* 348–362. doi.org/10.1037/0022-3514.85.2.348

Gross, J. J., & Thompson, R. A. (2007). Emotion regulation: Conceptual foundations. In J. J. Gross (Ed.), *Handbook of emotion regulation* (pp. 3–24). New York, NY: Guilford.

Hambleton, R. K. (2005). Issues, designs, and technical guidelines for adapting tests into multiple languages and cultures. In K. Hambleton, P. F. Merenda, & C. D. Spielberger (Eds.), *Adapting educational and psychological tests for cross-cultural assessment* (pp. 3–38). Mahwah, NJ: Erlbaum.

Hayes, S. C., Bissett, R., Korn, Z., Zettle, R. D., Rosenfarb, I., Cooper, L., & Grundt, A. (1999). The impact of acceptance versus control rationales on pain tolerance. *The Psychological Record, 49,* 33–47.

Heuven, E., Bakker, A. B., Schaufeli, W. B., & Huisman, N. (2006). The role of self-efficacy in performing emotion work. *Journal of Vocational Behavior, 69,* 222–235. doi.org/10.1016/j.jvb.2006.03.002

Hinderer, K. A., VonRueden, K. T., Friedmann, E., McQuillan, K. A., Gilmore, R., Kramer, B., & Murray, M. (2014). Burnout, compassion fatigue, compassion satisfaction, and secondary traumatic stress in trauma nurses. *Journal of Trauma Nursing, 21,* 160–169. doi.org/10.1097/JTN.0000000000000055

Hochschild, A. R. (2012). *The managed heart: Commercialization of human feeling.* Berkeley, CA: University of California Press.

Hooper, C., Craig, J., Janvrin, D. R., Wetsel, M. A., & Reimels, E. (2010). Compassion satisfaction, burnout, and compassion fatigue among emergency nurses compared with nurses in other selected inpatient specialties. *Journal of Emergency Nursing, 36,* 420–427. doi.org/10.1016/j.jen.2009.11.027

Hu, L. T., & Bentler, P. M. (1999). Cutoff criteria for fit indexes in covariance structure analysis: Conventional criteria versus new alternatives. *Structural Equation Modeling: A Multidisciplinary Journal, 6,* 1–55. doi.org/10.1080/10705519909540118

Jeon, S. Y., & Ha, J. Y. (2012). Traumatic events, professional quality of life and physical symptoms among emergency nurses. *Korean Journal of Adult Nursing, 24,* 64–73. doi.org/10.7475/kjan.2012.24.1.64

John, O. P., & Gross, J. J. (2004). Healthy and unhealthy emotion regulation: Personality processes, individual differences, and life span development. *Journal of Personality, 72,* 1301–1334. doi.org/10.1111/j.1467-6494.2004.00298.x

Langner, C. A., Epel, E., Matthews, K., Moskowitz, J. T., & Adler, N. (2012). Social hierarchy and depression: The role of emotion suppression. *Journal of Psychology: Interdisciplinary and Applied, 146,* 1–19. doi.org/10.1080/00223980.2011.652234

Larsen, D., & Stamm, B. H. (2008). Professional quality of life and trauma therapists. In S. Joseph & A. Lindley (Eds), *Trauma, recovery, and growth: Positive psychological perspectives on posttraumatic stress* (pp. 275–296). Hoboken, NJ: Wiley.

Lemaire, M., El-Hage, W., & Frangou, S. (2014). Reappraising suppression: subjective and physiological correlates of experiential suppression in healthy adults. *Frontiers in Psychology, 11,* 5–571. doi.org/10.3389/fpsyg.2014.00571

Liu, Y., Prati, M., Perrewe, P. L., & Brymer, R. A. (2010). Individual differences in emotional regulation, emotional experiences at work, and work related outcomes: A two study investigation. *Journal of Applied Social Psychology, 40,* 515–538. doi.org/10.1111/j.1559-1816.2010.00627.x

Măirean, C. (2016). Secondary traumatic stress and posttraumatic growth: Social support as a moderator. *The Social Science Journal, 53,* 14–21. doi.org/10.1016/j.soscij.2015.11.007

Măirean, C., & Turliuc, M. N. (2013). Predictors of vicarious trauma beliefs among medical staff. *Journal of Loss and Trauma, 18,* 414–428. doi.org/10.1080/15325024.2012.714200

Makic, M. B. (2015). Taking care of the caregiver: Compassion satisfaction and compassion fatigue. *Journal of Perianesthesia Nursing: Official Journal of the American Society of PeriAnesthesia Nurses, 30*, 546–547. doi.org/10.1016/j.jopan.2015.09.006

Mangoulia, P., Koukia, E., Alevizopoulos, G., Fildissis, G., & Katostaras, T. (2015). Prevalence of secondary traumatic stress among psychiatric nurses in greece. *Archives of Psychiatric Nursing, 29*, 333–338. doi.org/10.1016/j.apnu.2015.06.001

Matta, F. K., Erol-Korkmaz, T. H., Johnson, R. E., & Bıçaksız, P. (2014). Significant work events and counterproductive work behavior: The role of fairness, emotions, and emotion regulation. *Journal of Organizational Behavior, 35*, 920–944. doi.org/10.1002/job.1934

Moore, S. A., Zoellner, L. A., & Mollenholt, N. (2008). Are expressive suppression and cognitive reappraisal associated with stress-related symptoms? *Behaviour Research and Therapy, 46*, 993–1000. doi.org/10.1016/j.brat.2008.05.001

Morris, J. A., & Feldman, D. C. (1997). Managing emotions in the workplace. *Journal of Managerial Issues, 9*, 257–274.

Nolen-Hoeksema, S., & Watkins, E. R. (2011). A heuristic for developing transdiagnostic models of psychopathology: Explaining multifinality and divergent trajectories. *Perspectives on Psychological Science, 6*, 589–609. doi.org/10.1177/1745691611419672

Perron, B. E., & Hiltz, B. S. (2006). Burnout and secondary trauma among forensic interviewers of abused children. *Child and Adolescent Social Work Journal, 23*, 216–234. doi.org/10.1007/s10560-005-0044-3

Poulin, M. J., Brown, S. L., Dillard, A. J., & Smith, D. M. (2013). Giving to others and the association between stress and mortality. *American Journal of Public Health, 103*, 1649–1655. doi.org/10.2105/AJPH.2012.300876

Rottenberg, J., & Gross, J. J. (2003). When emotion goes wrong: Realizing the promise of affective science. *Clinical Psychology: Science and Practice, 10*, 227–232. doi.org/10.1093/clipsy.bpg012

Sansó, N., Galiana, L., Oliver, A., Pascual, A., Sinclair, S., & Benito, E. (2015). Palliative care professionals' inner life: Exploring the relationships among awareness, self-care, and compassion satisfaction and fatigue, burnout, and coping with death. *Journal of Pain and Symptom Management, 50*, 200–207. doi.org/10.1016/j.jpainsymman.2015.02.013

Sodeke-Gregson EA, Holttum S, & Billings J. (2013). Compassion satisfaction, burnout, and secondary traumatic stress in UK therapists who work with adult trauma clients. *European Journal of Psychotraumatology, 4*, 1–10. doi.org/10.3402/ejpt.v4i0.21869

Spânu, F., Baban, A., Bria, M., & Dumitrascu, D. L. (2013). What happens to health professionals when the ill patient is the health care system? Understanding the experience of practising medicine in the Romanian socio-cultural context. *British Journal of Health Psychology, 18*, 663–679. doi.org/10.1111/bjhp.12010

Stamm, B. H. (2010). *The concise ProQOL manual.* Pocatello, ID: ProQOL.org.

Tabachnick, B. G., & Fidell, L. S. (2007). *Using multivariate statistics.* Boston, MA: Pearson/Allyn & Bacon.

Tschan, F., Rochat, S., & Zapf, D. (2005). It's not only clients. Studying emotion work with clients and co-workers with an event-sampling approach. *Journal of Occupational & Organizational Psychology, 78*, 195–220. doi.org/10.1348/096317905X39666

Turliuc, M. N., Măirean, C., & Turliuc, M. D. (2015). Rumination and suppression as mediators of the relationship between dysfunctional beliefs and traumatic stress. *International Journal of Stress Management, 22*, 306–322. doi.org/10.1037/a0039272

Van der Wath, A., van Wyk, N., & Janse van Rensburg, E. (2013). Emergency nurses' experiences of caring for survivors of intimate partner violence. *Journal of Advanced Nursing, 69*, 2242–2252. doi.org/10.1111/jan.12099

Vujanovic, A. A., Bonn-Miller, M. O., Potter, C. M., Marshall, E. C., & Zvolensky, M. J. (2011). An evaluation of the association between distress tolerance and posttraumatic stress within a trauma-exposed sample. *Journal of Psychopathology and Behavioral Assessment, 33*, 129–135. doi.org/10.1007/s10862-010-9209-2

Young, J. L., Derr, D. M., Cicchillo, V. J., & Bressler, S. (2011). Compassion satisfaction, burnout, and secondary traumatic stress in heart and vascular nurses. *Critical Care Nursing Quarterly, 34*, 227–234. doi.org/10.1097/CNQ.0b013e31821c67d5.

Zlomke, K. R., & Hahn, K. S. (2010). Cognitive emotion regulation strategies: Gender differences and associations to worry. *Personality and Individual Differences, 48*, 408–413. doi.org/10.1016/j.paid.2009.11.007

Facial Expressions of Emotions: Recognition Accuracy and Affective Reactions During Late Childhood

GIACOMO MANCINI
SERGIO AGNOLI
BRUNO BALDARO
PIO E. RICCI BITTI
PAOLA SURCINELLI

ABSTRACT. The present study examined the development of recognition ability and affective reactions to emotional facial expressions in a large sample of school-aged children ($n = 504$, ages 8–11 years of age). Specifically, the study aimed to investigate if changes in the emotion recognition ability and the affective reactions associated with the viewing of facial expressions occur during late childhood. Moreover, because small but robust gender differences during late-childhood have been proposed, the effects of gender on the development of emotion recognition and affective responses were examined. The results showed an overall increase in emotional face recognition ability from 8 to 11 years of age, particularly for neutral and sad expressions. However, the increase in sadness recognition was primarily due to the development of this recognition in boys. Moreover, our results indicate different developmental trends in males and females regarding the recognition of disgust. Last, developmental changes in affective reactions to emotional facial expressions were found. Whereas recognition ability increased over the developmental time period studied, affective reactions elicited by facial expressions were characterized by a decrease in arousal over the course of late childhood.

THE ABILITY TO DISTINGUISH AND INTERPRET EMOTIONS from facial expressions is a main component of the nonverbal communication system and a crucial social ability for the development and the maintenance of human relations. The importance of decoding emotions from facial expressions is evident from the early social interactions of the infant. Indeed, the synchronization of expressive movements between mother and infant represents a key element of these early interactions (Garvey & Fogel, 2007; Lavelli & Fogel, 2002; Messinger & Fogel, 2007). Even if perceptual discrimination between different emotional expressions is present from the early stages of life, a more accurate interpretation of emotions appears between three and six years of age (Boyatzis, Chazan, & Ting, 1993; MacDonald, Kirkpatrick, & Sullivan, 1995; Widen & Russell, 2008). Indeed, through the preschool and early primary school years, increases in the ability to correctly recognize and label various emotional facial expressions have been observed (Camras & Allison, 1985; Harrigan 1984; Tremblay, Kirouac, & Dore, 2001) but there is also evidence that the developmental pattern of facial recognition ability is not uniform across emotions (De Sonneville et al., 2002; Vicari, Reilly, Pasqualetti, Vizzotto, & Caltagirone, 2000).

Whereas there is much research on facial expression recognition in infancy and early childhood, it is uncertain whether the facial emotion recognition ability continues to develop over this period. Few studies have investigated the ability to recognize emotions from facial expressions in late childhood, and these few studies have reported inconsistent findings. Indeed, some studies reported that there are few interesting changes in facial emotion recognition that occur after seven (Kirouac, Dore & Gosselin, 1985) or ten years of age (Tremblay et al., 2001), whereas others reported that recognition of facial emotions significantly improves between 6 and 15 years of age and adulthood (Herba, Landau, Russell, Ecker, & Phillips, 2006; Herba & Philipps, 2004; Montirosso, Peverelli, Frigerio, Crespi, & Brogatti, 2010; Vicari et al., 2000). Neurodevelopmental studies propose that brain areas involved in facial expression processing continue structural development throughout late childhood and adolescence (Kanwisher, McDermott, & Chun, 1997; Thomas et al., 2001), suggesting that emotional facial recognition abilities may not reach maturity until adulthood (Thomas, De Bellis, Graham, & LaBar, 2007). However, the majority of studies on emotion recognition have focused on the preschool period; thus, the extent and range of changes in the emotion recognition ability during late childhood and adolescence has been unclear.

Moreover, differences in the type of stimuli presented in the studies can make interpretation of the results difficult. Furthermore, studies differ in the types of responses they required from participants (Bruce et al., 2000; Markham & Adams, 1992). For example, a discrimination paradigm requires attentional and perceptual abilities (Walker-Andrews, 1997), a matching procedure relies more on visual and spatial abilities (Herba et al., 2006), and free labeling requires the ability to verbally identify facial expressions.

Other factors, such as gender, may affect the development of emotion processing (Herba & Philips, 2004). Women are usually considered more emotional than men (Fisher & Manstead, 2000) and, in the normal adult population, the majority of studies support the notion that females outperform males in the ability to accurately decode emotional facial expressions (Biele & Grabowska, 2006; Montagne, Kessels, Frigerio, de Haan, & Perrett, 2005; Hall & Matsumoto, 2004; Scholten, Aleman, Montagne, & Kahn, 2005; Thayer & Johnsen, 2000). However, a definitive female advantage has not been demonstrated across all investigations and all emotions (e.g., Biele & Grabowska, 2006; Calvo & Lundqvist, 2008; Montagne et al., 2005; Vassallo, Cooper, & Douglas, 2009).

With regard to preschool and school-aged children, in a meta-analysis McClure (2000) found evidence for a small, although robust, female advantage in emotion recognition over the developmental period (that is, from infancy to adolescence). However, later studies fail to report gender effects in childhood (De Sonneville et al., 2002; Vicari et al., 2000).

In the present study, the development of the ability to recognize emotions from facial expressions was investigated in a large sample of school-aged children using a multiple-choice categorization task. In particular, the study was aimed at investigating if changes in the emotion recognition ability occur during late childhood and if these changes can be observed for all emotions or only for specific emotion categories. Moreover, the effect of gender on the development of the emotion recognition ability was examined.

In addition, we also included a dimensional evaluation of subjective emotional reactions to faces by asking participants to rate their affective state in response to each facial expression in terms of valence and arousal. Indeed, another traditional approach to the study of emotional responses stipulates that emotions may be characterized along a smaller number of continuous psychological dimensions. One of the most familiar models is Russell's (1980) circumplex model of affect, which specifies that there are two main affective dimensions reflecting degrees of valence and arousal.

However, little research is available concerning what, or even if, dimensions are involved in children's interpretation of emotion and little work has been conducted to investigate the affective reactions elicited by facial expressions, using the dimensional model (Britton, Taylor, Sudheimer, & Liberzon, 2006). Studies on adult participants have found differences in self-reported intensity and physiological responses among emotional facial expressions (e.g., Vrana & Gross, 2004). For example, Springer and co-workers (Springer, Rosas, McGetrick, & Bowers, 2007) found that viewing angry facial expressions was associated with significantly larger acoustic startle eye blink responses than other types of facial expressions in adult participants (i.e., fear, neutral, and happy).

In the current study, we attempted to combine the categorical (discrete) and dimensional methodologies to investigate emotional perception in children. Indeed, each of these two accounts of emotion perception may be required to explain different properties of children's behavior. To our knowledge, no other study has examined the affective reactions elicited by the viewing of emotional facial expressions in children. In a previous study (McManis, Bradley, Berg, Cuthbert,

& Lang, 2001) investigating affective reactions using pictures of natural scenes, children's affective responses, in terms of valence and arousal, were similar to that of adolescent and adult participants. However, the expected increase in startle reflex magnitude during unpleasant pictures was observed only for girls and not for boys. In another study (Waters, Lipp, & Spence, 2005) the startle reflex magnitude did not differ significantly during viewing of unpleasant compared with neutral or pleasant pictures in 8- to 12-year-old children.

As a consequence, other aims of the present study include the following: whether subjective affective responses to emotional faces in children are comparable to those previously found in adults, if changes in subjective ratings occur between 8 and 11 years of age, and if these changes are related to the development of the emotion recognition ability.

Last, because gender differences have been found in affective responses to emotional pictures of natural scenes both in adult participants (Bradley, Codispoti, Sabatinelli & Lang, 2001) and in children (McManis, Bradley, Cuthbert, & Lang, 1995; McManis et al., 2001), with females showing enhanced reactivity to unpleasant pictures compared to males, gender differences in subjective evaluations of emotional faces were also investigated.

In summary, main aims of the current study were:

1. to investigate the development of the ability to recognise emotions from facial expressions during late childhood and the effect of gender on the development of the emotion recognition ability;
2. to investigate differences related to age and gender in affective evaluations of emotional faces;
3. to examine if changes in affective evaluations are related to the development of the emotion recognition ability.

Methods

Participants

The participants included 504 children (258 females) ranging in age from 8 to 11 years old (mean age 9.31 years). Participants were selected from six different state primary schools in Bologna city. The sample was composed of 173 participants (92 females) in the third grade, 168 participants (85 females) in the fourth grade, and 163 participants (81 females) in the fifth grade. Participants were in their normal school year. Children were excluded if they reported a diagnosis of mental retardation or psychological disabilities certified by the public mental health service or if their IQ score was below the normal range (IQ < 85). The present research was approved by the Ethical Committee of the Department of Psychology. The experimental procedure was explained to the children and their parents in a presentation session. Parents gave their written consent for the research, and children were freely allowed to participate in, or abstain from, the research.

Stimuli and Apparatus

Forty-eight color pictures of faces representing five basic emotions (anger, fear, sadness, happiness, and disgust) and neutral expressions were selected from the Karolinska Directed Emotional Face System (KDEF; Lundqvist, Flykt, & Öhman, 1998). Eight faces were selected for each emotional expression, and male and female presenters were included for each expression (half of the faces selected were male and half were female). The forty-eight pictures were divided into two sets of twenty-four facial expressions, and each set was arranged in four blocks of six expressions, such that there was one exemplar from each of the six stimulus types in each block. For each set, four different orders of picture presentation were constructed.

Stimulus presentation was conducted with an Acer laptop computer with a 2.4 GHz processor and a 21-inch monitor. A refresh rate of 60 Hz and a resolution of 1440 × 900 pixels were used.

Procedure

Participants were tested individually in a quiet room that was arranged for the experimental procedure. To assure a correct understanding of the task, the procedure was explained first to all participants in their classrooms and again to each participant through the presentation of two pictures. Participants were tested in a randomized order. Participants sat approximately 1 meter from the computer screen on which the pictures were presented. Each face was presented on the screen for a 6-second interval, and after each picture offset, participants were asked to complete a facial expression recognition task and to rate their emotional reactions in terms of valence and arousal. To complete the emotion recognition task, participants were asked to select one of six emotion labels (anger, sadness, happiness, fear, disgust, or neutral) that best described the emotional expression they just saw. The labels were shown on an answer sheet, and participants made their responses by writing a cross on the emotion label. Participants were given 10 seconds to make their selection, and they were asked to respond as accurate as possible. No feedback was given regarding the appropriateness of any response.

After the emotion recognition task, participants were also required to rate their emotional response on a 9-point scale using the paper and pencil version of the Self-Assessment Manikin (SAM; Bradley & Lang, 1994), which depicts a graphic figure that varies along two dimensions of pleasure and arousal. To represent the pleasure dimension, the SAM ranges from a smiling, happy figure to a frowning, unhappy figure; for the arousal dimension, it ranges from an excited, wide-eyed figure to a relaxed, sleepy figure. The pleasure dimension was presented first, and participants had 10 seconds to give their responses for each dimension.

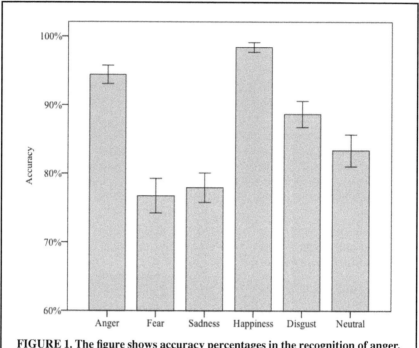

FIGURE 1. The figure shows accuracy percentages in the recognition of anger, fear, sadness, happiness, disgust, and neutral facial expressions.

A 30-second interval lapsed between the presentations of each picture. The order in which pictures were viewed was varied through eight possibilities across participants.

Results

Emotion Recognition Accuracy

A repeated measure analysis of variance (ANOVA) using emotional expression (anger, sadness, happiness, fear, disgust, and neutral face) as repeated factor was performed to explore the emotional facial expressions recognition accuracy during late childhood. A main effect of emotional expression was found $F(5, 496) = 137.05$, $p < .005$, $\eta^2 = .58$. As illustrated in Figure 1, angry and happy expressions were the most recognized emotions, followed by expressions of disgust and neutral expressions while facial expressions of fear and sadness were significantly less recognized as compared to all the other emotions ($ps < .001$).

TABLE 1. Number and Percentage of Responses to Each Emotion as a Function of the Facial Expression Presented

Facial expression presented	Emotion identified										
	Anger		Fear		Sadness		Happiness		Disgust		Neutral face	
	n	%	n	%	n	%	n	%	n	%	n	%
Anger	1902	94.3	27	1.3	18	0.9	6	0.3	44	2.2	19	0.9
Fear	17	0.8	1547	76.7	20	1.0	15	0.7	334	16.6	82	4.1
Sadness	22	1.1	146	7.2	1569	77.8	2	0.1	182	9.0	94	4.7
Happiness	4	0.2	5	0.2	5	0.2	1984	98.4	8	0.4	10	0.5
Disgust	54	2.7	17	0.8	140	6.9	3	0.1	1789	88.7	13	0.6
Neutral face	111	5.5	36	1.8	111	5.5	25	1.2	51	2.6	1681	83.4

Moreover, an analysis of the errors (Chi squared test) made from children in the recognition of the facial expressions highlighted that the mistakes were not distribute randomly ($p_s < .001$), except for the errors made in the recognition of happiness. The percentages of correct responses and errors in the recognition of each facial expression are presented in Table 1.

To analyze the development of emotional facial expression recognition accuracy during late childhood, a multivariate analysis of covariance (MANCOVA) was performed. Specifically, accuracy in recognizing the six facial expressions (anger, fear, sadness, happiness, disgust, and neutral face) was used as a dependent variable, gender (male or female) was used as an independent variable, and age (from 92 to 138 months) was used as a covariate variable (Figure 2). A statistically significant main effect of age on the accuracy of emotion recognition was determined ($F (6, 492) = 3.127, p < .005, \eta^2 = .037$). This effect highlighted an increase in the emotion recognition ability during these months. In particular, a statistically significant increase in recognition accuracy during these months was observed for sad and neutral expressions ($F (1, 497) = 14.155, p < .001, \eta^2 = .028$, and $F (1, 497) = 6.753, p < .01, \eta^2 = .013$, respectively). The slopes of the regression lines were positive ($b = .023$ and $b = .013$ for sadness and neutral face, respectively), showing an increase in the accuracy of the recognition of both facial expressions during these months.

A statistically significant effect of gender on emotion recognition was found for facial expressions of sadness and disgust ($F (1, 497) = 5.946, p = .015, \eta^2 = .12$, and $F (1, 497) = 5.368, p = .021, \eta^2 = .11$, respectively). This effect

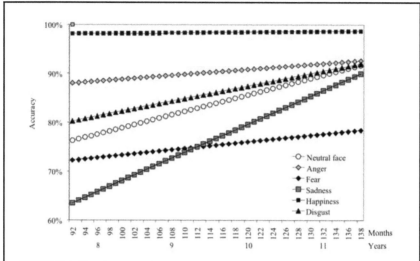

FIGURE 2. The figure depicts the development of accuracy in the recognition of neutral face, anger, fear, sadness, happiness, and disgust expressions from 8 (92 months) to 11.5 years (138 months) of age.

highlighted a greater recognition of facial expressions of sadness and disgust in girls than in boys. However, a significant interaction between age and gender was found in the recognition of sadness (F (1, 497) = 4.861, p = .028, η^2 = .010) and disgust (F (1, 497) = 4.044, p = .045, η^2 = .008), showing a difference between girls and boys in recognition accuracy development for both facial expressions. As shown in Figure 3, while girls displayed high accuracy levels in sadness recognition and their recognition ability showed only a slight increase from 8 to 11 years of age, boys showed a higher increase than girls over this time until their ability to recognize sad expressions overcame girls' performance when they reached approximately 11 years of age. Regarding disgust expressions, as shown in Figure 4, the development of the recognition ability showed an opposite trend in girls and boys. Indeed, in girls, the recognition of disgust expressions decreased over time (even if it was maintained at high levels), while in boys, the recognition of disgust expressions increased during these months until it overcame the level of the girls at approximately 11 years of age.

Affective Response

To explore the affective response (valence and arousal) to emotional facial expressions during late childhood, a repeated measures analysis of variance (ANOVA) was performed. A statistically significant main effect of emotional expression was found for both valence and arousal ratings (F (5, 499) = 157.41,

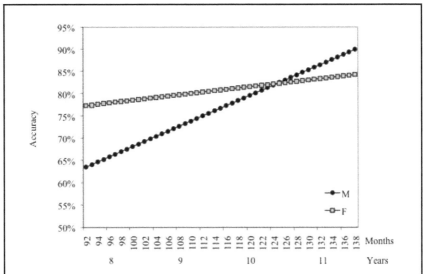

FIGURE 3. The figure depicts the accuracy in the recognition of sadness facial expression in females (grey squares) and males (black circles) from 8 (92 months) to 11.5 years (138 months) of age.

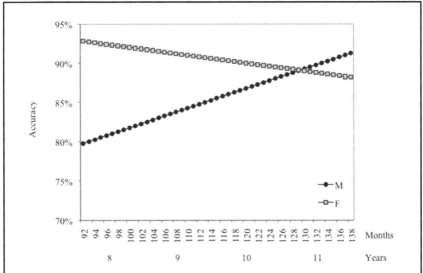

FIGURE 4. The figure depicts the accuracy in the recognition of disgust facial expression in females (grey squares) and males (black circles) from 8 (92 months) to 11.5 years (138 months) of age.

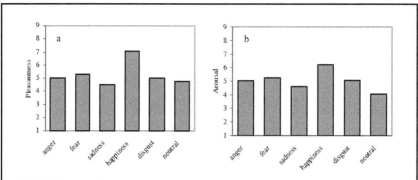

FIGURE 5. The figure shows valence ratings (a) and arousal ratings (b) associated to the viewing of the emotional facial expressions. The valence ratings ranged from 1 = very unpleasant to 9 = very pleasant. The arousal ratings ranged from 1 = calm to 9 = excited.

$p < .001$, $\eta^2 = .61$, and F (5, 499) = 121.60, $p < .001$, $\eta^2 = .55$, respectively). As expected, facial expressions of happiness were judged more pleasant than all of the other emotional expressions and neutral expressions ($ps < .001$). Among unpleasant emotions, facial expressions of fear were judged as more pleasant than the other emotional expressions and the neutral expressions ($ps < .001$), and facial expressions of anger and disgust were judged more pleasant than neutral and sad expressions ($ps < .005$ for all). Facial expressions of sadness were considered the most unpleasant facial expressions (see Figure 5a). Facial expressions of happiness were evaluated as significantly more arousing than all the other emotional expressions and neutral expressions ($ps < .001$), followed by facial expressions of fear, disgust, and anger. Facial expressions of sadness were evaluated as less arousing than all of the other emotional expressions ($ps < .001$) but more arousing than neutral expressions ($p < .001$, see Figure 5b).

To analyze the development of the affective response (valence and arousal) to facial emotional expressions during late childhood, a multivariate analysis of covariance (MANCOVA) was performed. Valence and arousal of the affective reactions to the viewing of the six emotional expressions (anger, sadness, happiness, fear, disgust, and neutral face) were used as dependent variables, gender (male or female) was used as independent variable, and age (from 92 to 138 months) was used as covariate.

The analyses performed on the subjective reports of valence showed only a near-significant effect of Age (F (6, 495) = 2.022, $p = .061$) with a tendency of the valence to become more negative over time. No gender effect was found.

The analyses performed on subjective reports of arousal showed a statistically significant effect of age (F (6, 495) = 2.170, $p = .045$, $\eta^2 = .026$). This

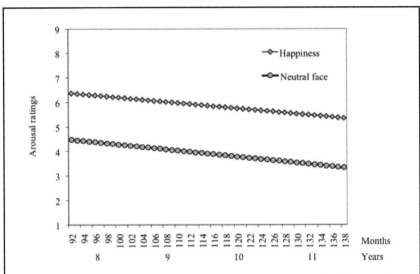

FIGURE 6. The figure depicts the activation (arousal) determined by the viewing of happiness (grey squares) and neutral face (grey circles) from 8 (92 months) to 11.5 years (138 months) of age.

effect highlighted a general decrease of the arousal induced by the viewing of the emotional expressions during the months examined. In particular, the analyses showed a significant effect of age on arousal responses to two specific emotional faces, happiness (F (1, 500) $= 4.327, p = .038, \eta^2 = .009$) and neutral expressions (F (1, 500) $= 7.984, p = .005, \eta^2 = .016$). In particular, the negative slopes of the regression lines ($b = -.022$ and $b = -.025$, for happiness and neutral face, respectively) showed that the arousal induced by both expressions decreased significantly during the months examined (Figure 6). No significant effect of gender was found.

Last, to explore the difference between the development of recognition accuracy and the development of subjective valence and arousal ratings, a repeated measures analysis of covariance (ANCOVA) was performed. In particular, task (accuracy scores, valence ratings, and arousal ratings) and facial expression (anger, sadness, happiness, fear, disgust, and neutral face) were used as dependent variables, and age (from 92 to 138 months) was used as covariate. The analysis revealed a significant task by age interaction (F (2, 998) $= 11.486, p < .001, \eta^2 = .023$). This result showed that the three measures covaried with age in different ways. Specifically, the contrasts showed that the developmental trend for accuracy was statistically different from the developmental trend for both valence (F (1, 499) $= 11.458, p = .001, \eta^2 = .022$) and arousal ($F$ (1, 499) $= 11.602, p = .001, \eta^2 = $

.023). While the recognition accuracy increased with age, the subjective reports of valence and arousal decreased with age.

Discussion

This study demonstrates that the recognition of emotions from facial expressions varies with the specific emotion presented and the age and gender of the observer. In particular we found different developmental trajectories in the recognition of specific emotions in boys and girls during late childhood. Moreover, we demonstrated that also the affective reactions to the emotional facial expressions are subjected to a developmental process during this age period.

Overall, and consistent with previous studies (Gosselin & Laroque, 2000; Herba et al., 2006), we found that the ability to recognize facial expressions increases between 8 and 11 years of age. This finding is consistent with the results of recent studies that demonstrated a constant increase in recognition ability throughout childhood (Herba et al., 2006; Montirosso et al., 2010; Vicari et al., 2000). At eleven years the children's ability to recognize emotions from facial expressions is similar to that found in adult samples. Indeed, looking at our findings in children aged 11 years and at findings of a previous study (Calvo & Lundqvist, 2008), which investigated emotion recognition in adults using the KDEF, percentages of correct recognition seem to be similar. Percentages of right recognition for facial expressions of sadness, happiness, and disgust seem to be quite similar in children and adults. Children seem to perform even better than adults in the recognition of facial expressions of anger and fear while they still show lower recognition accuracy as compared to adults for neutral expressions.

The emotion recognition improvement with age found in the present study should be seen in terms of specific expressions. Indeed, the greatest enhancements in recognition were observed for two specific facial expressions, neutral and sad expressions, while slower increases were observed for anger, fear, and disgust, and no effect of age was found for happiness.

These results bring new evidence in the understanding of the development of facial emotion recognition. In particular, the present study offers one of the first explorations of the recognition of neutral facial expressions during late childhood. Indeed, because the majority of previous studies did not include a neutral condition, our findings cannot be compared with previous results. Specifically, the recognition of neutral expressions was characterized by an evident increase in accuracy from 8 to 11 years of age. Previous studies have described neutral faces as emotionally ambiguous expressions (Thomas et al., 2001; Waters, Neumann, Henry, Craske, & Ornitz, 2008). In particular, children aged 4–8 were characterized by a low accuracy of recognition for this expression (Waters et al., 2008). Neutral faces are often misinterpreted as negative expressions, both in children (Waters et al., 2008) and adults (Lee, Kang, Park, Kim, & An, 2008). These data are also confirmed by the results of the present work since we found that the mistakes in neutral face recognition significantly favor expressions of anger and sadness.

The enhancement of neutral face recognition found in the present work suggests that late childhood could be considered a critical period for disambiguating this facial expression. However, because few studies have investigated neutral face processing during human development, further developmental investigations will be needed to delineate the developmental trend of neutral expression processing.

Sadness was the other emotion characterized by an evident improvement in recognition accuracy across late-childhood. The greatest enhancement found in sadness recognition is not consistent with some previous studies (Montirosso et al., 2010; Vicari et al., 2000). As previously discussed, it is possible that the variation of recognition development across studies is partially due to task demands and/or to the types of response required from subjects (Bruce et al., 2000; Markham & Adams, 1992). Moreover, our results, through a significant interaction between gender and age, showed that this trend essentially arises from the development of sadness recognition in boys. Girls already showed high accuracy in the recognition of sadness by the time they were 8 years old, and their performance underwent only a slight increase over time. On the contrary, boys started at a low level of accuracy and then showed a strong increase in performance over the months examined, finally displaying higher accuracies than girls at approximately 11.5 years of age. This gender difference could arise from the different pattern of adult-guided interaction that characterizes early childhood. For example, Fivush (1991) found specific differences in how mothers talk to their preschoolers about emotion, demonstrating that mothers talked more to their daughters than to their sons about sadness and its causes. Moreover, from infancy onwards, girls are exposed to a more expressive environment than are boys. As a consequence, girls are likely to develop initial emotion recognition abilities more rapidly than are boys (McClure, 2000). However, the results of the present study show that during late childhood, boys are able to close the gap that initially separates them from girls; from an initial disadvantage for sadness recognition, boys became as accurate as girls after reaching 11 years of age. However, the different development of recognition ability in boys and girls was not related exclusively to sadness; a similar trend was also found in disgust recognition. While, in girls, the recognition of the expression of disgust decreased over time (even if it was maintained at high levels), in boys, the recognition of disgust increased during the examined months until it surpassed that of girls at approximately 11 years of age. Even if previous studies (e.g., Campbell et al., 2002) already demonstrated gender-specific differences in adult and school-aged children for disgust recognition, our finding contrasts with that of previous works (Montirosso et al., 2010) that found no age-related improvement for disgust. The emotion of disgust is characterized by a complex development. Rozin (1990) demonstrated that some features of this emotion (e.g. the contagion feature) are absent until about 7 years of age. We could hypothesize that the sharpening in the emotional experience of disgust could produce new awareness also in the understanding of the expression associated to this emotion. The recognition of the facial expression of disgust could follow different developmental paths in boys and girls, because of the gender differences in the developmental transition characteristic of the late childhood (the juvenile transition; Del Giudice, Angeleri, & Manera, 2009). It could be hypothesized that the different physical and psychological maturation of boys and girls during this life stage, with an evident precocious maturation in girls, could affect also the recognition of complex emotions, like disgust. However this hypothesis should be tested in future studies with specific investigations on the influences of juvenile hormonal changes on the recognition of emotions.

The data of the present study do not indicate a constant female advantage during late childhood in the recognition of specific facial expressions, as suggested in previous works (Montirosso et al., 2010). Our results showed a developmental transition in the effect of gender on the recognition of specific facial expressions of emotions (sadness and disgust) during late childhood rather than a general stable effect of this variable. Gender could affect emotion recognition during late childhood through highly complex dynamical interactions between maturational and social factors. According to McClure (2000), it could be hypothesized that neurological maturation plays an important role in the early emergence of gender differences in facial expression recognition, whereas the social factors are central elements for maintaining, reinforcing, or changing the biologically determined differences. An approach of this type is consistent with the theorization of a juvenile transition during late childhood that integrates environmental and social factors with genotypic variation (in sexually differentiated ways) to explain the evolutionary trajectory followed by boys and girls during this life stage (Del Giudice et al., 2009).

In the present study, only the performance for happiness was flat and virtually at the ceiling. This finding could be interpreted as an effect of the forced-choice recognition task used in this study. Indeed, although this task minimizes verbal demands and may be less difficult than a free labeling task for younger children (Camras & Allison, 1985), it also could be prone to ceiling effects in older children (Thomas et al., 2007). However, it should be remembered that similar ceiling effects for happy expressions have been found in previous studies using different tasks (e.g., Vicari et al., 2000). The ceiling effect found for happiness could be explained by the fact that happiness was the only positive emotion presented and that the facial configuration for happiness is more distinctive than those of other facial expressions (Vicari et al., 2000).

Last, this study provides new data regarding subjective affective reactions to emotional facial expressions during late childhood. The present work represents a first exploration of the phenomenon during this period. As expected, significant differences among emotions were found in valence and arousal ratings. However, the differences we found in arousal ratings among the emotional expressions are relatively small. Even if this effect might be imputed to a difficulty in the understanding of the task by children, it represents a classical trend in the arousal assessment of emotional faces that emerged also in adult studies (Britton et al., 2006; Eisenbarth, Alpers, Segrè, Calogero, & Angrilli, 2008; Gerber et al., 2008; Goeleven, De Raedt, Leyman, & Vershuere, 2008). Moreover, valence and arousal cues have been found to be easily perceived by children as young as 3 years (Bullock & Russell, 1984). However, the self-assessed valence and arousal ratings resulting from the present work seem to be characterised by slightly higher ratings than previous findings in adults (Britton et al., 2006; Gerber et al., 2008). All facial expressions of emotion elicited more positive and arousing reactions than those usually described in adults. Nevertheless, our results showed that the affective space associated with the viewing of facial expressions is subjected to a developmental process during late childhood. Specifically, the self-reported arousal elicited by the faces was characterized by a negative trend, and the activation determined by the viewing of facial expressions showed a significant decrease over time. On the basis of these results, it could be hypothesized that the subjective affective space, and in particular the activation associated with emotional expressions, could be subjected to an accommodation process during late childhood. During this period, the affective reactions assume a more mature aspect, typical of the adult period. In particular, the decrease in arousal detected during late childhood is consistent with data regarding adults' arousal ratings of affective faces.

The same negative trend was detected in the valence data. However, the effect regarding the affective valence should be carefully considered because the results were only near-significant. The negative trend found for valence ratings could be interpreted as the result of a better comprehension of this affective dimension. Indeed, unpleasant emotions are evaluated by children in terms of valence similarly to neutral expressions and pleasantness scores for negative emotions are higher as compared to adult samples. Across months children's evaluations of unpleasant faces become gradually less positive and more similar to adults' ratings (e.g. Eisenbarth et al., 2008). Children, through constant exposure to emotional facial expressions and the gradual acquisition of social display rules (a process particularly evident during late childhood), could sharpen the monitoring of their affective states associated with the viewing of these emotional stimuli (Malatesta, 1982; Cole, 1986; De Paulo, Jordan, Irvine, & Laser, 1982).

The contrast between the developmental trends of recognition accuracy and valence and arousal ratings showed, in particular, that the recognition development was characterized by a trend opposite to that of both valence and arousal. The gradual incrementing of recognition ability corresponds to a gradual decrementing of valence and arousal ratings. However, as discussed previously, the observed negative trends for arousal and valence could be interpreted as the result of the children's acquisition of greater expertise and comprehension of these two emotional dimensions underlying facial expressions. Both categorical and dimensional accounts of emotion perception seem to show a developmental trend during late childhood that leads the emotional perception to a more mature form.

However, a direct comparison of the reactions of infants, children, adolescents and adults is needed to accurately delineate the changes due to age in the valence and arousal dimensions of the affective space associated with the viewing of facial expressions of emotion. In particular, a series of longitudinal studies investigating the affective space associated to the emotional face recognition could more specifically reveal the developmental changes in the affective meaning associated to facial expressions of emotion.

REFERENCES

Biele, C., & Grabowska, A. (2006). Sex differences in perception of emotion intensity in dynamic and static facial expressions. *Experimental Brain Research, 171,* 1–6. doi: 10.1007/s00221-005-0254-0

Boyatzis, C. J., Chazan, E., & Ting, C. (1993). Preschool children's decoding of facial emotions. *The Journal of Genetic Psychology, 154,* 375–382.

Bradley, M. M., Codispoti, M., Sabatinelli, D., & Lang, P. J. (2001). Emotion and motivation II: Sex differences in picture processing. *Emotion, 1,* 300–319.

Bradley, M. M., & Lang, P. J. (1994). Measuring emotion: The self-assessment manikin and the semantic differential. *Journal of Behavior Therapy and Experimental Psychiatry, 25,* 49–59. doi:10.1016/0005-7916(94)90063-9.

Britton, J. C., Taylor, S. F., Sudheimer, K. D., & Liberzon, I. (2006). Facial expressions and complex IAPS pictures: Common and differential networks. *Neuroimage, 31,* 906–919. doi:10.1016/j.neuroimage.2005.12.050.

Bruce, V., Campbell, R. N., Doherty-Sneddon, G., Import, A., Langton, S., McAuley, S., et al. (2000). Testing face processing skills in children. *British Journal of Developmental Psychology*, *18*, 319–333.

Bullock, M., & Russell, J. A. (1984). Preschool children's interpretation of facial expressions of emotion. *International Journal of Behavioral Development*, *7*, 193–214.

Calvo, M. G., & Lundqvist, D. (2008). Facial expressions of emotion (KDEF): Identification under different display-duration conditions. *Behavior Research Methods*, *40*, 109–115. doi: 10.3758/BRM.40.1.109.

Campbell, R., Elgar, K., Kuntsi, J., Akers, R., Terstegge, J., Coleman, M., et al. (2002). The classification of 'fear' from faces is associated with face recognition skill in women. *Neuropsychologia*, *40*, 575–584. doi:10.1016/S0028-3932(01)00164-6

Camras, L. A., & Allison, K. (1985). Children's understanding of emotional facial expressions and verbal labels. *Journal of Nonverbal Behavior*, *9*, 84–94.

Cole, P. M. (1986). Children's spontaneous control of facial expression. *Child Development*, *57*, 1309–1321.

Del Giudice, M., Angeleri, R., & Manera, V. (2009). The juvenile transition: A developmental switch point in human life history. *Developmental Review*, *29*, 1–31. doi:10.1016/j.dr.2008.09.001

De Paulo, B. M., Jordan, A., Irvine, A., & Laser P. S. (1982). Age changes in the detection of deception. *Child Development*, *53*, 701–709.

De Sonneville, L. M. J., Verschoor, C. A., Njiokiktjien, C., Op het Veld, V., Toorenaar, N., & Vranken, M. (2002). Facial identity and facial emotions: Speed, accuracy, and processing strategies in children and adults. *Journal of Clinical and Experimental Neuropsychology*, *24*, 200–213. doi:1380–3395/02/2402-2000 16.00.

Eisenbarth, H., Alpers, G. W., Segrè, D., Calogero, A., & Angrilli, A. (2008). Categorization and evaluation of emotional faces in psychopathic women. *Psychiatry Research*, *159*, 189–195. doi:10.1016/j.psychres.2007.09.001.

Fisher, A. H., & Manstead, A. (2000). The relation between gender and emotions in different cultures. In A. H. Fisher (Ed.), *Gender and emotion: Social psychological perspectives* (pp. 71–94). New York, NY: Cambridge University Press.

Fivush, R. (1991). Gender and emotion in mother-child conversations about the past. *Journal of Narrative and Life History*, *4*, 325–341.

Garvey, A., & Fogel, A. (2007). Dialogical change processes, emotions, and the early emergence of self. *International Journal for Dialogical Science*, *2*, 51–76.

Gerber, A. J., Posner, J., Gorman, D., Colibazzi, T., Yu, S., Wang, Z., et al. (2008). An affective circumplex model of neural systems subserving valence, arousal, and cognitive overlay during the appraisal of emotional faces. *Neuropsychologia*, *46*, 2129–2139. doi:10.1016/j.neuropsychologia.2008.02.032.

Goeleven, E., De Raedt, R., Leyman, L., & Vershuere, B. (2008). The Karolinska Directed Emotional Faces: A validation study. *Cognition and Emotion*, *22*, 1094–1118.doi:10.1080/02699930701626582.

Gosselin, P., & Larocque, C. (2000). Facial morphology and children's categorization of facial expressions of emotions: A comparison between Asian and Caucasian faces. *The Journal of Genetic Psychology*, *161*, 346–358. doi:10.1080/00221320009596717.

Hall, J. A., & Matsumoto, D. (2004). Gender differences in judgments of multiple emotions from facial expressions. *Emotion*, *4*, 201–206. doi:10.1037/1528-3542.4.2.201 201.

Harrigan, J. A. (1984). The effects of task order on children's identification of facial expressions. *Motivation and Emotion*, *8*, 157–169.

Herba, C. M., Landau, S., Russell, T., Ecker, C., & Phillips, M. L. (2006). The development of emotion-processing in children: Effects of age, emotion, and intensity. *Journal of Child Psychology and Psychiatry*, *47*, 1098–1106. doi: 10.1111/j.1469-7610.2006.01652.x.

Herba, C., & Phillips, M. (2004). Annotation: Development of facial expression recognition from childhood to adolescence: Behavioural and neurological perspectives. *Journal of Child Psychology and Psychiatry, 45*, 1185–1198.

Kanwisher, N., McDermott, J., & Chun, M. M. (1997). The fusiform face area: A module in human extrastriate cortex specialized for face perception. *Journal of Neuroscience, 17*, 4302–4311. doi:0270-6474/97/174302-10005.00/0.

Kirouac, G., Dore, F. Y., & Gosselin, F. (1985). The recognition of facial expressions of emotions. In R. E. Tremblay, M. A. Porovost, & F. F. Strayer (Eds.), *Ethologie et development de l' enfant* (pp. 131–147). Paris: Stock.

Lavelli, M., & Fogel, A. (2002). Developmental changes in mother-infant face-to-face communication: Birth to 3 months. *Developmental Psychology, 38*, 288–305. doi:10.1037//0012-1649.38.2.288.

Lee, E., Kang, J. I., Park, I., Kim, J. J., & An, S. K. (2008). Is a neutral face really evaluated as being emotionally neutral? *Psychiatry Research, 157*, 77–85. doi:10.1016/j.psychres.2007.02.005.

Lundqvist, D., Flykt, A., & Öhman, A. (1998). *The karolinska directed emotional faces.* Stockholm: Karolinska Institutet.

MacDonald, P. M., Kirkpatrick, S. W., & Sullivan, L. A. (1995). Schematic drawings of facial expressions for emotion recognition and interpretation by preschool-aged children. *Genetic, Social, and General Psychology Monographs, 122*, 375–388.

Malatesta, C. Z. (1982). The expression and regulation of emotion: A lifespan perspective. In T. Field & A. Fogel (Eds.), *Emotion and early interaction* (pp. 1–25). Hillsdale: Lawrence Erlbaum.

Markham, R., & Adams, K. (1992). The effect of type of task on children's identification of facial expressions. *Journal of Nonverbal Behavior, 16*, 21–39.

McClure, E. B. (2000). A meta-analytic review of sex differences in facial expression processing and their development in infants, children and adolescents. *Psychogical Bulletin, 126*, 424–453. doi: 10.1037/0033-2909.126.3.424.

McManis, M. H., Bradley, M. M., Berg, W. K., Cuthbert, B. N., & Lang, P. J. (2001). Emotional reactions in children: verbal, physiological, and behavioral responses to affective pictures. *Psychophysiology, 38*, 222–231. doi:10.1111/1469-8986.3820222.

McManis, M. H., Bradley, M. M., Cuthbert, B. N., & Lang, P. J. (1995). Kids have feelings too: children's physiological responses to affective pictures. *Psychophysiology, 33*, S53 (Abstract).

Messinger, D., & Fogel, A. (2007). The interactive development of social smiling. In R. V. Kail (Ed.), *Advances in child development and behavior* (pp. 327–366). Amsterdam, NL: Elsevier.

Montagne, B., Kessels, R. P., Frigerio, E., de Haan, E. H., & Perrett, D. I. (2005). Sex differences in the perception of affective facial expressions: Do men really lack emotional sensitivity? *Cognitive Processes, 6*, 136–141. doi:10.1007/s10339-005-0050-6.

Montirosso, R., Peverelli, M., Frigerio, E., Crespi, M., & Brogatti, R. (2010). The development of dynamic facial expression recognition at different intensities in 4- to 18-year-olds. *Social Development, 19*, 71–92. doi: 10.1111/j.1467-9507.2008.00527.x.

Rozin, P. (1990). Development in the food domain. *Developmental Psychology, 26*, 555–562. doi:0012-1649/90/000.75.

Russell, J. A. (1980). A circumplex model of affect. *Journal of Personality and Social Psychology, 39*, 1161–1178.

Scholten, M. R. M., Aleman, A., Montagne, B., & Kahn, R.S. (2005). Schizophrenia and processing of facial emotions: Sex matters. *Schizophrenia Research, 78*, 61–67. doi:10.1016/j.schres.2005.06.019.

Springer, U. S., Rosas, A., McGetrick, J., & Bowers, D. (2007). Differences in startle reactivity during the perception of angry and fearful faces. *Emotion*, *7*, 516–525. doi:10.1037/1528-3542.7.3.516 516.

Thayer, J. F., & Johnsen, B. H. (2000). Sex differences in judgment of facial affect. A multivariate analysis of recognition errors. *Scandinavian Journal of Psychology*, *41*, 243–246. doi:10.1016/j.paid.2005.12.014.

Thomas, L. A., De Bellis, M. D., Graham, R., & LaBar, K. (2007). Development of emotional facial recognition in late childhood and adolescence. *Developmental Science*, *10*, 547–558. doi: 10.1111/j.1467-7687.2007.00614.x

Thomas, K. M., Drevets, W. C., Whalen, P. J., Eccard, C. H., Dahl, R. E., Ryan, N. D., & Casey, B. J. (2001). Amygdala response to facial expressions in children and adults. *Biological Psychiatry*, *49*, 309–316. doi:10.1016/S0006-3223(00)01066-0.

Tremblay, C., Kirouac, G., & Dore, F.Y. (2001). The recognition of adults' and children's facial expressions of emotions. *The Journal of Psychology*, *121*, 341–350.

Vassallo, S., Cooper, S. L. C., & Douglas, J. M. (2009). Visual scanning in the recognition of facial affect: Is there an observer sex difference? *Journal of Vision*, *9*, 1–10.

Vicari, S., Reilly, J. S., Pasqualetti, P., Vizzotto, A., & Caltagirone, C. (2000). Recognition of facial expressions of emotions in school-age children: The intersection of perceptual and semantic categories. *Acta Paediatrica*, *89*, 836–845. doi:10.1111/j.1651-2227.2000.tb00392.x

Vrana, S. R., & Gross, D. (2004). Reactions to facial expressions: Effects of neutral expressions, gender, speech anxiety. *Biological Psychology*, *66*, 63–78. doi:10.1016/j.biopsycho.2003.07.004.

Walker-Andrews, A. S. (1997). Infants' perception of expressive behaviors: Differentiation of multimodal information. *Psychological Bulletin*, *121*, 437–456. doi: 10.1037/0033-2909.121.3.437.

Waters, A. M., Lipp, O. V., & Spence, S. H. (2005). The effects of affective picture stimuli on blink modulation in adults and children. *Biological Psychology*, *68*, 257–281. doi:10.1016/j.biopsycho.2004.05.002.

Waters, A. M., Neumann, D. L., Henry, J., Craske, M. G., & Ornitz, E. M. (2008). Baseline and affective startle modulation by emotional faces in 4–8 year old high and low anxious children. *Biological Psychology*, *78*, 10–19. doi:10.1016/j.biopsycho.2007.12.005.

Widen, S. C., & Russell, J. A. (2008). Young children's understanding of others' emotions. In M. Lewis & J. M. Haviland-Jones (Eds.), *Handbook of Emotions* (pp. 348–363). New York, NY: Guilford.

The Effect of Death Anxiety and Age on Health-Promoting Behaviors: A Terror-Management Theory Perspective

ÖZLEM BOZO
AYÇA TUNCA
YELİZ ŞİMŞEK

ABSTRACT. The authors aimed to examine the effect of death anxiety on the reports of health-promoting behaviors and to determine the role of age in this relation using a terror-management theory perspective. Participants were 100 individuals from young adult (those who were 20–35 years of age) and older adult (those who were 60 years of age and older) groups whom the authors assigned to the death anxiety or control conditions. The questionnaire set included a demographic information sheet and the Health-Promoting Lifestyle Profile II (S. Walker, K. R. Sechrist, & N. J. Pender, 1987). Before administering the scales, the authors gave the participants in the experimental condition a brief excerpt whose content induced death-related thoughts and led the participants to think about their own death. The authors calculated a 2 (young adults vs. older adults) × 2 (death anxiety vs. no death anxiety) between-subjects factorial analysis of variance (ANOVA) to test their hypotheses. Although ANOVA results did not yield a significant main effect for age, the main effect of the conditions was significant, indicating that people in the death anxiety condition reported more health-promoting behaviors than did people in the control condition. The interaction of the age and conditions was also significant. The authors discuss the strengths, limitations, and implications of the findings.

DURING THE 20TH CENTURY, THE LEADING CAUSE of death changed from infectious diseases such as pneumonia and tuberculosis to chronic diseases such as heart disease and cancer, which are closely related to unhealthy behaviors and lifestyle (Brannon & Feist, 2007). Although most people are presumably aware of the protective effects of health-promoting behaviors against those chronic diseases, many people still do not engage in them.

40

Few researchers have examined the effect of providing mortality-related information on health-promoting behaviors of different age groups, especially of older adults, from a terror-management theory (TMT) perspective (Greenberg, Pyszczynski, & Solomon, 1986). From the TMT perspective, human beings share the most common and simplest instinct, self-preservation, with other species. However, humans' intellectual capacities force them to recognize their inescapable mortality (Pyszczynski, Greenberg, & Solomon, 1997). The awareness of unavoidable death leads to possible paralyzing terror, which would generate continued goal-directed behavior that may be manifested in many ways. Researchers studying TMT claimed that people tend to show different reactions to death-related thoughts (Pyszczynski et al.). That is, when people face anxiety of death, they show different reactions. On the one hand, they tend to increase their health-promoting behaviors. On the other hand, they may increase their health-threatening behaviors (Arndt, Routledge, & Goldenberg, 2006). Thus, in addition to many other determinants such as age, people's reports of health-promoting behaviors may also be affected by death anxiety.

According to the dual-process model (Pyszczynski, Greenberg, & Solomon, 1999), which is an extension of TMT (Greenberg et al., 1986), people use different defense mechanisms against conscious and unconscious death-related thoughts. When the death-related thoughts are conscious, people use proximal defenses that involve active suppression of such thoughts or cognitive distortions that push the problem of death into the distant future in an apparently rational manner. Alternatively, when the death-related thoughts are unconscious, people use distal defenses that—on the surface—have no rational or logical relation to the problem of death. However, distal defenses defend people against death by making them capable of construing themselves to be valuable participants in a meaningful universe. Thus, health-promoting behaviors can be considered to be a proximal defense used to alleviate conscious death-related thoughts, and we intended to examine the effect of death anxiety—specifically, the fear of dying horribly—on one of the proximal defenses: health-promoting behaviors of young and older adults.

The literature has revealed that age could be one of the important determinants of health-promoting behaviors. Older adults tended to show higher scores than did young and middle-aged adults in different dimensions of health-promoting behaviors (Arnold & Becker, 2004). Out of six subscales, Arnold and Becker found significant age group differences in five subscales of the Health-Promoting Lifestyle Profile II (HPLP II; Walker, Sechrist, & Pender, 1987); namely, health responsibility, physical activity, nutrition, interpersonal relationships, and stress management. However, there was no significant age group difference in terms of spiritual growth. In another study, compared with younger adults, older adults had lower scores on physical activity; and younger adults' needs for health programming were less, compared with that of older adults (Bagwell & Bush, 2000). Although Arras, Ogletree, and Welshimer (2006) found no significant relations between total health-promoting behaviors and age, they detected a meaningful relation among advanced age, stress management, and health responsibility among male adults who were older than 45 years of age. Likewise, in another study, female participants tended to show better health behaviors than did their younger and less-educated counterparts (Jackson, 2006). In addition, researchers found that age was strongly associated with health-seeking behaviors. For example, as women's age increased, their mammography experiences also increased (Ham, 2006). Thus, it can be suggested that older adults, compared with their younger counterparts, tend to exhibit more health-promoting behaviors when there is no mortality salience.

When the effects of age and death anxiety on health-promoting behaviors were examined together in the literature, we encountered contradictory results. Different age groups have different levels of death anxiety, and these differences result in a variety of health-related behaviors (Ben-Ari & Findler, 2005). According to Ben-Ari and Findler's study, younger and middle-aged adults tended to promote health, more than did older adults, when death anxiety was consciously remembered. For the older group, a reminder of death was not a surprise because at older ages, people are familiar with the idea of impending death. In addition to their knowledge, older adults exhibited considerable preparation for death in terms of the care that hospices offer. Similarly, in another study, younger cancer patients had a stronger tendency to receive care than did the older ones (Catt et al., 2005). Parallel with the previous findings, age was found to be negatively associated with the fear of being destroyed; that is, the fear of "being cremated after death or donated to medical research" (Depaola, Griffin, Young, & Neimeyer, 2003, p. 346). However, some other studies indicated that the experience of embodied ill health, rather than age, seems to be important in terms of health-promoting behaviors (Lawton, 2002). Thus, it is difficult to figure out the common effect of age and death anxiety on health-promoting behaviors.

In summary, the literature revealed conflicting findings on the relation among age, death anxiety, and health-promoting behaviors. Therefore, the present study aimed to explore this relation among a Turkish sample with a newly adapted scale (i.e., the HPLP II), a direct measure of health-promoting behaviors. We hypothesized that death anxiety leads people to engage in health-promoting behaviors more frequently. Furthermore, older people engage in health-promoting behaviors more frequently than do younger people when there is no death anxiety. Last, compared with older adults in the death anxiety condition, young adults in the same condition engage in health-promoting behaviors more frequently.

Method

Participants

Participants were 100 individuals who did not receive any compensation for participation. We selected these participants through a convenience sampling procedure. We conducted the research with the available sample and kept constant all variables except age. Of participants, 50 were young adults between the ages of 25 and 35 years ($M = 29.6$ years, $SD = 3.6$ years), whereas the other 50 were older adults between the ages of 60 and 80 years ($M = 63.9$ years, $SD = 5.6$ years). There were 51 (51%) women and 49 (49%) men in the sample, and they were not significantly different from each other in terms of their reports of health-promoting behaviors, $t(98) = -.74$, $p > .05$; and death anxiety, $t(98) = -.48$, $p > .05$. We determined the social status of participants by their responses to two separate questions about their education and perceived SES. Accordingly, the participants of the present study were primarily from middle-class backgrounds ($n = 79$; 79%), whereas the rest were from lower class ($n = 17$; 17%), and upper class ($n = 4$; 4%) backgrounds. Approximately half of the sample comprised university graduates ($n = 53$; 53%), whereas the remaining participants were distributed across primary school graduates ($n = 23$; 23%), high school graduates ($n = 14$; 14%), graduate school graduates ($n = 7$; 7%), and secondary degree holders ($n = 3$; 3%).

Measures

HPLP II (Walker et al., 1987). We used the HPLP II to measure the frequency of participants' self-reported healthy behaviors. This instrument was designed to provide information about health-promoting lifestyle activities. The HPLP II is a 52-item scale comprising the following six subscales: self-actualization (13 items), health responsibility (10 items), exercise (5 items), stress management (7 items), interpersonal support (7 items), and nutrition (6 items). Examples of behaviors measured are the following: eating breakfast and taking time for relaxation. The items are rated on a 4-point Likert-type scale ranging from 1 (*never*) to 4 (*routinely*). Total possible scores ranged from 52 to 208. We adapted the HPLP II to Turkish culture by using individuals from different ages and SES. The Turkish version of the scale had the same number of items as did the original one, and each item was translated word by word. However, during the translation process, on the basis of the daily use of the terms, different serving sizes were adapted (e.g., serving to exact grams, slices). The Turkish version of the HPLP II has a high internal consistency reliability of .93 for the present sample. Higher scores on the HPLP II indicate a lifestyle with higher self-reported health-promoting behaviors.

Thorson–Powell's Death Anxiety Scale (Yıldız & Karaca, 2001). A Turkish adaptation of Thorson and Powell's (1994) Death Anxiety scale comprised 25 items rated on a 5-point Likert-type type scale ranging from 1 (*not true to me*) to 5 (*very true to me*). Higher scores on this scale reflected higher death anxiety. The reliability of the scale in terms of Cronbach's alpha coefficient was .84. To test the validity of the scale, we examined its correlation with Templer's (1970) Death Anxiety scale, $r = .28$, $p < .01$, and concluded that Thorson–Powell's Death Anxiety scale seems to have convergent validity. Thorson–Powell's Death

Anxiety scale has a high internal consistency reliability of .89 for the present sample. We used this scale in the present study for manipulation check.

Procedure

Before we conducted the main study, we conducted two pilot studies. The aim of the first pilot study was to verify that the scenario—which would be used in the main study—engenders death anxiety. To verify that older adults did not experience more trait death anxiety than did young adults, the death anxiety scores of age groups were compared in another pilot study.

We recruited participants of the main study from different age groups (younger vs. older adults) through a convenience sampling procedure. First, we found 50 young adults and 50 older adults and randomly assigned them to the two experimental conditions (death anxiety vs. control). With this approach, we created four cells of the present study: 2 (age: young adults vs. older adults) × 2 (experimental conditions: death anxiety vs. control). After the random assignment of the participants to the conditions, each cell comprised 25 participants. The participants did not know whether they were in the death anxiety or control condition. They were given informed consent forms to sign to assure that they participated in the study voluntarily. Once they accepted to participate, participants completed the questionnaires in approximately 20–30 min.

Before the administration of the questionnaires, participants in the death anxiety condition were presented with a scenario including several reminders of death. Recent death anxiety literature suggested that death anxiety is a multi-dimensional construct (Henley & Donovan, 1999). Apart from the fear of one's own death, it also includes fear of missing out on a full life, fear of the death of loved ones, fear of causing death, and fear of the process of dying or fear of dying horribly. The fear of the process of dying or dying horribly was the theme of the present scenario. The researchers tried to increase the participants' feelings of anxiety about death through this scenario by permitting them to assume that they were the protagonist of the story (see the Appendix). After being exposed to a death anxiety-inducing scenario, participants in the death anxiety condition completed the HPLP II. The participants in the control group were administered all the scales that the experimental group completed except for the scenario with the death reminders. In other words, for the control group, no death anxiety-inducing cues were provided. After the completion of the study, the participants were debriefed and assured that the information gathered would remain anonymous.

Results

To verify that the scenario engenders death anxiety, we compared death anxiety pre- and posttests scores of 19 older adults using paired samples *t* test. The analysis revealed that the scenario engendered death anxiety among older

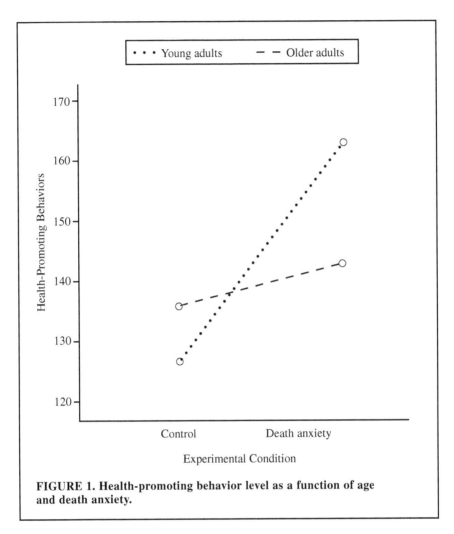

FIGURE 1. Health-promoting behavior level as a function of age and death anxiety.

adults, $t(19) = -2.23$, $p < .05$, $d = -0.54$. To confirm that young and older adults were not significantly different from each other in terms of death anxiety before the exposure to death anxiety condition (i.e., to verify that older adults did not experience more trait death anxiety), the pretest death anxiety scores of age groups were compared in another pilot study. An independent samples t test analysis revealed that before the exposure to the scenario, older adults were not experiencing more trait death anxiety, $t(33) = -.80$, $p = .43$.

We conducted a 2 (young vs. older adults) $\times$ 2 (death anxiety vs. no death anxiety) between-subjects factorial analysis of variance (ANOVA) to examine the main effects of death anxiety and age, and their interaction effects on health-promoting behaviors. ANOVA results did not yield a significant main effect for age, $F(1, 96) = 1.83$, $p = .18$, meaning that people's health-promoting behaviors did not seem to change as a function of their age. However, we found a significant main effect for the conditions, $F(1, 96) = 31.92$, $p < .001$, $\eta^2 = .25$, suggesting that people in the death anxiety condition ($M = 152.38$, $SD = 22.08$) engaged in health-promoting behaviors more frequently than did people in the control condition ($M = 131.40$, $SD = 17.43$). The interaction of the age and conditions was also significant, $F(1, 96) = 14.67$, $p < .001$, $\eta^2 = .13$, indicating that young adults in the death anxiety condition ($M = 162.00$, $SD = 20.95$) reported more health-promoting behaviors than did older adults in the same condition ($M = 142.76$, $SD = 19.06$). However, young adults in control condition ($M = 126.80$, $SD = 10.79$) reported less health-promoting behaviors than did older adults in the same condition ($M = 136.00$, $SD = 21.45$). Post hoc Tukey HSD tests showed that young adults in the death anxiety condition reported more health-promoting behaviors than young adults in control condition. We found no significant differences in terms of older adults' health-promoting behaviors in experimental and control conditions. Furthermore, a post hoc comparison with Tukey HSD test showed that the reports of health-promoting behaviors by older and younger adults were not significantly different from each other in the control condition but were significant in the death anxiety condition. Figure 1 represents the interaction effect.

Discussion

The present study examined the effect of age and death anxiety on the frequency of engaging in health-promoting activities. Although ANOVA results did not yield a significant main effect for age, the main effect of the conditions was significant, indicating that participants in the death anxiety condition tended to report more health-promoting behaviors than did those in the control condition. The interaction of the age and conditions was also significant, meaning that young adults in the death anxiety condition reported more health-promoting behaviors than did older adults in the same condition. However, young adults in the control condition reported less health-promoting behaviors than did older adults in the same condition. Moreover, young adults in the experimental condition engaged in more health-promoting behaviors than did young adults in the control condition. Nevertheless, we found no significant differences in terms of older adults' health-promoting behaviors in the experimental and control conditions. According to the results of the analyses, all hypotheses of the study were verified.

We found that death anxiety had an important effect on the reports of health-promoting behaviors, but only of the young adults. This finding further supports previous research suggesting age differences in responses to death reminders (Gesser, Wong, & Reker, 1988; Maxfield et al., 2007; Rasmussen, & Brems, 1996). These studies showed that despite the temporal proximity to death, older adults were somehow less defensive against the reminders of death. As Hecken-hausen and Schulz (1995) stated, increased frequency and potency of mortality reminders, together with decreased effectiveness of long-standing strategies for protecting oneself from the awareness of death and accompanying anxiety, may lead older adults to adopt newer and more age-appropriate strategies to protect themselves from the awareness of their mortality and accompanying anxiety. Researchers have suggested that as people get older, death becomes an expected and normative event, and this makes the death less stressful and easier to cope with (Ryff & Dunn, 1985; Ryff & Heidrich, 1997).

The finding that older adults report less health-promoting behaviors than do young adults in the death anxiety condition can also be explained by the nature of the scenerio that we used in the present study. As the TMT literature suggested, subtle mortality salience inductions produce stronger effects than do obstrusive and powerful inductions (Greenberg, Pyszczynski, Solomon, Simon, & Breus, 1994). Similarly, researchers have found that whereas younger adults make harsher judgements in response to typical mortality salience inductions, older adults do not (Maxfield et al., 2007). Thus, because the scenerio we used in the present study was a typical mortality salience induction, older adults may not have been affected by it as much as the younger adults. This same finding that older adults reported less health-promoting behaviors than did young adults in the death anxiety condition can be explained by the fact that older adults have a lower fear of death than do both middle-aged and younger adults (Gesser et al., 1988). As previously mentioned, as people get older, death becomes an expected and normative event, and this makes the death less stressful and easier to cope with (Ryff & Dunn, 1985; Ryff & Heidrich, 1997).

As previously stated, young adults in the death anxiety conditon reported significantly more health-promoting behaviors than did their counterparts in the control condition. This finding is contrary to the popular notion that young people feel that they are immortal. As Henley and Donovan (2003) stated, young people thought they were immortal until they were exposed to death reminders. Thus, young people are responsive to messeges about death. Therefore, to pro-mote young adults' willingness and motivation to engage in health-promoting behaviors, reminders of death may be used. However, death reminders need to be carefully used in health-promoting campaigns. As Routledge, Arndt, and Goldenberg (2004) indicated, reactions to unconscious death concerns may actu-ally threathen one's health. Routledge et al. stated that when the death-related concerns function below the level of consciousness, the most important deter-minant of defensive behavior becomes the potential of that behavior to increase self-esteem, regardless of how healthy or physically protective that behavior is. That is, mortality concerns, depending on where they are in their consciousness, may produce contradictory defenses (Routledge et al.).

We found that older adults were better than younger adults in terms of practicing health-promoting behaviors without a reminder of death (in the control condition). This may be because of several possible underlying mechanisms. Arras et al. (2006) found that older male adults have a higher responsibility for health and better stress-management strategies. Moreover, older people believe that their control over their health is higher (Arnold & Becker, 2004; Arras et al.). Several studies supported this finding that older adults engage in more health-promoting behaviors when there is no death anxiety. Jackson (2006) found that older female adults tend to show better health behaviors than do younger ones. Similarly, Ham (2006) found that as women's age increases, their mammography experiences also increase. Thus, regardless of their gender, when older people do not feel death anxiety, they engage in health-promoting behaviors more frequently than do younger ones because of the following three reasons: higher responsibility of health, better stress-management strategies (Arras et al.), and higher control over their health (Arnold & Becker; Arras et al.).

Although the findings on the relation between age and health-promoting behaviors conflict, most of the findings suggested that as age increases, the frequency of engaging in health-promoting behaviors also increases (Arnold & Becker, 2004; Arras et al., 2006; Ham, 2006; Jackson, 2006). However, in the present study, we did not obtain a significant difference between young and older adults' scores on health-promoting behaviors as a function of their age. This may be because of the limited age range of the present sample. HPLP II was originally developed using individuals between the ages of 18 and 92 years. However, this study did not take middle-age groups into the scope of existing experimental conditions. Further studies may need to include adolescents (those who are between the ages of 15–25 years) and middle-aged individuals (those who are between the ages of 35–60 years) to have more generalizable results.

In previous studies, there has been a significant relation between an individual's own perception of health and his or her health-promoting behaviors. Older adults are more concerned with their health and have more ability to perform tasks that enhance their well-being (Bagwell & Bush, 2000). In addition, death reminders do not result in a change in the behaviors of older adults who already take care of their health (Ben-Ari & Findler, 2005). Similarly, the present study found that different conditions (death anxiety vs. control) make no difference in the frequency of engagement in health-promoting behaviors of older adults. On the contrary, younger adults in the present study showed significantly higher health-promoting behaviors in the death anxiety condition than in the control condition. According to the study by Gailliot, Schmeichel, and Baumeister (2006), awareness of death and mortality is frightening to people, and self-regulation prevents them from awareness of death and mortality's aversiveness. In Gailliot et al.'s study, self-regulation meant controlling various elements of one's life successfully. Because of their being able to avoid this aversive consciousness of death, younger people in the present study may have reported higher performance on health-promoting behaviors. Last, we found that older adults engaged in less health-promoting behaviors than did younger adults in the death anxiety condition, which may be explained by older adults' familiarity with the idea of death (Ben-Ari & Findler).

Limitations

There were several limitations of the present study. One of these limitations was the sample size. We used only 100 participants to test the hypotheses of the study. An increased number of participants would yield more reliable results. Also, the reminder of death was followed by 2 min of thinking time. This time delay may have also affected the results of the study. As Greenberg et al. (1994) suggested, to affect individuals' interpersonal judgments and behavior after the problem of death is activated, it should be removed from consciousness. They stated that the receptibility of death-related themes is higher after a delay and distraction than it is immediately after the mortality salience. Thus, further studies may prolong the time following the death reminder and then measure the reports of health-promoting behaviors of participants. Moreover, although death anxiety is a multidimensional construct (Henley & Donovan, 1999), the present study examined the effect of only one of those dimensions—fear of the process of dying or fear of dying horribly—on the reports of health-promoting behaviors. Future studies need to examine the effect of all of the dimensions of death anxiety on individuals' reports of health-promoting behaviors. Specifically, because the effect of reminders related to the death of loved ones may be more dramatic than the effect of reminders related to one's own death (Henley & Donovan, 2003), the observed age-related differences in the experimental condition may be more dramatic. Furthermore, because the present study was cross-sectional, the observed age-related differences may be the results of the differences between the older and younger samples rather than the age per se. Another limitation of the study was that we used a composite score of all the subscales of HPLP II rather than individual subscales. In the future, researchers need to use individual subscales to get information about specific types of health-promoting behaviors. Last, researchers have suggested that self-esteem is another factor that may affect the effect of age and death anxiety on the performance of health-promoting behaviors (Ben-Ari & Findler, 2005). Therefore, further studies need to investigate the possible moderator–mediator effect of self-esteem of individuals in relation to age and death anxiety on the people's willingness to engage in health-promoting behaviors.

To conclude, the finding that death anxiety and its interaction with age are important predictors of health-promoting behaviors reveals much about humans' most common and simplest instinct—self-preservation—and their reactions to the fear of unavoidable death. However, as Lester (1967) stated, compared with the progress in other areas of psychology, the understanding of the fear of death has increased little, and for this reason, researchers need to conduct more studies to have a better understanding of the subject of interest.

REFERENCES

Arndt, J., Routledge, C., & Goldenberg, J. L. (2006). Predicting proximal health responses to reminders of death: The influence of coping style and health optimism. *Psychology and Health, 21,* 593–614.

Arnold, W., & Becker, C. M. (2004). Health-promoting behaviors of older Americans versus young and middle aged adults. *Educational Gerontology, 30,* 835–844.

Arras, R. E., Ogletree, R. J., & Welshimer, K. J. (2006). Health-promoting behaviors in men age 45 and above. *International Journal of Men's Health, 5*(1), 65–79.

Bagwell, M. M., & Bush, H. A. (2000). Improving health promotion for blue-collar workers. *Journal of Nursing Care Quality, 14*(4), 65–71.

Ben-Ari, O. T., & Findler, L. (2005). Proximal and distal effects of mortality salience on willingness to engage in health-promoting behavior along the life span. *Psychology and Health, 20,* 303–318.

Brannon, L., & Feist, J. (2007). *Health psychology: An introduction to behavior and health* (6th ed.). Belmont, CA: Wadsworth.

Catt, S., Blanchard, M., Hall, J. A., Zis, M., Blizard, R., & King, M. (2005). Older adults' attitudes to death, palliative treatment and hospice care. *Palliative Medicine, 19,* 402–410.

Depaola, S. J., Griffin, M., Young, J. R., & Neimeyer, R. A. (2003). Death anxiety and attitudes toward the elderly among older adults: The role of gender and ethnicity. *Death Studies, 27,* 335–354.

Gailliot, M. T., Schmeichel, B. J., & Baumeister R. F. (2006). Self-regulatory processes defend against the threat of death: Effects of self-control depletion and trait self-control on thoughts and fears of dying. *Journal of Personality and Social Psychology, 91,* 49–62.

Gesser, G., Wong, P. T., & Reker, G. T. (1988). Death attitudes across the life span: The development and validation of the Death Attitude Profile (DAP). *Omega: Journal of Death and Dying, 18,* 113–128.

Greenberg, J., Pyszczynski, T., & Solomon, S. (1986). The causes and consequences of a need for self-esteem: A terror-management theory. In R. F. Baumeister (Ed.), *Public self and private self* (pp. 189–212). New York: Springer-Verlag.

Greenberg, J., Pyszczynski, T., Solomon, S., Simon, L., & Breus, M. (1994). The role of consciousness and the specificity to death of mortality salience effects. *Journal of Personality and Social Psychology, 67,* 627–637.

Ham, O. K. (2006). Factors affecting mammography behavior and intention among Korean women. *Oncology Nursing Forum, 33*(1), 113–119.

Heckenhausen, J., & Schulz, R. (1995). A life-span theory of control. *Psychological Review, 102,* 284–304.

Henley, N., & Donovan, R. (1999). Threat appeals in social marketing: Death as a 'special case.' *International Journal of Nonprofit and Voluntary Sector Marketing, 4*, 1–20.

Henley, N., & Donovan, R. (2003). Young people's response to death threat appeals: Do they really feel immortal? *Health Education Research: Theory & Practice, 18*(1), 1–14.

Jackson, T. (2006). Relationships between perceived close social support and health practices within community samples of American women and men. *The Journal of Psychology, 140*, 229–246.

Lawton, J. (2002). Colonising the future: Temporal perceptions and health-relevant behaviours across the adult lifecourse. *Sociology of Health & Illness, 24*, 714–733.

Lester, D. (1967). Experimental and correlational studies of the fear of death. *Psychological Bulletin, 67*, 27–36.

Maxfield, M., Pyszczynski, T., Kluck, B., Cox, C. R., Greenberg, J., & Solomon, S. (2007). Age-related differences in responses to thoughts of one's own death: Mortality salience and judgements of moral transgressions. *Psychology & Aging, 22*, 341–353.

Pyszczynski, T., Greenberg, J., & Solomon S. (1997). Why do we need what we need? A terror-management perspective on the roots of human social motivation. *Psychological Inquiry, 8*, 1–20.

Pyszczynski, T., Greenberg, J., & Solomon S. (1999). A dual-process model of defense against conscious and unconscious death-related thoughts: An extension of terror-management theory. *Psychological Review, 106*, 835–845.

Rasmussen, C. A., & Brems, C. (1996). The relationship of death anxiety to age and psychosocial maturity. *The Journal of Psychology, 130*, 141–144.

Routledge, C., Arndt, J., & Goldenberg, J. L. (2004). A time to tan: Proximal and distal effects of mortality salience on sun exposure intentions. *Personality and Social Psychology Bulletin, 30*, 1347–1358.

Ryff, C. D., & Dunn, D. D. (1985). A life-span developmental approach to the study of stressful events. *Journal of Applied Developmental Psychology, 6*, 113–127.

Ryff, C. D., & Heidrich, S. M. (1997). Experience and well-being: Explorations on domains of life and how they matter. *International Journal of Behavioral Development, 20*, 193–206.

Templer, D. I. (1970). The construction and validation of a death anxiety scale. *The Journal of General Psychology, 82*, 165–177.

Thorson, J. A., & Powell, F. C. (1994). A revised death anxiety scale. In R. A. Neimeyer (Ed.), *Death anxiety handbook* (pp. 31–43). Washington, DC: Taylor & Francis.

Walker, S., Sechrist, K. R., & Pender, N. J. (1987). The Health-Promoting Lifestyle Profile development and psychometric characteristics. *Nursing Research, 36*(2), 76–81.

Yıldız, M., & Karaca, F. (2001). Thorson–Powell Ölüm Kaygısı Ölçeği'nin Türkçe çevirisinin normal populasyonda geçerlik ve güvenilirlik çalışması [The validity and reliability study of Turkish version of Thorson–Powell Death Anxiety scale in a normal population]. *Tabula Rasa, 1*(1), 43–55.

APPENDIX
Short Story Involving Feelings of Anxiety About Death

Please read the following short story. After you read the story, assume that you are the protagonist and think about your feelings of anxiety about death.

He was no more making plans, for everything happened spontaneously. Beyond his awareness, just ordinarily. . . Moreover, he was not only already familiar with the darkness in his heart but also, surely, with death, which was breathing at his nape. He put his legs—which were heavy due to illness—on the ground by the help of his hands. He could hardly straighten after he mustered up all his strength and stooped. He walked towards the window with his very little steps, sipped some water to remove the bitter taste and smell of the medicines in his mouth. Just for a moment, he tried to find peace in the splashing sound of the water, which occurred while he was pouring the water into the glass. Then he opened the thick curtain of the window; the glass of which he stubbornly kept closed every night. Jesus! All darkness on Earth flowed inside him in one second. The feeling of drowning . . . He was in the throes of death. . . . It was morning; it was the hour when the sun was at its brightest state, which illuminated the room even from behind the thick curtain. Alas, the sun was also gone from his eyes as the curtain was drawn, never to rise again. He couldn't gulp. He was feeling guilty as he breathed because he had despicably treated his young body, his greatest treasure. A most vigorous scream left inside and arrived to his throat yet could not go out, which further drowned him. The bottom of all his hair was hurting as if he was hung by his hair. He felt a pressure on his heart. As life continued at its most beauty beyond the window, he was, between his own room and the hospital corridors, which smelt medicine, just waiting for the moment when death would take him away.

The Effects of Material and Experiential Discretionary Purchases on Consumer Happiness: Moderators and Mediators

REBECCA THOMAS
MURRAY MILLAR

ABSTRACT. Experiential purchases are differentiated from material purchases in terms of objective; experiential purchases serve the purpose of acquiring a life experience, while material purchases serve the purpose of acquiring an object. Research has demonstrated that experiential purchases are associated with more happiness than material purchases. The current study investigated two explanations for this relationship that focused on the how the purchase influenced the self and how the purchase influenced interpersonal relationships. In addition, the study explored whether social economic status would influence the strength of the relationship between the type of purchase and happiness. Participants were required to recall either a recent experiential or material purchase and rate their happiness with the purchase. Then participants completed scales designed to measure the purchase's impact on the self and interpersonal relationships. Last, participants completed a scale to measure social economic status. It was found that Impacts on the Self mediated the relationship between purchase type and happiness and Socioeconomic Status moderated the relationship.

WESTERN CULTURE IS CURRENTLY IMBUED WITH the materialistic idea that possessions produce happiness with strong forces in the culture promoting and supporting this idea. For example, the average American is exposed to an astonishing 3,000 advertisements each day (Kilbourne & Jhally, 2000); and Kasser (2002) suggests the media is saturated with images of material excess. Not surprisingly, vast amounts of discretionary money and time are used for the acquisition of material possessions (Franco, 2004). Despite the ascendancy of materialism, persistent voices from both religious and humanistic traditions have disputed the notion that the acquisition of discretionary possessions brings happiness. For example, Erick Fromm (1976) proposed that acquiring possessions could inhibit self–actualization and happiness. Further, research examining the effects of material possessions on happiness has failed to find a straightforward relationship between discretionary possessions and happiness.

At the societal level, both Hellevik (2003) and Frank (1999, 2005) found that in wealthy western nations, increases in material possessions were not associated with gains in happiness. Correspondingly, both Diener and Oishi (2000), and Myers (2000) found that increases in material possessions were not associated with increases in well-being across a number of nations. At a more ideographic level, persons who placed more importance on material possessions reported less happiness and were less psychologically healthy than persons who placed less importance on possessions (Kasser & Ahuvia, 2002). Other researchers have produced similar findings (e.g., Richins and Dawson, 1992; Sirgy, 1998; Van Boven, 2000; and Wright and Larson, 1993). Scholars offer a variety of explanations for this absent relationship. For example, Myers suggests that the pursuit of material goals my cause other social and emotional goals to remain unmet (Myers & Diener, 1995; Myers, 2000). Perhaps social writer Eric Hoffer was correct when he observed, "You can never get enough of what you don't need to make you happy" (Shachtman, 2011).

Material and Experiential Purchases

Controversy over the effects of material possessions on happiness has inspired social scientists to closely examine the relationship between discretionary purchases and happiness. As part of this endeavor, Van Boven and his colleagues have distinguished between discretionary purchases of material objects and discretionary purchases of experiences (Van Boven & Gilovich, 2003). Material purchases have the purpose of acquiring a material object, are tangible, and remain in the present. The most common material purchases recalled by participants in empirical studies are electronics and jewelry (Van Boven & Gilovich). Conversely, experiential purchases have the purpose of acquiring a life experience through participation in an event, are not tangible, are episodic, and are experienced by the person for a finite amount of time. Examples of experiential purchases include vacations, admissions to an amusement park, or dinner at a restaurant. Experiential purchases are distinguished from material purchases in terms of the goal, i.e., experiential purchases have the goal of acquiring a life experience while a material purchases have the goal of acquiring an object. Research examining the relationship between happiness and these two types of discretionary purchases has consistently found that experiential purchases are associated with more happiness than material purchases (Millar & Thomas, 2009; Van Boven & Gilovich, 2003).

Although there is evidence that experiential purchases are associated with more happiness than material purchases no research has examined why experiential purchases produce more happiness or when this relationship will be strong or weak. The present study explored two mediating variables that might cause the relationship between experiential purchases and happiness. In addition, the study examined a potential moderating variable that might influence the strength of the relationship between experiential purchases and happiness.

Mediating Role of Impact on Self and Interpersonal Relationships

There are two potential causal explanations for why there is a strong relationship between experiential purchases and happiness: Impact on the Self and Interpersonal Relationships. First, discretionary experiential purchases may be more central to positive self-identity than discretionary material purchases because a large part of one's self-concept is made-up of experiences. Indeed, when one describes life it tends to be a series of experiences (e.g., obtained degree, fell in love, had children). Although material purchases are often used to signal to others elements of your identity, they tend not to be incorporated into descriptions of the self (Belk, 1988). The acquisition of experiences may lead a person to view the self more favorably, due to positive stereotypes associated with experiential people who are often viewed as learned or cultured (Van Boven, 2005). Persons who are primarily interested in the acquisition of material objects are often viewed as superficial and unintelligent (Van Boven). Furthermore, experiential purchases may satisfy the personal needs of self–actualization and personal growth more than material acquisitions (Kasser & Ryan, 1996). For example, experiential purchases, such as tickets to a museum, are often viewed as more meaningful than material purchases because of their ostensible ability to contribute to self-growth and development (Kasser, 2002).

Second, discretionary experiential purchases may foster more social contact than discretionary material purchases, that is, experiences are more likely to involve significant interactions with other persons. In the literature examining purchases and happiness, the most commonly described experiences are dating, dining, and dancing purchases, whereas the most commonly described material purchases are clothes, jewelry, and electronics (Van Boven, 2005). Each of the most commonly referred to experiential purchases requires some form of social interaction by their nature. Although purchasing clothes may involve other persons, the primary feature of experiential experiences, such as dating, is interacting with another person. It is possible that most experiential purchases inherently require social interaction. A number of lines of research have demonstrated that increases in social interactions are associated with increases in happiness (e.g., Argyle, 1987; Diener & Seligman, 2002; Kasser, 2002; Oishi & Koo, 2008).

Moderating Effect of SES

There is reason to believe there are factors that might make the relationship between experiential purchases and happiness either stronger or weaker, such as socioeconomic status. Socioeconomic status (SES) most often refers to a person's position within a hierarchical social structure and is a distribution in relation to others based on opportunity, prosperity, and standing (Mirowsky & Ross, 2003).

Overall, the research examining the psychological consequences of SES has produced inconsistent results. Some research indicates that people high in SES report higher levels of positive psychological outcomes such as happiness and life satisfaction compared to people low in SES (Argyle, 1987; Myers & Diener, 1995; Mirowsky & Ross). Other research indicates that little to no relationship between income and feelings of well–being or happiness (Ahuvia & Friedman, 1998; Csikszentmihalyi, 1999; Diener, 2000; Myers, 2000; Oishi, Diener, Lucas, & Such 1999; Oropesa, 1995; Richins & Rudmin, 1994; Schyns, 1998, 2000). However, most theorizing and data indicate that persons low in SES would be happier with material purchases compared to persons higher in SES. Kasser (2002) posits that low SES leads to insecurity due to the worry and preoccupation with basic needs such as physical safety and comfort. It is possible that low SES persons cope with this insecurity by focusing on the acquisition of possessions. Further, it is possible that low SES persons use possessions as a means of improving their SES standing. Sangkhawasi and Johri (2007) have found that people with lower incomes acquire material possessions to gain the perception of higher status.

Hypotheses

In order to examine both why there is a relationship between experiential purchases and happiness and when this relationship will be strong or weak the current study examined four hypotheses. First, experiential purchases will produce more self–reported happiness compared to material purchases. Second and third, Impact on the Self and Interpersonal Relationships will mediate purchase type and happiness, respectively. Fourth, SES will moderate the relationship between purchase type and happiness. Specifically, persons lower in SES will report more happiness with material purchases; persons higher in SES will report more happiness with experiential purchases.

Method

Participants

Participants were 80 females and males recruited from undergraduates at a large university located in the southwestern United States. Participants received no monetary compensation and the student participants received class credit in exchange for participation. The average age of the participants was 23. Seventy-three percent of the participants were of European descent, 12% were of Hispanic descent, 7% were of Asian descent, 4% were of African descent, and 4% were from other groups.

Procedure

The experimenter informed the participants that the purpose of the study is to explore his/her reaction to a recent life event and that all of their responses would be anonymous. Participants were then randomly assigned to either the material purchase or experiential purchase conditions. In the material purchase condition, the instructions asked the participants to recall their most recent material purchase for more than $100. That is, think about a recent discretionary purchase of an object that you obtained and kept in your possession. In the experiential purchase condition, the instructions asked the participants to recall their most recent experiential purchase for more than $100 where the primary purpose of the purchase was to acquire a life experience. That is, think about some recent discretionary activity you paid to participate in. The directions in this study for the purchase conditions were modeled from Van Boven and Gilovich (2003).

Happiness Measures. After the participants completed the written description of the event, they completed the questionnaire designed to measure happiness. On the first scale, participants were asked to indicate how happy the purchase made them feel on a nine–point scale with end–points of 1 (*not happy*) and 9 (*very happy*). On the second scale, participants were asked to indicate how much the event contributed to their happiness, and on a third scale, whether they would have been more happy doing something else. This method has shown to be a reliable and valid way to measure happiness in regards to purchase typologies and allows for a check of internal consistency (Millar & Thomas, 2009; Van Boven & Gilovich, 2003).

Mediating Variables Measures. Impact on the Self was measured using self–report scales with end points of 1 (*no contribution to the self*) and 9 (*contributes highly to the self*). Participants were asked how much the purchase contributed to their self–concept, self–image, self–growth, how important the purchase was to them as a person, how meaningful the purchase was to them, and if the purchase made them feel more positive about themselves. In addition, the degree to which the purchase was associated with Interpersonal Relationships was measured on three nine–point scales with end–points of 1 (*no interactions*) and 9 (*many interactions*). Participants were asked to indicate how much time was spent with another person in relation to the purchase, how much the purchase fostered a relationship with another person, and how much the purchase contributed to conversation and/or discussions with others. The order of the Impact on the Self and Interpersonal Relationships scales were counter balanced.

Moderating SES Variable Measure In the social sciences SES has been most often conceptualized as a psychosocial variable consisting of where one views oneself in relationship to others in terms of education, income, occupation, and wealth (Mirowsky & Ross, 2003; Rindfleisch, Burroughs, & Denton, 1997; Twenge & Campbell, 2002). To measure SES participants were asked to complete six items. Participants were asked to indicate maternal and paternal educational attainment on separate scales with end points ranging from 1 (*no school*) to 9 (*completed graduate degree*). Third, participants were asked to indicate their perceived wealth, from 1 (*lowest wealth*) and 9 (*highest wealth*). Perceived wealth was explored to avoid potential recall problems regarding a specific dollar amount; and has been found to be a better predictor than more objective dollar measures

(Ghiselli, 1964; O'Guinn & Faber, 1989; Rindfleisch et al., 1997). Fourth, participants were asked their housing status from 1 the (*lowest status*) and 9 (*highest status*). The fifth and six items asked participants how much of their own income consists of discretionary funds from 1 (*low amount*) to 9 (*high amount*), and how much of their parents' income consists of discretionary funds with the same endpoints, respectively.

Results

To investigate the impact of the type of purchase on self–reports of happiness, a happiness measure was created by summing the participant's responses to the three questions of happiness associated with the purchase (Cronbach's alpha = .82). This happiness measure was analyzed using an independent t–test contrasting experiential purchase with material purchase. As predicted, and consistent with past research, a significant effect for Purchase Type was obtained, $t(78) = 2.83, p$ <.01. Experiential purchases were associated with more of happiness ($M = 7.50$, $SD = 1.19$) than material purchases ($M = 6.62, SD = 1.22$).

Mediating Role of Impact on the Self

An impact-on-self measure was created by summing each participant's responses to the questions related to the construct (Cronbach's alpha = .87). This measure was analyzed using an independent t–test contrasting experiential purchase with material purchase. Consistent with the mediation prediction, there was a statistically significant difference between Purchase Types on Impact-on-Self, $t(78) = 5.70, p < .01$, with experiential purchases ($M = 6.94, SD = 1.01$) having a higher propensity to associate with Impact-on-Self compared to material purchases ($M = 4.57, SD = 1.03$). However, to demonstrate the meditational role of Impact-on-Self, we must show that when the effect of the mediator (Impact-on-Self) is controlled for the relationship between the independent variable (type of purchase) and happiness is reduced. To accomplish this we used the analytic strategy outlined by Baron and Kenny (1986) and conducted three regression analyses. First, the relationship between the mediator (Impact-on-Self) and happiness was established by regressing on Happiness and on Impact-on-Self. As expected there was a significant association, (*standardized beta* = .42, $t =$ 4.08, $p < .0001$). Second, Happiness was regressed on the Purchase Type. As expected and consistent with the original t–test, Purchase Type was significantly related to Happiness (*standardized beta* = .31, $t = 2.83, p < .01$). Third, Happiness was regressed on both Impact-on-Self and Purchase Type. In this analysis, the effects of the mediator (Impact-on-Self) are removed from the relationship between the independent variable (Purchase Type) and the dependent variable (Happiness). As predicted when the effects of the mediator (Impact-on-Self) were controlled for, the relationship between the Type of Purchase and Happiness became non-significant (*standardized beta* = .10, $t = -.82, p = .42$). A Sobel's

Test indicated, the beta from this equation (*standardized beta* = .10) was significantly smaller than the beta for Purchase Type when the mediator was not controlled for (*standardized beta* = .31, t = 2.83, p < .01), (Sobel's Test, Z = 2.63, p < .01).

Mediating Role of Interpersonal Relationships

An interpersonal relationships measure was created by summing each participant's responses to the questions related to the construct (Cronbach's alpha = .80). When this measure was analyzed using an independent t-test contrasting experiential purchase with material purchase a statistically significant difference between Purchase Types on Interpersonal Relationships was found, $t(78)$ = 3.45, p < .01. As expected, experiential purchases were associated more with interpersonal relationships (M = 6.58) than material purchases (M = 4.83). To demonstrate mediation, the three regression analyses outlined by Baron and Kenny (1986) were conducted. First, when Interpersonal Relationships were regressed on Happiness, a significant relationship was found (*standardized beta* = .31, t = 2.83, p < .01). Second, happiness was regressed on the Purchase Type and as expected and consistent with the original t-test, Purchase Type was significantly related to Happiness (*standardized beta* = .36, t = 3.45, p < .01). Third, Happiness was regressed on both Interpersonal Relationships and Purchase Type. However, contrary to expectations, when the effects of the mediator (Interpersonal Relationships) were controlled for, the relationship between the Type of Purchase and Happiness remained significant (*standardized beta* = .24, t = 2.11, p < .05). Moreover, the beta from this equation (*standardized beta* = .24) was not significantly smaller than the beta for Purchase Type when the mediator was not controlled for (*standardized beta* = .31, t = 2.83, p < .01), (Sobel's Test, Z = 1.37, p = .17).

Moderating Role of SES

It was hypothesized that experiential purchases would produce more happiness than material purchases in persons high in SES, and material purchases would produce more happiness than experiential purchases in persons low in SES. A SES measure was created by summing each participant's responses to the questions related to SES (Cronbach alpha = .61). This hypothesis was examined in a three–step hierarchical regression analysis (see Aiken and West, 1991 for a description of this procedure). In this analysis three regressions analyses were performed in which purchase type, SES, and the interaction term (purchase type X SES) were added into the equation used to predict happiness. As expected, the addition of the interaction term (Purchase Type by SES) produced a significant increase in prediction over the main effects model, *standardized beta* = −1.41, t = −2.89, p < .005, ΔR^2 = .09, p < .005, (see Table 1).

The interaction of Purchase Type and SES was probed by examining the values for each of the two groups when SES was high (1 standard deviation (SD)

TABLE 1. Summary of Hierarchical Regression Analysis for SES Moderator Variable

Variable	B	Beta	ΔR
Step 1			
Purchase Type	.47	.33*	
Step 2			
Purchase Type	.49	.35*	.016
SES	.17	.13	
Step 3			
Purchase Type	2.45	1.73*	.090*
SES	.17	.13	
Purchase X SES	−.39	−1.41*	

*$p < .05$.

above the mean) and when SES was low (1 SD below the mean), (see Aiken and West, 1991 for an explanation of the procedure). There was a statistically significant difference in low SES persons on purchase happiness, *standardized beta* $= -1.53$, $t = -4.92$, $p < .0001$. Persons low in SES reported more happiness with material purchases ($M = 8.33$, $SD = 2.40$) than experiential purchases ($M = 5.27$, $SD = 2.01$). There was not difference in high SES persons on purchase happiness. That is, persons high in SES did not report more happiness associated with experiential purchases.

Control Analyses

An analysis was performed to examine the amount of money spent by participants on the reported purchases. The amount of money spent was analyzed using an independent t–test contrasting experiential purchase with material purchase no statistically significant difference was found. An additional analysis was performed to examine the differences of SES between participants on purchase type. SES was analyzed using an independent t–test contrasting experiential purchase with material purchase. There was not a statistically significant difference between the conditions for SES indicating that there were no inherent differences between the groups on SES.

Discussion

The purpose of this study was to investigate the relationship between the type of purchase and happiness by exploring two variables that might cause the relationship and a variable that might influence the strength of the relationship. The findings from the study provided partial support for the predictions. The results replicated the finding in the extant literature that persons report more happiness after experiential purchases than after material purchases. In addition, impact on the self was found to mediate the relationship between purchase type and happiness. That is, when the variance associated with impact on the self was removed, the relationship between purchase type and happiness was significantly reduced. Lastly, SES was found to moderate the relationship between purchase type and happiness with persons low in SES reporting more happiness with material purchases than experiential purchases.

Contrary to predictions, little support was found for the mediating role of interpersonal relationships. The removal of the variance associated with interpersonal relations failed to reduce the relationship between purchase type and happiness. It is tempting to simply conclude that interpersonal relationships do not mediate the effects of purchase type on happiness. However, caution is in order when interpreting null results. It is possible the failure to find mediating effects for interpersonal relationships was caused by problems associated with the how we measured interpersonal relationships. For example, it may be more important to focus on whether the purchase was performed alone or with other persons than to focus on the number of social interactions associated with the purchase.

Although, this research produced a number of significant findings, the current study has limitations. First, the study used retrospective self–reports to measure happiness and the mediating variables, impact on self and interpersonal relationships. This type of self-report measure is susceptible to a variety of memory biases that cause evaluations of events and objects to change as a function of time. For example, research on attitude polarization has demonstrated that attitudes can become more extreme as persons think about the event or object (Clarkson, Tormala, & Leone, 2011). It is possible that this polarizing effect also occurs with happiness ratings. Did the purchase actually produce more happiness or do participants just remember it producing happiness? Perhaps, self-reports only tap retrospective associations between activity types and happiness. Despite this, these recollections are important because they may motivate future behavior. That is, if persons associate a particular type of discretionary activity with happiness then they may perform the activity in the future in an effort to become happy. Regardless, in future research, the addition of a more concurrent measure of happiness would enrich our understanding of the relationship between discretionary activity and happiness.

Second, the distinction between experiential activity and material purchase is not always straightforward. It is possible to think of ambiguous situations that could be construed as both an experiential and material purchase, (e.g., purchasing a car part to rebuild an engine, musical instruments, sporting goods). To cope with this ambiguity we had participants self–define the activity based on their goals, that is, experiential purchases have the goal purchasing something you pay to participate in. Using goals to distinguish these behaviors can create difficulties because it is tricky to measure intentions objectively. Yet, motivations and intentions have been successfully used in other lines of psychological research, for example, aggression has been defined as behavior performed with the *intention* to harm another (Anderson & Bushman, 2002).

Although goals and intentions can readily be used to distinguish between types of discretionary purchases, there are other dimensions that differentiate the two types of purchases examined in the current study. One dimension that may influence how these discretionary purchases relate to happiness is the presence of an object. Both types of purchases produce memories but only material purchases lead to the possession of an object whereas experiential purchases are less likely to lead to the ownership of an object. Consequently, material purchases may be more susceptible to unfavorable comparisons and interpretations than experiential purchases, that is, a person can easily compare his/her object with someone else's and find it lacking. It is possible that with material purchase, the qualities of the object may affect happiness. How the qualities of the object and type of purchase interact to influence happiness is another question that needs to be explored.

Conclusions and Future Directions

The present research addressed the important question of why experiential purchases are associated with more happiness than material purchases. The results indicated that experiential purchases have more impact on the self and that this impact is associated with increased happiness. This is consistent with the notion that experiential purchase may be more effective that material purchases at satisfying needs for personal growth and self-actualization. In addition, the present research found that SES influences the relationship between purchase type and happiness.

However, as often happens in research, the current findings create more questions that should stimulate future research. One question would be whether there are other individual differences beyond SES that moderate the relationship between purchase type and happiness. For example, it is possible that persons high in materialism would be more satisfied and happy with material purchases than experiential purchases. Another set of questions focus on other types of purchases. That is, while the current research focused on material vs. experiential purchases, it is clear that there are other types of discretionary purchases that need to be investigated. For example, beyond purchasing objects and experiences, another common discretionary activity has the primary goal of creation. Persons engage in an extensive range of discretionary creative activity (e.g., folk art, crafts). What are the relative effects of purchases associated with creative activities on happiness compared to experiential and material purchases?

REFERENCES

Ahuvia, A., & Friedman D.A. (1998). Income, consumption, and subjective well–being, *Journal of Macromarketing*, *18*(2), 153–168. doi: 10.1177/027614679801800207

Aiken, L. S., & West, S. G. (1991). *Multiple regression: Testing and interpreting interactions*. Newbury Park, CA: Sage.

Anderson, C. A., & Bushman, B. J. (2002). Human Aggression. *Annual Review of Psychology*, *53*(3), 27–51. doi:10.1146/annurev.psych.53.100901.135231

Argyle, M. (1987). *The psychology of happiness*. London: Methuen.

Baron, R. M., & Kenny, D. (1986). The moderator–mediator distinction in social psychological research: Conceptual, strategic, and statistical considerations. *Journal of Personality and Social Psychology*, *51*(6), 1173–1182. doi:10.1037/0022-3514.51.6.1173

Belk, R. (1988). Possessions and the extended self. *Journal of Consumer Research*, *15*, 139–68. doi: 10.1086/209154

Clarkson, J., Tormala, Z., & Leone, C. (2011). A self–validation perspective on the mere thought effect. *Journal of Experimental Social Psychology*, *47*(2), 449–454. doi:10.1016/j.jesp.2010.12.003f

Csikszentmihalyi, M. (1999). If we are so rich, why aren't we happy? *American Psychologist*, *54*(10), 821–827. doi:10.1037/0003-066X.54.10.821

Diener, E. (2000). Subjective well–being: The science of happiness and a proposal for a nation index. *American Psychologist*, *55*, 34–43. doi:10.1037/0003-066X.55.1.34

Diener, E., & Oishi, S. (2000). Money and happiness: Income and subjective well–being across nations. In E. Diener and S. Oishi (Eds.), *Culture and subjective well–being* (pp 185–218). MA, US: The MIT Press.

Diener, E., & Seligman, E. P. (2002). Very happy people. *Psychological Science*, *13*, 81–84. doi:10.1111/1467-9280.00415

Franco, L. (2004). A Marketer's Guide to Discretionary Income. *Consumer Research Center*, The Conference Board.

Frank, R. (1999). *Luxury fever: Why money fails to satisfy in an era of success*. New York: Free Press.

Frank, R. (2005). Does money buy happiness? In F. Huppert, N. Baylis, and B. Keverne (Eds.), *The science of well–being* (pp. 461–473). New York, NY: Oxford University Press.

Fromm, E. (1976). *To have or to be?* New York: Harper & Row.

Ghiselli, E. E. (1964). *Theory of Psychological Measurement*, New York: McGraw Hill.

Hellevik, O. (2003). Economy, values and happiness in Norway. *Journal of Happiness Studies*, *4*(3), 243–283. doi:10.1023/A:1026232018534

Kasser, T. (2002). *The high price of materialism*. Cambridge, MA: MIT Press.

Kasser, T., & Ahuvia, A. (2002). Materialistic values and well–being in business students. *European Journal of Social Psychology*, *32*, 137–146. doi:10.1002/ejsp.85

Kasser, T., & Ryan, R. (1996). Further examining the American dream: Differential correlates of intrinsic and extrinsic goals. *Personality and Social Psychology Bulletin*, *22*, 280–287. doi:10.1177/0146167296223006

Kilbourne, J., & Jhally, S. (2000). *Killing us softly*. Northampton, MA: Media Education Foundation.

Millar, M. G., & Thomas, R. L. (2009). Discretionary activity and happiness: The role of materialism. *Journal of Research in Personality.* *43*(4), 699–702. doi:10.1016/j.jrp.2009.03.012

Mirowsky, J. R., & Ross, C. E. (2003). *Education, social status, and health*. Hawthorne, NY, US: Kluwer Academic/Plenum Publishers, 411–447.

Myers, D. (2000). The funds, friends, and faith of happy people. *American Psychologist, 55*, 56–67. doi:10.1037/0003-066X.55.1.56

Myers, D., & Diener, E. (1995). Who is happy? *Psychological Science, 6*, 10–19. doi:10.1111/j.1467-9280.1995.tb00298.x

O'Guinn, T. C., & Faber, R. J. (1989). Compulsive buying: A phenomenological exploration. *Journal of Consumer Research, 16*, 147–157. doi:10.1086/209204

Oishi, S., Diener, E. F., Lucas, R. E., & Such, E. M. (1999). Cross–cultural variations in predictors of life satisfaction: Perspectives from needs and values. *Personality and Social Psychology Bulletin, 25*(8), 980–990. doi:10.1177/01461672992511006

Oishi, S., & Koo, M. (2008). Culture, interpersonal perceptions, and happiness in social interactions. *Personality and Social Psychology Bulletin, 34*, 307–320. doi:10.1177/0146167207311198

Oropesa, R. S. (1995). Consumer possessions, consumer passions, and subjective well–being. *Sociological Forum, 10*(2), 215–244. doi:10.1007/BF02095959

Richins, M., & Dawson, S. (1992). Consumer values orientation for materialism and its measurement: Scale development and validation. *Journal of Consumer Research, 19*, 303–316. doi:10.1086/209304

Richins, M., & Rudmin, F. (1994). Materialism and economic psychology, *Journal of Economic Psychology, 15*, 217–231. doi:10.1016/0167-4870(94)90001-9

Rindfleisch, A., Burroughs, J., & Denton, F. (1997). Family structure, materialism, and compulsive consumption. *Journal of Consumer Research, 23*, 312–325.

Sangkhawasi, T., & Johri, L. M. (2007). Impact of brand status on materialism in Thailand. *Journal of Consumer Marketing, 24*(5), 275–282. doi: 10.1108/07363760710773094

Schyns, P. (1998). Crossnational differences in happiness: Economic and cultural factors explored. *Social Indicators Research, 43*, 3–26. doi:10.1023/A:1006814424293

Schyns, P. (2000). The relationship between income, changes in income and life satisfaction in West Germany and the Russian Federation: Relative, absolute, or a combination of both? In E. Diener & D.R. Rahtz (Eds.), *Advances in Quality of Life Theory and Research* (pp. 203–207). Dordrecht, the Netherlands: Kluwer Academic Publishers.

Shachtman, T. (2011). *American Iconoclast: The Life and Times of Eric Hoffer*. Titusville, NJ: Hopewell Publications.

Sirgy, J. (1998). Materialism and quality of life. *Social Indicators Research, 43*, 227–260. doi:10.1023/A:1006820429653

Twenge, J. M., & Campbell, K. W. (2002). Self–esteem and socioeconomic status: A meta–analytic review. *Personality and Social Psychology Review, 6*(1), 59–71. doi:10.1207/S15327957PSPR0601_3

Van Boven, L. (2000). Living "the good life": The hedonic superiority of experiential versus material purchases. *Dissertation Abstracts International: Section B: The Sciences and Engineering, 61*(5–B), 2821.

Van Boven, L. (2005). Experientialism, materialism, and the pursuit of happiness. *Review of General Psychology, 9*, 132–142. doi:10.1037/1089-2680.9.2.132

Van Boven, L., & Gilovich, T. (2003). To do or to have: That is the question. *Journal of Personality and Social Psychology, 85*, 1193–202. doi:10.1037/0022-3514.85.6.1193

Wright, N., & Larson, V. (1993). Materialism and life satisfaction: A meta–analysis. *Journal of Consumer Satisfaction, Dissatisfaction, and Complaining Behavior, 6*, 158–165.

Aggression among Male Alcohol-Dependent Inpatients who Smoke Cigarettes

OMER SAATCIOGLU
RAHSAN ERIM

ABSTRACT. The authors aimed to explore the relation between nicotine dependence and the severity of aggression among Turkish male alcohol-dependent inpatients who smoked cigarettes, as well as the effect of aggression in these groups. Participants were 126 male alcohol-dependent inpatients who were given the Structured Clinical Interview for *DSM-IV*, Substance Use Disorder Module (A. Corapcioglu, O. Aydemir, & M. Yildiz, 1999; M. B. First, R. L. Spitzer, & J. B. W. Williams, 1997), the Fagerstrom Test for Nicotine Dependence (K. O. Fagerstrom, 1978), and the Overt Aggression Scale (OAS; S. C. Yudofsky, J. M. Silver, W. Jackson, J. Endicott, & D. Williams, 1986). The authors found differences between male alcohol-dependent inpatients with nicotine dependence ($n = 94$) and those with nondependence ($n = 32$) in OAS subtypes. The authors' findings showed that smoking cigarettes—an addiction frequently observed with alcoholism—was positively correlated with aggressive behaviors. The authors suggest that smoking cigarettes may cause aggression or aggression may cause smoking. Observing and evaluating how aggression and smoking cigarettes are associated with alcohol dependence may help relapse prevention and improve effectiveness of treatment interventions in alcoholism.

THE RELATION BETWEEN ALCOHOL CONSUMPTION and violent action, including aggressive behavior, has been well accepted by scientists and the public in general (Fagan, 1993). Many researchers have developed and used various methods as early as 35 years ago, and they have explored the aforementioned interrelationship (Gustafson, 1993; Lang, 1993). An important result was found in Bushman's (1997) study in which the participants showed increased aggressiveness as the level of alcohol consumption increased.

Because the relation between alcohol consumption and aggression or violence is complex, researchers have recommended several models to try to highlight this subject. Violence is a significant problem among some individuals with psychiatric disorders and alcoholism or other substance use disorders (Giancola & Zeichner, 1997; Moss & Tarter, 1997). The role of alcohol in aggression or violence is attributed to the disruption in normal brain functions. A good example of this is the *disinhibition hypothesis*, which suggests that alcohol weakens brain mechanisms that control impulsive behaviors, including inappropriate aggression under normal circumstances (Borders, Barnwell, & Earleywine, 2007; Gustafson, 1994). Alcohol consumption can cause misjudgment of social cues and thus overreaction to a perceived threat through impairing the information processing (Miczek, DeBold, Van Erp, & Tornatzky, 1997). At the same time, an assessment of forthcoming risks on the basis of impulsive violent behavior may well be a direct result of narrowing attention (Cook & Moore, 1993).

Aggressive behaviors of alcohol users are generally revealed under the influence of alcohol (Gordis, 1997). These aggressive behaviors are generally directed against others (Roizen, 1997) or the self (Borders, Barnwell, & Earleywine, 2007; Gustafson, 1994). Regarding types of aggression or violence, no model can be applied to all people. However, the association between violent behaviors, alcoholism, and male gender is well documented (Borges, Cherpitel, & Rosovsky, 1998). Whereas some violent behaviors require treatment some others are easily preventable according to the research, much remains to be learned. Either the widespread of alcohol use and aggression or the associations between two have been well known in society at large (Lipsey, Wilson, Cohen, & Derzon, 1997).

Animal experiments revealed the purpose of aggressive type smoking as a part of reducing the anger by titration of nicotine intake; hence withdrawal demonstrates increased hostility and irritability (Miczek, DeBold, et al., 1994). Smoking nicotine among human participants decreased aggression in a competitive task per experimental measures. Low-tar cigarettes introduced to human experiments resulted in meaningful decreases in two types of aggressive responses caused by low and high frequency of money takeaways related to another party (Cherek, 1984). By no means can the therapeutic potential use of nicotine in controlling the aggressive or violent behavior overshadow the high risks of tobacco smoking to health (Miczek, Haney, Tidey, Vivian, & Weerts, 1994).

Nicotine is one substance that is ingested most frequently with alcohol. In the present study, we explored the question "What are the effects of addiction to nicotine on aggression patterns of alcohol-dependent individuals when they are not under influence of alcohol?" We aimed to explore the relation between the severity of nicotine dependence and aggression among alcohol-dependent inpatients.

Method

Participants and Setting

Participants were 126 consecutive male inpatients who smoked cigarettes and were hospitalized at the Alcohol and Drug Treatment, Education and Research Center at the Bakirkoy Research and Training Hospital for Psychiatry, Neurology, and Neurosurgery in Istanbul, Turkey. Istanbul is a city with a population of more than 10 million people, and it has one specialized center for the treatment of alcohol and drug addiction. All participants were diagnosed as having alcohol dependency. We conducted interviews with participants after detoxification, which occurred 4 weeks following the last use of alcohol. We applied measures during this period. We excluded participants who were under the age of 18 years or had mental retardation or cognitive impairment. None of the participants had comorbid psychiatric disorders. We obtained patients' informed consent after they were fully informed about the study.

The age range of participants was 26–61 years ($M = 42.51$ years, $SD = 7.19$ years). Of all participants, 81 (64.2%) reported that they were married, 56 (42.9%) reported that they were educated at primary school level or below, and 88 (69.9%) reported that they were self-employed. For all participants, the mean age of beginning alcohol use was 18.98 years ($SD = 4.72$ years, range $= 12$–30 years), the mean duration of intensive alcohol use was 3.41 years ($SD = 4.53$ years, range $= 0.5$–25 years), the mean age of beginning smoking cigarettes was 17.26 years ($SD = 4.22$ years, range $= 8$–30 years), and the mean duration of smoking cigarettes was 25.27 years ($SD = 7.94$ years, range $= 13$–44 years). Of the 126 alcohol-dependent inpatients, 94 (74.6%) were nicotine dependent.

Measures

We collected sociodemographic data directly from participants by using a form, and we used other sources (e.g., family and hospital records) as much as possible to gain reliable information about the participants' sociodemographic and clinical backgrounds. We diagnosed alcohol use disorder using the Turkish version of the Structured Clinical Interview for DSM-IV (SCID-I), Substance Use Disorder Module (Corapcioglu, Aydemir, & Yildiz, 1999; First, Spitzer, & Williams, 1997). We assessed participants by using the following scales 15 days after disappearance of withdrawal symptoms, on the basis of the observations that detoxification requires an average of 7–10 days for alcohol addiction, and that anxiety and mood disorders occur more frequently during the initial 2 weeks after ceasing the use of alcohol (Swift, 1999).

Fagerstrom Test for Nicotine Dependence (FTND). Fagerstrom (1978) structured the Fagerstrom Tolerance Questionnaire (FTQ) to assess various components of smoking. Fagerstrom and Schneider (1989) reviewed and redeveloped the questionnaire in assessing the nicotine dependence rates caused by cigarette smoking. Heatherton, Kozlowski, Frecker, and Fagerstrom (1991) further examined and refined the FTQ and developed the FTND, which can be used as a subsection of any general health and lifestyle-screening questionnaire in and out of health facilities. The FTND comprises four yes–no items and two multiple-choice items and can be used in an interview or self-report format. The items on the FTND are scored 0 and 1 for *yes* and *no* responses, respectively, and are scored from 0 to 3 for multiple-choice items. The items are summed to yield a total score of 0–10, in which a score of 7 or greater suggests physical dependence on nicotine. For the present study, we accepted an FTND score of 7 or greater for physical dependence on nicotine. The range of 4.0–4.5 is accepted to be the cut-off score. In samples of cigarette smokers seeking treatment, mean scores have ranged from 5.2 to 6.3. Cronbach's alpha internal consistency reliability coefficients from three clinical samples ranged from .56 to .64 (Pomerleau, Carton, Lutzke, Flessland, & Pomerleau, 1994).

Overt Aggression Scale (OAS; Yudofsky, Silver, Jackson, Endicott, & Williams, 1986). Yudofsky et al. described the design and reliability of a scale for rating aggressive behavior of adults and children. On the OAS, which was specific to inpatient populations, aggression is measured using four subscales: verbal aggression, physical aggression against objects, physical aggression against self, and physical aggression against others. Seven characteristic behaviors, according to the severity, are identified in each of the four aggression subscales, thus weighted accordingly. Subscale items are not mutually exclusive, and scoring is based on the weighted sum of all endorsed behaviors. Cronbach's alpha coefficients ranged from .79 to .83 for OAS. The OAS is used to evaluate four dimensions of current aggressive behavior. Norms are unavailable, and Yudofsky et al. did not present sample means.

Statistical Analysis

We performed a multivariate analysis of variance to compare overall differences between nicotine dependent and nondependent participants on aggression subscales. We then used follow-up analyses of variance to compare group means on each dimension and computed the means for groups in homogeneous subsets. For all statistical analyses, p values were two-tailed, and differences were considered significant at $p < .05$. We used the coefficient of determination (r^2), which is the strength of the relation between two variables. This is a measure of the proportion of variance shared by the two variables, and it varies from 0 to 1.

Results

A comparison of the sociodemographic features among alcohol-dependent individuals with and without nicotine dependence revealed no statistically

TABLE 1. Comparison of the Sociodemographic Variables in Male Alcohol-Dependent Inpatients With Nicotine Nondependence and Dependence ($N = 126$)

Variable	FTND		χ^2	df	p
	Nondependence ($n = 32$)	Dependence ($n = 94$)			
Marital status			2.20	2	.33
Married	24	57			
Unmarried	6	26			
Single	2	11			
Residence			2.27	1	.13
Urban	29	74			
Rural	3	20			
Occupation			2.99	3	.39
Unemployed	4	16			
Self-employed	21	67			
Retired	7	10			
Education			5.48	2	.07
Primary school or less	14	42			
Secondary school	13	21			
High school	5	31			

Note: FTND = Fagerstrom Test for Nicotine Dependence (T.F. Heatherton, L.T. Kozlowski, R.C. Frecker, & K.O. Fagerstrom, 1991).

significant differences in marital status, domicile, occupation, and education level (see Table 1).

There were positive correlations between smoking (FTND total score) and OAS total score ($r = .48$, $p < .0001$), verbal aggression ($r = .45$, $p < .0001$), physical aggression against objects ($r = .48$, $p < .0001$), physical aggression against self ($r = .38$, $p < .0001$), and physical aggression against others ($r = .35$, $p < .0001$).

We found positive correlations between the total aggression score on the OAS and verbal aggression, physical aggression against objects, physical aggression against self, and physical aggression against others. The OAS and OAS subscales for our sample demonstrated internal consistency; Cronbach's alphas ranged from .76 to .82. There were correlations between OAS subscales for all participants (see Table 2).

The smoking status of participants had a significant effect on the four types of aggression, Wilks's $\lambda = .65$; $F(4, 121) = 16.62$, $p < .01$. The strength of the relation between two variables was low, according to r^2 values. We found a statistically significant difference between the two groups in the severity of verbal

TABLE 2. Correlations between Subscales of the OAS and Total Scores Among Alcohol-Dependant Inpatients ($N = 126$)

OAS subscale	1	2	3	4
1. Verbal aggression	—	.71	.63	.64
2. Physical aggression against objects		—	.68	.57
3. Physical aggression against self			—	.92
4. Physical aggression against others				—
Total scores	.89	.85	.89	.86

Note. Correlation is significant at the $p < .01$ level. OAS = Overt Aggression Scale (S.C. Yudofsky. J.M. Silver, W. Jackson, J. Endicott, & D. Williams, 1986).

aggression, physical aggression against objects, and aggression against self but not aggression against others (see Table 3).

Discussion

We found no statistically significant differences between sociodemographic characteristics of male alcohol-dependent inpatients with and without nicotine dependence, and this fact may be attributable to the fundamental characteristic of alcohol addiction. There are no studies in the literature regarding correlation between nicotine addiction and alcoholism in terms of sociodemographic characteristics.

In previous studies, the severity of nicotine addiction was higher among users of alcohol compared with the overall population (Borges et al., 1998; De Leon et al., 2007; Lipsey et al., 1997; Meyerhoff et al., 2006; Shiffman & Balabanis, 1995). More than 90% of alcohol users also smoke cigarettes, and this rate is higher than the rate of smoking in the overall population. Individuals consuming considerable amounts of alcohol make much less effort to quit smoking (Hughes, 1995; Hurt et al., 1994). Researchers have shown that users of alcohol among hospitalized patients, psychiatric patients, and adolescents smoke much more than those who do not use alcohol (Ceballos, 2006; Hughes; Hurt et al.). These studies investigating smoking rates between alcohol users and the overall population were different from our study in sample characteristics. In the present study, the majority of participants with alcohol dependence were also nicotine dependent. We identified nicotine-dependent individuals among patients with alcohol dependence.

The objective of our study was to evaluate aggressive behaviors of alcohol-dependent individuals under treatment and not under the influence of alcohol. Our findings suggest that smoking—an addiction that is observed frequently with alcoholism—is positively correlated with current aggressive behaviors. Other

TABLE 3. Comparison of the Violence Scores in Male Alcohol-Dependent In-patients with Nicotine Dependence and Nondependence ($N = 126$)

Subscale of the Overt Aggression Scale	M	SD	95% confidence interval Lower	Upper	R^2	F	p
Verbal aggression					.04	5.44	.02*
Nondependence	1.84	1.53	1.29	2.39			
Dependence	3.46	3.80	2.68	4.24			
Total	3.05	3.44	2.44	3.65			
Physical aggression against objects					.05	5.89	.02*
Nondependence	0.50	0.80	0.21	0.79			
Dependence	1.79	2.95	1.18	2.39			
Total	1.46	2.64	0.99	1.93			
Physical aggression against self					.03	3.94	.05*
Nondependence	0.06	0.25	−0.03	0.15			
Dependence	0.93	2.45	0.42	1.43			
Total	0.71	2.15	0.33	1.09			
Physical aggression against others					.02	2.55	.11
Nondependence	0.28	0.89	−0.04	0.60			
Dependence	0.97	2.37	0.48	1.45			
Total	0.79	2.11	0.42	1.17			

Note. We used a one-way analysis of variance. For nicotine dependence, $n = 94$; for nicotine nondependence, $n = 32$. For nondependence, $df = 93$; for dependence, $df = 31$.
*$p < .05$.

researchers have shown that the suppressing effects of smoking on aggressive responses is dose dependent in that smoking high doses of nicotine produces more suppression than does smoking lower doses (Cherek, 1984). Cherek suggested that doses of nicotine that suppressed aggressive responding also increased nonaggressive monetary reinforcement responses. This indicates that the suppressing effects of nicotine on human aggressive responses are not due to a nonspecific and generalized depression of response. It is interesting to note that our results do not support findings that nicotine cigarettes decrease aggressive and violent behavior among alcohol users. In the present study, it is worth noting that the mean scores of four dimensions of the aggression scale tended to be higher in male alcohol-dependent inpatients with nicotine dependence, compared with the nicotine nondependence group. The difference did not reach the significance level between the groups only in the dimension of physical aggression against others. This suggests that participants made considerable efforts to control themselves against others, especially during the treatment process.

Our study has several limitations. Although we conducted the study after detoxification, recently detoxified patients may still have some cognitive problems affecting their evaluation of themselves. These measurement errors may have affected the scores on self-rating scales. Another limitation of the present study is that all of the participants were male patients. The study group was restricted to a population of individuals who were seeking treatment, and, therefore, it is not possible to generalize the findings to nontreatment groups. Further studies are required to confirm these results on larger clinical samples.

In the typology of alcohol dependence, our study group's characteristics seemed to be similar to some characteristics of Cloninger's Type 2 (Cloninger, Bohmann, & Sigvardsson, 1981) and Babor's Type B (Babor et al., 1992). Both of these types involve men: They exhibit alcohol-seeking behavior early in life (age of onset is less than 25 years), tend to be impulsive and risk taking, and display antisocial behavior. Furthermore, some characteristics of our participants were similar to those of young antisocial and chronic severe subtypes, as described in a new study by scientists at the National Institute for Alcohol Abuse and Alcoholism (Moss, Chen, & Yi, 2007). In the present study, we did not evaluate participants on antisocial features or personality disorder. Our study sample did not meet all of the characteristics of any subtypes of alcoholism. We suggest that future researchers address the relations among smoking, aggression, and subtypes of alcoholism. In addition, there could be another subtype in addition to subtypes of alcohol dependence that researchers have previously identified.

There is no published research on how nicotine changes behavioral patterns in alcohol-dependent inpatients. Although the effects of reducing and increasing concentration of nicotine are mentioned, at present, there is no finding about aggressive behaviors. How do smoking cigarettes and alcohol use—two types of addiction that are observed together—affect aggressive behaviors? Could this dual use play a role in aggressive behaviors? Our results do not provide complete answers to these questions, but they give some clues. Could it be beneficial to treat addiction to nicotine and alcohol together in patients with aggressive behaviors? All of these questions need to be answered in planned follow-up studies.

REFERENCES

Babor, T. F., Hofmann, M., Del Broka, F. K., Hesselbrock, V., Meyer, R. E., Dolinsky, Z. S., et al. (1992). Types of alcoholics: I. Evidence for an empirically derived typology based on indicators of vulnerability and severity. *Archives of General Psychiatry, 49,* 599–608.

Borders, A., Barnwell, S. S., & Earleywine, M. (2007). Alcohol-aggression expectancies and dispositional rumination moderate the effect of alcohol consumption on alcohol-related aggression and hostility. *Aggressive Behavior, 33,* 327–338.

Borges, G., Cherpitel, C. J., & Rosovsky, H. (1998). Male drinking and violence-related injury in the emergency room. *Addiction, 93,* 103–112.

Bushman, B. J. (1997). Effects of alcohol on human aggression: Validity of proposed explanations. In M. Galanter (Ed.), *Recent developments in alcoholism* (Vol. 13, pp. 227–243). New York: Plenum Press.

Ceballos, N. A. (2006). Tobacco use, alcohol dependence, and cognitive performance. *Journal of General Psychology, 133,* 375–388.

Cherek, D. R. (1984). Effects of cigarette smoking on human aggressive behavior. *Progressive Clinical Biology Research, 169,* 333–344.

Cloninger, C. R., Bohmann, M., & Sigvardsson, S. (1981). Inheritance of alcohol abuse, cross-fostering analysis of adopted men. *Archives of General Psychiatry, 38,* 861–868.

Cook, P. J., & Moore, M. J. (1993). Economic perspectives on reducing alcohol-related violence. In S. E. Martin (Ed.), *Alcohol and interpersonal violence* (pp. 193–212, NIAAA Research Monograph No. 24, NIH Pub. No. 93-3496). Rockville, MD: National Institute on Alcohol Abuse and Alcoholism.

Corapcioglu, A., Aydemir, O., & Yildiz, M. (1999). *DSM-IV Eksen I bozuklukları için yapılandırılmış klinik görüşme, Kullanım kılavuzu* [Structured clinical interview for DSM-IV (*SCID*-I), Turkish version]. Ankara, Turkey: Hekimler Yayin Birligi.

De Leon, J., Rendon, D. M., Baca-Garcia, E., Aizpuru, F., Gonzalez-Pinto, A., Anitua, C., et al. (2007). Association between smoking and alcohol use in the general population: Stable and unstable odds ratios across two years in two different countries. *Alcohol & Alcoholism, 42,* 252–257.

Fagan, J. (1993). Interactions among drugs, alcohol, and violence. *Health Affairs, 12,* 65–79.

Fagerstrom, K. O. (1978). Measuring degree of physical dependence to tobacco smoking with reference to individualization of treatment. *Addictive Behavior, 3,* 235–241.

Fagerstrom, K. O., & Schneider, N. G. (1989). Measuring nicotine dependence: A review of the Fagerstrom Tolerance Questionnaire. *Journal of Behavior Medicine, 12,* 159–182.

First, M. B., Spitzer, R. L., & Williams, J. B. W. (1997). *Structured Clinical Interview for DSM-IV (SCID).* Washington, DC: American Psychiatric Association.

Giancola, P. A., & Zeichner, A. (1997). The biphasic effects of alcohol on human physical aggression. *Journal of Abnormal Psychology, 106,* 598–607.

Gordis, E. (1997). Alcohol, violence, and aggression. *Alcohol Alert.* Retrieved February 16, 2009, from http://pubs.niaaa.nih.gov/publications/aa38.htm

Gustafson, R. (1993). What do experimental paradigms tell us about alcohol-related aggressive responding? *Journal of Studies on Alcohol, 11*(Suppl.), 20–29.

Gustafson, R. (1994). Alcohol and aggression. *Journal of Offender Rehabilitation, 21,* 41–80.

Heatherton, T. F., Kozlowski, L. T., Frecker, R. C., & Fagerstrom, K. O. (1991). The Fagerstrom Test for Nicotine Dependence: A revision of the Fagerstrom Tolerance Questionnaire. *British Journal of Addiction, 86,* 1119–1127.

Hughes, J. R. (1995). Clinical implications of the association between smoking and alcoholism. In J. B. Fertig & J. P. Allen (Eds.), *Alcohol and tobacco: From basic science to clinical practice* (pp. 171–185, NIAAA Research Monograph No. 30, NIH Pub. No. 95-3931). Washington, DC: U.S. Government Printing Office.

Hurt, R. D., Eberman, K. M., Croghan, I. T., Offord, K. P., Davis, L. J., Jr., Morse, R. M., et al. (1994). Nicotine dependence treatment during inpatient treatment for other addictions: A prospective intervention trial. *Alcoholism: Clinical and Experimental Research, 18,* 867–872.

Lang, A. R. (1993). Alcohol-related violence: Psychological perspectives. In S. E. Martin (Ed.), *Alcohol and interpersonal violence* (pp. 121–148, NIAAA Research Monograph No. 24, NIH Pub. No. 93–3496). Rockville, MD: National Institute on Alcohol Abuse and Alcoholism.

Lipsey, M. W., Wilson, D. B., Cohen, M. A., & Derzon, J. H. (1997). Is there a causal relationship between alcohol use and violence? A synthesis of evidence. In M. Galanter (Ed.), *Recent developments in alcoholism* (Vol. 13, pp. 245–282). New York: Plenum Press.

Meyerhoff, D. J., Tizabi, Y., Staley, J. K., Durazzo, T. C., Glass, J. M., & Nixon, S. J. (2006). Smoking comorbidity in alcoholism: Neurobiological and neurocognitive consequences. *Alcoholism: Clinical and Experimental Research, 30,* 253–264.

Miczek, K. A., DeBold, J. F., Haney, M., Tidey, J., Vivian, J., & Weerts, E. M. (1994). Alcohol, drugs of abuse, aggression, and violence. In A. J. Reiss Jr. & J. A. Roth (Eds.), *Understanding and preventing violence: Social influences* (Vol. 3, pp. 377–570). Washington, DC: National Academy Press.

Miczek, K. A., DeBold, J. F., Van Erp, A. M., & Tornatzky, W. (1997). Alcohol, GABAA-benzodiazepine receptor complex, and aggression. In M. Galanter (Ed.), *Recent developments in alcoholism* (Vol. 13, pp. 139–171). New York: Plenum Press.

Miczek, K. A., Haney, M., Tidey, J., Vivian, J., & Weerts, E. M. (1994). Neurochemistry and pharmacotherapeutic management of aggression and violence. In A. J. Reiss Jr., K. A. Miczek, & J. A. Roth (Eds.), *Understanding and preventing violence: Biobehavioral influences* (Vol. 2, pp. 245–514). Washington, DC: National Academy Press.

Moss, H. B., Chen, C. M., & Yi, H. (2007). Subtypes of alcohol dependence in a nationally representative sample. *Drug and Alcohol Dependence, 91,* 149–158.

Moss, H. B., & Tarter, R. E. (1997). Substance abuse, aggression, and violence. *American Journal on Addiction, 2,* 149–160.

Pomerleau, C. S., Carton, S. M., Lutzke, M. L., Flessland, K. L., & Pomerleau, O. F. (1994). Reliability of the Fagerstrom Tolerance Questionnaire and the Fagerstrom Test for Nicotine Dependence. *Addictive Behavior, 19,* 33–39.

Roizen, J. (1997). Epidemiological issues in alcohol-related violence. In M. Galanter (Ed.), *Recent developments in alcoholism* (Vol. 13, pp. 7–40). New York: Plenum Press.

Shiffman, S., & Balabanis, M. (1995). Associations between alcohol and tobacco. In J. B. Fertig & J. P. Allen (Eds.), *Alcohol and tobacco: From basic science to clinical practice* (pp. 17–36, NIAAA Research Monograph No. 30, NIH Pub. No. 95–3931). Washington, DC: U.S. Government Printing Office.

Swift, R. M. (1999). Drug therapy for alcohol dependence. *New England Journal of Medicine, 40,* 1482–1487.

Yudofsky, S. C., Silver, J. M., Jackson, W., Endicott, J., & Williams, D. (1986). The Overt Aggression Scale for the objective rating of verbal and physical aggression. *American Journal of Psychiatry, 143,* 35–39.

Angry Versus Furious: A Comparison Between Valence and Arousal in Dimensional Models of Emotions

L. Y. Lo, N. L. Hung, and M. Lin

ABSTRACT

The present study compared the roles of valence and arousal, proposed by the dimensional models of emotions, in recognizing emotional expressions. It was hypothesized that the dimension of valence, due to its functional significance, would be more salient in the recognition of emotional expressions than the dimension of arousal would be. The results of the current study supported this hypothesis. The participants in all age groups were more accurate and quicker in recognizing an emotion when the expression was paired up with another emotional expression that was different in the polarity of the valence dimension than with this similar polarity difference in the arousal dimension. The insignificant difference in recognizing the positive and negative emotional expressions in the group of elders also rejected the Socio-Emotional Selectivity Theory.

Introduction

The phrase "No Man Is an Island" is possibly correct because no human being can survive alone in the wild. Humans need to form groups and cooperate with each other in order to maximize their chance of living. In the ancient past before the development of any formal language system, the ability of displaying emotional expressions and reading emotional expressions in others certainly aids all kinds of interactions among group members. The perceived emotions influence the way to interact, express, and anticipate others' behaviors. Thus, emotion recognition is thought to be a crucial factor in social and interpersonal functioning, which is highly related to social interest and life satisfaction (Demenescu, Mathiak, & Mathiak, 2014).

Discrete Versus Dimensional

Two major theoretical models, namely the discrete (or basic) emotion model and the dimensional emotion model, are commonly adopted when explaining emotion perception. The discrete emotion model emphasizes the uniqueness of each emotional state, which stems from the adaptive responses of cognitive appraisal (Frijda, 2007; Frijda & Scherer, 2009). Each emotional expression carries its own function for tackling specific challenges throughout one's life (Adolphs, Tranel, & Damasio, 1998; Wicker et al., 2003; Wilensky, Schafe, Kristensen, & LeDoux, 2006). For example, anger is usually represented by enlarging the body size and intensifying the vocal sound (Chuen-wattanapranithi, Xu, Thipakorn, & Maneewongvatana, 2008; Hauser, 1997; Ohala, 1984; Siegman, Anderson, & Berger, 1990). All these signals alert the intruder about the physical strength of the exhibitors (Moradian & Walker, 2008) and warn them about the potential cost (i.e., being injured) if the exhibitor is offended. On the other hand, fear is usually indicated by, for example, paleness in appearance and shivering (Darwin, 2009). This is compatible with the conservation-withdrawal strategy (Engel & Schmale, 1972), which tries to reserve energy for either withdrawal or repairing any damage. Because of the functional specificity, these basic emotions are believed to be independently processed. For example, the amygdala is one of the key physiological components that responds specifically to the emotion of fear (Ledoux, 2003). With damage to that particular region, patients have exhibited different levels of difficulty in responding to threatening signals (Adolphs et al., 1998).

In contrast to the discrete emotion model, the dimensional emotion model conceptualizes emotions as emerging from several basic dimensions. Russell and Barrett (1999) proposed a concrete dimensional structure, named circumplex, to indicate a schematic map of core affect. The construction of circumplex is based on the results from the factor analysis and semantic differential analysis of the linguistic recording and vocal and facial expressions of different types of emotion. Two major dimensions, valence (or pleasantness) and activation (or arousal), have been consistently found in the conceptualization of emotions across cultures (Bolls, 2010; Russell & Barrett, 1999). Each dimension yields two polarities, (i.e., positive and negative, indicated as "+" and "−" signs, respectively), so it is impossible to imagine an emotion being positive (e.g., pleasant) and negative (e.g., unpleasant) simultaneously. With this 2×2 dimensional design, each emotion can be identified and located into one of the quarters; that is, pleasant and active, pleasant and inactive, unpleasant and active, or unpleasant and inactive. As each quarter in the circumplex represents a specific combination of valence and activation, emotions in the same quarter can be inferred to contain similar qualities. In other words, emotional expressions located in the same quarter should be more similar than the emotional expressions in different quarters.

Emotion Recognition

Based on the discrete emotion model, each emotional expression has its own specific function for survival. Exhibitors can display each emotional expression as distinctively as possible. And the expressions themselves should be highly discriminative which largely enhances the recognition process and minimizes the chance of confusion or misinterpretation. In other words, discrete emotion model implies that an angry face can be recognized as easy or as difficult as recognizing a happy face as both expressions bear their own discrete functional significance.

However, it is easy to imagine that an angry face could be quickly spotted in a crowd of happy faces, but not faces showing disgust. The dimensional model therefore asserts that not all emotional expressions are highly distinctive from each other. If two expressions are located in the same quarter in the circumplex, they should be more similar than any two that are located in different quarters. This proposition has been supported by some physiological evidence. For example, the insula is found to be closely related to disgust; however, this relationship is not an exclusive one as the insula is also found to be activated when an individual sees frightening pictures (Schienle et al., 2002). Furthermore, the amygdala is found to be responsive to an expression of not only fear but also anger. Some studies have even suggested that the amygdala responds significantly when any strong emotion is triggered (Cunningham, Van Bavel, & Johnsen, 2008). Patients with a damaged amygdala have been found to be less capable of identifying fear, disgust, surprise, and guilt (Boucsein, Weniger, Mursch, Steinhoff, & Irle, 2001). In cognitive performances relating to emotional processing, a wide variety of negative emotional stimulation, such as fear and anger, can induce similar types of behavior including withdrawal or reduction in reaction time (Isaacowitz & Stanley, 2011). This is fully compatible with the proposition of the dimensional model as both fear and anger are at the same polarity (i.e., unpleasantness) in the dimension of valence. No reviewed empirical study has attempted to investigate the differences between the discrete emotion model and the dimensional model in relation to individuals' abilities to recognize basic emotions. The present study therefore tried to fill the research gap.

Present Study

The discrete emotion model suggests that emotional expressions are highly discriminative from each other, which enhances the recognition efficiency of all emotional expressions; whereas, the dimensional model asserts that the recognizability depends on where the emotions are located in the circumplex. In a traditional recognition test, the participants are usually given a set of emotional expressions, including all five to six discrete emotion, one by one and are asked to categorize or name the emotional expressions in each of the pictures shown (e.g., Etcoff & Magee, 1992; Kirita & Endo, 1995). With this standard procedure, researchers can tell whether the pictures are explicit enough to deliver the intended emotional content and whether the participants are sensitive enough to capture the emotion being reflected in the pictures. A modification was suggested and carried out for this study whereby participants were told beforehand what two types of emotional expressions that they would see (e.g., angry vs. disgust or angry vs. happy) in each session. They were asked to identify the expressions in each of these sessions. If the discrete emotion model is correct, then the accuracy in recognizing the angry face in the session with angry and disgust faces and the session with angry and happy faces should be similar. It is because each discrete emotional expression bears the unique functional significance. On the other hand, if the dimensional model is correct, the accuracy should be lower in the angry and disgust paired expressions than the other pair as anger and disgust are located in the same quarter in the circumplex (i.e., negative in valence and positive in arousal). By comparing the recognition accuracy of the emotional expression pairs, which are either in the same quarter or different quarters, it is possible to examine whether the discrete emotion model or the dimensional model is more suitable for explaining emotion recognition.

With a 2 × 2 design in the circumplex model, emotional expressions can differ in one single dimension or both dimensions. It is predicted that expressions with different polarities in both dimensions should be highly recognizable; for example, sadness (i.e., unpleasant and low arousal) and happiness (i.e., pleasant and high arousal). It is uncertain whether a similar accuracy could be yielded in the condition where the expressions only differ in any one of the dimensions. The ability of identifying emotional valence is believed to be an important skill in survival. In the example of anger, it is more rewarding to automatically detect whether your neighbor, no matter whether he or she is a barbarian or a lion, is in an unpleasant state so you can decide on and prepare for the most appropriate action. The cost of not being able to detect the valence can be extremely high when compared to a failure in detecting whether your neighbor is just annoyed or furious. In line with this reasoning, the exhibitor would also like to express a contrastive physical difference between the emotions with different polarities in the valence dimension. In other words, the present study hypothesized that emotional expressions with different polarities in the dimension of valence have greater physical contrast than the expressions with different polarities in the dimension of arousal. Hence, the recognition accuracy in the former condition was expected to be higher than in the latter condition.

If the detection of the difference in the valence dimension is important for survival, this processing preference should be kept throughout one's entire life once it has been established. Due to neurodegeneration, elders are found to experience deterioration in emotion recognition (Orgeta & Phillips, 2008; Ruffman, Sullivan, & Dittrich, 2009). Compared to young adults, elders have been shown to respond slower and make more errors when recognizing emotional expressions. These results seem to suggest that the elders' degree of deterioration in recognition accuracy is similar across all discrete emotional expressions. Yet, if valence carries a significant role in survival, it is still expected that elders, even with their deteriorated recognition ability, should exhibit a better performance in recognizing the emotional expressions that are different in the dimension of valence than in the dimension of arousal. In other words, the salience of the valence dimension in emotion recognition can be revealed regardless of the age of the perceivers. Due to constraints in the experimental designs, the reviewed past studies could not examine this speculation; therefore, we examined this speculation in the present study.

Methodology

Participants

Thirty young adults aged between 20 and 25 (Mean = 23.77, SD = 1.53), 25 adults aged between 40 and 45 (Mean = 43.47, SD = 1.22), and 25 elders aged 60 and above (Mean = 67.89, SD = 3.74) were recruited by convenient sampling in the present study. The ratio of males to females in each age group was 0.74. All participants were Hong Kong Chinese and had normal or correct-to-normal vision and hearing ability. No dementia cases were reported among the elder participants.

Stimuli

Two male and two female models, aged between 20 and 28, were recruited to generate the emotional facial stimuli for the present study. They were asked to demonstrate five emotional expressions, including happy, interested, bored, sad, and angry expressions, in addition to a neutral expression. Though interested and bored are not commonly studied in emotion research, they are regarded as affective components that strongly influence learning progress and work performance (Ainley, 2007). All photographs were taken with a 12M pixel digital camera and further processed in Photoshop. Each photo was 4 cm (width) × 5 cm (height) and was digitized as grayscale. Facial components were clearly shown in each of the photographs and neither glasses nor accessories were worn in the photographs. Twenty undergraduate raters, with an equal number of males and females, were recruited to evaluate the typicality of the emotional expressions. Emotional expressions would only be adopted when they were rated, on average, above 4 in a 7-point Likert scale (i.e., 1: least representative; 7: most representative). All emotional expressions of the four models passed this criterion and the mean rating scores ranged from 4.65 to 5.80 (i.e., happy: 5.80, interested: 4.65, sad: 4.92, bored: 5.08, and angry: 5.72). Furthermore, the raters were briefly introduced to the circumplex model of emotion, and they were asked to put the emotional expressions into the four quarters based on their understanding of valence and arousal. All emotional expressions were placed correctly as suggested by Russell and Barrett (1999).

Faces displaying neutral expressions were rated for the attractiveness and the mean score was 5.40 ($SD = 0.37$) in a 10-point Likert scale, which suggested an average level of attractiveness with little variation among the models. Finally, 20 emotional photographs (4 models × 5 emotional expressions) were generated for the present study. Three testing conditions with different types of emotional expression pairings were constructed as detailed in the following section.

Valence Condition: Testing the Strength of the Valence Dimension

The participants in this condition were told beforehand about the two types of the emotional expressions that they would be shown and that they should identify each of the presented expressions by pressing the assigned keys as accurately and quickly as possible. There were two sessions in this valence condition. The participants were required to identify the expressions of happiness (+valence and +arousal) and anger (−valence and +arousal), and the expressions of interested (+valence and +arousal) and anger (−valence and +arousal) in the corresponding sessions. A key difference between emotional expressions in each of the sessions is the polarity in the valence dimension. Furthermore, the polarities of all four emotional expressions are identical in the dimension of arousal.

Each pairing was shown twice to all participants, and therefore, 16 trials (2 emotional expressions × 2 presentation times × 4 models) were generated for each of the sessions in this condition.

Arousal Condition: Testing the Strength of the Arousal Dimension

Similar to the valence condition, there were also two sessions in this condition. The participants were required to identify the expressions of anger (+arousal and −valence) and sadness (−arousal and −valence) in one session, and the expressions of anger (+arousal and −valence) and boredom (−arousal and −valence) in another session. The emotional expressions in each of the sessions differed in the polarity in the arousal dimension but retained the same polarity in the dimension of valence. Similarly, 16 trials were generated for each of the subdivisions in this condition.

Combined Condition: Testing the Strength of Both the Valence and Arousal Dimensions

Sharing the design of the valence and arousal conditions, combined condition reflects the joint effects of both the dimensions of valence and arousal. The participants were required to identify the expressions in the sessions with 1: happiness (+arousal and +valence) and sadness (−arousal and −valence), 2: happiness (+arousal and +valence) and boredom (-arousal and −valence), 3: interested (+arousal and +valence) and sadness (−arousal and −valence), and 4: interested (+arousal and +valence) and boredom (−arousal and −valence). The emotional expressions in each of the four sessions had different polarities in both dimensions. Sixteen trials were constructed for each of the sessions, and therefore, a total of 64 trials were included in this condition.

By comparing the accuracy and reaction time among these three conditions, it was possible to identify whether polarity difference in the dimension of valence, but not the dimension of arousal, could lead to a faster reaction time and higher accuracy in emotion recognition. It was further expected that the highest accuracy and fastest reaction time would be yielded in the combined condition.

Procedures

The participants were randomly assigned to one of the three conditions to start with. They were arranged to sit 65 cm in front of a 15″ computer screen. At the beginning of each trial, a fixation point "*" was shown for one second in the middle of the screen, and an emotional expression was then shown to the participants. In the valence condition, the participants were required to recognize the shown emotional expression by pressing the corresponding keys on a standard keyboard. A new emotional expression was shown after a keystroke response was received. In order to reduce the memory workload for the participants, there were stickers beside the computer to remind the participants what the corresponding response keys were. Similar procedures were executed in both sessions. The sequence of the sessions was counterbalanced. All trials were randomly presented by a program, namely Direct RT.

In the condition of arousal, the procedure was highly similar to that of the valence condition except that the participants were shown angry and sad faces in one session and angry and bored expressions in another session.

A similar procedure was applied to the combined condition. The participants were required to recognize the shown emotional expressions in each of the four sessions by pressing the corresponding keys.

A 2-minute break was given between these conditions. The participants were reminded to respond to the emotional expressions as quickly and accurately as possible at the beginning of each condition. All keystroke responses and reaction times were recorded by Direct RT.

Results and Analysis

The descriptive findings among the three conditions are presented in **Table 1**. A 3 (age group) × 3 (experimental condition) ANOVA was conducted. The main effects of age and experimental condition were found to be significant ($F(2, 213) = 45.41$, $p < 0.01$ and

Table 1. Means and standard deviation of the accuracy (in %) and reaction time (in seconds) among the three experimental conditions.

Age groups	Conditions	Mean of accuracy (SD)	Mean of reaction time (SD)
Young adults	Valence	90.8 (7.1)	1616.2 (615.8)
	Activation	76.5 (15.8)	2116.7 (876.7)
	Cross	92.0 (6.3)	1546.1 (692.1)
Middle-age adults	Valence	93.8 (6.1)	2411.3 (1031.2)
	Activation	77.3 (11.7)	2861.1 (860.0)
	Cross	90.6 (6.3)	2358.5 (962.3)
Elderly	Valence	92.0 (6.3)	4426.5 (1352.0)
	Activation	66.5 (10.5)	5673.6 (1954.5)
	Cross	73.4 (12.2)	4457.8 (1112.9)

$F(2, 213) = 37.93$, $p < 0.01$, respectively). The group of elders was found to be significantly less accurate than the other two age groups in the recognition test ($p < 0.01$). No significant difference in accuracy was found between the groups with young adults and middle-age adults (Tukey HSD $= 0.08$, $p = 0.884$). Moreover, the accuracy in the arousal condition was the lowest compared to the other two experimental conditions ($p < 0.01$); whereas there was no significant accuracy difference between the valence and combined conditions (Tukey HSD $= 0.02$, $p = 0.65$). In other words, the participants were less capable of distinguishing between the emotional expressions in the arousal condition than the valence condition. An insignificant interaction effect ($F(4, 213) = 1.346$, $p = 0.254$) implied that this performance pattern was found in all age groups in the present study.

A similar pattern was also observed in the analysis of the reaction time. Significant main effects of age ($F(2, 213) = 161.17$, $p < 0.01$) and experimental condition ($F(2, 213) = 11.56$, $p < 0.01$) were found. The reaction time in the group of elders was, as expected, slower than the other two age groups ($p < 0.01$). The young adults were also found to perform signifi-cantly faster than the middle-age adults (Tukey HSD $= 783.96$, $p < 0.01$). The participants again performed slowest in the arousal condition when compared to the valence condition (Tukey HSD $= 707.38$, $p < 0.01$) and combined condition (Tukey HSD $= 742.18$, $p < 0.01$), yet no significant difference in reaction time was found between the latter two conditions (Tukey HSD $= 34.79$, $p < 0.01$). No significant interaction effect was obtained ($F(4, 213) = 1.17$, $p = 0.327$).

Discussion

The primary goal of the present study was to investigate the effects of the dimensions of valence and arousal in relation to emotion recognition. In general, it was found that the par-ticipants, regardless of age, performed better in the recognition task where the emotional expressions differed in the dimension of valence (e.g., angry vs. happy) rather than in the dimension of arousal (e.g., anger vs. sadness). The participants performed more accurately and quickly in the former condition than the latter condition. The facilitation effect resulting from the difference in valence was also found to be similar to the joint effect of valence and arousal in the combined condition. This again illustrated the prominent role of valence when processing emotional expressions.

The Importance of Valence

Emotion recognition is one of the crucial skills in conducting daily social interactions. Dis-playing and understanding emotional expressions aid the flow in social interactions as they help in judging the attitudes as well as the feelings of others and generating real-time appro-priate responses (Gao & Maurer, 2009; Watling, Workman, & Bourne, 2012). The partici-pants in the different age groups in the present study were more capable of distinguishing between the emotional expressions that differed in valence but not in arousal. These findings echo the functional role of valence from an evolutionary perspective. Animals try to avoid anything that leads to injury or death. With this reasoning, detecting whether someone is experiencing an unpleasant state (such as rage), is particularly crucial in survival as approaching any individual who is experiencing rage may heighten the risk of being injured. It is certain that both valence and arousal levels are important as the risk of being injured would also vary with the degree of anger being perceived. Nevertheless, it seems that, with the support of the present findings, valence is shown to be a more salient dimension that can be detected in emotional perception. This proposition is also in line with studies in communication. Cognitive expectancy and the pleasantness of emotional feedback are strong predictors of the degree of involvement in the communication (Le Poire & Yoshimura, 1999). If the emotional feedback is perceived to be unpleasant, it greatly affects the intention to continue the interaction between the involved parties.

Similar findings were also obtained in the study of memory. Adelman and Estes (2013) investigated how emotional connotations affected memory under different conditions, and tested whether arousal and valence predicted recognition memory for over 2,500 words. The results indicated that both negative and positive words were remembered better than neutral words. Importantly, the advantage of remembering the emotional words was independent to their arousal (or activity) level. It was also found that the emotional words generated a higher level of perceptual fluency than neutral words (Becker et al., 2001). Similarly, the fluency was highly determined by the valence level, but not by the arousal level, of the words.

There are numerous studies investigating the neurological module that specifically processes threatening signals (Adolphs, 2002; Öhman & Mineka, 2001). The detection process is almost automatic (LeDoux, 2003). The response, no matter fight or flight, to the threatening signals is triggered instantly, and the intensity of the signal is usually not particularly considered. The specificity of the physiological designs to the stimuli with different valence but not arousal levels is also compatible with the salient role of valence in emotional perception. All these findings jointly suggest the importance of valence detection in survival.

Physical Features and Functionality

Emotional expressions differing in the valence dimension were recognized faster and more accurately than the expressions differing in the arousal dimension. However, the results could be alternatively interpreted as follows: the physical difference in the facial features within the pairs in the valence condition could be larger than the difference in the arousal condition. Therefore, expressions in the valence condition were more quickly recognized than the expressions in the other condition. It is inevitable that there could be unstandardized physical differences within the pairs between the two conditions. This, however, also echoes the functional significance that is entailed in the nature of emotional valence. Given that emotional valence is important to survival, the perceivers would be first alerted by the valence cues when perceiving emotional expressions. When reciprocating and displaying emotional expressions, they would also try to make a larger contrast between positive and negative emotional expressions compared to the expressions with different arousal levels. Consequently, the physical difference between the emotional expressions in the valence condition is expectedly larger than the difference in the arousal condition. Still, in order to minimize the confounding effect due to the physical features, possible controls for the facial differences between the valence and arousal conditions would be welcome in future studies.

Socio-Emotional Selectivity Theory

The elders in the present study were generally found to be slower and less accurate in the recognition test compared to the younger age groups. This partially supports the neurodegeneration theory, which suggests a general decline in the ability to recognize different types of emotional expression as one ages. The present results further suggest that the effect of deterioration was not the same across all three experimental conditions. Similar to the younger age groups, emotional expressions differing in the valence dimension can still be better recognized by the elders than the expressions differing in the arousal dimension.

On the other hand, the socio-emotional selectivity theory suggests that older adults are more likely to attempt to regulate their emotional experiences and to maintain the feeling of well-being than younger adults (Charles & Campos, 2011). By increasingly attending to positive emotion rather than negative emotion, an approachable manner can be fostered that facilitates social interactions and functioning (Lockenhoff & Carstensen, 2007). Elders are therefore more prone to interpret the perceived emotion as pleasant even if this may deviate from the actual meaning carried by the expression (Keightley, Winocur, Burianova, Hongwanishkul, & Grady, 2006). In other words, there is a high chance that the elders would mis-recognize the unpleasant emotional expressions as pleasant. This hypothesis however was not supported by the results of the present study. No significant performance difference between recognizing the positive and negative emotional expressions in the elder group was obtained (accuracy: $t = 1.33$, $p = 0.20$; RT: $t = 0.98$, $p = 0.37$). The insignificant difference seems to provide better support to the neurological degeneration theory that affects elders' overall emotion recognition ability.

Exclusive or Complementary

Basic emotion model has been studied and validated for decades; whereas a dimensional model is usually regarded as a reductionist perspective of basic emotions that suggests basic emotions can be characterized by a few distinctive dimensions, such as valence and arousal. At a quick glance, both accounts seem to be contradictory to each other, yet these two accounts are not mutually exclusive. It is always possible to talk about two discrete concepts (e.g., flower and bus) based on a dimension (e.g., in a spatial dimension, both objects occupy space). Similarly, the dimensional model does not necessarily reject the uniqueness of the basic emotions but provides a way of describing the relationships among the emotions. In other words, categorizing the basic emotions with specific dimensions does not refute the discreteness of the emotions and the expressions. Previous studies on basic emotions (e.g., Wicker et al., 2003) have included thorough explanations about the functional and physical differences among the basic emotions and the expressions but they have seldom focused on the similarities and differences among them. Results of the present study explored and demonstrated the relationships among the basic emotions and their expressions in the context of emotion recognition.

Potential Implication

People with ASD are generally found to be less accurate in identifying emotional expressions (Celani, Battacchi, & Arcidiacono, 1999; Walsh, Vida, & Rutherford, 2014). They are less capable of identifying or labeling both basic and secondary emotional expressions (Bolte & Poustka, 2003; Rump, Giovannelli, Minshew, & Strauss, 2009). Hence, there are different exercises helping these individuals to learn different emotional expressions. One of the general methods is to let the people with ASD to be extensively exposed to a pool of emotional faces so that they may internally generalize cues for recognizing different types of expressions. If valence dimension is crucial in emotional recognition as suggested by the present study, it is therefore recommended that the emotional faces being exposed to the people with ASD should be differing in valence dimension in the beginning of the learning phase. It is because the difference in valence dimension, in terms of facial features and functionality, should be more noticeable than the difference in the arousal dimension. This would help people with ASD to be more readily to capture different cues in perceiving emotional expressions as a start and pave the way for them to understand other expressions with less contrast in later learning stages.

References

Adolphs, R. (2002). Recognizing emotion from facial expressions: Psychological and neurological mechanisms. *Behavioral and Cognitive Neuroscience Reviews*, *1*(1), 21–62. doi.org/10.1177/1534582302001001003

Adolphs, R., Tranel, D., & Damasio, A. R. (1998). The human amygdala in social judgment. *Nature*, *129*(3), 470–474. doi.org/10.1038/30982

Adelman, J. S., & Estes, Z. (2013). Emotion and memory: A recognition advantage for positive and negative words independent of arousal. *Cognition*, *129*, 530–535. doi.org/10.1016/j.cognition.2013.08.014

Ainley, M. (2007). Being and feeling interested: Transient state, mood, and disposition. In P. A. Schutz & R. Pekrun (Eds.), *Emotion in education* (pp. 147–163). San Diego, CA: Academic Press. doi.org/10.1016/B978-012372545-5/50010-1

Becker, E. S., Rinck, M., Margraf, J., & Roth, W. T. (2001). The emotional Stroop effect in anxiety disorders: general emotional or disorder specificity? *Journal of Anxiety Disorder*, *15*, 147–159. doi: 10.1038/npjschz.2016.18

Bolls, P. D. (2010). Understanding emotion from a superordinate dimensional perspective: A productive way forward for communication processes and effects studies. *Communication Monographs*, *77*(2), 146–152. doi.org/10.1080/03637751003790477

Bolte, S., & Poustka, F. (2003). The recognition of facial affect in autistic and schizophrenic subjects and their first-degree relatives. *Psychological Medicine*, *33*(5), 907–915. doi.org/10.1017/S0033291703007438

Boucsein, K., Weniger, G., Mursch, K., Steinhoff, B. J., & Irle, E. (2001). Amygdala lesion in temporal lobe epilepsy subjects impairs associative learning of emotional facial expressions. *Neuropsychologia*, *39*(3), 231–236. doi.org/10.1016/S0924-977X(11)70015-3

Celani, G., Battacchi, M. W., & Arcidiacono, L. (1999). The understanding of the emotional meaning of facial expressions in people with autism. *Journal of Autism and Developmental Disorders*, *29*, 57–66. doi.org/10.1023/A:1025970600181

Charles, S. T., & Campos, B. (2011). Age-related changes in emotion recognition: How, why, and how much of a problem? *Journal Of Nonverbal Behavior*, *35*(4), 287–295. doi.org/10.1007/s10919-011-0117-2

Chuenwattanapranithi, S., Xu, Y., Thipakorn, B., & Maneewongvatana, S. (2008). Encoding emotions in speech with the size code. A perceptual investigation. *Phonetica*, *65*(4), 210–230. doi.org/10.1159/000192793

Cunningham, W. A., Van Bavel, J. J., & Johnsen, I. R. (2008). Affective flexibility: Evaluative processing goals shape amygdala activity. *Psychological Science*, *19*, 152–160. doi.org/10.1111/j.1467-9280.2008.02061.x

Darwin, C. (2009). *The Expression of the emotion in man and animals.* London, UK: Penguin.

Demenescu, L. R., Mathiak, K. A., & Mathiak, K. (2014). Age- and gender-related variations of emotion recognition in pseudowords and faces. *Experimental Aging Research*, *40*(2), 187–207. doi.org/10.1080/0361073X.2014.882210

Engel, G. L., & Schmale, A. H. (1972). Conservation withdrawal: A primary regulatory process for organic homeostasis. In R. Porter & J. Knight (Eds.), *Physiology, emotions and psychosomatic illness* (pp. 57–88). New York, NY: Elsevier.

Etcoff, N. L., & Magee, J. J. (1992). Categorical perception of facial expression. *Cognition*, *44*, 227–240. doi.org/10.1037/a0025336

Frijda, N. H. (2007). *The laws of emotion.* Mahwah, NJ: Lawrence Erlbaum.

Frijda, N. H., & Scherer, K. R. (2009). Emotion definition. In D. Sander, & K. R. Scherer (Eds.), *Oxford companion to emotion and the affective sciences* (pp. 142–143). Oxford, UK: Oxford University Press.

Gao, X., & Maurer, D. (2009). Influence of intensity on children's sensitivity to happy, sad, and fearful facial expressions. *Journal of Experimental Children Psychology*, *102*, 503–521. doi.org/10.1016/j.jecp.2008.11.002

Hauser, M. D. (1997). Artifactual kinds and functional design features: what a primate understands without language. *Cognition*, *64*, 285–308. doi.org/10.1016/S0010-0277(97)00028-0

Isaacowitz, D. M., & Stanley, J. (2011). Bringing an ecological perspective to the study of aging and recognition of emotional facial expressions: Past, current, and future methods. *Journal of Nonverbal Behavior*, *35*, 261–278. doi.org/10.1007/s10919-011-0113-6

Keightley, M. L., Winocur, G., Burianova, H., Hongwanishkul, D., & Grady, C. L. (2006). Age effects on social cognition: Faces tell a different story. *Psychology and Aging*, *21*(3), 558–572. doi.org/10.1037/0882-7974.21.3.558

Kirita, T., & Endo, M. (1995). Happy face advantage in recognizing facial expressions. *Acta Psychologica*, *89*(2), 149–163. doi.org/10.1016/0001-6918(94)00021-8

LeDoux, J. (2003). *Synaptic self.* New York: Penguin.

Le Poire, B. A., & Yoshimura, S. M. (1999). The effects of expectancies and actual communication on nonverbal adaptation and communication outcomes: A test of interaction adaptation theory. *Communication Monographs*, *66*(1), 1–30. doi.org/10.1080/03637759909376460

Lockenhoff, C. E., & Carstensen, L. L. (2007). Aging, emotion, and health-related decision strategies: Motivational manipulations can reduce age differences. *Psychology and Aging*, *22*(1), 134–146. doi.org/10.1037/0882-7974.22.1.134

Moradian, N. R., & Walker, S. E. (2008). Relationships between body size and sound-producing structures in crickets: Do large males have large harps? *Invertebrate Biology*, *127*(4), 444–451. doi.org/10.1111/j.1744-7410.2008.00142.x

Ohala, J. J. (1984). An ethological perspective on common cross-language utilization of F0 of voice. *Phonetica*, *41*, 1–16.

Öhman, A., & Mineka, S. (2001). Fears, phobias, and preparedness. Toward an evolved module of fear and fear learning. *Psychological Review*, *108*, 483–522. doi.org/10.1037//0033-295X.108.3.483

Orgeta, V., & Phillips, L. H. (2008). Effects of age and emotional intensity on the recognition of facial emotion. *Experimental Aging Research*, *34*, 63–79. doi.org/110.:1080/03610730701.762047

Ruffman, T., Sullivan, S., & Dittrich, W. (2009). Older adults' recognition of bodily and auditory expressions of emotion. *Psychology and Aging*, *24*(3), 614–622. doi.org/10.1037/a0016356

Rump, K. M., Giovannelli, J. L., Minshew, N. J., & Strauss, M. S. (2009). The development of emotion recognition in individuals with autism. *Child Development*, *80*(5), 1434–1447. doi.org/10.1111/j.1467-8624.2009.01343.x

Russell, J. A., & Barrett, L. (1999). Core affect, prototypical emotional episodes, and other things called emotion: Dissecting the elephant. *Journal of Personality and Social Psychology*, *76*(5), 805–819. doi.org/10.1007/BF00992253

Siegman, A. W., Anderson, R. A., & Berger, T. (1990). The angry voice: its effects on the experience of anger and cardiovascular reactivity. *Psychosomatic Medicine*, *52*(6), 631–642.

Schienle, A., Stark, R., Walter, B., Blecker, C., Kirsch, P., Sammer, G., & Vaitl, D. (2002). The insula is not specifically involved in disgust processing: an fMRI study. *Neuroreport*, *13*, 2023–2026. doi.org/10.1097/00001756-200211150-00006

Walsh, J. A., Vida, M. D., & Rutherford, M. D. (2014). Strategies for perceiving facial expressions in adults with autism spectrum disorder. *Journal of Autism and Developmental Disorders*, *44*, 1018–1026.

Watling D., Workman L, Bourne V. J. (2012). Emotion lateralisation: Developments throughout the lifespan. *Laterality*, *17*(4), 389–411. doi.org/10.1080/1357650X.2012.682160

Wicker, B., Keysers, C., Plailly, J., Royet, J. P., Gallese, V., & Rizzolatti, G. (2003). Both of us disgusted in my insula: The common neural basis of seeing and feeling disgust. *Neuron*, *40*, 655–664.

Wilensky, A. E., Schafe, G. E., Kristensen, M. P., & LeDoux, J. E. (2006). Rethinking the fear circuit: The central nucleus of the amygdala is required for the acquisition, consolidation, and expression of Pavlovian fear conditioning. *Journal of Neuroscience*, *48*, 12387–12396. doi.org/10.1523/JNEUROSCI.4316-06.2006

Faces of Shame: Implications for Self-Esteem, Emotion Regulation, Aggression, and Well-Being

Patrizia Velotti, Carlo Garofalo ⓘ, Federica Bottazzi, and Vincenzo Caretti

ABSTRACT
There is an increasing interest in psychological research on shame experiences and their associations with other aspects of psychological functioning and well-being, as well as with possible maladaptive outcomes. In an attempt to confirm and extend previous knowledge on this topic, we investigated the nomological network of shame experiences in a large community sample ($N = 380$; 66.1% females), adopting a multidimensional conceptualization of shame. Females reported higher levels of shame (in particular, bodily and behavioral shame), guilt, psychological distress, emotional reappraisal, and hostility. Males had higher levels of self-esteem, emotional suppression, and physical aggression. Shame feelings were associated with low self-esteem, hostility, and psychological distress in a consistent way across gender. Associations between characterological shame and emotional suppression, as well as between bodily shame and anger occurred only among females. Moreover, characterological and bodily shame added to the prediction of low self-esteem, hostility, and psychological distress above and beyond the influence of trait shame. Finally, among females, emotional suppression mediated the influence of characterological shame on hostility and psychological distress. These findings extend current knowledge on the nomological net surrounding shame experiences in everyday life, supporting the added value of a multidimensional conceptualization of shame feelings.

Shame is commonly defined as an intense negative emotion characterized by the perception of a global devaluation of the self (Tangney & Dearing, 2002). Shame feelings are often triggered by social events in which a drop of personal status or feelings of rejection are perceived. Of note, rather than representing a unidimensional construct, shame could actually refer to different aspects of the self, such as behaviors or body characteristics, as well to the broader identity (Andrews, Qian, & Valentine, 2002; Hejdenberg & Andrews, 2011). Specifically, a multidimensional conceptualization of shame has been proposed (Andrews et al., 2002) to identify: (a) experiences of characterological shame (i.e., regarding personal habits, manner with others, the kind of person one is, and personal skills); (b) experiences of behavioral shame (i.e., referred to doing something wrong, saying something stupid, and failing in competitive contexts); and (c) bodily shame (i.e., referred to being ashamed of one's physical appearance). There is substantial evidence linking shame with psychopathology in general, and internalizing symptoms in particular (Andrews et al., 2002; Velotti, Elison, & Garofalo, 2014). Yet, associations between specific experiences of shame and other psychological mechanisms have sparsely been investigated. In the current study, we sought to provide a fine-grained analysis of the nomological network surrounding shame feelings, adopting a multidimensional conceptualization of shame experiences. The concept of nomological network refers to a group of constructs that are theoretically or empirically expected to show consistent linkages, and as such nomological network analysis is used to measure construct validity (Cronbach & Meehl, 1955). Specifically, we aimed at confirming associations between shame feelings and psychopathological distress (Andrews et al., 2002). Furthermore, we sought to expand current knowledge broadening the scope of the nomological network of shame. To this end, we first reviewed prior literature to identify possible correlates of shame experiences.

Shame and Self-Esteem

Frequent experiences of shame may eventually crystallize into trait-like shame prone-ness. Trait shame, in turn, involves a particularly painful, and often incapacitating, negative feeling involving a sense of inferiority, hopelessness, and helplessness, as well as a desire to hide personal flaws (Andrews et al., 2002). Accordingly, it has been pro-posed that experiences of shame are tightly linked with fluctuation in self-esteem, and it is plausible that frequent experiences of shame could be conceptually related to chronically low levels of self-esteem (Elison, Garofalo, & Velotti, 2014). Furthermore, low levels of self-esteem could increase the individual vulnerability to experience nega-tive emotional states, including shame. Accordingly, although the directionality of their association is not clear, several studies have reported a substantial relation between low self-esteem and negative emotions, such as guilt and shame (Garofalo, 2015; Marshall, Marshall, Serran, & O'Brien, 2009). Of note, both self-esteem and negative emotions have been linked to increased aggressive tendencies, yet few studies have empirically tested associations between shame and aggression.

Shame and Aggression

The link between shame and aggression was proposed by several scholars, and some went so far as to say that all forms of violence are anticipated by feelings of shame and humiliation (Gilligan, 1996). From this perspective, early experiences of rejection and abuse might lead to shame-proneness in adulthood. In turn, individuals with high levels of shame-proneness may believe that resorting to aggression and violence is the only possible way to get rid of their shame feelings. From an evolutionary perspective, the experience of shame early in the development may be later replaced by a condition of chronic anger, adopted as a means to keep others away so that shame feelings cannot be detected or triggered (Farmer & Andrews, 2009). Alternatively, the perception of self-devaluation – which is implicit in shame experiences – may represent the first step of a chain that connects shame and aggression (Elison et al., 2014). Specifically, the sequence could begin with a devaluation of the self that causes shame; in turn, shame feelings can lead to the experience of substantial anger and to the expression of aggressive behavior towards the source of the initial devaluation (Elison et al., 2014; Velotti et al., 2014). In line with this assumption, in a recent study shame experiences were associated with trait anger, and this relation was accounted for by the role of angry reactions to criticisms (Hejdenberg & Andrews, 2011). Specifically, behavioral shame was linked to both proneness toward angry reactions and trait anger, whereas characterological and bodily shame were only related to angry reactions to criticisms (Hejdenberg & Andrews, 2011). In this chain, maladaptive emotion regulation may play a mediating role (Garofalo, Holden, Zeigler-Hill, & Velotti, 2016; Roberton, Daffern & Bucks, 2012). Yet, this possibility has not been empirically tested so far.

Shame and Emotion Regulation

Shame is considered among the emotions that are more difficult to regulate (Elison et al., 2014). Of note, the way people regulate emotions has important consequences for their well-being (Gross & John, 2003). Cognitive reappraisal and expressive suppression have been identified among the emotion regulation strategies that people use more often (Gross & John, 2003; Gross & Levenson, 1993). Cognitive reappraisal entails thinking about an upsetting situation from a different angle in order to alter its meaning and modulate its emotional impact. Expressive suppression involves an attempt to inhibit or reduce the outward expression of an ongoing emotional experience (i.e., not showing the emotion that one is feeling). In general, reappraisal and suppression are inversely related to a wide range of outcomes in the domains of subjective well-being, affectivity, and social relationships. Specifically, reappraisal is typically associated with better, and suppression with poorer, outcomes (Gross & John, 2003). A recent experimental study has shown that trait shame was linked with emotional suppression (Lanteigne, Flynn, Eastabrook, & Hollenstein, 2014). This is important, because adopting maladaptive emotion regulation strategies for shame may ultimately lead to both internalizing (e.g., psychological distress) and externalizing (e.g., aggression) psychopathological symptoms (Elison, Pulos, & Lennon, 2006; Velotti et al., 2014). Therefore, it is possible that shame is associated with maladaptive emotion regulation, which in turn may explain the associations that shame has with psychopathological symptoms and aggression.

Overview of the Current Study

In the present study we sought to: (1) confirm and extend prior research on the nomological network of shame, investigating its associations with measures of psychological distress; self-esteem, aggression, and emotion regulation; and (2) examine the possible mediating role of maladaptive emotion regulation (i.e., emotional suppression) in the association between trait shame and external correlates (i.e., self-esteem, aggression and general psychopathology). Since gender differences in shame experiences (Andrews et al., 2002), emotion regulation (John & Gross, 2003), aggression (Fossati, Maffei, Acquarini, & Di Ceglie, 2003), and psychopathological distress (Prunas, Sarno, Preti, Madeddu, & Perugini, 2012) have consistenly been reported, we also examined gender differences in mean levels and patterns of associations.

Method

Participants and Procedures

The total sample comprised 380 adult participants (66.1% women, $N = 251$) recruited from the community. Participants were recruited by psychology graduate students with a snowball sampling technique: they started recruiting 5 participants from their acquaintances and asked them to recruit participants among their social networks. Men ($M_{age} = 31.00$, $SD = 11.42$, range 19–63) were slightly but significantly older than women ($M_{age} = 28.50$, $SD = 9.88$, range 18–58), $t(225.85) = 2.11, p = .04$. All participants were Italian. The majority of participants were university students ($N = 225$, 59.2%), whereas 6.3% ($N = 24$) were unemployed, 23.9% ($N = 91$) were employees, 9.5% ($N = 36$) were self-employed, and 1.1% ($N = 4$) were retired. Most participants ($N = 313$, 82.4%) reported to be (or to had been in the past) in a significant intimate relationship lasted at least 6 months. Finally, 64 participants (16.8%) did not have children, whereas 316 of them (83.2%) had at least one kid. All participants voluntarily and anonymously took part in the study and provided written informed consent. Participants were administered the questionnaires described below and returned them in a sealed envelope to ensure confidentiality. The local Institutional Review Board formally approved all procedures.

Measures

All measures were self-report Likert-type questionnaires. Participants were administered the Italian versions of the following measures. The translated items of all measures were obtained by the authors of the corresponding published Italian adaptations (see references below).

Experience of Shame Scale (ESS; Andrews et al., 2002)
The ESS is a 25-item questionnaire designed to capture the experience of shame across three components: characterological shame (sample item: 'Have you felt ashamed of any of your personal habits?'; $\alpha = .85$), behavioral shame (sample item: 'Do you feel ashamed when you do something wrong?'; $\alpha = .85$), and bodily shame (sample item: 'Have you felt ashamed of your body or any part of it?'; $\alpha = .87$). The sum of these three components provides an overall index of shame feelings ($\alpha = .91$). In the present study, the Italian version of the ESS was used (Caretti, Craparo, & Schimmenti, 2010), which substantially replicated the psychometric properties of the original version.

Differential Emotions Scale-IV (DES-IV; Izard et al., 1993)
The DES-IV consists of 36 items aimed at capturing the frequency of the experience of specific positive and negative emotions in the daily life. For the purpose of this study, only the six items assessing shame (e.g., 'Feel embarrassed when anybody sees you make a mistake'; $\alpha = .63$) and guilt (e.g., 'Feel regret, sorry about something you did'; $\alpha = .68$) of the Italian adaptation of the DES-IV (Zavattini et al., 2015) were administered.

Rosenberg Self-Esteem Scale (RSES; Rosenberg, 1965)
The 10-item RSES was used to assess the general level of self-esteem (e.g., 'On the whole, I am satisfied with myself'). The Italian version of the RSES has shown sound psychometric properties (Prezza, Trombaccia, & Armento, 1997). Cronbach's alpha was .88 in the present study.

Symptom Checklist-90-Revised (SCL-90-R; Derogatis, 1994)

The SCL-90-R is a 90-item inventory designed to measure general psychopathological distress suffered in the past month. The SCL-90-R estimates a global index of psychopathology (Global Severity Index, GSI), by averaging all item scores (e.g., 'To what extent do you feel/have you felt blue in the last month?'), rated on a Likert scale ($\alpha = .97$). The Italian adaptation of the SCL-R-90 was used in this study (Prunas et al., 2012).

Emotion Regulation Questionnaire (ERQ; Gross & John, 2003)

The 10-item ERQ was administered to assess individual differences in two emotion regulation strategies: cognitive reappraisal (e.g., 'I control my emotions by changing the way I think about the situation I'm in'; $\alpha = .87$) and expressive suppression (e.g., 'I keep my emotions to myself'; $\alpha = .79$). For the purpose of this study, we used the Italian version of the ERQ (Balzarotti, John, & Gross, 2010), which has shown adequate psychometric properties.

Aggression Questionnaire (AQ; Buss & Perry, 1992)

The AQ is a 29-item instrument composed by four subscales: physical aggression (e.g., 'Once in a while I can't control the urge to strike another person'; $\alpha = .83$); verbal aggression (e.g., 'I can't help getting into arguments when people disagree with me'; $\alpha = .76$); anger ('I sometimes feel like a powder keg ready to explode'; $\alpha = 80$); and hostility (e.g., 'When people are especially nice, I wonder what they want'; $\alpha = .81$). The AQ total score represent an index of trait aggression ($\alpha = 90$). The Italian version of the AQ has shown good reliability and validity (Fossati et al., 2003), and has been used in the present study.

Data Analytic Strategy

Descriptive statistics were computed for all study variables. Gender differences and associations with socio-demographic variables of interest were evaluated with one-way between-groups univariate or multivariate analyses of covariance (i.e., ANCOVA or MANCOVA, respectively). Pillai's Trace was used as the most robust test statistic, and Partial Eta squared ($\eta^2_{partial}$) was chosen as an estimate of the effect size of the univariate F tests. Pearson product-moment correlation coefficients among all measures were calculated. The homogeneity of correlation coefficients across gender was tested using the appropriate z statistic (Cohen, Cohen, West, & Aiken, 2003). To test whether the ESS scales explained additional variance in previously significant correlates, above and beyond the effect of DES-IV-assessed shame, hierarchical multiple regression analyses were conducted. The Variance Inflation Factor (VIF) was adopted to assess collinearity. Finally, to test the hypothesized indirect effect of shame on both aggression and psychopathological distress through the mediation of maladaptive emotion regulation, hierarchical regression and bootstrap analyses were conducted using the PROCESS Macro for SPSS (Hayes, 2013). All analyses were carried out holding constant the effect of age.

Results

Descriptive Analyses and Gender Differences

Descriptive statistics and gender differences are presented in Table 1.

Table 1. Means, Standard Deviations (*SD*), and Gender Comparisons (Controlling for Age) for All Study Variables (*N* = 380).

	Male participants (*N* = 129) Mean (*SD*)	Female participants (*N* = 251) Mean (*SD*)	Whole sample (*N* = 380) Mean (*SD*)	*F*	df	η^2 partial
ESS total score	46.89(11.79)	**52.96(12.48)**	50.89(12.57)	17.15***	1, 375	.04
ESS characterological	21.63(6.09)	22.73(6.49)	22.36(6.37)	1.37	1, 375	.00
ESS behavioral	18.70(5.15)	**20.65(5.41)**	19.99(5.40)	9.79**	1, 375	.03
ESS bodily	6.57(2.53)	**9.54(3.45)**	8.53(3.46)	69.34***	1, 375	.16
DES-IV shame	5.24(1.71)	**6.03(2.11)**	5.75(2.01)	9.85**	1, 342	.03
DES-IV guilt	6.24(1.75)	**6.79(1.97)**	6.59(1.91)	4.45*	1, 342	.01
Self-esteem	**32.00(4.75)**	30.50(5.49)	31.01(5.29)	6.62*	1, 377	.02
SCL-90-R GSI	.54(.38)	**.76(.53)**	.69(.49)	15.55***	1, 377	.04
ERQ reappraisal	4.71(1.02)	**4.97(1.05)**	4.88(1.05)	4.93*	1, 377	.13
ERQ suppression	**3.70(1.19)**	3.18(1.24)	3.36(1.25)	12.98***	1, 377	.03
AQ total score	63.57(16.51)	62.18(15.75)	62.65(16.00)	1.14	1, 377	.00
AQ physical aggression	**17.42(6.50)**	14.13(5.34)	15.25(5.96)	29.26***	1, 377	.07
AQ verbal aggression	14.37(3.74)	13.67(4.24)	13.91(4.09)	2.59	1, 377	.01
AQ anger	15.47(5.24)	16.09(5.30)	15.88(5.28)	0.82	1, 377	.00
AQ hostility	16.33(5.02)	**18.29(5.73)**	17.63(5.57)	8.44**	1, 377	.02

Note. ESS = Experience of Shame Scale; DES-IV = Differential Emotions Scale-IV; SCL-90-R = Symptom Checklist-90-Revised; ERQ = Emotion Regulation Questionnaire; AQ = Aggression Questionnaire. Bolded mean values are significantly greater than the corresponding value in the opposite gender.
*$p < .05$. **$p < .01$. ***$p < .001$.

Females reported an overall greater level of ESS-assessed shame than males, and lower levels of self-esteem. Also, MANCOVA results revealed that there was a statistically significant difference between male and female participants on the combined ESS scale scores, $F(3, 372) = 26.57$, $p < .001$, Pillai's Trace = .18, $\eta^2_{partial} = .18$. Specifically, females scored higher than males on behavioral and bodily shame. Females also reported significantly greater levels of DES-IV-assessed guilt and shame, multivariate $F(2, 340) = 5.12$, $p < .01$, Pillai's Trace = .03, $\eta^2_{partial} = .03$. A subsequent ANCOVA revealed a significant gender difference on the SCL-90-R GSI score. Furthermore, a significant multivariate effect of gender occurred on the combined ERQ scales, $F(2, 375) = 9.52$, $p < .001$, Pillai's Trace = .05, $\eta^2_{partial} = .05$; in particular, females reported higher levels of cognitive reappraisal, and lower levels of expressive suppression than males. Finally, a significant difference across gender occurred when the AQ subscales were entered as combined dependent variables, $F(4, 373) = 19.28$, $p < .001$, Pillai's Trace = .17, $\eta^2_{partial} = .17$, but not when males and females when compared on the AQ total score using an ANCOVA design. When the AQ subscales were considered separately, only two differences reached statistical significance, in opposite directions: males reported higher levels of physical aggression, but lower levels of hostility, than females.

Furthermore, we tested whether levels of shame differed between people with and without children, as well as between people who reported to be (or to had been in the past) in a long lasting romantic relationship and people who did not. Controlling for gender and age, participants with children reported significantly lower scores on the ESS total score, $F(1, 373) = 3.95$, $p > .05$, $\eta^2_{partial} = .01$. However, the multivariate main effect of the parental condition (i.e., children yes/no) on the combined ESS scale scores was only approaching significance, $F(3, 371) = 2.22$, $p = .08$, Pillai's Trace = .02, $\eta^2_{partial} = .02$. Specifically, although participants with children reported lower levels of shame on all three dimensions, these differences were significant for characterological shame, $F(1, 373) = 3.98$, $p < .05$, $\eta^2_{partial} = .01$, and behavioral shame, $F(1, 373) = 4.79$, $p < .05$, $\eta^2_{partial} = .01$. On the other hand, although there was not significant difference on the ESS total score, $F(2, 372) = 1.49$, $p > .05$, $\eta^2_{partial} = .01$, a significant multivariate effect between participants with and without a current or past intimate relationship occurred on the combined ESS scales, $F(6, 742) = 2.57$, $p < .05$, Pillai's Trace $= .04$, $\eta^2_{partial} = .02$. Specifically, controlling for gender and age, individuals who had never had a long lasting intimate relationship reported significantly greater scores of bodily shame, $F(2, 372) = 4.33$, $p < .05$, $\eta^2_{partial} = .02$. The analyses in this paragraph were exploratory in nature, to test for associations between the ESS and demographics. However, since an interesting pattern of results occurred, we opted for reporting and discussing them, to stimulate further research in this area.

ESS Nomological Network

Correlation analysis results are displayed in Table 2. Of note, the ESS scales were all strongly related to the ESS total score (controlling for age, partial rs were .89, .84. and .63 for the characterologial shame, behavioral shame, and bodily shame scales, respectively). Further, the ESS scales were significantly associated to each other (rs ranging between .33 and .60). All ESS scales were significantly and positively related to the DES-IV shame and guilt scales. Of note, homogeneity tests did not show significant differences in correlation coefficient values of any ESS scale with shame *versus* guilt scale from the DES-IV, min. $z = 0.24$, max $z = 1.53$, all $ps > .05$. Conversely, homogeneity tests across gender revealed that only 1 out 8 pairs of correlation coefficients (12.5%) significantly differed across gender, with the association between bodily shame and guilt being stronger among males ($z = 2.27$, $p < .05$). All the ESS scales were also significantly and negatively associated with levels of self-esteem. As for the associations between the ESS and the ERQ, no significant correlations were found with cognitive reappraisal. Among females only, a significant positive correlations emerged between emotional suppression and both characterological shame and the ESS total score. Among males, no significant associations occurred between the ESS and the AQ total score; on the other hand, the AQ total score was significantly and positively related to the ESS bodily shame scale and the ESS total score among females. Physical aggression was negatively related with characerological shame among males. Among females, the direction of the association was inverse, but nonsignificant. Of note, correlation coefficients between physical aggression and ESS total and characerological shame scores significantly differed across gender ($z = 2.12$ and 2.41, respectively, both $ps < .05$). Verbal aggression was only significantly related to characerological shame (negatively) among females. Among females, anger showed a positive association with bodily shame. Moreover, the ESS total and subscale scores were significantly and positively related to hostility across gender. Finally, significant positive correlations were found between all ESS scales and the GSI scale of the SCL-90-R. Overall, only 3 out of 44 comparisons between correlation coefficients (across gender) turned out to be significant (6.82%), suggesting that the patterns of correlations between the ESS scales and external correlates are largely invariant across gender (min. $z = 0.00$, max $z = 1.68$, all $ps > .05$).

Incremental Variance of ESS Dimensions on Relevant Outcomes

We then tested whether the ESS scales significantly explained a portion of additional variance in self-esteem, hostility, and psychopathological distress (as these were the variables

Table 2. Partial Correlations (Controlling for Age) of the ESS Total and Scale Scores with the DES-IV Guilt and Shame Scales, Self-Esteem Level, Emotion Regulation Strategies, and Aggression Dimensions, in Both Male (N = 129) and Female (N = 251) Participants (Total N = 380).

		DES-IV shame	DES-IV guilt	Self-esteem	ERQ reappraisal	ERQ suppression	AQ total	AQ physical aggression	AQ verbal aggression	AQ anger	AQ hostility	SCL-90-R GSI
ESS total	Males	.45***	.56***	-.42***	.01	.03	.04	-.16[a]	-.04	.02	.37***	.43***
	Females	.51***	.54***	-.51***	-.06	.19**	.16*	.07[a]	-.12	.07	.41***	.52***
ESS characterological	Males	.40***	.54***	-.46***	.02	.12	.01	-.21*[a]	-.03	-.01	.34***	.45***
	Females	.50***	.59***	-.54***	-.05	.22**	.12	.05[a]	-.15*	.05	.34***	.52***
ESS behavioral	Males	.39***	.40***	-.25***	.02	-.04	.06	-.09	-.01	.05	.31***	.26***
	Females	.38***	.36***	-.30***	-.01	.12	.09	.03	-.12	-.02	.33***	.33***
ESS bodily	Males	.33**	.49***[a]	-.35***	-.04	-.06	.04	-.06	-.10	.01	.29**	.36***
	Females	.30***	.28***[a]	-.37***	-.11	.09	.22***	.12	.03	.17**	.33***	.39***

Note. ESS = Experience of Shame Scale; DES-IV = Differential Emotions Scale-IV; ERQ = Emotion Regulation Questionnaire; AQ = Aggression Questionnaire; SCL-90-R = Symptom Checklist-90-Revised; GSI = Global Severity Index scale of the SCL-90-R.

[a]Significant difference in correlation coefficients between male and female participants.

* p < .05. ** p < .01. *** p < .001.

Table 3. Hierarchical Multiple Regression Analyses Predicting Self-Esteem, Hostility, and Psychopathological Distress ($N = 380$).

	Self-esteem B	AQ Hostility β	GSI β
Step 1			
Age	.21***	−.20***	−.10
Gender	.13*	−.15**	−.20***
Adjusted R2change	.06***	.06***	.05***
Step 2			
DES-IV shame	−.38***	.60***	.54***
Adjusted R2change	.13***	.33***	.27***
Step 3			
ESS characterological shame	−.39***	−.02	.30***
ESS behavioral shame	−.09	.08	−.08
ESS bodily shame	−.17***	.15**	.18***
Adjusted R2change	.13***	.02**	.10***

Note. AQ = Aggression Questionnaire; GSI = Global Severity Index of the Symtpom Checklist-90-Revised; DES-IV = Differential Emotions Scale-IV; ESS = Experience of Shame Scale. Gender was dummy-coded with 0 = females.

most strongly associated at the bivariate level with the ESS scales), above and beyond the influence of DES-IV-assessed shame (see Table 3). None of the VIF values suggested that collinearity among predictors could have biased regression results. Hierarchical multiple regression analyses revealed that, controlling for age and gender, the ESS scales significantly explained a portion of incremental variance in all of the outcomes considered. Specifically, after removing the shared variance among ESS scales, characteriological and bodily shame scales significantly and independently predicted self-esteem level (negatively) and global psychopathological distress (positively). Further, bodily shame uniquely and positively predicted hostility, over and above the influence of the shame scale of the DES-IV.

Does Emotional Suppression Account for an Indirect Relationship between Sshame and Maladaptive Outcomes?

Based on partial correlation results (see Table 2), the significance of statistical indirect effects was assessed only among female participants (i.e., because among males the association between shame and emotional suppression was not significant, ruling out the possibility of any indirect effect of the former through the latter). A summary of the indirect effect analyses conducted is presented in Table 4. A total of seven indirect effects were tested, four of which yielded significant results with small effect size. Specifically, emotion suppression mediated the effect of ESS total score and characterological shame on both hostility and psychopathological distress. The other indirect effects (involving self-esteem and overall trait aggression) did not reach statistical significance.

Discussion

The aim of the current study was to confirm and extend previous knowledge on the nomological net surrounding the multidimensional construct of shame, also testing for invariance across gender. Further, the possible mechanisms underlying the association between shame and maladaptive outcomes were investigated, examining the mediating role of maladaptive emotion regulation (i.e., emotional suppression).

Table 4. Summary of Bootstrapping Analyses Examining the Indirect Effect of Shame on Self-Esteem, Aggression, and Psychopathological Distress Through the Role of Emotional Suppression, Controlling for Age (Among Females Only; $N = 251$; 5,000 Bootstrap Samples).

Predictor Variable(PV)	Mediating variable(M)	Criterion Variable (CV)	Effect of PV on M (a)	Effect of M on CV, controlling for the PV (b)	Total effect (c)	Direct effect (c')	Indirect effect (bias corrected intervals)		abcs [95% bias corrected CI]
							(a × b)	95% CI	
ESS total	Emotional suppression	Self-esteem	.02**	−.39	−.23***	−.22***	−.007	[−.021, .000]	
ESS total	Emotional suppression	AQ total	.02**	.68	.21**	.20*	.012	[−.015, .053]	
ESS characterological shame	Emotional suppression	AQ total	.04**	.75	.31*	.28	.028	[−.028, .111]	
ESS total score	Emotional suppression	AQ hostility	.02**	.87**	.20***	.18***	.016	[.005, .035]	.034 [.009, .075]
ESS characterological shame	Emotional suppression	AQ hostility	.04**	.90**	.32***	.28***	.034	[.012, .075]	.039 [.013, .084]
ESS total score	Emotional suppression	GSI	.02**	.10***	.02***	.02***	.002	[.001, .003]	.041 [.012, .081]
ESS characterological shame	Emotional suppression	GSI	.04**	.09***	.04***	.04***	.003	[.001, .007]	.042 [.015, .085]

Note. ESS = Experience of Shame Scale; AQ = Aggression Questionnaire; GSI = Global Severity Index scale of the Symptom Checklist-90-Revised; CI = Confidence Intervals. Unstandardized coefficients are reported. ab_{cs} = completely standardized indirect effect, measure of the effect size for significant indirect effects.
*$p < .05.$ **$p < .01.$ ***$p < .001.$

In line with the expectations, women reported greater levels of shame (specifically: behavioral and bodily shame), and lower levels of self-esteem, than men. Women also reported greater levels of psychopathological distress, cognitive reappraisal, and hostility, whereas men had greater levels of emotional suppression and physical aggression. Taken together, these findings are in line with prior findings (Andrews et al., 2002; Fossati et al., 2003; John & Gross, 2003) on gender differences in emotional experience, emotion regulation styles, as well as in the expression of aggressive tendencies. Notably, levels of characterological and behavioral shame were higher among people who did not have kids, and levels of bodily shame were higher among people who never had a significant romantic relationship. The correlational nature of the study did not allow to speculate about causal effects, but the interesting link between intimate attachment relationships (with children and/or romantic partners) and shame feelings in different domains warrants future investigation.

The nomological network surrounding shame experiences was largely consistent across gender. Behavioral, characterological, and bodily shame feelings were all related with trait shame and trait guilt. Furthermore, shame feelings were associated with decreased self-esteem, and with higher levels of hostility and psychological distress. This is consistent with previous literature (Garofalo, 2015; Elison, 2005; Gilligan, 1996; Marshall et al., 2009) and suggests that the experience of shame does not come in isolation. Rather, feelings of shame are likely associated with a more general lack of confidence in the self as well as in the outside world. As such, it is not surprising that feelings of shame and lack of confidence in the self and the others can be accompanied by overall psychological distress. Some gender differences in the nomological net emerged, suggesting that the experience of shame might have more pronounced consequences in women. Indeed, characterological shame was related with emotional suppression, indicating that women who are more prone to experience feeling of shame about their own personality may tend to adopt maladaptive emotion regulation strategies (Nyström & Mikkelsen, 2013). This might be due to an attempt to protect themselves from the effects of such unbearable feelings (Elison et al., 2014), which would probably increase the experience of shame itself. Therefore, it appears that women who experience characterological shame are likely to suppress, rather than show, their own emotions. In line with this, higher levels of characterological shame were also associated with lower levels of verbal aggression. Further, bodily shame was associated with angry feelings, suggesting that the perception of flaws in their physical aspect could be a trigger for angry and aggressive outbursts especially in females (Hejdenberg & Andrews, 2011). Finally, physical aggression was negatively related to characterological shame in men, indicating a possible inhibiting effect of shame toward aggressive tendencies. This is consistent with the idea that shame feelings are not always bad, and that the experience of shame might have healthy and adaptive consequences (Farmer & Andrews, 2009). For example, feeling ashamed about a previous aggressive behavior can have the positive consequence of inhibiting the same behavior in the future. As a whole, although all others coefficients were nonsignificant, the trends seem to indicate that shame is negatively associated with aggression among men, but positively related (or unrelated) to aggression among women. Future examinations of the possible differential effects of shame on aggression across gender are required to obtain a deeper insight into the shame-aggression link.

Our findings also supported the importance of adopting a multidimensional conceptualization of shame (Andrews et al., 2002). Indeed, over and above the influence of trait shame, characterological and bodily shame were independently associated with low self-esteem and psychological distress. Further, bodily shame was independently related to hostility. This suggests that, even after controlling for individual differences in the experience of shame in daily life, specific feelings of shame referred to one's identity or body might add to the explanation of internalizing and externalizing symptoms. As a last step, we aimed at exploring possible mechanisms linking shame feelings with maladaptive outcomes. Mediation analyses revealed that—among women—the associations of shame feelings (and, in particular, characterological shame) with hostility and psychological distress was accounted for by emotional suppression. This might indicate that both the externalization (i.e., hostility) and internalization (i.e., psychological distress) of shame feelings could be explained by poor emotion regulation, rather than being an effect of shame *per se*. In other words, shame feelings are likely to increase the individual difficulty in regulating emotions, and this in turn could lead to an increase in hostile attitudes and psychopathological symptoms (Garofalo et al., 2016; Velotti et al., 2014). On the other hand, the same pattern did not explain the association between shame and low self-esteem, suggesting that their shared variance was not accounted for by emotional suppression.

This study presented several limitations. First, the reliance on self-report questionnaires may have inflated correlations due to the spurious effect of common method variance. Second, the generalization of these results is limited by the recruitment of a convenience sample of community individuals, the majority of whom where university students. One possible problem in relying on convenience samples comprising a strong component of university students is a restriction in the variance of several demographic (e.g., Socio Economic Status) and personality (e.g., impulsive or antisocial traits) characteristics that may be linked to some of the variables examined in the present study (e.g., aggression). Third, the correlational design prevents us from drawing conclusions about the causal relations among study variables. Nevertheless, the present findings may help design longitudinal studies to test prospective associations among shame experiences and related constructs over time. Finally, the use of single measures for each construct of interest raises the possibility that results would not generalize to other operationalizations of the same constructs.

Nonetheless, we believe these findings extend current knowledge on the nomological network of shame feelings, providing novel insight on the role of specific shame experiences. Specifically, the present findings suggest that conceptualizing shame as a multidimensional construct may be helpful in delineating the associations between shame and maladaptive outcomes. Notably, our study also provides additional support for the use of the ESS as a brief multidimensional measure of shame experiences. From a clinical point of view, this is important as a focus on specific 'faces' of shame can be appropriate to target psychopathological symptoms and aggression. Finally, the current study advanced prior knowledge indicating that fostering the use of adaptive emotion regulation strategies could be an important target to prevent or reduce psychopathological symptoms and aggression.

ORCID

Carlo Garofalo (iD) http://orcid.org/0000-0003-2306-6961

References

Andrews, B., Qian, M., & Valentine, J. D. (2002). Predicting depressive symptoms with a new measure of shame: The experience of shame scale. *British Journal of Clinical Psychology, 41*, 29–42.

Balzarotti, S., John, O. P., & Gross, J. J. (2010). An Italian adaptation of the Emotion Regulation Questionnaire. *European Journal of Psychological Assessment, 26*, 61–67.

Buss, A. H., & Perry, M. (1992). The aggression questionnaire. *Journal of Personality and Social Psychology, 63*, 452–459. doi: 10.1037/0022-3514.63.3.452

Caretti, V., Craparo, G., & Schimmenti, A. (2010). Il ruolo della disregolazione affettiva, della dissociazione e della vergogna nei disturbi del comportamento alimentare. [The role of affective dysregulation, dissociation and shame in eating disorders]. In V. Caretti, & D. La Barbera (eds.), *Addiction. Aspetti Biologici e di Ricerca* [*Addiction. Biological and Research Aspects*] (pp. 135–165). Milano, IT: Raffaello Cortina Editore.

Cohen, J., Cohen, P., West, S. G., & Aiken, L. S. (2003). *Applied multiple regression/ correlation analysis for the behavioral sciences (3rd ed.).* Hillsdale, NJ: Erlbaum.

Cronbach, L. J., & Meehl, P. E. (1955). Construct validity in psychological tests. *Psychological Bulletin, 52*(4), 281–302.

Derogatis, L. R. (1994). *SCL-90-R, administration, scoring and procedures manual for the revised version (3rd ed.).* Minneapolis, MN: National Computer Systems.

Elison, J. (2005). Shame and guilt: A hundred years of apples and oranges. *New Ideas in Psychology, 23*, 5–32.

Elison, J., Garofalo, C., & Velotti, P. (2014). Shame and aggression: Theoretical considerations. *Aggression and Violent Behavior, 19*, 447–453.

Elison, J., Pulos, S., & Lennon, R. (2006). Shame-focused coping: An empirical study of the compass of shame. *Social Behavior and Personality, 34*, 161–168.

Farmer, E., & Andrews, B. (2009). Shameless yet angry: shame and its relationship to anger in male young offenders and undergraduate controls. *Journal of Forensic Psychiatry & Psychology, 20*, 48–65.

Fossati, A., Maffei, C., Acquarini, E., & Di Ceglie, A. (2003). Multigroup confirmatory component and factor analyses of the Italian version of the aggression questionnaire. *European Journal of Psychological Assessment, 19*, 54–65.

Garofalo, C. (2015). Emozionalità negativa ed autostima in un campione di offender detenuti: Uno studio preliminare [Negative emotionality and self-esteem in an incarcerated offender sample: Preliminary investigation]. *Giornale Italiano di Psicologia [Italian Journal of Psychology], 42*, 363–371.

Garofalo, C., Holden, C. J., Zeigler-Hill, V., & Velotti, P. (2016). Understanding the connection between self-esteem and aggression: The mediating role of emotion dysregulation. *Aggressive Behavior, 42,* 3–15.

Gilligan, J. (1996). *Violence. Reflections on a National Epidemic.* New York, NY: Vintage Books.

Gross, J. J., & John, O. P. (2003). Individual differences in two emotion regulation processes: Implications for affect, relationships, and well-being. *Journal of Personality and Social Psychology, 85,* 348–362.

Gross, J. J., & Levenson, R. W. (1993). Emotional suppression: Physiology, self-report, and expressive behavior. *Journal of Personality and Social Psychology, 64,* 970–986.

Hayes, A. F. (2013). *Introduction to mediation, moderation, and conditional process analysis: A regression-based approach.* New York, NY: Guilford Press.

Hejdenberg, J., & Andrews, B. (2011). The relationship between shame and different types of anger: A theory-based investigation. *Personality and Individual Differences, 50,* 1278–1282.

Izard, C. E., Libero, D. Z., Putnam, P., Haynes, O. M. (1993). Stability of emotion experiences and their relations to traits of personality. *Journal of Personality and Social Psychology, 64*(5), 847–860.

Lanteigne, D. M., Flynn, J. J., Eastabrook, J. M., & Hollenstein, T. (2014). Discordant patterns among emotional experience, Arousal, and expression in adolescence: Relations with emotion regulation and internalizing problems. *Canadian Journal of Behavioural Science / Revue canadienne des sciences du comportement, 46,* 29–39.

Marshall, W. L., Marshall, L. E, Serran, G. A., & O'Brien, M. D. (2009). Self-esteem, shame, cognitive distorsions and empathy in sexual offenders: Their integration and treatment implications. *Psychology, Crime & Law, 15,* 217–234.

Nyström, M. B. T., & Mikkelsen, F. (2013). Psychopathy-related personality traits and shame management strategies in adolescents. *Journal of Interpersonal Violence, 28,* 519–537.

Prezza, M., Trombaccia, F. R., & Armento, L. (1997). La scala dell'autostima di Rosenberg: Traduzione e validazione Italiana. [The Rosenberg self-esteem Scale: Italian translation and validation.]. *Bollettino di Psicologia Applicata [Applied Psychology Bulletin], 223,* 35–44.

Prunas, A., Sarno, I., Preti, E., Madeddu, F., & Perugini, M. (2012). Psychometric properties of the Italian version of the SCL-90-R: A study on a large community sample. *European Psychiatry, 27,* 591–597.

Roberton, T., Daffern, M., & Bucks, R. S. (2012). Emotion regulation and aggression. *Aggression and Violent Behavior, 17,* 72–82.

Rosenberg, M. (1965). *Society and the adolescent self-image.* Princeton, NJ: Princeton University Press.

Tangney, J. P., & Dearing, R. L. (2002). *Shame and guilt.* New York, NY: Guilford Press.

Velotti, P., Elison, J., & Garofalo, C. (2014). Shame and aggression: Different trajectories and implications. *Aggression and Violent Behavior, 19,* 454–461.

Zavattini, G. C., Garofalo, C., Velotti, P., Tommasi, M., Romanelli, R., Espirito Santo, H., & Saggino, A. (2015). Dissociative experiences and psychopathology among inmates in Italian and Portuguese prisons. *International Journal of Offender Therapy and Comparative Criminology.* Advance online publication. doi.org/10.1177/0306624X15617256.

The Myth of the Angry Atheist

BRIAN P. MEIER

ADAM K. FETTERMAN
MICHAEL D. ROBINSON

COURTNEY M. LAPPAS

ABSTRACT. Atheists are often portrayed in the media and elsewhere as angry individuals. Although atheists disagree with the pillar of many religions, namely the existence of a God, it may not necessarily be the case that they are angry individuals. The prevalence and accuracy of angry-atheist perceptions were examined in 7 studies with 1,677 participants from multiple institutions and locations in the United States. Studies 1–3 revealed that people believe atheists are angrier than believers, people in general, and other minority groups, both explicitly and implicitly. Studies 4–7 then examined the accuracy of these beliefs. Belief in God, state anger, and trait anger were assessed in multiple ways and contexts. None of these studies supported the idea that atheists are particularly angry individuals. Rather, these results support the idea that people believe atheists are angry individuals, but they do not appear to be angrier than other individuals in reality.

MOST PEOPLE IN THE UNITED STATES BELIEVE IN GOD. A 2008 survey of 35,000 Americans found that approximately 95% of people believe in God (Pew Research Center, 2008). The percentage of people who espouse a belief in a God varies widely across countries (Zuckerman, 2007, 2009) and even though there are hundreds of millions of nonbelievers wordwide (Zuckerman, 2007; Newport, 2011), they represent a minority. The term "atheist" is generally used to describe individuals who, given the available evidence, conclude that there are no Gods or creators, and the term "agnostic" is used to describe people who are unsure, undecided, or apathetic about the existence or nonexistence of a God or a creator (Zuckerman, 2009). The focus in this article is on people's belief or disbelief in

God (e.g., believers, atheists, and agnostics) and their perceived and actual anger levels.

Atheists are a minority group in the United States. Typically, overt discrimination or unjustifiable negative behavior toward minorities is not explicitly tolerated in many societies (e.g., in regards to race or gender). However, discrimination against atheists appears to be somewhat acceptable. For example, atheists are distrusted (Gervais, Shariff, & Norenzayan, 2011) and considered to be lacking in morality (Zuckerman, 2009). More consequential, less than 50% of Americans state that they would vote for an atheist presidential candidate (Jones, 2007) and 48% of individuals in one sample said they would disapprove if their child chose to marry an atheist (Edgell, Gerteis, & Hartmann, 2006). Another study found that people would discriminate against atheists in important medical treatments (Furnham, Meader, & McClelland, 1998).

Discrimination can be rationalized on the basis of the supposed undesirable stereotypes or generalized beliefs about a given group of people. For example, the belief that obese people are lazy and lacking in personal responsibility may bolster the tendency to discriminate against them (Puhl & Heuer, 2010). Stereotypes can also lead to a type of self-fulfilling prophecy that has been labeled "stereotype threat" (Spencer, Steele, & Quinn, 1999). For example, the belief that women are worse at math compared to men can actually cause women to perform more poorly on math exams (Spencer et al.). Therefore, identifying and correcting inaccurate stereotypes could be a useful strategy in reducing the negative outcomes of stereotypes. In this article, we examine the prevalence and accuracy of an angry-atheist stereotype.

One potential stereotype about atheists is that they are particularly angry individuals. Countless media reports, internet postings, interviewers, and authors have used the angry-atheist label (e.g., Adams, 2011; Gellman, 2006; Lurie, 2010; Shaha, 2010). A self-proscribed atheist has even written a book that attempts to explain why atheists are so angry (Christina, 2012). A general theme in these anecdotal examples is that atheists are particularly angry people and that they challenge religion and believers in an angry and confrontational manner. Advocates of a "New Atheist" movement (e.g., atheist groups and well-known commentators like Richard Dawkins or Sam Harris) challenge religion and the existence of a creator in a passionate manner, and they do so in more public settings than the more underground conversations of atheists from the past. Such public discussions may contribute to the general perception that, overall, atheists are exceptionally angry individuals. On the basis of such confrontational case examples and media depictions, but also in part to justify discriminatory behavior, we hypothesized that atheists would be viewed as angrier than other individuals (which is a systematic focus of Studies 1–3 of our investigation).

Researchers have examined stereotypes about atheists (e.g., Ehrlich & Van Tubergen, 1971; Gervais et al., 2011) as well as relations between religiosity and mood (e.g., Diener, Tay, & Myers, 2011; Jonas & Fischer, 2006; Koenig

& Larson, 2001; Shreve-Neiger & Edelstein, 2004), but we are unaware of any work that has specifically examined stereotypes about anger and belief in God or the actual relationship between these variables. Some stereotypes have a basis in reality. Research shows some support for the "beauty is good" stereotype linking attractiveness to friendliness (Meier, Robinson, Carter, & Hinsz, 2010). We suspect that the angry-atheist stereotype, if it exists and is robust, is unlikely to be a stereotype of this type. Media portrayals of the angry atheist almost surely focus on confirmatory cases and ignore cases that disconfirm the stereotype. As such, these confirmatory cases are unlikely to characterize the behaviors of the average non-believer. One's doubt about the existence of God is likely motivated by other considerations rather than anger or hostility. Religion can be a touchy subject to both believers and non-believers, but touchiness in this context need not imply touchiness in others. For all of these reasons, we doubted whether atheists would be angrier than believers (a focus of Studies 4–7 of our investigation).

All told, then, we expected greater myth than reality to the angry-atheist stereotype. The value of this work is both scientific and potentially societal. Negative stereotypes fuel discriminatory behavior (Correll, Park, Judd, & Wittenbrink, 2002) and misperceptions of anger can engender hostile behaviors on the part of perceivers (Orobio de Castro, Veerman, Koops, Bosch, & Monshouwer, 2002), both of which are problematic outcomes. By both documenting and disconfirming the angry-atheist stereotype, then, it is possible that our findings could contribute to a more civil discourse between believers and nonbelievers who are informed of such findings.

Overview of Studies

Studies 1–3 focus on the question of whether people ascribe higher levels of anger to atheists than to believers or people in general. Studies 4–7 focus on the question of whether there is in fact a relationship between people's belief in God and their levels of trait and state anger. Both questions will be pursued in multiple ways with different types of designs for the sake of comprehensiveness.

Study 1

Study 1 sought to determine whether people perceive atheists to be angrier than theists (i.e., people who belief in a God). We asked people to rate the average level of anger of both atheists and theists. We hypothesized that people would rate atheists as angrier than theists.

Method
Participants

Participants were 93 individuals (58 females; age $M = 36.82$ years; $SD = 12.82$ years). The self-reported race breakdown of participants was as follows:

87.10% Caucasian, 4.30% African-American, 4.30% Asian or Pacific Islander, 2.20% Hispanic, 1.10% American Indian or Alaskan Native, and 1.10% mixed race.

Materials and Procedure

Participants were recruited from Amazon.com's Mechanical Turk, which has been shown to be a valid way to collect online data (Paolacci, Chandler, & Ipeirotis, 2010). The advantages of this recruitment procedure are diversity in age and geographical location. Participants were asked two straightforward questions that examined their explicit beliefs about the anger of atheists and theists. They were asked to rate the level of anger of the average atheist ("I think the average atheist—a person who does not believe in God—is") and believer ("I think the average theist or believer—a person who believes in God—is") using a 7-point scale (1 = not at all angry; 7 = very angry). In addition to the questions about atheists and believers, participants completed a number of questionnaires that were not relevant to the present study.

Results and Discussion

Participant gender did not interact or modify the findings in any of the studies so we do not discuss it. We used a paired-samples t-test to determine if the perceived level of anger differed for atheists and theists. Atheists were perceived to be angrier ($M = 3.48$; $SD = 1.49$) than theists ($M = 2.37$; $SD = 1.26$), $t(92) = 5.80$, $p < .001$, $d = 0.60$. Study 1 provided initial support for an angry-atheist stereotype in people's explicit beliefs.

Study 2

People are sometimes reluctant to explicitly (consciously and in self-reported terms) endorse negative beliefs about minority groups (Greenwald et al., 2002). For this reason, it is useful to assess stereotypes based on group membership using implicit (possibly unconscious, performance-based) measures as well (Greenwald et al., 2002). Implicit measures examine associations between concepts without directly or explicitly asking participants for such information with the goal of ascertaining an accurate picture of people's beliefs about sensitive subjects such as racial attitudes (Fazio & Olson, 2003). Following this literature, Study 2 sought to examine if, and the extent to which, the angry-atheist stereotype characterizes implicit associations in addition to self-reported beliefs (i.e., the results of Study 1). To examine this question, we used the implicit association test (IAT), which has been used in hundreds of studies and has displayed admirable levels of predictive validity (Greenwald, Poehlman, Uhlmann, & Banaji, 2009). We hypothesized that participants would display implicit associations consistent with the angry-atheist stereotype.

Method

Participants

Participants were 111 North Dakota State University undergraduates (52 females; age $M = 19.38$ years; $SD = 1.88$ years). The original sample included 115 participants, but 4 participants were dropped because of incomplete data or task errors. The self-reported race breakdown of participants was as follows: 73.00% Caucasian, 13.50% African-American, 8.10% Asian or Pacific Islander, 1.80% Hispanic, 1.80% American Indian or Alaskan Native, 0.90% Creole, and 0.90% nonreport.

Materials and Procedure

Participants completed an IAT and answered demographic questions in private rooms with computers. The IAT is used to examine associations among concepts in an indirect manner (Greenwald, McGhee, & Schwartz, 1998). Our version of the IAT required participants to categorize randomly presented words in terms of four categories: atheist, believer, angry, and calm. We used the word "atheist" for the atheist category and the word "believer" for the believer category as these words directly targeted the categories of interest and there are few synonyms. With respect to the angry versus calm distinction, five angry (angry, annoyed, bitter, hostile, and irritable) and five calm (calm, easygoing, peaceful, relaxed, and restful) words were presented in different trials. The latter comparison category was used because calmness is antithetical to anger (Berkowitz, 1993).

Across numerous trials, participants were asked to categorize a randomly presented word quickly and accurately one at a time. Category names appeared on the upper left and right of a screen. Individuals pressed the "q" key of the keyboard if the word belonged to the category (or categories) on the left and the "p" key of the keyboard if the word belonged to the category (or categories) on the right. Incorrect categorizations (e.g., categorizing the word "hostile" as a "calm" word instead of an "angry" word) were followed by the word INCORRECT in red font for 1,500 milli-seconds (ms) or 1.50 seconds. Correct categorizations were followed by a 150 ms blank screen until the next word appeared.

The IAT had five blocks; three of them were practice blocks. The critical comparison was between block 3, which included the combined compatible categories of "believer-calm" and "atheist-angry," and block 5, which included the combined incompatible categories of "believer-angry" and "atheist-calm". In these blocks, two categories were mapped onto one response button. For example, in block 3, participants pressed the "q" key if the word presented on any given trial was "believer" or had a calm meaning (e.g., peaceful), but they pressed the "p" key if the word presented on any given trial was "atheist" or had an angry meaning (e.g., annoyed). In block 5, participants pressed the "q" key if the word presented on any given trial was "atheist" or had a calm meaning, but they pressed the "p" key if the word presented on any given trial was "believer" or had an angry meaning. The purpose of these blocks was to determine if participants were faster when atheist-angry and believer-calm were paired (block 3) compared to when atheist-calm and believer-angry are paired (block 5). In the IAT, blocks with faster average categorizations times are a sign of associations that are formed in memory. Participants completed 60 trials in each of these blocks.

We administered the compatible block involving atheist-angry and believer-calm before the incompatible block involving atheist-calm and believer-angry. A meta-analysis has established that variations in the order of compatible and incompatible blocks minimally influence the size of implicit associations as determined by the IAT (Nosek, Greenwald, & Banaji, 2005).

Results and Discussion

Quantification procedures were consistent with the original IAT (Greenwald et al., 1998). We deleted inaccurate trials (7.2% of trials) and replaced trials faster than 300 ms or slower than 3,000 ms with these actual values. In other words, all trials slower than 300 ms were recoded to 300 ms and all trials faster than 3,000 ms were recoded to 3,000 ms. A log-transformation was then performed to reduce the positive skew inherent to reaction-time data. Analyses were performed on log-transformed values, but results are reported in terms of ms for ease of interpretation. We used a paired-samples t-test to examine categorization times by block type. Participants were much faster categorizing words in the atheist-angry/believer-calm block ($M = 742$ ms; $SD = 106$ ms) than in the atheist-calm/believer-angry block ($M = 984$ ms; $SD = 170$ ms), $t(110) = -19.61$, $p < .001$, $d = -1.86$. The effect size for this result was large suggesting that the angry-atheist stereotype appears robust in terms of implicit associations.

Studies 1 and 2 provide evidence for a stereotype in which atheists were viewed as angrier compared to believers. This conclusion would be bolstered if replicated with a different block order, but it is unlikely that a different result would have been found given prior results (Greenwald et al., 1998; Nosek et al. 2005). Nonetheless, the invariant block order chosen could be viewed as a limitation of Study 2 or at least an area for future investigation. All told, then, people appear to associate atheism with anger in terms of implicit associations.

Study 3

In Study 3, we sought to replicate and extend the results from Studies 1 and 2 in a number of ways. First, in order to ensure that the results from Studies 1 and 2 were reliable and generalizable, we collected data from a nationally representative sample of participants from the United States who were recruited by the survey company Qualtrics. Second, the comparison group for Studies 1 and 2 was believers or theists. Although the vast majority of Americans are in fact believers in God (Pew Research Center, 2008), it is possible that this label rendered anger judgments (or implicit associations involving anger) lower than they otherwise might be. Accordingly, the control target group for Study 3 was "people in general." We hypothesized that atheists would be rated as angrier than people in general, thus confirming a particular sort of link between perceptions of atheists and the emotion of anger.

Third, we wanted to establish that ascriptions of anger to atheists do not occur simply because of the minority status of this group. To make this point, Study 3 included another minority target group—gay and lesbian individuals—for comparison purposes. This comparison group is similar in size and familiarity to the atheist group and has been used effectively in previous stereotype research (e.g., Gervais et al., 2011). We hypothesized that participants would perceive atheists to be angrier than gay and lesbian individuals, which are results that would support the specificity of the angry-atheist stereotype. Study 3 also assessed participants' own beliefs in God as a potential moderating factor.

Method

Participants

Participants were 196 individuals (99 females; age $M = 45.09$ years; $SD = 16.28$ years). The self-reported race breakdown of participants was as follows: 73.50% Caucasian, 10.20% African-American, 9.20% Hispanic, 6.60% Asian or Pacific Islander, and 0.50% no answer. As an indicator of the national scope of the data collection effort, responses were obtained from participants in 40 different states.

Materials and Procedure

The participants completed a number of questionnaires, many of which were not relevant to the present study. The participants were asked three questions that examined their explicit beliefs about the anger of atheists, people in general, and gay and lesbian individuals (1 = not at all angry; 7 = extremely angry). They later also completed a single-item belief in God scale. They were asked to answer this question: I believe God exists (1 = strongly disagree; 5 = neither disagree nor agree; 9 = strongly agree). Single-item continuous belief in God measures like this one are frequently used in the religiosity literature to assess the extent to which people believe in God (Gervais & Norenzayan, 2012a; Inzlicht & Tullett, 2010; Shariff & Norenzayan, 2007).

Results and Discussion

The mean of the single-item belief in God measure was 7.32 ($SD = 2.35$). We examined anger perceptions by group (i.e., atheists, people in general, and gay and lesbian individuals) and belief in God (z-scored) using a General Linear Model analysis. The main effect of belief in God was not significant, $F(1, 194) = 3.10$, $p = .08$. Both the main effect of group, $F(2, 388) = 24.40$, $p < .001$, partial eta squared = .11, and the interaction between group and belief in God, $F(2, 388) = 11.96$, $p < .001$, partial eta squared = .06, were significant. We ran

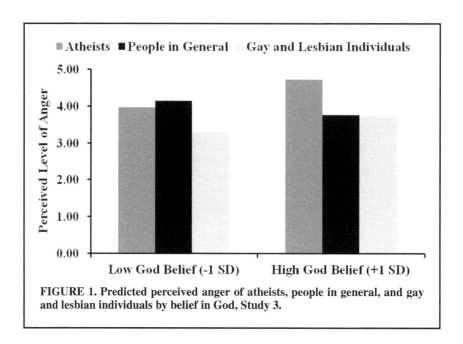

FIGURE 1. Predicted perceived anger of atheists, people in general, and gay and lesbian individuals by belief in God, Study 3.

multiple paired-samples t-tests in order to examine the target group main effect. Participants rated atheists as angrier ($M = 4.35$; $SD = 1.55$) than people in general ($M = 3.95$; $SD = 1.31$), $t(195) = 3.16$, $p = .002$, $d = 0.23$, and gay and lesbian individuals ($M = 3.51$; $SD = 1.55$), $t(195) = 7.10$, $p < .001$, $d = 0.51$. Gay and lesbian individuals were perceived to be less angry than people in general, $t(195) = -3.50$, $p = .001$, $d = -0.25$, which is interesting, but not particularly relevant to the predictions in the current study.

The procedures of Aiken and West (1991) were used to understand the significant interaction. As shown in Figure 1, participants scoring high (+1 SD) in belief in God rated atheists as angrier than people in general, $F(1, 194) = 33.59$, $p < .001$, partial eta squared $= .15$, and the gay and lesbian target group, $F(1, 194) = 36.14$, $p < .001$, partial eta squared $= .16$, with no difference between the latter two groups, $F < 1$. The pattern differed somewhat for those participants scoring low (−1 SD) in belief in God. At this low level of belief, estimated means did not differ for the atheist and people in general target groups, $F < 1.20$, though the gay and lesbian target group was perceived to be less angry than atheists, $F(1, 194) = 16.27$, $p < .001$, partial eta squared $= .08$, and people in general, $F(1, 194) = 23.32$, $p < .001$, partial eta squared $= .11$.

As might be expected, then, the tendency to perceive atheists as angrier than people in general was more pronounced at higher levels of belief in God. Irrespective of belief in God, though, atheists were perceived to be angrier than both people in general and a comparison minority group, thereby replicating and extending the results of Studies 1 and 2. The latter result is an important one in suggesting that there is some specificity to the angry-atheist stereotype, though other target group comparisons might be used in the future.

Study 4

Studies 1–3 establish the existence of an angry-atheist stereotype. In Studies 4–7, we examined whether this stereotype is accurate. Studies 4–7 could quite conceivably involve null effects. Although any particular null effect might be questioned, we took steps to ensure that appropriate conclusions could be drawn. Convergence across studies was emphasized, and beliefs in God and experiences of anger were assessed in multiple ways. In addition, the sample sizes (in Studies 4–6) were such that the statistical power was in the range of approximately .70 to .80, which is sufficient to detect a medium effect. Therefore, the power of these studies was adequate (Aron, Aron, & Coups, 2009; Cohen, 1992).

Study 4 offers perhaps the strongest test of the angry-atheist hypothesis because participants were asked to categorize their religious affiliation (i.e., one's self identification of being an atheist, Christian, etc.). Few individuals self-identify as atheists in a strict sense of the term (Pew Research Center, 2008). Accordingly, a large sample size was collected to identify such individuals. Participants completed a trait anger scale and categorized their religious affiliation. Three different results are possible: (1) atheists score higher in trait anger than believers, (2) atheists score lower in trait anger than believers, or (3) or atheists do not differ in trait anger compared to believers.

Method

Participants

Over several semesters from 2007 to 2012, we recruited 1,009 Gettysburg College undergraduates (612 females; age $M = 18.94$; $SD = 2.03$ years). The self-reported race breakdown of participants was as follows: 89.10% Caucasian, 3.80% African-American, 3.20% Asian or Pacific Islander, 2.20% Hispanic, .20% American Indian or Alaskan Native, and 1.60% other or a race that was not listed.

Materials and Procedure

Participants were asked to list their religious affiliation as a category (e.g., atheist, Christian, or Jewish). Participants also reported on their levels of anger in relation to the commonly used Buss-Perry Trait Anger Scale (Buss & Perry, 1992). This scale taps trait anger or the extent to which individuals become angry across situations and contexts; it measures anger in terms of a personality trait. The scale consists of seven items (e.g., "I have trouble controlling my temper") rated along a 5-point continuum (1 = strongly disagree; 5 = strongly agree). We averaged the items to form a measure of trait anger ($\alpha = .78$; $M = 2.20$; $SD =$

0.68). The participants completed other questionnaires and tasks not related to the current hypothesis.

Results and Discussion

Seventy participants classified themselves as atheists and 757 participants classified themselves as believers or theists (a Christian or Jewish faith). The remaining 182 participants categorized themselves as something other than an atheist or theist (e.g., a Hindu or they chose an other category). We used a one-way ANOVA to examine whether atheists had higher trait anger than theists. We did not find an effect of religious category, $F(1, 825) = 0.12$, $p = .73$; the trait anger means of the atheists ($M = 2.23$; $SD = 0.76$) and theists ($M = 2.20$; $SD = 0.68$) were similar. These results were nearly identical when we compared atheists to everyone else in the sample, $F(1, 1007) = 0.13$, $p = .72$; the trait anger means of the atheists ($M = 2.23$; $SD = 0.76$) and everyone else ($M = 2.20$; $SD = 0.68$) were similar.

We next examined the equivalency of the trait anger means between atheists and believers and atheists and everyone else using the equivalency between means testing procedures of Rogers, Howard, and Vessey (1993). We found that the differences between the atheist and believer groups and the atheist and everyone else groups were within 10% of the smaller mean (approximately .22) in each case, $ps < .05$. In other words, the means were equivalent. Both ANOVA and equivalency testing procedures revealed that, when defined in a strictly categorical sense, atheists do not appear to be angrier than other individuals.

Study 5

Study 4 revealed that atheists were not higher in trait anger than believers in God. Even though the study was adequately powered, additional data are warranted given that null relations were obtained. For power-related considerations, and because the results could be different, more continuous measures of belief in God were used in Studies 5–7. In Study 5, participants completed two measures of belief in God and two measures of trait anger. The results of Study 4 led us to believe that we would not find a significant relationship between belief in God and trait anger.

Method
Participants

Participants were 89 Gettysburg College undergraduates (49 females; age $M = 18.67$ years; $SD = 2.52$ years). The self-reported race breakdown of participants was as follows: 92.10% Caucasian, 2.20% African-American, 2.20% Asian or Pacific Islander, 1.10% Hispanic, and 2.20% other or a race that was not listed. We also collected a categorical measure of religiosity. The breakdown of participants' categorical religiosity was as follows: 66.30% Christian, 7.90% atheist, 6.70% agnostic, 5.60% Jewish, and 13.50% other or a category that was not listed.

Materials and Procedure

Participants completed tasks and questionnaires (many of which were not relevant to the present studies) on a computer. Participants completed four trait scales relevant to the present study. To assess belief in God, participants completed the Nearness to God Scale (Gorsuch & Smith, 1983), which has six items rated on a 4-point continuum (1 = strong disagreement; 4 = strong agreement). The items were averaged to form a belief in God score ($\alpha = .93$; $M = 2.62$; $SD = 0.90$). Although the scale is labeled Nearness to God, the items tap belief in God ("God is very real to me", "Because of his presence, we can know that God exists"). Indeed, Toburen and Meier (2010) found that self-identified theists scored much higher on this scale than self-identified atheists ($d = 1.30$). Nonetheless, we also used the face-valid and more direct belief in God measure from Study 3: "I believe God exists" (1 = strongly disagree; 9 = strongly agree; $M = 5.94$; $SD = 2.77$).

To measure anger, participants completed the Buss-Perry Trait Anger Scale (Buss & Perry, 1992) used in Study 4 as well as the commonly used Spielberger Trait Anger scale (Spielberger, 1988), which consists of 10 items (e.g., "I have a fiery temper") rated along a 4-point continuum (1 = almost never; 4 = almost always). The items were averaged to form two scores, Buss-Perry scale ($\alpha = .79$; $M = 2.11$; $SD = 0.62$); Spielberger scale ($\alpha = .82$; $M = 1.88$; $SD = 0.47$).

Results and Discussion

We computed Pearson correlations to determine the direction and strength of relations between belief in God and trait anger. As shown in Table 1, neither

---

TABLE 1. Correlations among Variables, Study 5 (Above the Diagonal) and Study 6 (Below the Diagonal)

	Nearness to God	Direct God Belief	Buss-Perry Trait Anger	Spielberger Trait Anger
Nearness to God	–	.62*	.06	.13
Direct God Belief	.93*	–	.01	−.01
Buss-Perry Trait Anger	−.04	−.05	–	.71*
Spielberger Trait Anger	−.07	−.08	.77*	–

* $= p < .01$.

---

belief in God measure was significantly related to either trait anger measure. Not only were these correlations nonsignificant, but they tended to be in the opposite direction of the angry-atheist stereotype. Study 5 provides converging validity for the idea that the angry-atheist stereotype does not appear to be accurate.

Study 6

We wanted to substantiate the findings of Study 5 using a more generalizable sample of individuals in the United States. Study 5 consisted of college undergraduates. Such individuals, typically away from their parents for the first time, are likely to question prior religious beliefs (Brown & Lowe, 1951). Accordingly, it was deemed important to examine relations between belief in God and trait anger among an older group of individuals. Participants from Amazon.com's Mechanical Turk completed the same questionnaires from Study 5. We did not expect to find significant relationships between belief in God and anger.

Method
Participants

Participants were 108 individuals (73 females; age $M = 34.37$ years; $SD = 13.03$ years) who lived in 28 different U.S. states. The self-reported race breakdown of participants was as follows: 79.60% Caucasian, 13.90% Asian or Pacific Islander, 4.60% Hispanic, and 1.90% African-American. We also collected a categorical measure of religiosity. The breakdown of participants' categorical religiosity was as follows: 63.00% Christian, 16.70% agnostic, 8.30% atheist, 1.90% Jewish, 1.90% Buddhist, 0.90% Hindu, and 7.40% other or a category that was not listed.

Materials and Procedure

The participants completed the same scales administered in Study 5 as well as other questionnaires not relevant to this study. They completed the Nearness to God ($\alpha = .97$; $M = 2.71$; $SD = 1.12$), direct belief in God ($M = 6.27$; $SD = 3.05$), Spielberger ($\alpha = .87$; $M = 1.77$; $SD = 0.53$), and Buss-Perry ($\alpha = .88$; $M = 2.42$; $SD = 0.82$) scales.

Results and Discussion

In this more diverse sample in terms of age and location, the results were similar to Study 5. As shown in Table 1, neither belief in God measure significantly correlated with either measure of trait anger. However, the two belief in God measures were strongly correlated as were the two trait anger measures, which coincides with the results of Study 5. Accordingly, variations in belief in God appear nonpredictive of trait anger among an older sample.

Study 7

Studies 4–6 examined belief in God and trait anger. People higher in trait anger have more experiences of state or momentary anger as well (Deffenbacher, 1992). State anger, though, is particularly apparent in aversive or provoking contexts (Berkowitz & Harmon-Jones, 2004). In order to provide additional converging validity to Studies 4–6, we assessed belief in God and state anger following an anger induction in Study 7. We hypothesized that state anger would be higher following an anger-induction manipulation, but we did not expect belief in God to have an influence on this effect.

Method
Participants

Participants were 71 Gettysburg College undergraduates (43 females; age $M = 18.72$ years; $SD = 1.09$ years). The original sample included 76 participants, but 5 participants were dropped because of incomplete data or because they did not complete the task properly. The self-reported race breakdown of participants was as follows: 94.40% Caucasian, 4.20% African-American, and 1.40% American Indian or Alaskan Native. We also collected a categorical measure of religiosity. The breakdown of participants' categorical religiosity was as follows: 66.20% Christian, 9.90% atheist, 8.50% agnostic, 7.00% Jewish, and 8.50% other or a category that was not listed.

Materials and Procedure

Belief in God was assessed in terms of the Nearness to God Scale ($\alpha = .94$; $M = 2.74$; $SD = 0.95$), which correlated strongly with the direct belief in God measure in Studies 5 and 6. Participants also completed a state anger scale after the manipulation. They rated their current feelings across six items (e.g., angry, hostile) of the PANAS-X State Anger Scale (Watson & Clark, 1994) using an 11-point response scale (0 = not at all; 10 = extremely). We averaged across these markers to quantify state anger ($\alpha = .81$; $M = 1.57$; $SD = 1.54$).

The emotion induction literature has shown that autobiographical writing manipulations are effective in targeting an emotional state of interest (Lerner & Keltner, 2001; Moons & Mackie, 2007) and we, therefore, used such a manipulation. By random assignment, individuals were asked to spend 6 minutes writing about a previous event that had made them extremely angry (the anger induction condition) or about their activities during the previous day (the control condition). Subsequently, individuals reported on their momentary anger using the PANAS-X scales. They also completed the Nearness to God scale.

Results and Discussion

A General Linear Model analysis was conducted with state anger as the dependent variable and the anger induction and z-scored belief in God as the

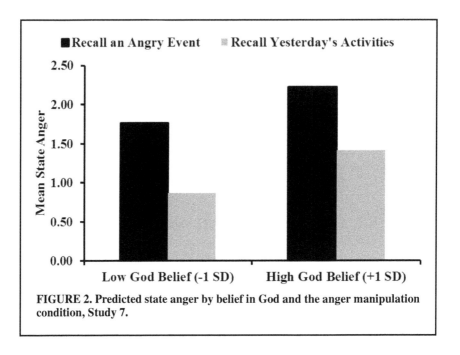

FIGURE 2. Predicted state anger by belief in God and the anger manipulation condition, Study 7.

independent variables. As expected, participants in the anger condition reported more state anger ($M = 1.99$; $SD = 1.79$) than participants in the control condition ($M = 1.14$; $SD = 1.09$), $F(1, 67) = 5.81$, $p = .019$, partial eta squared $= .08$. This effect reveals that the anger manipulation was effective. The main effect for belief in God was not significant, $F(1, 67) = 1.95$, $p = .17$ (the predicted means were in the opposite direction of the angry-atheist stereotype). Importantly, belief in God did not moderate or buffer the impact of the anger manipulation, $F < 1$. For the sake of complete reporting, Figure 2 displays estimated means (Aiken & West, 1991) as a function of condition and low (-1 SD) versus high ($+1$ SD) levels of beliefs in God. Accordingly, it appears equally easy to induce anger among individuals low versus high in belief in God.

General Discussion

Our studies revealed that people believe that atheists are angrier than believers, people in general, and another minority group of comparable size. Yet, we did not find any evidence to suggest that atheists—or those people believing in God to a lesser extent—are particularly angry individuals. In the following sections, we discuss implications, outline some future directions of research, and address potential limitations.

Implications and Future Considerations

First and foremost, our results suggest that the idea of the angry-atheist is a myth. Although people espouse the view that atheists are angry, and although such associations are embedded at an implicit level of cognition, the idea simply does not appear to be true. For this reason, we would encourage people to challenge this idea when expressed by communication partners or when encountered in popular media sources. It is a misperception that should be corrected rather than endorsed.

Indeed, it is important to correct negative stereotypes that are not true because they can have unfortunate consequences. For example, research has shown that perceiving other people as angry can make us hostile and set the stage for conflicts that need not happen (Berkowitz, 2012; Orobio de Castro et al., 2002). Such conflicts may be especially likely with atheists because this group appears to be stigmatized in some unique ways (Gervais et al., 2011; Gervais & Norenzayan, 2012b) and because society does not seem to censure the disparagement of atheists in the same way that it might censure the disparagement of other minorities. Stereotypes are detrimental to stigmatized groups because they create expectations about how people should treat out-group individuals (Bahns & Branscombe, 2010). Future research should focus on whether the angry-atheist stereotype actually drives discriminatory behavior. For example, does an angry-atheist perception correlate with a tendency to withhold rights from atheists? Or, perhaps, does an angry-atheist perception lead others to start arguments with atheists leading to an induced confirmation of the stereotype? In sum, the angry-atheist perception might partially drive discriminatory behavior against atheists. Studies that assess both variables will be useful in examining this idea.

Our studies were not designed to identify the factors that drive an angry-atheist stereotype. Indeed, our research question was purposely simple: does the angry-atheist stereotype exist and to what extent is it accurate? However, we can speculate on some potential causes. One potential cause relates to passionate atheists who discuss religion in public settings. These individuals are typically open, forceful, and fervent about their beliefs. Such discussions about religion and God go against what most Americans believe. These portrayals could drive people's beliefs that atheists are angry. Furthermore, media brings to mind this stereotype when they use the term "angry atheist" to describe this passionate communication style.

Another potential cause relates to perceivers potentially projecting their own anger onto atheists. Religion is a major source of meaning and comfort to a large number of Americans (Pew Research Center, 2008). Atheists may be perceived to threaten this source of meaning, thereby triggering anger and the defensive sorts of processes identified by existential psychologists (e.g., Solomon, Greenberg, & Pyszczynski, 2000). Research has indeed shown that people can project anger onto other individuals. For example, Schimel, Greenberg, and Martens (2003) found that participants who were told that they scored high versus low on a measure of anger subsequently rated a hypothetical person as higher in anger. Other work has shown that participants who underwent an angry versus a sad or neutral mood induction were more likely to use stereotypes when making judgments about a hypothetical individual (Bodenhausen, Sheppard, & Kramer, 1994). Furthermore, prominent models of aggression suggest that experiencing provocation and anger can bias people into perceiving subsequent events in a hostile manner (Berkowitz, 2012; Meier & Wilkowski, 2013). Future work should examine if anger in perceivers is related to the tendency to engage in the angry-atheist stereotype. For example, researchers could examine the extent to which state or trait anger predicts the tendency to use the angry-atheist stereotype.

It is also possible that there is a type of "focalism" to the angry-atheist stereo-type and to why it is not correct. Atheists are a small minority and many people may have few interactions with them (Zuckerman, 2007). Research suggests that it is precisely under such conditions that stereotypes can thrive even if incorrect (Dovidio, Gaertner, & Kawakami, 2003). That is, they thrive when people have preconceived ideas about a group of people that are not updated in the context of "individuating" information concerning particular people from that group. The same principles can explain why negative stereotypes could persist even *with* rela-tively friendly encounters because we are often unaware of the religious beliefs of the people with whom we interact. Such a tendency can be magnified considering that people tend to seek information that confirms rather than disconfirms their initial beliefs (Nickerson, 1998).

We assessed trait anger because trait anger encompasses the most general anger-related tendencies of individuals (Wilkowski & Robinson, 2010). We also assessed state anger in relation to prototypical elicitors of it (Lerner & Keltner, 2001). However, we cannot conclude that there will never be differences in anger between believers and nonbelievers. Indeed, it would be interesting to examine anger in the context of religious settings or disagreements. On the one hand, one might predict that, in these contexts at least, atheists might experience anger more intensely in reaction to what they perceive to be an erroneous belief system. On the other hand, though, there are reasons for thinking that belief in God can serve a defensive function and that, for this reason, believers might become more angry if they think that their beliefs are being challenged (Solomon et al., 2000). Creative research designs would be needed to examine this more specific research question, though the results would have value in extending the present analysis in a more nuanced fashion.

Limitations

Our studies included some limitations that are worth discussing. First, larger sample sizes can be advocated for some purposes at least. In more particular terms, the statistical power in Study 7 was lower than the other studies and would benefit from a larger sample size (though note that the direction of the believer/non-believer difference was counter to the angry-atheist stereotype). Second, some of the dependent measures involved one item. Although single-item measures of religious orientation are often used, they may not be the most reliable ones.

Third, with the exception of Study 2, all of our dependent measures were self-reported in nature. We do regard this reliance on self-report as a limitation and would use behavioral paradigms, observer reports, or peer reports in extensions of the present work. Fourth, we briefly remind the reader that block order was not counterbalanced in Study 2. Doing so could be useful in supporting the results of Study 2 (though see Nosek et al., 2003). In the context of these limitations, we emphasize the convergence of the conclusions across multiple studies using multiple methods and sample types.

Summary and Conclusions

We examined the prevalence and accuracy of an angry-atheist stereotype in seven studies. We found that people believe atheists are angrier than believers, people in general, and another minority group, both explicitly and implicitly. However, none of our studies supported the idea that atheists are angrier than other individuals. Our work, in sum, suggests that the angry-atheist stereotype exists, but that it does not match reality. Dissemination of the present results may be useful in correcting misperceptions while averting potential unwarranted and harmful consequences.

REFERENCES

Adams, G. (2011, December 11). Santa Monica's angry atheists declare a real war on Christmas. *The Independent*. Retrieved from http://www.independent.co.uk/news/world/americas/santa-monicas-angry-atheists-declare-a-real-war-on-christmas-6276970.html

Aiken, L. S., & West, S. G. (1991). *Multiple regression: Testing and interpreting interactions*. Newbury Park, CA: Sage Publications.

Aron, A., Aron, E. N., & Coups, E. J. (2009). *Statistics for psychology (5th Edition)*. Upper Saddle River, NJ: Prentice Hall.

Bahns, A. J., & Branscombe, N. R. (2010). Effects of legitimizing discrimination against homosexuals on gay bashing. *European Journal of Social Psychology*, *41*, 388–396. doi: 10.1002/ejsp.784

Berkowitz, L. (1993). *Aggression: Its causes, consequences, and control*. New York, NY: McGraw Hill.

Berkowitz, L. (2012). A different view of anger: The cognitive-neoassociation conception of the relation of anger to aggression. *Aggressive Behavior*, *38*, 322–333. doi: 10.1002/ab.21432

Berkowitz, L., & Harmon-Jones, E. (2004). Toward an understanding of the determinants of anger. *Emotion*, *4*, 107–130. doi: 10.1037/1528-3542.4.2.107

Bodenhausen, G. V., Sheppard, L. A., & Kramer, G. P. (1994). Negative affect and social judgment: The differential impact of anger and sadness. *European Journal of Social Psychology*, *24*, 45–62. doi: 10.1002/ejsp.2420240104

Brown, D. G., & Lowe, W. L. (1951). Religious beliefs and personality characteristics of college students. *Journal of Social Psychology*, *33*, 103–129. doi: 10.1080/00224545.1951.9921803

Buss, A. H., & Perry, M. (1992). The aggression questionnaire. *Journal of Personality and Social Psychology*, *63*, 452–459. doi: 10.1037/0022-3514.63.3.452

Christina, G. (2012). *Why are you atheists so angry? 99 things that piss off the Godless*. San Francisco, CA: Dirty Heathen Publishing.

Cohen, J. (1992). A power primer. *Psychological Bulletin*, *112*, 155–159. doi: 10.1037/0033-2909.112.1.155

Correll, J., Park, B., Judd, C. M., & Wittenbrink, B. (2002). The police officer's dilemma: Using ethnicity to disambiguate potentially threatening individuals. *Journal of Personality and Social Psychology*, *83*, 1314–1329. doi: 10.1037/0022-3514.83.6.1314

Deffenbacher, J. L. (1992). Trait anger: Theory, findings, and implications. In C. D. Spielberger & J. N. Butcher (Eds.), *Advances in personality assessment*, Vol. 9. (pp. 177–201). Hillsdale, NJ: Erlbaum.

Diener, E., Tay, L., & Myers, D. G. (2011). The religion paradox: If religion makes people happy, why are so many dropping out? *Journal of Personality and Social Psychology*, *101*, 1278–1290. doi: 10.1037/a0024402

Dovidio, J. F., Gaertner, S. L., & Kawakami, K. (2003). Intergroup contact: The past, present, and the future. *Group Processes and Intergroup Relations*, *6*, 5–21. doi: 10.1177/1368430203006001009

Edgell, P., Gerteis, J., & Hartmann, D. (2006). Atheists as "other": Moral boundaries and cultural membership in American society. *American Sociological Review*, *71*, 211–234. doi: 10.1177/000312240607100203

Ehrlich, H. J., & Van Tubergen, G. N. (1971). Exploring the structure and salience of stereotypes. *Journal of Social Psychology*, *83*, 113–127. doi: 10.1080/00224545.1971.9919979

Fazio, R. H., & Olson, M. A. (2003). Implicit measures in social cognition research: Their meaning and use. *Annual Review of Psychology*, *54*, 297–327. doi: 10.1146/annurev.psych.54.101601.145225

Furnham, A., Meader, N., & McClelland, A. (1998). Factors affecting nonmedical participants' allocation of scarce medical resources. *Journal of Social Behavior and Personality*, *12*, 735–736.

Gellman, M. (2006, April 25). Rabbi Gellman tries to understand angry Atheists. *Newsweek*. Retrieved from http://www.newsweek.com/2006/04/25/trying-to-understand-angry-atheists.html

Gervais, W. M., & Norenzayan, A. (2012a). Like a camera in the sky? Thinking about God increases public self-awareness and socially desirable responding. *Journal of Experimental Social Psychology*, *48*, 298–302. doi: 10.1016/j.jesp.2011.09.006

Gervais, W. M., & Norenzayan, A. (2012b). Reminders of secular authority reduce believers' distrust of atheists. *Psychological Science, 23*, 483–491. doi: 10.1177/0956797611429711

Gervais, W. M., Shariff, A. F., & Norenzayan, A. (2011). Do you believe in atheists? Distrust is central to anti-atheist prejudice. *Journal of Personality and Social Psychology, 101*, 1189–1206. doi: 10.1037/a0025882

Gorsuch, R. L., & Smith, C. S. (1983). Attributions of responsibility to God: An interaction of religious beliefs and outcomes. *Journal for the Scientific Study of Religion, 22*, 340–352.

Greenwald, A. G., Banaji, M. R., Rudman, L. A., Farnham, S. D., Nosek, B. A., & Mellott, D. S. (2002). A unified theory of implicit attitudes, stereotypes, self-esteem, and self-concept. *Psychological Review, 109*, 3–25. doi: 10.1037//0033-295X.109.1.3

Greenwald, A. G., McGhee, D. D., & Schwartz, J. L. K. (1998). Measuring individual differences in implicit cognition: The implicit association test. *Journal of Personality and Social Psychology, 74*, 1464–1480. doi: 10.1037/0022-3514.74.6.1464

Greenwald, A. G., Poehlman, T. A., Uhlmann, E., & Banaji, M. R. (2009). Understanding and using the Implicit Association Test: III. Meta-analysis of predictive validity. *Journal of Personality and Social Psychology, 97*, 17–41. doi: 10.1037/a0015575

Inzlicht, M., & Tullett, A. M. (2010). Reflecting on God: Religious primes can reduce neurophysiological response to errors. *Psychological Science, 21*, 1184–1190. doi: 10.1177/0956797610375451

Jonas, E., & Fischer, P. (2006). Terror management and religion: Evidence that intrinsic religiousness mitigates worldview defense following mortality salience. *Journal of Personality and Social Psychology, 91*, 553–567. doi: 10.1037/0022-3514.91.3.553

Jones, J. (2007, February 20). Some Americans reluctant to vote for Mormon, 72-year-old presidential candidates. *Gallup News Service.* Retrieved from http://www.gallup.com/poll/26611/some-americans-reluctant-vote-mormon-72yearold-presidential-candidates.aspx

Koenig, H. G., & Larson, D. B. (2001). Religion and mental health: evidence for an association. *International Review of Psychiatry, 13*, 67–78. doi: 10.1080/09540260124661

Lerner, J. S., & Keltner, D. (2001). Fear, anger, and risk. *Journal of Personality and Social Psychology, 81*, 146–159. doi. 10.1037//O022-3514.81.1.146

Lurie, A. (2010, August 3). Anatomy of an angry atheist. *The Huffington Post.* Retrieved from http://www.huffingtonpost.com/alan-lurie/anatomy-of-an-angry-athei_b_668720.html

Meier, B. P., Robinson, M. D., Carter, M. S., & Hinsz, V. B. (2010). Are sociable people more beautiful? A zero-acquaintance analysis of agreeableness, extraversion, and attractiveness. *Journal of Research in Personality, 44*, 293–296. doi: org/10.1016/j.jrp.2010.02.002

Meier, B. P., & Wilkowski, B. M. (2013). Reducing the tendency to aggress: Insights from social and personality psychology. *Social and Personality Psychology Compass, 7*, 343–354. doi: 10.1111/spc3.12029

Moons, W. G., & Mackie, D. M. (2007). Thinking straight while seeing red: The influence of anger on information processing. *Personality and Social Psychology Bulletin, 33*, 706–720. doi: 10.1177/0146167206298566

Newport, F. (2011, June 3). More than 9 in 10 Americans continue to believe in God. *Gallup News Service.* Retrieved from http://www.gallup.com/poll/147887/americans-continue-believe-god.aspx

Nickerson, R. S. (1998). Confirmation bias: A ubiquitous phenomenon in many guises. *Review of General Psychology, 2*, 175–220. doi: 10.1037/1089-2680.2.2.175

Nosek, B. A., Greenwald, A. G., & Banaji, M. R. (2005). Understanding and using the implicit association test: II. Method variables and construct validity. *Personality and Social Psychology Bulletin, 31*, 166–180. doi: 10.1177/0146167204271418

Orobio de Castro, B., Veerman, J. W., Koops, W., Bosch, J. D., & Monshouwer, H. J. (2002). Hostile attribution of intent and aggressive behavior: A meta-analysis. *Child Development, 73*, 916–934. doi: 10.1111/1467-8624.00447

Paolacci, G., Chandler, J., & Ipeirotis, P. G. (2010). Running experiments on Amazon Mechanical Turk. *Judgment and Decision Making, 5*, 411–419.

Pew Research Center. (2008). *U.S. religion landscape survey. Religious affiliation: Diverse and dynamic. February 2008.* Washington, DC: Pew Research Center.

Puhl, R. M., & Heuer, C. A. (2010). Obesity stigma: Important considerations for public health. *American Journal of Public Health, 100*, 1019–1028. doi: 10.2105/AJPH.2009. 159491

Rogers, J. L., Howard, K. I., & Vessey, J. T. (1993). Using significance tests to evaluate equivalence between two experimental groups. *Psychological Bulletin, 113*, 553–565. doi: 10.1037/0033-2909.113.3.553

Schimel, J., Greenberg, J., & Martens, A. (2003). Evidence that projection of a feared trait can serve a defensive function. *Personality and Social Psychology Bulletin, 29*, 969–979. doi: 10.1177/0146167203252969

Shaha, A. (2010, September 10). Thank god (and Richard Dawkins) I'm no longer an 'angry atheist.' *The Guardian.* Retrieved from http://www.guardian.co.uk/science/blog/ 2010/sep/09/god-richard-dawkins-angry-atheist

Shariff, A. F., & Norenzayan, A. (2007). God is watching you: Priming God concepts increases prosocial behavior in an anonymous economic game. *Psychological Science, 18*, 803–809. doi: 10.1111/j.1467-9280.2007.01983.x

Shreve-Neiger, A. K., & Edelstein, B. A. (2004). Religion and anxiety: A critical review of the literature. *Clinical Psychology Review, 24*, 379–397.

Solomon, S., Greenberg, J., & Pyszczynski, T. (2000). Pride and prejudice: Fear of death and social behavior. *Current Directions in Psychological Science, 9*, 200–204. doi: 10.1111/1467-8721.00094

Spencer, S. J., Steele, C. M., & Quinn, D. M. (1999). Stereotype threat and women's math performance. *Journal of Experimental Social Psychology, 35*, 4–28. doi: org/10.1006/jesp.1998.1373

Spielberger, C. D. (1988). *Manual for the state-trait anger expression inventory.* Odessa, FL: PAR.

Toburen, T., & Meier, B. R. (2010). Priming God-related concepts increases anxiety and task persistence. *Journal of Social and Clinical Psychology, 29*, 127–143. doi: 10.1521/jscp.2010.29.2.127

Watson, D., & Clark, L. A. (1994). *The PANAS-X: Manual for the positive and negative affect schedule-Expanded Form.* Iowa City, IA: University of Iowa.

Wilkowski, B. M., & Robinson, M. D. (2010). The anatomy of anger: An integrative cognitive model of trait anger and reactive aggression. *Journal of Personality, 78*, 9–38. doi: 10.1111/j.1467-6494.2009.00607.x

Zuckerman, P. (2007). Atheism: Contemporary numbers and patterns. In M. Martin (Ed.), *The Cambridge companion to atheism* (pp. 47–66). Cambridge, England: Cambridge University Press.

Zuckerman, P. (2009). Atheism, secularity, and well-being: How the findings of social science counter negative stereotypes and assumptions. *Sociology Compass, 3–6*, 949–971. doi: 10.1111/j.1751-9020.2009.00247.x

Assessment of Anger Terms in Hebrew:
A Gender Comparison

ORLY SARID

ABSTRACT. Appraisal of anger terms is based on past experience recollections, social norms, and gender roles. The objectives of this study were to find combinations of emotional components presented by a new composite variable that will exhibit differences between genders and differentiate between anger terms in Hebrew. The sample was comprised of forty students, Hebrew native speakers who participated in a web based study. Participants were asked to rate eight anger terms in Hebrew on a number of features that comprised five emotional components: subjective feelings states body reactions, expressions, action tendencies, and cognitive evaluations. A two-factor between-subjects multivariate analysis of variance (MANOVA) was conducted. A simplified multivariate composite, defined as subjective experience minus regulation, explained 10% of the gender difference. Another simplified composite, which combines the additive effect of the subjective experience and the actions that accompany this emotional state, explained 14% of difference between the anger terms. The findings are discussed with respect to appraisal theory and social constructivist conceptualization.

THIS ARTICLE FOCUSES ON THE RATINGS given by young Israeli women and men to a number of features in the meaning of eight anger terms in Hebrew *ko'es*/angry, *me'utzban*/annoyed, *metuskal*/frustrated, *merugaz*/irritated, *zo'em*/furious, *marir*/bitter, *mitraem*/resentful, and *nakmani*/revengeful. The features belong to several emotional components reported, in psychology, as central in the experience of emotion: subjective feelings states (also referred to as subjective experience), body reactions, expressions (facial, gestural), action tendencies, and cognitive evaluations.

Appraisal component theory emphasizes the process through which emotions contribute to the formation of distinct attitudes and behavioral responses. Within this process, the individual detects and assesses the environment by attaching sig-nificance, valence, and intensity to an emotional experience (Moors, Ellsworth, Scherer, & Frijda, 2013; Parrot, 2004). Appraisal process represents a continu-ous evaluation of an emotional experience including appraisal of changes in the quality and intensity of physiological responses, expressions, action tendencies, and subjective feelings. All of which, facilitates differentiation between emotional experiences (Clore & Ortony, 2000; Frijda, 2009; Scherer, 2001) and elucidates response patterning specific to a certain emotion.

One of the limitations of appraisal componential theory is its inability to determine a sequential process of the components that comprise an emotional experience. Scherer (2005), for example, views emotions as a collection of com-ponents being processed in parallel. Each component can be activated by separate external conditions or aspects. Within a certain context interactions of component –context are appraised by the individual (Aue, Flykt, & Scherer, 2007; Grandjean & Scherer, 2008; Moors et al., 2013).

Anger is categorized by several researchers as a basic (Ekman, 1999; Ortony & Turner, 1990) universal emotion (Hupka, Lenton, & Hutchison, 1999) elicited when an individual identifies actions as unjust and conflicting with conventional norms. Yet, other researchers would argue that to a large extent anger's response patterning such as physiological reaction, expression and actions, accepted in one's culture, is "socially constructed," and its manifestation is unique to that culture (Johnson-Laird & Oatley, 2000). Furthermore, cultural researchers claim that even in the presence of certain universal physiological reactions, the response patterning of anger depends on social norms, cultural meaning, and practices (Barrett, 2006; Crump, Logan, & McIlroy, 2007; Kelan, 2008; Russell, 2003). According to this perspective, an anger experience can be appraised through a combination of several components within a certain cultural or social context. A major strength of componential conceptualization is its ability to compare emotional patterning between social and cultural context and to better understand how values and norms, specific to one's culture, might be differently reflected in the individual response patterning in another culture.

Hofstede (1997) suggested several dimensions to characterize and compare between cultures, among them: individualism vs. collectivism, masculinity versus femininity, and degrees of power distance between members of a certain culture. Within individualistic cultures, people are expected to look solely after one's self or immediate family, whereas collectivistic values imply that people are integrated from birth into cohesive groups that protect them in exchange for loyalty. Masculinity and femininity refer to gender roles, whereas traditional assignment to masculine roles of aggressiveness and competition compared to feminine roles concerned with children, caring for people and tenderness, are preserved (Marcus & Gould, 2000).

When researchers looked at the aforementioned cultural aspects and exam-ined emotional components that construct an emotional experience, they noticed that across cultures certain emotions have a distinct response patterning (Ellsworth & Scherer, 2003; Frijda, 2009; Roseman & Smith, 2001; Scherer, 2001). A culture that emphasizes masculine orientation encourages a traditional female role. Within this culture, it is expected to find gender differences in beliefs and behaviors pertaining to an emotion such as anger. However, with respect to an anger response, findings from previous studies, across different social and cultural contexts, yielded mixed results and were dependent on the specific emotional component that was comparatively analyzed. Within the component of subjective feelings, which is considered in psychological literature to consist of valence (feeling good–bad), arousal (feeling aroused–relaxed), and potency (feeling strong–weak) (Fontaine, Scherer, Roesch, & Ellsworth, 2007), men and women did not report any substantial differences (Barrett, Robin, Pietromonaco, & Eyssell, 1998; Grossman & Wood, 1993). Findings from a comparative study, conducted among university students from 37 different countries, showed that women and men reported similar anger intensity toward other people within individualistic societies, such as the United States and Canada (Archer, 2004; Fischer, Rodriguez-Mosquera, van Vianen, & Manstead, 2004; Fischer & Manstead, 2008).

Unlike the component of subjective feeling of anger which is fairly stable across genders and cultures, the reaction to anger is an active process influenced by the beliefs, values, and social environment pertaining to one's culture. Reaction tendencies are considered in the literature as more variable because they involve culturally accepted ways of responses to correct the perceived offense (Roseman & Smith, 2001; Russell, 2003; Scherer, Schorr, & Johnstone, 2001). Actions can be confrontational (Berkowitz, 1993; Mackie, Devos, & Smith, 2000), aggressive (Averill, 1982; Halperin, Russell, Dweck, & Gross, 2011), or non-aggressive, such as avoiding contact with the provoker or leaving the scene (Campbell & Muncer, 2008; Timmers, Fischer, & Manstead, 1998). Previous findings have shown that actions of anger depend on the gender, social status, and control within a certain culture (Mauro, Sato, & Tucker, 1992; Parrot, 2004; Van Kleef, 2009). The implication is that cultural beliefs and values seem to influence the way women and men express and act on emotional experience of anger, and cultural norms permit a somewhat different set of emotional responses to men and women. In individualistic cultures, emotions are perceived as important personal experiences, and acts of anger are considered appropriate when they clarify self-assertion and protect the individuals' rights, as long as they are expressed in suitable social manner (Eid & Diener, 2001). Safdar et al. (2009) claims that several individualistic cultures even set rules that support an outward expression of anger as a way to emphasize the strength of the emotion. Exaggerated expressions of anger are reinforced in the U.S. individualistic culture as a way to communicate individuality. The expression of anger is less acceptable in collectivistic cultures where social manners favor harmony within relationships and respect for authority (Koopmann-Holm & Matsumoto, 2011; Safdar et al., 2009).

Within a masculine society aimed at competition and power, men seem to reinforce an overt expression of anger, whereas a low status female role seems to discourage an overt expression of anger among women (Brody & Hall, 2008; Fischer et al., 2004; Rivers, Brackett, Katulak, & Salovey, 2007). However, in individualistic-masculine cultures where women have higher status and power positions, their open expression of anger is more tolerated (Alonso-Arbiol et al., 2011).

The ways anger expressions are regulated, after the anger eliciting incident, also differ among genders across social and cultural contexts (Brody & Hall, 2008). For example, findings from a study conducted in Great Britain among undergraduate students showed that women compared to men reported they tend to divert the expression of aggressive behavior and exert stronger control on their outward behavior (Campbell & Muncer, 2008).

In sum, while subjective experience of anger is a rather stable and similar reaction for both genders, expressions, action tendencies and regulation of anger are seem to be dependent and affected by cultural norms.

One of the means to convey cultural beliefs and ideology is through the use of language and lexical terms (Armon-Jones, 1986; Mesquita, 2003). Thus, appraisal of emotion terms that belong to the same construct (e.g., "anger" across the same emotional components) will enable the identification of specific components that the individual uses to describe the physiological responses and expressive behaviors that each term evokes. Furthermore, it will show if a similar response patterning exists in appraisals of anger terms as in anger experiences. In the scientific literature, this issue has not been thoroughly explored (Glenberg, Jaworski, Rischal, & Levin, 2007; Niedenthal, 2007; Cox & Harrison, 2008; Scherer, 2001, 2005), and, to the best of our knowledge, it is the first time a comparative analysis has been conducted between anger terms in Hebrew among young Israeli men and women.

Cultural Background

The Israeli culture embraces western individualism while also emphasizing masculine norms of behavior (Shulman, Blatt, & Walsh, 2006; Levin 2011). The Israeli Jewish society was shaped by the Kibbutz' egalitarian ideology, wherein gender equality has been influential on women. Despite this egalitarian ideology, the Israeli Jewish society is characterized by male dominance in most settings (Barzilai, 2001; Kulik, 2001, 2005; Sasson-Levy, 2003a, 2003b; Wood & Eagly, 2002).

In the last decades, gender role definitions, influenced by age, education, concepts of masculinity, and femininity, have been challenged in western societies, among them the Israeli society (Ritter, 2004). Indeed, findings from a recent Israeli study have suggested that the higher the level of a woman's education, the more liberal her gender role ideology (Kulik, 2000).

Israeli culture also tends to legitimatize open communication, frankness, and straightforwardness and places value on the open expression of anger (Margalit & Mauger, 1984). Results from a recent study showed that within mundane conversation, young Israeli women made high use of masculine grammatical forms and tend to avoid feminine grammatical terms (Sa'ar, 2007). Women's use of masculine terms is explained as a way to integrate into the masculine Israeli society. Within the Israeli culture, conflict is perceived as a part of human relationships and is not regarded as threatening, because resolving the conflict enables people to move on (Gershenson, 2003). In a similar manner, social expectations in Israel do not assume high levels of politeness, and Israelis have been described as having weak "expressive boundaries" (Shamir & Melnik, 2002), meaning that people easily carry over their thoughts and feelings into their overt behavior (Ravid, Rafaeli, & Grandey, 2010). This cultural aspect, together with a cultural value of relatively low hierarchical distance which prevails within social structures in Israel, contributes to open expression of anger among men and women (House, Hanges, Javidan, Dorfman, & Gupta, 2004) of appraisal.

Taking into account, the componential aspects of anger response, social constructivist conceptualization and based on the literature on gender, and the Israeli culture, it is suggested that ratings of features within each component, respective to each anger term, is a highly complex process. It is assumed that rating anger terms across the same components involves the individual's understanding of the specific states and actions that each term induces within a broader body of knowledge, including past experience recollections, social norms, and gender roles (Niedenthal, Barsalou, Winkielman, Krauth-Gruber, & Ric, 2005; Robinson & Clore, 2002; Russell, 2003).

Due to the complexity of the appraisal process, it is expected that rather than an isolated component, a combination of components may offer a better way to examine differences between genders and across anger terms. The objectives are to find combinations of emotional components presented by a new composite variable that will exhibit differences between genders and differentiate between anger terms in Hebrew.

Method

Participants

Forty participants, 20 men and 20 women, completed the web questionnaire. All indicated they spoke, read, and wrote fluently in Hebrew. The women's mean age was 23.71 years (SD = 1.74 years), and the men's mean age was 24.10 (SD = 1.66 years). All participants were single with Jewish religious orientation, born and raised in Israel. Among the participants 22.5% ($n = 9$) of the women and 17.5% of the men ($n = 7$) were bilingual and spoke, in addition to Hebrew,

TABLE 1. Distribution Percentages of Participants by Demographic Variables

Gender	Women	Men
Percentages (number)	50 (20)	50 (20)
Age		
M	23.71	24.10
SD	1.74	1.66
Religion		
Jewish	50 (20)	50 (20)
Family Status		
Single	50 (20)	50 (20)
Country of origin		
Israel	50 (20)	50 (20)
Languages		
Hebrew	50 (20)	50 (20)
Other languages	22.5 (9)	17.5 (7)
Russian	4 (44)	3 (43)
English	2 (22)	2 (29)
French	2 (22)	1 (14)
Spanish	1 (12)	1 (14)

Absolute numbers appears in parenthesis.

either Russian (44% vs. 43%), English (22% vs. 29%), French (22% vs. 14%), or Spanish (1% vs. 14%). Please see Table 1.

Procedure and Materials

The present study was performed as part of the ELIN cross cultural project ("the impact of emotion language on international negotiation") coordinated by the Swiss Center for Affective Sciences at the University of Geneva (ELIN, 2012). The Israeli study was administered according to the instructions provide by the ELIN team.

In the first stage, a preliminary psycholinguistic study was designed to select a representative set of terms which represent "anger" construct. In this preliminary study, anger scenarios were translated from the original English version to: Hebrew, French, Chinese, German, Spanish, and Russian. Twenty Israeli Jewish students, all of whom speak, read, and write fluently in Hebrew, were recruited with a snowball technique. They were presented with "anger"-eliciting situations designed to delineate anger terms that portray the way they would feel in each of the situations. Within the analysis process, the words offered in each scenario were grouped and eight anger terms in Hebrew were selected. An elaborate description of this procedure is provided by Ogarkova, Soriano, and Lehr (2012a, 2012b). The most prevalent terms used in this pre-study, in descending order of frequency of appearance were: *Ko'es*/angry and *merugaz*/irritated; *me'utzban*/annoyed and *zo'em*/furious; *metuskal*/frustrated, *mitraem*/resentful, *marir*/bitter, and *nakmani* /revengeful.

In the second stage of the ELIN study, the ELIN-GRID questionnaire was translated from English to Hebrew, and an independent bilingual person back translated the Hebrew version to English. The two English versions were compared and modifications applied. The authors of the original version helped in critical cases. The study was approved by an ethical committee.

An invitation to participate in the Israeli study was advertised on two academic campuses in the southern part of Israel: Ben-Gurion University of the Negev and Sapir College. In the invitation, it was stated that the study is a web based study in which Hebrew native speakers are asked to rate anger terms in Hebrew. Explicit inclusion criteria were: age 20–29, being a student who speaks, reads and writes fluently in Hebrew. A quota of 20 men and 20 women was sought. Respondents were told their participation in the study was voluntary, were notified that their e-mail address needed to be attached to their response, and were assured that their emails would be kept confidential (as suggested by Granello & Wheaton, 2004). Upon receiving oral informed consent, respondents were referred to a web site constructed by the ELIN team to fill out the ELIN-GRID questionnaire. The online questionnaire was created in HTML format.

All participants had access to the internet and answered the questionnaire from their own computer in their free time, while the research assistants were available on line to answer questions if raised. Upon completing the questionnaire, the respondent informed the research assistant who made sure that all answers were given to all questions. Respondents did not receive any compensation for their participation. Completion of the questionnaire, including the instructions, took approximately one hour. The data were collected between October and December 2008.

The ELIN-GRID questionnaire (Fontaine, Scherer, & Soriano, 2013) was administered in the current study. The ELIN team added to a reliable and valid GRID questionnaire (Scherer & Fontaine, 2013; Scherer & Meuleman, 2013) several features to better capture the distinctions between emotion terms. The analysis of the ELIN-GRID questionnaire is reported by the ELIN team (ELIN, 2012). They conducted hierarchical cluster analysis and principal component analysis on the features which were rated by Spanish and Russian speakers on "anger" terms in their language (ELIN, 2012). Participants were asked to rate each of the terms on the 95 emotion features which were presented in six emotional components. Using a 9-point Likert scale ranging from extremely unlikely (1) to extremely likely (9), they rated the likelihood with which each emotion feature can be inferred from each of the anger terms that appeared on the screen (ELIN, 2012).

In the current study a similar procedure took place using the same features. The features have proven to be effective as a way to evaluate the degree to which proposed theoretical components are part of the meaning of anger terms.

However, in the current study the feature were grouped into components following the conceptualization of the componential model (Ellsworth & Scherer, 2003; Fontaine et al., 2007; Grandjean, Sander, & Scherer, 2008; Scherer, 2001; Scherer & Ellgring, 2007). The scores for each of the six components were summed and a total score for each of the six components served as the dependent variables. A high overall score in a component means that many of the features are rated as likely to apply. This means that the component is perceived to be highly relevant to the meaning of the term. A term obtaining a comparatively lower overall score would be less characterized by this component.

The components are detailed hereby:

The *subjective experience* component includes 10 features that characterize the overall feeling of the emotional state. Participants were asked: "when you hear/read this word in your language, how likely is it, as inferred from the meaning of the word, that the person undergoing the emotional experience, e.g., 'felt bad,' 'felt good,' 'felt strong'?" The total sum of ratings ranged between10 and 90.

The *bodily experiences* component was assessed by 13 features that tend to occur during the emotional state. Participants were asked, for example: "when you hear/read this word in your language, how likely is it, as inferred from the meaning of the word, that the person undergoing the emotional experience, e.g., 'blushed,' 'perspired,' 'had moist hands'?" The total sum of ratings ranged between 11 and 99.

The *expressions* component was assessed by 14 features (vocal, gestural, and facial), typically shown during an anger emotional state. Participants were asked, for example: "when you hear/read this word in your language, how likely is it, as inferred from the meaning of the word that the person undergoing the emotional experience, e.g., 'spoke louder,' 'spoke faster,' 'frowned'?" The total sum of ratings ranged between 13 and 117.

The *action tendency* component was assessed by 13 features regarding typical actions or desires to act that usually occur during the emotional state. Participants were asked, for example: "when you hear/read this word in your language, how likely is it, as inferred from the meaning of the word, that the person undergoing the emotional experience wanted to 'damage, hit or say something that hurts to the person who had caused the emotion,' 'wanted to hit or damage the things nearby,' 'wanted to damage or say something hurtful to whoever was nearby'?" The total sum of rates ranged between 13 and 117.

The *regulation* component was assessed by three features regarding the regulation one may exert over the emotional state. Participants were asked: "when you hear/read this word in your language, how likely is it, as inferred from the meaning of the word, that the person undergoing the emotional experience will 'hide the emotion from others by smiling,' 'show her/his emotion more than she/he felt it,' 'show her/his emotion less than she/he felt it'?" The total sum of ratings ranged between 3 and 27.

TABLE 2. Internal Reliability for Each of the Six Components Cronbach α

Component	Cronbach's alpha
Subjective Experience	0.84 (*nakmani*/revengeful) $\leq \alpha \leq$ 0.97 (*marir*/bitter)
Bodily Experiences	0.91 (*nakmani*/revengeful) $\leq \alpha \leq$ 0.98 (*zo'em*/furious)
Expressions	0.93 (*nakmani*/revengeful) $\leq \alpha \leq$ 0.98 (*me'utzban*/annoyed, *zo'em*/furious, *mitraem*/resentment)
Action Tendency	0.91 (*nakmani*/revengeful) $\leq \alpha \leq$ 0.98 (*marir*/bitter, *zo'em*/furious)
Regulation	0.75 (*nakmani*/revengeful) $\leq \alpha \leq$ 0.89 (*metuskal*/frustrated)
Cognitive Evaluation	0.96 (*nakmani*/revengeful) $\leq \alpha \leq$ 0.99 (*ko'es*/angry, *me'utzban*/annoyed)

The *cognitive evaluation* component was assessed by 25 features regarding the cognitive evaluations one may have toward each term. Participants were asked, for example: "when you hear/read this word in your language, how likely is it, as inferred from the meaning of the word, that the person undergoing the emotional experience will make, consciously or not, the following evaluations or appraisals, e.g., 'was caused intentionally,' 'was caused by the person's behavior,' 'was caused by an intrinsic quality of the person'?" The total sum of ratings ranged between 25 and 225.

Data Analysis

Data analysis was performed using statistical software SPSS 19.0 (SPSS Science, Chicago, IL, USA). As previously noted, the theoretical conceptualization postulates that each of the six components measure separate and distinct features. Thus, in the first step, internal reliability was calculated for each of the six components. Cronbach's alpha are presented in Table 2. Each of the eight anger terms results were obtained from twenty participants; thus overall, there were 160 answers that were scored for each of the six components. A two-factor between-subjects multivariate analysis of variance (MANOVA) was performed. The features that comprise the emotional components served as the dependent variables in the analysis. The gender of the respondents (women, men) and the eight anger terms presented to them (*ko'es*/angry, *merugaz*/irritated, *me'utzban*/annoyed, *zo'em*/furious, *metuskal*/frustrated, *mitraem*/resentful, *marir*/bitter, *nakmani* /revengeful) comprised the independent variables. Evaluation of the homogeneity of variance-covariance matrices and normality assumptions underlying MANOVA

TABLE 3. Intercorrelations Among the Emotion Components

Emotion component	Subjective experience	Body experiences	Expressions	Action tendency	Regulation	Evaluation
Subjective experience	1.00	−.17*	.28**	−.14	.23**	−.16*
Body experiences		1.00	.13	.84**	−.18*	.96**
Expressions			1.00	−.02	−.16*	−.05
Action tendency				1.00	−.05	.87**
Regulation					1.00	−.13
Evaluation						1.00

$*p \leq .05.$ $**p \leq .001.$

was calculated to find possible substantial anomalies. The alpha level of significance was set to .05. Bivariate correlations were calculated to see if any dependent variables were highly correlated (Schmitt, 1996).

MANOVA analysis for both the gender and the anger terms variables were calculated. Partial Eta squared was calculated and the contribution of gender and anger terms to the explained variance in the dependent variable was calculated as well.

In order to answer the aim of the study, we looked for combinations of components presented by a composite variable to exhibit differences between the genders and anger terms. Following the MANOVA analysis recommended by Grice and Iwasaki (2007) and Harris (2001), we checked whether the same simplified multivariate composite explained the gender difference and differentiated between anger terms.

Results

Internal reliability for each of the six components is presented in Table 2.

For each component, high Alpha values were obtained. High Cronbach Alpha values do not necessarily indicate one measure but can indicate several different domains within a specific construct (Green, Lissitz, & Mulaik, 1977; Schmitt, 1996).

Before answering the study aim, a two-factor, between-subjects multivariate analysis of variance (MANOVA) was conducted. Evaluation of the homogeneity of variance-covariance matrices and normality assumptions underlying MANOVA did not reveal any substantial anomalies and the alpha level of significance was set to .05. The bivariate correlations among the dependent variables are presented in Table 3.

From Table 3, we can see that some of the dependent variables are highly correlated, especially significant are the high correlations (r > .80) between body experiences and action tendency, body experiences and evaluations, action tendency, and evaluations. The significance level is that appropriate to $n = 160$ (each one of the eight anger term was rated by 20 participants).

Results from the MANOVA for both the gender and the anger terms variables were statistically significant. The corresponding Wilks' Λ was (.87), $F(6,139) = 3.59, p < .001$) for gender and (.38), $F(42,655) = 3.57, p < .001$) for anger terms. The interaction between gender and anger terms was not statistically significant. Partial Eta squared indicated that gender explained 13.4% and anger terms 15% of the variance in the dependent variable.

Univariate means (M) and standard deviations (SD) are reported in Table 4.

In Table 5, the values of the unstandardized discriminant function coefficients ($sdfc$) for the first multivariate combination for both gender and anger terms, are presented. We do not present the discriminant function coefficient for the interaction between gender and anger terms that was found to be insignificant. Also presented are the correlations (c_{cd}) between the canonical variables and each of the dependent variables.

In order to answer the aim of the study a combination of components was conducted, presented by a composite variable, to exhibit differences between the genders and anger terms. Table 5 presents which emotion components contribute most to the difference between the genders and the anger terms. From the table we can see that for gender, regulation and subjective experience have the largest coefficient, but with opposite signs. A simplified multivariate composite, defined as subjective experience minus regulation, still explains the gender difference. This combination of components might be thought of as the gap or distance between the intensity of the emotional state and the effort to regulate it. Univariate analysis on this variable showed $F(1,144) = 15.90, p < .01$). Partial Eta squared indicated that this combination explains 10% of the variance in the dependent variables. A large gap or distance would mean poor regulation of the subjective feeling. Examining the mean values of this new variable for men and women shows that this gap or distance was larger for women than for men 'in regard to all eight anger terms'. This gap would mean women perceive more than men that the anger terms entail very distinct feelings and the regulatory effort in their opinion is poor.

However, the composite variable that differentiated between the genders did not significantly differentiate between the anger terms, $F(7,144) = 1.6, NS$). As for the gender case, we checked whether a simplified composite variable can be constructed to differentiate between the anger terms. This time, based on the coefficients in Table 5, we used the composite variable subjective experience plus action tendency. This composite variable represents the additive effect of the subjective emotional experience and the actions that accompany this emotional state. To elaborate, participants distinguish between anger terms based their opinions on the distinct emotional subjective experience and the actions re-attached to this

TABLE 4. Means and Standard Deviations of the Emotion Components

Components	Emotion terms	Gender	M	SD
Subjective experience	*ko'es*/angry	women	54.70	3.90
		men	47.50	9.94
	merugaz/irritated	women	56.20	5.22
		men	52.70	9.35
	me'utzban/annoyed	women	55.80	5.55
		men	53.60	5.83
	zo'em/furious	women	53.60	8.36
		men	52.20	7.96
	metuskal/frustrated	women	48.66	4.71
		men	48.63	8.70
	mitraem/resentful	women	49.22	5.73
		men	47.54	8.34
	marir/bitter	women	58.88	5.34
		men	47.18	6.67
	nakmani/revengeful	women	52.00	8.06
		men	47.27	9.01
Body experiences	*ko'es*/angry	women	44.40	31.15
		men	31.10	33.16
	merugaz/irritated	women	12.20	25.71
		men	26.70	28.53
	me'utzban/annoyed	women	29.20	26.50
		men	43.50	32.13
	zo'em/furious	women	39.10	27.14
		men	21.80	28.80
	metuskal/frustrated	women	39.66	30.27
		men	36.18	34.82
	mitraem/resentful	women	39.66	30.27
		men	36.18	34.82
	marir/bitter	women	39.66	30.27
		men	36.18	34.82
	nakmani/revengeful	women	51.66	29.69
		men	59.18	15.71
Expressions	*ko'es*/angry	women	82.70	9.78
		men	77.00	14.39
	merugaz/irritated	women	69.60	11.32
		men	69.80	9.34
	me'utzban/annoyed	women	82.20	11.28
		men	78.70	11.36
	zo'em/furious	women	76.30	11.69
		men	74.40	11.99
	metuskal/frustrated	women	78.22	16.50
		men	78.81	8.37
	mitraem/resentful	women	84.77	16.49
		men	81.63	8.09

(Continued on next page)

TABLE 4. Means and Standard Deviations of the Emotion Components (Continued)

Components	Emotion terms	Gender	M	SD
	marir/bitter	women	79.73	16.71
		men	75.36	9.14
	nakmani/revengeful	women	82.22	5.33
		men	76.18	11.25
Action tendency	*ko'es*/angry	women	54.20	38.39
		men	37.90	40.51
	merugaz/irritated	women	15.20	32.09
		men	38.80	41.31
	me'utzban/annoyed	women	46.90	40.96
		men	60.10	41.92
	zo'em/furious	women	76.30	11.69
		men	74.40	11.99
	metuskal/frustrated	women	51.44	39.05
		men	41.63	40.38
	mitraem/resentful	women	51.44	39.65
		men	41.63	40.38
	marir/bitter	women	58.55	39.98
		men	70.72	9.98
	nakmani/revengeful	women	50.55	37.56
		men	50.76	37.03
Regulation	*ko'es*/angry	women	13.50	3.97
		men	15.20	3.08
	merugaz/irritated	women	14.30	3.43
		men	17.40	4.06
	me'utzban/annoyed	women	14.00	3.39
		men	18.70	4.96
	zo'em/furious	women	14.80	3.29
		men	18.70	3.30
	metuskal/frustrated	women	14.22	4.17
		men	15.09	2.94
	mitraem/resentful	women	12.55	4.85
		men	14.72	3.55
	marir/bitter	women	15.44	5.43
		men	15.00	3.09
	nakmani/revengeful	women	15.44	4.89
		men	14.54	3.61
Evaluation	*ko'es*/angry	women	114.60	81.75
		men	74.90	79.76
	merugaz/irritated	women	28.70	20.52
		men	72.70	70.65
	me'utzban/annoyed	women	85.10	74.12
		men	107.10	78.12
	zo'em/furious	women	101.30	71.21
		men	59.00	40.15

(Continued on next page)

TABLE 4. Means and Standard Deviations of the Emotion Components (Continued)

Components	Emotion terms	Gender	M	SD
	metuskal/frustrated	women	100.88	77.68
		men	89.72	87.40
	mitraem/resentful	women	100.88	77.68
		men	89.72	87.40
	marir/bitter	women	100.88	77.68
		men	89.72	87.40
	nakmani/revengeful	women	117.11	66.90
		men	145.90	23.51

state. Univariate analysis on this variable showed $F(7,144) = 3.40, p < .01$). Partial Eta square indicated that this combination explain 14% of the variance in the dependent variables. On the other hand, this composite did not differentiate in a statistically significant way between men and women.

It is interesting to note that the subjective experience component was part of both simplified composite variables; therefore, opposed to the aim of the study that searches for a combination of components, it was worthwhile checking whether, by itself, it can also differentiate between the gender and the emotion terms categories. Subjective experience alone explain 4% of the variance in gender $F(1,144) = 5.90$, $p < .01$) and 8.1% of the variance in the emotion terms $F(7,144) = 2.76, p < .01$).

TABLE 5. Unstandardized Discriminant Function Coefficients for Gender and Emotion Terms and Correlations between the Canonical Variables and Each of the Dependent Variables

Components	Sdfc-gender	c_{cd}-gender	Sdfc–emotion terms	c_{cd}–emotion terms
Subjective experience	−.10	−.51	.05	.23
Body experiences	.04	−.03	−.02	−.13
Expressions	−.01	−.34	−.02	−.14
Action tendency	−.00	.01	.06	.28
Regulation	.24	.65	.02	−.10
Evaluation	−.01	−.05	−.02	.24

Note. sdfc = coefficients from first unstandardized discriminant function; c_{cd} = correlations between the dependent variables and the canonical variable.

Discussion

The current study investigates young Israeli adults, men and women, in-terpretation of several emotional components regarding eight anger terms. Forty participants reported their opinions on the meaning of eight anger words. In partic-ular about the likelihood that combination of components is part of the meaning of those words. The anger terms rated by participants were as follows: *ko'es/*angry, *merugaz/*irritated, *me'utzban/*annoyed, *zo'em/*furious, *metuskal/*frustrated, *mi-traem/*resentful, *marir/*bitter, *and nakmani/*revengeful.

Several interesting findings emerge from this study. A multivariate analysis was employed and made use of the inter-correlations among all the dependent variables (six emotional components). Accordingly, results from the MANOVA, for both the gender and the anger terms, were statistically significant. Partial Eta squared indicated that gender explained 13.4% of the variance in the dependent variable, and emotion terms explained 15% of the variance. A new simplified de-pendent variable was comprised, based on the MANOVA results which represent a concept different from analyzing each emotional component individually. The new combination of components was based on the discriminant function coeffi-cients for gender. A composite of two components, subjective experience minus regulation, explained 10% of the variance between men and women. This is al-most as high as the eta squared of the full composite variable that was found by the MANOVA procedure. For women, the mean values of this new composite across all anger terms showed higher ratings. This implies that the anger terms did not elicit a vague or undefined subjective experience. The subjective experi-ence, designated by the words, is appraised as eliciting a very distinct feeling for women. Furthermore, for women, a larger gap or distance was found between the appraised emotional experience and the appraised need to regulate the response. In other words, women, more than men, perceive that the anger terms lead to a higher intensive subjective experience, whereas they appraise regulatory efforts rather low. The inferences of our participants, men and women, as reflected by the new composite variable, may represent the discord that accompanies women's role in the Israeli society. It is possible that the new composite points to the conflict that Israeli women have between individualism and masculinity. On one hand, women are entitled to their subjective experiences, but, on the other hand they need to conform to their role in the masculine oriented Israeli society. Women believe, as inferred from their ratings across all anger terms, that they poorly regulate their response (Sasson-Levy, 2011).

The new simplified composite that differentiates between the genders did not explain the differences among the anger terms. Another new composite variable emerged by examining the discriminant function coefficients, subjective experi-ence plus action tendencies. The new simplified variable explained 14% of the variance between anger terms. Again, this is almost as high as the eta squared of the full composite variable that was found by the MANOVA procedure. This may imply that our participants' capability to differentiate anger terms is modeled by an additive combination of the subjective experience inferred in the anger term, and the actions that are inferred from the term.

The findings of the current study corroborate findings from a previous study which compared between anger labeling in English, Chinese, Japanese, and Hungarian. Anger labeling was found to be neither a universal concept nor solely a cultural construction, but a combined body-based and social construction (Koävecses, 2000). It is thereby suggested that, due to the complexity of the appraisal process, a distinct combination of components may offer a better and simplified way to shed light on appraisal differences between men and women. However, as a consequence of the complexity of the appraisal process, a different composite was constructed to explain the differences between anger terms. This new composite point to the idea that in the process of appraisal and interpretation of anger terms, the subjective experience is a crucial component, but it, by itself, explains a rather small percentage of the variance. It is the combination of the appraised subjective experience with actions that give a fuller picture of how differentiation of the meaning of the terms is appraised. This idea corroborates with Ravid and colleagues reasoning that within the Israeli culture people easily carry over their thoughts and feelings into their overt behavior (Ravid et al., 2010). Furthermore, previous findings have shown that greater intensity of anger and outward behavioral responses are associated with masculinity (Brody & Hall, 2008; Fischer et al., 2004; Rivers et al., 2007). The new composite that differentiates between anger terms may point to the masculine norms that prevail in the Israeli society and in this study are singled out by inferences toward anger labeling.

As previously noted, the component of subjective experience differentiates between the anger terms and between men and women's appraisals. This component, that characterizes the emotional state, elucidates that, in the process of appraisal and attaching significance to emotional semantic knowledge, subjective experience is a pertinent component in understanding gender opinions and cultural beliefs and norms.

The two simplified composites that emerged from the analysis also corroborate the ideas presented in componential models of emotions. These ideas state that emotional processes are dynamically patterned as the individual continuously appraises objects, behaviors, and situations with respect to their effect on his/her values (Ellsworth & Scherer, 2003; Scherer et al., 2001). Our two composites enable us to clearly explain that assessment of semantic knowledge can to be conducted on a simplified multi-modal basis. A theoretical contribution of this study is its ability to study linear combinations of variables rather than single variables, for example, subjective experience, action tendency and regulation components are not analyzed separately as dependent variables but depend on the interaction among themselves.

It is interesting to note that the emotional components which were examined in this study differentiated between the genders' ratings and between several anger terms. However, a simplified combination of the components provided a better understanding of the ability of the new comprised dependent variable to differentiate between the genders and the emotional labeling.

The limitations of this study need to be stated as well. The first limitation is that the measures used in the present study are based on a self-reporting scale. Participants reported their opinions on the meaning of eight anger terms, but the current study did not examine the actual responses of men and women in real time situations that involve their differential use of distinct anger terms. For this, laboratory experiments and analysis of real time encounters can provide further evidence for culture and gender effect. Second, the representativeness of the sample, based on a web-based recruited survey, is limited. Thus, the generalizability of the results can be compromised. Moreover, the sample is not a representative sample of Israeli society which is comprised of diverse cultural and ethnic groups, but rather a homogenous sample of young undergraduate Israeli students that study in the southern part of Israel. Their ratings of semantic terms point to the effect that gender and cultural norms have, in appraisal processes and semantic labeling. Further studies are called for to examine appraisals of Israeli men and women on appraisals of other emotional constructs such as "shame" or "guilt" and towards positive constructs such as "pride." Additional investigations are needed to determine whether the same simplified composite that differentiates between Israeli men and women ratings of anger terms, is useful in the appraisal analysis of other emotional labeling.

Conclusions

This study provides preliminary evidence that emotional components, which usually measure emotional experiences, are effective in measuring distinct opinions toward emotional labeling. The findings also showed that when measuring opinions towards specific anger terms, new composites comprised of combined components effectively portray differences between the genders and emotion terms. The simplified composites that were found to have the differentiating power correspond with common social norms (Barrett, 2006; Crump et al., 2007; Kelan, 2008; Russell, 2003). The combination 'subjective experience minus regulation' is suggested to reflect social norms regarding gender roles whereas the other combination 'subjective experience plus with action tendency' reflects cultural norms that differentiate between anger terms.

This work emphasizes the importance of multivariate analysis when dealing with a cluster of emotional components. It also shows that different combinations of emotional components are needed to differentiate between men and women and between anger terms. The current findings point to the idea that we restructure our reality differently and give support to the re-constructionist view of reality that serves as social regulatory functions for gender roles and cultural norms (Russell, 1994, 2003).

REFERENCES

Alonso-Arbiol, I., van de Vijver, F. J., Fernandez, I., Paez, D., Campos, M., & Carrera, P. (2011). Implicit theories about interrelations of anger components in 25 countries. *Emotion, 11*(1), 1–11.

Archer, J. (2004). Sex differences in aggression in real-world settings: A meta-analytic review. *Review of General Psychology, 8*(4), 291–322.

Armon-Jones, C. (1986). The social functions of emotions. In R. Harré (Ed.), *The social construction of emotions* (pp. 57–82). Oxford, England: Basil Blackwell.

Aue, T., Flykt, A., & Scherer, K. R. (2007). First evidence for differential and sequential efferent effects of stimulus relevance and goal conduciveness appraisal. *Biological psychology, 74*(3), 347–357.

Averill, J. R. (1982). *Anger and aggression: An essay on emotion.* New York, NY: Springer-Verlag.

Barrett, L. F. (2006). Solving the emotion paradox: Categorization and the experience of emotion. *Personality and Social Psychology Review, 10*, 20–26.

Barrett, L. F., Robin, L., Pietromonaco, P. R., & Eyssell, K. M. (1998). Are women the "more emotional" sex? Evidence from emotional experiences in social context. *Cognition & Emotion, 12*(4), 555–578.

Barzilai, G. (2001). A political and legal culture. In E. Yuchtman-Yaar & Z. Shavit (Eds.), *Trends in Israeli society* (pp. 52–64). Tel Aviv: The Open University Press. (Hebrew)

Berkowitz, L. (1993). Aggression: Its causes, consequences, and control. In *McGraw-Hill series in social psychology.* New York, NY/England: McGraw-Hill Book Company.

Brody, L. R., & Hall, J. A. (2008). Gender and emotion in context. In M. Lewis, J. M. Haviland-Jones, & L. Feldman-Barrett (Eds.), *Handbook of emotions* (pp. 395–407). New York, NY: Guilford.

Campbell, A., & Muncer, S. (2008). Intent to harm or injure? Gender and the expression of anger. *Aggressive Behavior, 34*, 282–293.

Clore, G. L., & Ortony, A. (2000). *Cognition in emotion: Always, sometimes, or never. Cognitive neuroscience of emotion.* New York, NY: Oxford University Press.

Cox, D. E., & Harrison, D. W. (2008). Models of anger: contributions from psychophysiology, neuropsychology and the cognitive behavioral perspective. *Brain Structure & Function, 212*, 371–385.

Crump, B. J., Logan, K. A., & McIlroy, A. (2007). Does gender still matter? A study of the views of women in the ICT industry in New Zealand. *Gender, Work & Organization, 14*(4), 349–370.

Eid, M., & Diener, E. (2001). Norms for experiencing emotions in different cultures: Inter- and intranational differences. *Journal of Personality and Social Psychology, 81*, 869–885.

Ekman, P. (1999). Basic emotions. In T. Dalgleish & M. Power (Eds.), *Handbook of cognition and emotion* (Chapter 3). Sussex, UK: John Wiley & Sons.

ELIN. (2012). *The impact of emotion language on international negotiation.* Swiss network for international studies. Available at http://www.snis.ch/system/files/working_paper_the_impact_of_emotion_language.pdf

Ellsworth, P. C., & Scherer, K. R. (2003). Appraisal processes in emotion. In R. J. Davidson, K. R. Scherer, & H. Goldsmith (Eds.), *Handbook of affective sciences* (pp. 572–595). New York, NY: Oxford University Press.

Fischer, A. H., & Manstead, A. S. R. (2008). Social functions of emotion. In M. Lewis, J. M. Haviland-Jones, & L. Feldman-Barrett (Eds.), *Handbook of emotions* (pp. 456–468). New York, NY: Guilford.

Fischer, A. H., Rodriguez-Mosquera, P. M., van Vianen, A. E., & Manstead, A. S. (2004). Gender and culture differences in emotion. *Emotion, 4*(1), 87–94.

Fontaine, J. R. J., Scherer, K. R., Roesch, E. B., & Ellsworth, P. C. (2007). The world of emotions is not two-dimensional. *Psychological Science, 18*, 1050–1057.

Fontaine, J., Scherer, K. R., & Soriano, C. (Eds.). (2013). *Components of emotional meaning: A sourcebook*. Oxford: Oxford University Press.

Frijda, N. H. (2009). Emotion experience and its varieties. *Emotion Review, 1*(3), 264–271.

Gershenson, O. (2003). Misunderstanding between Israelis and Soviet immigrants: Linguistic and cultural factors. *Multilingua, 22*(3), 275–290.

Glenberg, A. M., Jaworski, B., Rischal, M., & Levin, J. R. (2007). What brains are for: Action, meaning, and reading comprehension. In D. McNamara (Ed.), *Reading comprehension strategies: Theories, interventions, and technologies* (pp. 221–240). Mahwah, NJ: Erlbaum.

Grandjean, D., Sander, D., & Scherer, K. R. (2008). Conscious emotional experience emerges as a function of multilevel, appraisal-driven response synchronization. *Consciousness & Cognition, 17*(2), 484–495.

Grandjean, D., & Scherer, K. R. (2008). Unpacking the cognitive architecture of emotion processes. *Emotion, 8*(3), 341.

Granello, D. H., & Wheaton, J. E. (2004). Online data collection: strategies for research. *Journal of Counseling & Development, 82*, 387–393.

Green, S. B., Lissitz, R. W., & Mulaik, S. A. (1977). Limitations of coefficient alpha as an index of test unidimensionality. *Educational and Psychological Measurement, 37*, 827–838.

Grice, J. W., & Iwasaki, M. (2007). A truly multivariate approach to MANOVA. *Applied Multivariate Research, 12*, 199–226.

Grossman, M., & Wood, W. (1993). Sex differences in intensity of emotional experience: A social role interpretation. *Journal of Personality and Social Psychology, 65*, 1010–1022.

Halperin, E., Russell, A. G., Dweck, C. S., & Gross, J. J. (2011). Anger, hatred, and the quest for peace: Anger can be constructive in the absence of hatred. *Journal of Peace Research, 48*, 637–651.

Harris, R. J. (2001). *A primer of multivariate statistics* (3rd ed.). Mahwah, NJ: Lawrence Erlbaum.

Hofstede, G. (1997). *Cultures and organizations: Software of the mind*. New York, NY: McGraw-Hill.

House, R., Hanges, P. J., Javidan, M., Dorfman, P. W., & Gupta, V. (Eds.). (2004). *Culture, leadership and organizations: The GLOBE study of 62 societies*. Beverly Hills, CA: Sage Publications.

Hupka, R. B., Lenton, A. P., & Hutchison, K. A. (1999). Universal development of emotion categories in natural language. *Journal of Personality and Social Psychology, 77*(2), 247–278.

Johnson-Laird, P. N., & Oatley, K. (2000). The cognitive and social construction of emotions. In M. Lewis & J. M. Haviland-Jones (Eds.), *Handbook of emotions* (2nd ed., pp. 458–475). New York, NY: Guilford Press.

Kelan, E. (2008). Gender, risk and employment insecurity: The masculine breadwinner subtext. *Human Relations, 61*, 1171–1202.

Koopmann-Holm, B., & Matsumoto, D. (2011). Values and display rules for specific emotions. *Journal of Cross-Cultural Psychology*, *42*, 355–371.

Koävecses, Z. (2000). *Metaphor and emotion: Language, culture, and body in human feeling.* Cambridge, England: Cambridge University Press.

Kulik, L. (2000). Intra-familiar congruence in gender role ideology: Husband–wife versus parents–offspring. *Journal of Comparative Family Studies*, *31*, 91–107.

Kulik, L. (2001). Assessing job search intensity and unemployment-related attitudes among young adults. *Journal of Career Assessment*, *9*, 156–167.

Kulik, L. (2005). The impact of families on gender identity and on sex-typing of household tasks in Israel. *Journal of Social Psychology*, *145*(3), 299–316.

Levin, D. S. (2011). You're always first a girl: Emerging adult women, gender, and sexuality in the Israeli army. *Journal of Adolescent Research*, *26*(1), 3–29.

Mackie, D. M., Devos, T. , & Smith, E. R. (2000). Intergroup emotions: Explaining offensive action tendencies in an intergroup context. *Journal of Personality and Social Psychology*, *79*(4), 602–616.

Marcus, A., & Gould, E. W. (2000). Crosscurrents: cultural dimensions and global Web user-interface design. *Interactions*, *7*(4), 32–46.

Margalit, B. A., & Mauger, P. A. (1984). Cross-cultural demonstration of orthogonality of assertiveness and aggressiveness - comparison between Israel and the United States. *Journal of Personality and Social Psychology*, *46*(6), 1414–1421.

Mauro, R., Sato, K., & Tucker, J. (1992). The role of appraisal in human emotions: A cross-cultural study. *Journal of Personality and Social Psychology*, *62*(2), 301–317.

Mesquita, B. (2003). Emotions as dynamic cultural phenomena. In H. Goldsmith, R. Davidson, & K. Scherer (Eds.), *Handbook of the affective sciences* (pp. 871–890). New York, NY: Oxford.

Moors, A., Ellsworth, P. C., Scherer, K. R., & Frijda, N. H. (2013). Appraisal theories of emotion: State of the art and future development. *Emotion Review*, *5*(2), 119–124.

Niedenthal, P. M. (2007). Embodying emotion. *Science*, *316*(5827), 1002–1005.

Niedenthal, P. M., Barsalou, L. W., Winkielman, P., Krauth-Gruber, S., & Ric, F. (2005). Embodiment in attitudes, social perception, and emotion. *Personality and Social Psychology Review*, *9*(3), 184–211.

Ogarkova, A., Soriano, C., & Lehr, C. (2012a). Naming feelings: exploring the equivalence of emotion terms in five European languages. *Lodz Studies in Language*, *24*, 3–35.

Ogarkova, A., Soriano, C., & Lehr, C. (2012b). Cultural specificity in labeling emotional scenarios: A case study of ANGER, SHAME, GUILT, and PRIDE in five European languages. In V. I. Shakhovskyy (Ed.), *Human communication: Motives strategies, tactics.* Volgograd: Peremena.

Ortony, A., & Turner, T. J. (1990). What's basic about basic emotions? *Psychological Review*, *97*(3), 315–333.

Parrot, W. R. (2004). The nature of emotion. In M. B. Brewer & M. Hewstone (Eds.), *Emotion and motivation* (pp. 5–20). Malden, MA: Blackwell.

Ravid, S., Rafaeli, A., & Grandey, A. (2010). Expressions of anger in Israeli workplaces: The special place of customer interactions. *Human Resource Management Review*, *20*(3), 224–234.

Ritter, D. (2004). Gender role orientation and performance on stereotypically feminine and masculine cognitive tasks. *Sex Roles*, *50*(7–8), 583–591.

Rivers, S. E., Brackett, M. A., Katulak, N. A., & Salovey, P. (2007). Regulating anger and sadness: An exploration of discrete emotions in emotion regulation. *Journal of Happiness Studies, 8*(3), 393–427.

Robinson, M. D., & Clore, G. L. (2002). Belief and feeling: Evidence for an accessibility model of emotional self-report. *Psychological Bulletin, 128*, 934–960.

Roseman, I. J., & Smith, C. A. (2001). Appraisal theory: Overview, assumptions, varieties, controversies. In K. R. Scherer, A. Schorr, & T. Johnstone (Eds.), *Appraisal processes in emotion: Theory, methods, research. Series in affective science* (pp. 3–19). New York, NY: Oxford University Press.

Russell, J. A. (1994). Is there universal recognition of emotion from facial expressions? A review of cross-cultural studies. *Psychological Bulletin, 115*, 102–141.

Russell, J. A. (2003). Core affect and the psychological construction of emotion. *Psychological Review, 110*, 145–172.

Sa'ar, A. (2007). Masculine talk: On the subconscious use of masculine linguistic form among Hebrew-and Arabic-speaking women in Israel. *Signs: Journal of Women in Culture and Society, 32*(2), 405–429.

Safdar, S., Friedlmeier, W., Matsumoto, D., Yoo, S. H., Kwantes, C. T., & Kakai, H. (2009). Variations of emotional display rules within and across cultures: A comparison between Canada, USA, and Japan. *Canadian Journal of Behavioral Science, 41*(1), 1–10.

Sasson-Levy, O. (2003a). Feminism and military gender practices: Israeli women soldiers in "Masculine" roles. *The Sociological Inquiry, 73*(3), 440–465.

Sasson-Levy, O. (2003b). Military, masculinity and citizenship: Tensions and contradictions in the experience of blue-collar soldiers. *Identities: Global Studies in Culture and Power, 10*(3), 319–345.

Sasson-Levy, O. (2011). The military in a globalized environment: Perpetuating an extremely gendered organization. In E. Jeanes, D. Knights, & P. Y. Martin (Eds.), *Handbook of gender, work and organization* (pp. 391–410). London: Sage.

Shamir, B., & Melnik, Y. (2002). Boundary permeability as a cultural dimension: A study of cross cultural working relations between American and Israelis in high-tech organizations. *Journal of Cross-Cultural Management, 2*(2), 219–238.

Scherer, K. R. (2001). Appraisal considered as a process of multilevel sequential checking. In K. R. Scherer, A. Schorr, & T. Johnstone (Eds.), *Appraisal processes in emotion: Theory, methods, research* (pp. 92–120). Oxford: Oxford University Press.

Scherer, K. R. (2005). What are emotions? And how can they be measured? *Social Science Information, 44*, 693–727.

Scherer, K. R., Schorr, A., & Johnstone, T. (Eds.). (2001). *Appraisal processes in emotion: Theory, methods, research.* New York, NY: Oxford University Press.

Scherer, K. R., & Ellgring, H. (2007). Multimodal expression of emotion: Affect programs or componential appraisal patterns? *Emotion, 7*(1), 158–171.

Scherer, K. R., & Fontaine, J. R. F. (2013). Embodied emotions: The bodily reaction component. In J. R. F. Fontaine, K. R. Scherer, & C. Soriano (Eds.), *Components of emotional meaning.* Oxford: Oxford University Press.

Scherer, K. R., & Meuleman, B. (2013). Human emotion experiences can be predicted on theoretical grounds: Evidence from verbal labeling. *PloS one, 8*(3), e58166.

Schmitt, N. (1996). Uses and abuses of coefficient alpha. *Psychological assessment, 8*(4), 350.

Shulman, S., Blatt, S. J., & Walsh, S. (2006). The extended journey and transition to adulthood: The case of Israeli backpackers. *Journal of Youth Studies, 9*(2), 231–246.

Timmers, M., Fischer, A. H., & Manstead, A. S. R. (1998). *Gender differences in motives for regulating emotions. Personality & Social Psychology Bulletin, 24*, 974–985.

Van Kleef, G. A. (2009). How emotions regulate social life: The emotions as social information (EASI) model. *Current Directions in Psychological Science, 18*, 184–188.

Wood, W., & Eagly, A. H. (2002). A cross-cultural analysis of the behavior of women and men: Implications for the origins of sex differences. *Psychological Bulletin, 128*(5), 699–727.

The Effects of Dysphoria and Personality on Negative Self-Referent Attitudes and Perceptions of the Attitudes of Others

SHADI BESHAI
JENNIFER L. PRENTICE
JENNIFER L. SWAN
KEITH S. DOBSON

ABSTRACT. The cognitive model of depression posits that depressed individuals harbor more dysfunctional self-referent attitudes, but little is known about how depressed individuals perceive the attitudes and perceptions of others in their social arena. This study examined whether dysphoric individuals perceive others to hold equally negative attitudes about themselves, and whether such perceptions depend on sociotropic (i.e., highly invested in social approval and relationship success) and autonomous (i.e., highly invested in vocational or academic achievement and goal attainment) personality styles. A sample of undergraduate students ($N = 197$) was recruited, and after the assessment of their depression symptoms and personality style, participants read vignettes that described negative scenarios, and imagined that these scenarios occurred to themselves or the general university student. After reading each vignette, participants also rated their agreement with a number of statements that assessed dysfunctional attitudes. Results indicated that elevated dysphoria (i.e., showing signs of depression) scores were positively associated with dysfunctional self-referent attitudes. Further, moderational analyses examining the interaction of sociotropy and dysphoria did not support the hypothesis that individuals higher on dysphoria *and* sociotropy were less likely to perceive others as harboring negative attitudes about themselves in comparison to those with elevated dysphoria and lower levels of sociotropy. Last, individuals showing elevated dysphoria *and* higher scores on subdomains of autonomy were more likely to perceive others as exhibiting negative attitudes about themselves than those with low levels of the trait. These findings, their implications, and strengths and limitations of the current investigation are further discussed.

DEPRESSION IS OFTEN REFERRED TO AS THE COMMON COLD OF PSY-CHOPATHOLOGY. This unfortunate analogy tends to minimize the clinically significant impairment associated with the disorder in a variety of domains, including disturbances in psychological functioning and social relationships. Research indicates that depression is ubiquitous, regardless of ethnicity or geographical region, as it has been identified in a number of countries (Simon, Goldberg, Von Korff, & Üstün, 2002). For instance, the lifetime prevalence rates of depression are approximately 17% in the United States and 9% worldwide, while the one-year prevalence of the condition is estimated to be 5–6% worldwide (Kessler, Chiu, Demler, & Walters, 2005; Kessler et al., 2003; Dobson & Dozois, 2008). The cost of depression is not only emotional, but also economical, when healthcare costs as well as work productivity loss, disability claims, and other issues are considered (Stephens & Joubert, 2001). Given the detrimental and pervasive costs of depression, ongoing examination of the constructs that are associated with depressed mood, such as dysfunctional attitudes, biases, and personality styles, is warranted.

Beck's (1967) cognitive model of depression contends that individuals with depression experience a variety of depressogenic schemas (or core beliefs), cognitive biases, dysfunctional attitudes, and negative thoughts. This negative bent in the information processing system of individual sufferers serves to perpetuate or maintain a depressed mood (Beck, 2005). In accordance with Beck's formulation, a number of investigations (Haaga, Dyck, & Ernst, 1991; Dozois & Beck, 2008) have found that depressed individuals report significantly more acute negative thoughts towards the self than nondepressed individuals. Of particular relevance to the present study, multiple researchers (Beshai, Dobson, & Adel, 2012; Dobson, Pusch, Ardo, & Murphy, 1998; Blatt, Quinlan, Chevron, McDonald, & Zuroff, 1982) have also found that dysphoric participants (or those showing elevated depression symptoms without meeting formal diagnostic criteria for clinical depression) harbor significantly more negative self-critical thoughts than nondysphoric individuals.

Similarly, Beck (1967) maintained that dysphoric and depressed individuals hold self-referent dysfunctional attitudes. These attitudes, which Beck believed to manifest as "if – then" statements in the depressive cognitive system, are predominantly rigid and unrealistic. Weissman and Beck (1978) have created the Dysfunctional Attitudes Scale (DAS) to test the validity of this hypothesis. Since its development, the DAS has been widely used in depression and dysphoria studies. Thus far, Beck's hypothesis has consistently been supported among studies that have employed the instrument (e.g., Crandell & Chambless, 1986; Dobson & Shaw, 1986; Goldberg, Gerstein, Wenze, Welker, & Beck, 2008). For instance, Garber, Weiss, and Shanley (1993) found that depressed individuals scored significantly higher than their nondepressed counterparts on the DAS.

The majority of studies in the depression literature have focused on self-referent thoughts and attitudes exhibited by depressed or dysphoric individuals. In contrast, little is known regarding how individuals with depression perceive the attitudes and thoughts of others. Studies of the extent to which depressed and dysphoric individuals perceive similar negative attitudes in others are needed. For instance, if depressed individuals expect others to either be cool and distant, or even potentially hostile toward them, such perceptions would likely contribute to a lack of willingness to engage in social interactions. Further, depressed individuals may expect social interactions to be negative in tone, and thus their avoidance of these situations could become a self-fulfilling prophecy.

In the arena of social psychology, multiple investigations regarding how individuals perceive others' attitudes have focused on the false consensus bias. The false consensus bias, also termed the self-referent bias, is similar to the availability heuristic, wherein a decision-making "shortcut" is adopted. This shortcut allows decisions to be made based on the greater accessibility of an individual's recent experiences and attitudes that are directly relevant to the situation at hand (Haynes, Smith, & Hunsley, 2011). Since information about the self is most accessible when making judgements about others, individuals tend to think of others as similar to themselves. Individuals who employ the false consensus bias rely on self-referent attitudes and beliefs to judge the frequency of similar attitudes held by others.

As an example of the false consensus bias, Stanford undergraduate students were asked to indicate whether or not they would wear a sandwich board around campus for 30 minutes (L. Ross, Greene, & House, 1977). To increase the generalizability of the findings, two signs were used that stated either "Eat at Joe's" or "Repent." After students indicated whether they would or would not participate, students were also asked to estimate the percentage of students who would agree and who would refuse to carry the sandwich board. L. Ross et al. (1977) found that participants who agreed to wear the sign predicted that 62.2% of peers would also comply with the task. In contrast, students who refused to wear the sign predicted only a 33% compliance rate. This study supports the presence and salience of the false consensus bias, as it appears that participants' prediction of other's behaviors and attitudes were directly related to their own attitudes regarding the board. Moreover, Krueger and Clement (1994) asked participants to indicate their agreement with 40 personality items. After completing an unrelated task, participants were asked to estimate the percentage of students who would agree with each of the personality items. The authors found that even when participants were educated on the false consensus bias and provided with representative data of the phenomenon, their responses still evidenced the bias. These studies lend credence to the robust nature of the false consensus bias.

Although the false consensus bias has been supported by a number of studies with healthy participants, investigations of this phenomenon with depressed individuals have been more equivocal. For instance, depressed individuals believe that negative events, and depressive reactions to such events, occur to others more frequently than do nondepressed individuals (Kuiper & MacDonald, 1983). Other data suggests that depressed individuals judge others' performance as more positive than nondepressed participants (Lobitz & Post, 1979). Thus, it is unclear whether individuals with depression judge others' experiences and reactions as more or less negative relative to their own experiences. Research that further elucidates the relationship between individuals with depression and their judgments and attitudes toward others is needed.

Research suggests that personality factors play an important role in the development of depression. In a refinement of his cognitive model, Beck postulated the existence of the personality characteristics of sociotropy and autonomy, which result in differential risk for depression, particularly when combined with negative life events (Beck, Rush, Shaw, & Emery, 1979; Beck, 1983). Individuals who are high on sociotropy place considerable value on dependable interpersonal relationships, acceptance by others, and supportive relationships. When relationships fail to meet these criteria, individuals high on sociotropy are at an increased risk for depression (Coyne & Whiffen, 1995). In contrast, individuals who are more autonomous are concerned with the promotion of personal goals and successes and are argued to be self-critical. When these individuals are confronted with personal failures, they are at a greater risk for developing depression (Coyne & Whiffen).

Based on these conceptualizations of personality, individuals are more vulnerable to depression when the theme of a negative life event (i.e., whether the life stressor is predominately characterized by personal failure or the loss of a social relationship) is congruent with their dominant personality trait. For example, individuals who score high on autonomy may be more likely to develop depression when a personal goal is thwarted. In contrast, the deterioration of an intimate relationship may increase the risk for depression in individuals high on sociotropy. The interaction between the theme of a negative life event and personality variable is referred to as the congruency hypothesis (Clark, Beck, & Brown, 1992).

A number of investigations have found support for sociotropy and autonomy as vulnerability factors for depression. Morse and Robins (2005) investigated the role of sociotropy and autonomy in predicting depressive symptoms in a sample of remitted depressed older adults. These authors found strong support for the congruency hypothesis: increases in depressive symptoms were preceded by negative life events with themes, social or achievement, congruent with the individual's personality (i.e., high sociotropy or autonomy). The interaction between sociotropy or autonomy and concordant stressful life events has also been identified as a risk factor for relapse into depression (Segal, Shaw, Vella, & Katz, 1992). It has further been postulated that sociotropic and autonomous personality styles moderate the relationship between dysphoria and cognitive biases. For example, Dobson and colleagues (1998) used priming tasks designed to induce sociotropy and autonomy in individuals showing elevated baseline levels of these traits. They found that when dysphoric students were personally invested in the sociotropy and autonomy priming tasks, they were more likely to exhibit negative distortions. These findings indicate that negative biases are activated when a task challenges the core beliefs associated with an individual's dominant personality style.

In accordance with the congruency hypothesis, and given the hypothesized need of individuals high on sociotropy to preserve social bonds and foster approval, it is likely that individuals high on this trait may perceive fewer negative attitudes in others. In contrast, highly autonomous individuals may benefit from seeing negative attitudes in others, as the generalized other may be perceived as less of a potential threat to their personal success if they are regarded as inferior. Given these ideas, the purpose of the present investigation was to assess the association of personality style on dysphoric individuals' tendency to perceive similar negative attitudes in others. In accordance with Beck's cognitive model of depression (1967; Beck et al., 1979), it was hypothesized that dysphoria, regardless of personality style, would be positively associated with dysfunctional attitudes toward the self. Second, and consistent with Beck's (1983) conceptualization of sociotropy and autonomy, it was predicted that students exhibiting heightened dysphoria *and* sociotropy would be less likely to perceive the generalized other as possessing dysfunctional attitudes. Alternatively, it was predicted that individuals showing high dysphoria *and* autonomy would be more likely to perceive heightened dysfunctional attitudes in the generalized other. As such, personality style (e.g., sociotropy/autonomy) is predicted to moderate the relationship between dysphoria and perceived dysfunctional attitudes in the generalized other. That is, the interaction of personality and depressive symptoms is predicted to account for a significant portion of the variance beyond what is predicted by personality *and/or* dysphoria alone. To the authors' knowledge, there is no previous research that examines the link between the perceptions of attitudes in others and dimensions of personality related to dysphoria.

Research of this nature is important for both theoretical and practical reasons. First, if the hypotheses presented above are supported, then refinements to both the congruency hypothesis and false consensus bias model in depression are in order. Second, and given the social impact of depression, this study may be used to inform the design and tailoring of extant treatments for the disorder. For instance, if individuals high on autonomy are found to see negative attitudes in others more than their nonautonomous counterparts, then the psychoeducational and thought cognitive restructuring portion therapy may be fine-tuned to accommodate such findings.

Method

Participants

A total of 197 undergraduate students were recruited through the University of Calgary, Department of Psychology's Research Participant System. Participants were provided partial course credit for their participation. Following the consent process, participants completed a form to collect basic demographic variables (e.g., age, gender, academic major and year of study, religious affiliation, etc.). Descriptive statistics revealed that the sample consisted of approximately an equal

TABLE 1. Means and Standard Deviations for Demographic Variables

	M	SD
Age (years)	21.17	4.52
Education		
(years of postsecondary)	2.50	1.29
Gender		
% female	55.80%	n = 110

number of females (55.80%) and males (44.20%), was predominantly Caucasian (98.00%), and most students had completed less than two years of post-secondary education (52.80%). The combined mean age for the entire sample was 21.17 (*SD* = 4.52). A summary of pertinent demographic variables is displayed in Table 1.

Measures

The Center for Epidemiological Studies Depression Scale (CES–D; Radloff, 1977)

The CES-D is a 20-item self-report measure designed to assess current levels of depressive symptomatology in the general population. Participants indicate the extent to which they endorse statements such as "I felt depressed," "I talked less than usual," "I had trouble keeping my mind on what I was doing," and "I thought my life had been a failure" during the past week on a 4-point Likert scale from 0 (or "rarely or none of the time/less than once a day"), to 3 (or "most or all of the time/5–7 days"). Scores on this instrument range from 0–60 with higher scores indicating greater depressive symptomatology. The CES-D has been found to reliably assess symptoms of depression and can accurately discriminate between psychiatric and community samples (Radloff). The CES-D has demonstrated high internal consistency ($\alpha = .85$) and sound concurrent validity in the general population (e.g., C. E. Ross & Mirowsky, 1984). Further, the CES-D has demonstrated high internal consistency ($\alpha = .93$) among university samples (e.g., Devins et al., 1988), and adequate convergent validity (Radloff). In the current sample, the CES-D demonstrated excellent internal consistency ($\alpha = .91$).

Dysfunctional Attitudes Scale (DAS; Weissman & Beck, 1978)

The DAS consists of 40 depressive attitudes, such as "I cannot be happy unless most people I know admire me". Respondents indicate, on a 7-point Likert scale ranging from 1 "totally agree" to 7 "totally disagree," the degree to which they endorse each statement. Scores on this instrument range from 40–280, with higher scores indicating greater negative attitudes (after the reversal of negatively worded items). Cane, Olinger, Gotlib, and Kuiper (1986) conducted a factor analysis on the DAS using a student population and found a two–factor structure that explained 61% of the variance. These researchers labeled the factors Performance Evaluation and Approval by Others. The two–factor structure of the DAS has generally been accepted in the depression literature (Dozois, Covin, & Brinker, 2003), and closely resembles the sociotropy and autonomy constructs identified by Beck (1983).

The Dysfunctional Attitudes Scale (DAS) was used to create the Self-Other Dysfunctional Scenarios scale (SODS) in the present study. A number of items from the DAS with interpersonal (e.g., "If others dislike you, you cannot be happy."; "Being alone leads to unhappiness.") and academic/ vocational (e.g., "If I fail at my work, then I am a failure as a person."; "If I don't set the highest standards for myself, I am likely to end up a second-rate person.") themes were reworded to create 12 hypothetical scenarios. These 12 scenarios were subdivided into two six-scenario sets. The first set of six scenarios asked participants to imagine the situations as if they are occurring to themselves (SODS-SELF), whereas the second set of six scenarios asked participants to imagine the situations as if they are occurring to "the average university student" (SODS-OTHER). Consistent with the DAS, each of the two six-scenario sets can be further subdivided into two three-scenario segments dealing either with themes of interpersonal or vocational/academic failure.

After each scenario, participants were asked to indicate how much they agree, on a 7-point Likert scale (1 "totally agree" to 7 "totally disagree"), with two statements associated with the scenario. As such, there were two response items for each of the 12 scenarios for a total of 24 items and a range of scores from 24–168. With the reversal of negatively worded items, higher scores were indicative of a higher frequency of dysfunctional attitudes. For example, the second scenario, which was related to the theme of vocational failure, asked respondents to rate their attitudes toward the generalized other if they had experienced the following scenario:

> Situation 2: Imagine that you're walking to class. One of your classmates greets you and begins to express her reactions about her job. She tells you that she's absolutely terrible at what she does, and that she overheard her employer talking about her termination to another supervisor.
>
> How much do you agree (from 1–7) with the following statements *regarding the average university student* if they have experienced the same situation as the person above?
>
> - They are successful as human beings.
> - They will never be happy in their life.

The SODS-OTHER and SODS-SELF subscales demonstrated adequate to good internal consistency, with alpha coefficients of .83 and .79, respectively. Further, and as a partial test of the construct validity of the SODS, it was found that total scores on the SODS significantly and positively correlated with scores on the CES–D, $r = .32$, $p < .01$.

The Revised Sociotropy–Autonomy Scale (SAS-R; Clark & Beck, 1991)

The Sociotropy-Autonomy Scale (SAS; Beck, Epstein, Harrison, & Emery, 1983) is a 60-item self-report measure designed to assess two personality factors: sociotropy and autonomy. The SAS consists of two subscales, namely sociotropy and autonomy, and each are comprised of 30 items (e.g., "I am afraid of hurting other people's feelings"', and "It is more important to get a job done than to worry about other people's reactions", for sociotropy and autonomy, respectively). Both the sociotropy and autonomy scales demonstrate high internal consistency, with coefficients of 0.90 and 0.83, respectively (Beck et al., 1983). The SAS-R was created to improve the validity of the autonomy subscales of the SAS. Ten of the original items were removed, and 24 new items were added for a total of 74 items. The SAS-R has four factors: sociotropy, solitude/interpersonal insensitivity, independence, and individualistic achievement. The sociotropy subscale contains 28 items dealing with disapproval, pleasing others, and attachment issues. The other subscales were designed to approximate Beck's (1983) autonomy construct. The solitude/interpersonal insensitivity subscale consists of 16 items assessing preference for solitary activities, or an insensitivity to the needs and wishes of others. The third subscale, independence, includes 16 items measuring independent orientation. Last, the individualistic achievement subscale contains 14 items measuring goal obtainment and other achievement-related concerns.

The SAS-R demonstrates improved psychometric properties compared to the original SAS, and exhibited a stronger association with negative mood states (Clark & Beck, 1991). For this sample, the sociotropy scale demonstrated good internal validity with an alpha of .83. The solitude or interpersonal insensitivity, individualistic achievement, and independence subscales demonstrated adequate internal consistency with alphas of .71, .78, and .71, respectively. The individualistic achievement and independence subscales of the SAS-R were moderately correlated, indicating that they are tapping a similar construct (Clark & Beck, 1991). However, the solitude/interpersonal insensitivity subscale showed minimal correlation with the other two autonomy subscales, indicating that this scale may assess a separate personality construct. For this reason, it has been advised that the autonomy subscales be evaluated separately and not as a single autonomy score (Clark & Beck, 1991).

Procedure

Ethics approval was obtained from the University of Calgary Conjoint Faculties Research Ethics Board. After offering consent, all participants completed a battery of questionnaires including a demographic information form, the CES-D,

TABLE 2. Correlation Coefficients Among Dysphoria, Self-Referent Dysfunctional Attitudes, and Personality Orientation ($N = 197$)

Measure	CES–D	SODS-SELF	Sociotropy	Independence	Solitude
CES–D					
SODS-SELF	.38**				
Sociotropy	.20**	.47**			
Independence	.06	−.04	−.09		
Solitude	.21**	−.03	−.18*	.50**	
Achievement	−.18*	−.36**	−.41**	−.04	.03

Note. CES-D = Center for Epidemiologic Study Depression Scale; SODS-SELF = Self-Other Dysfunctional Scenarios Scale–Self Subscale.
* = Significant at the .05 level. ** = Significant at the .01 level.

the SAS-R, and the SODS. After completing the questionnaires, participants were debriefed and thanked for their participation.

Results

Preliminary Data Analyses

Before the analyses were conducted, the data were reviewed for completeness, and internal consistency coefficients were calculated for the CES-D, all four subscales of the SAS-R, and the SODS-SELF and SODS-OTHER subscales. An *a priori* alpha level of .05 was used to examine planned hypotheses.

Analyses followed several steps. First, a correlational analysis was conducted in order to calculate Pearson's correlation coefficients for the relationships between the various personality styles (as calculated by the four subscales of the SAS), dysphoria (CES-D), and dysfunctional self-referent attitudes (SODS-SELF). Second, a partial correlation analysis was conducted to tease apart the variance accounted for by personality in the relationship between dysfunctional self-referent attitudes and dysphoria. Last, and to test the predicted interaction between personality and dysphoria in predicting perceptions of dysfunctional attitudes in others, moderator analyses were conducted using depressive symptoms and personality as predictors of SODS-OTHER scores.

Relationships Between Dysphoria, Personality, and Self-Referent Attitudes

The mean score for all participants on the CES-D was 12.60 ($SD = 8.85$). As planned, a zero-order correlational analysis was conducted to measure the degree and direction of association between sociotropy, independence, solitude, achievement, dysphoria, and SODS-SELF scores (see Table 2). The analysis revealed a significant and positive relationship between CES-D and SODS-SELF scores,

$r = .38, p < .01$. Similarly, there was a significant and positive relationship between CES-D and sociotropy, and CES-D and solitude scores, $r = .20$ and $r = .21, p < .01$, respectively. There was a significant, negative relationship between CES-D and achievement scores, $r = -.18, p < .05$. Furthermore, there was a significant and positive relationship between SODS-SELF and sociotropy scores, $r = .47, p < .01$, whereas there was a significant and negative relationship between SODS-SELF and achievement scores, $r = -.36, p < .05$.

Significant correlations were found between scores on the various SAS–R subscales. For instance, sociotropy was significantly and negatively correlated with both solitude and achievement, $r = -.18, p < .05$, and $r = -.41, p < .01$, respectively. Last, the analysis revealed a significant, positive relationship between independence and solitude, $r = .5, p < .01$.

Given the results of the above analyses, wherein significant relationships were found between scores on the CES-D, SODS-SELF, and the subscales of the SAS-R, a partial correlation analysis was conducted to partial out the variance of personality in the relationship between CES-D and SODS-SELF. Specifically, this analysis partialled out the variances of sociotropy, solitude, and achievement to determine the strength of the relationship between dysphoria and self-referent negative attitudes. This analysis revealed that, even after removing the variance of sociotropy, solitude, and achievement, scores on the CES-D and SODS-SELF were still significantly and positively correlated, $r = .29, p < .01$.

Moderating Effect of Sociotropy, Achievement, Independence, and Solitude

To investigate whether the association between dysphoria and perceptions of attitudes of the generalized other depends on personality constructs, four moderator regression models were tested using hierarchical multiple regression analyses. That is, independent moderator regression models for sociotropy, achievement, independence, and solitude were tested. To increase the interpretability of the findings, all independent variables were mean-centered before analysis (Dalal & Zickar, 2012). Table 3 summarizes data obtained from the four hierarchical multiple regression analyses. In the first analysis, sociotropy and dysphoria were entered as Step 1, and the interaction term of sociotropy by dysphoria was then entered in the equation as Step 2. This pattern (i.e., personality subfactor and dysphoria scores entered as Step 1, and then interaction term of the personality subfactor $\times$ dysphoria as Step 2) was followed for the three subsequent hierarchical regression analyses. The first analysis revealed that the main effects of sociotropy and dysphoria (Step 1) predicted 1.7% of the variance in SODS-OTHER scores, $p > .05$. In Step 2, the interaction of sociotropy by dysphoria accounted for 3.5% of the variance, which represented a non-significant change in variance accounted for ($\Delta R^2 = .02, p > .05$).

Results from the second analysis revealed that the main effects of achievement and dysphoria (Step 1) accounted for 3% of the variance in SODS-OTHER scores, $p < .05$. The interaction of achievement by dysphoria entered in Step 2 accounted

TABLE 3. Summary of the Hierarchical Multiple Regression Analyses for the Interaction of Personality Subfactors and Dysphoria in Predicting Perceived Dysfunctional Attitudes in Other

Predictor	B	$SE\ B$	β	R	R^2	AdjR^2	ΔR^2	ΔF (df)
Sociotropy								
Step 1				.131	.017	.007	.017	1.702 (2, 194)
Sociotropy	−.001	.052	−.001					
Dysphoria	.148	.082	.132					
Step 2				.188	.035	.020	.018	3.636 (1, 193)
Sociotropy	−.005	.052	−.007					
Dysphoria	.171	.082	.152*					
Sociotropy × Dysphoria	−.001	.006	−.136					
Achievement								
Step 1				.174	.030	.020	.030	3.032 (2, 194)
Achievement	−.167	.103	−.116					
Dysphoria	.125	.081	.111					
Step 2				.268	.072	.057	.041	8.581** (1, 193)
Achievement	−.195	.102	−.135					
Dysphoria	.160	.080	.142*					
Achievement × Dysphoria	.034	.011	.207**					
Independence								
Step 1				.134	.018	.008	.018	1.776 (2, 194)
Independence	−.038	.100	−.027					
Dysphoria	.149	.080	.133					
Step 2				.268	.072	.057	.058	11.154** (1, 193)
Independence	.010	.098	.007					
Dysphoria	.161	.078	.143*					
Independence × Dysphoria	.038	.012	.234**					
Solitude								
Step 1				.168	.028	.018	.028	2.816 (2, 194)
Solitude	.139	.094	.107					
Dysphoria	.122	.081	.108					
Step 2				.261	.068	.054	.040	8.258** (1, 193)
Solitude	.166	.093	.128					
Dysphoria	.096	.080	.085					
Solitude × Dysphoria	.028	.010	.202**					

Note. * = Significant at the .05 level. ** = Significant at the .01 level.

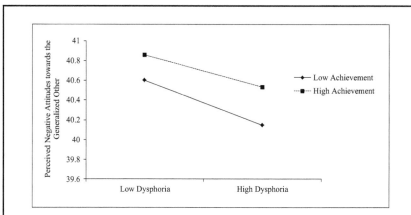

FIGURE 1. Effects of dysphoria by achievement levels on perceived negative attitudes toward the generalized other.

for a significant change in the variance accounted for ($\Delta R^2 = .04$, $p < .05$). The second model which incorporated the interaction term was significant, $F(3, 194) = 4.96$, $p < .01$ (see Figure 1).

Results from the third hierarchical regression analysis revealed that the main effects of independence and dysphoria (Step 1) accounted for 1.8% of the variance in SODS-OTHER scores, $p > .05$. When the interaction term of independence by dysphoria is introduced to the equation in Step 2, this accounted for a significant change in variance ($\Delta R^2 = .07$, $p < .05$). The second model in the equation which incorporated the interaction term was significant, $F(3, 194) = 4.96$, $p < .01$ (see Figure 2).

Last, results from the fourth hierarchical regression analysis revealed that the main effects of solitude and dysphoria together (Step 1) accounted for 2.8% of the variance in SODS-OTHER scores, $p > .05$. The interaction of solitude by dysphoria entered in Step 2 produced a significant change in variance accounted for in SODS-OTHER scores, $\Delta R^2 = .07$, $p < .05$. Further, the second model, which incorporated the interaction term, was significant, $F(3, 194) = 4.70$, $p < .01$ (see Figure 3).

Discussion

This study investigated the relationship between depressive symptoms and personality orientations in predicting dysfunctional attitudes. Specifically, the false consensus effect was examined in a university student sample. Consistent with a large body of empirical literature (see Clark, Beck, & Alford, 1999, for a review), and in support of our first hypothesis, it appears that depression symptoms were

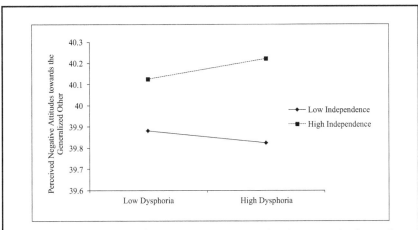

FIGURE 2. Effects of dysphoria by independence levels on perceived negative attitudes toward the generalized other.

significantly and positively correlated with dysfunctional self-referent attitudes. As such, individuals endorsing elevated depression symptoms were more likely to endorse more dysfunctional attitudes related to the self (or vice versa). The significance of this relationship between dysphoria and attitudes was maintained even after partialling out the variances accounted for by personality orientation. Second, no support was found for the hypothesis that individuals showing elevated

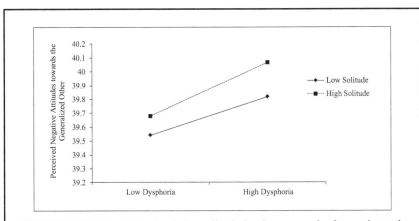

FIGURE 3. Effects of dysphoria by solitude levels on perceived negative attitudes toward the generalized other.

depression scores who also scored high on sociotropy view fewer negative attitudes harbored by the generalized other than dysphoric students low on sociotropy, as the interaction between sociotropy and dysphoria was nonsignificant. The hierarchical analysis revealed that the interaction of sociotropy by dysphoria scores was not able to predict a significant portion of the variance in perceived dysfunctional attitudes toward others over and above what is predicted by sociotropy and dysphoria as separate terms.

Last, and in support of the study predictions, students exhibiting elevated depressive symptoms who were also high on autonomy, as measured by the in-dependence, solitude, and individualistic achievement subscales on the SAS-R, were more likely to view negative attitudes exhibited by the generalized other than students high on depression and low on autonomy. The analysis conducted above revealed that the interaction of autonomy subfactors by dysphoria were able to account for a unique portion of variance in scores on the SODS-OTHER, over and above what can be predicted by the main effects of autonomy subfactors and dysphoria scores taken separately. The results of this study generally support the cognitive model of depression (Beck, 1967; Beck et al., 1979), as it posits that depressed individuals tend to harbor more dysfunctional attitudes about the self. These unrealistic if–then statements are seen to be the product of the individual's core beliefs or schemas. Students who reported elevated depression, as measured by the CES-D, also tended to report more negative attitudes toward the self. This result indicates that Beck's theory applies to dysphoric individuals independently of their dominant personality style.

The moderator analyses revealed that those who reported elevated auton-omy (in combination with elevated depressive symptoms) were more likely to report perceived dysfunctional attitudes in the generalized other. There are several possible explanations for this pattern of results. For example, differences in the experience and expression of depression between individuals high on sociotropy and those high on autonomy may moderate the relationship between dysphoria and the views of negative attitudes in others. More specifically, Robins, Hayes, Block, Kramer, and Villena (1995; Robins, Block, & Peselow, 1989) found sup-port for two distinct presentations of depression that may be accounted for by individual differences in sociotropy and autonomy. The researchers suggested that depressed individuals high on sociotropy evidence greater efforts to solicit help from others, and are more optimistic in regards to the positive outcomes that may result from their help-seeking. In contrast, individuals high on autonomy tend to participate in fewer help-seeking behaviors that involve others; fewer requests for help are likely the result of greater pessimism about the likelihood of the aid being beneficial (Robins et al., 1995).

It is conceivable then that differences in the experience of depression may in-fluence an individual's tendency to imagine that others will hold negative attitudes. For instance, Robins and colleagues' (1995) research suggests that individuals high on autonomy are more likely to view negative attitudes in others compared to individuals who have a high level of sociotropy, given that they are not personally invested in viewing others positively. Highly autonomous individuals are personally invested in maintaining control of their environment, and reliance on others would relinquish this control and ultimately threaten their independence. Furthermore, individuals who are high on autonomy are more often self-critical, and as a result of the false consensus effect may assume that other individuals are equally self-critical and rigid in their evaluations of themselves. Last, judging others as weaker may simultaneously contribute to the individual's perception of themselves as more successful than others, which ultimately contributes to their need for personal achievement.

Similarly, some research of the false consensus bias indicates that the strength and consistency of this bias depend on a number of moderators, one of which is personality (Marks & Miller, 1987). Depression has also been shown to moderate the effects of this bias in previous research (Lobitz & Post, 1979; Tabachnik, Crocker, & Alloy, 1983). To date, there have been no studies that look at both depression and personality conjointly in the moderation of the false consensus effect. The results of the present study revealed that dysphoric individuals may only exhibit the false consensus bias regarding perceptions of attitudes in others when they are high on autonomy.

As there is relatively little research on the predictors of how individuals view negative attitudes in others, the novel results of this experiment represent a significant addition to the literature. The analyses showed that the interaction between dysphoria and facets of autonomy are significant predictors of individuals' tendency to view negative attitudes in others. This finding is in line with previous research that has found that depressed or dysphoric individuals report more dysfunctional attitudes relative to their nondepressed counterparts (Beshai et al., 2012; Dobson et al., 1998; Blatt et al., 1982). These results are further consistent with those found by L. Ross and colleagues (1977), Krueger and Clement (1994) and Kuiper and MacDonald (1983), which support the validity of the false consensus bias. Specifically, our results suggest that dysphoric individuals high on autonomy may primarily rely on their own experiences, attitudes, and beliefs when asked to judge whether other individuals hold similar maladaptive attitudes. Greater reliance on their personal attitudes may then serve as the impetus to view others as holding equally negative views of the self.

This study is the first to examine the relationship among dysphoria, autonomy, and the false consensus bias in regards to perceptions of negative attitudes in others. While there is strong support for the role of sociotropy in dysphoria the literature is more inconsistent in regards to the role of autonomy. However, the present results suggest that dysphoria and autonomy can interact to change the social experience of depression, as evidenced by the frequency of negative attitudes perceived in others. A notable strength of the present study is its use of the CES-D, rather than the BDI, in the assessment of depression symptoms. Sato and McCann (2000) contend that the BDI's items better represent sociotropy than autonomy. In fact, these researchers suggested investigations examining the association between depression and the personality styles should employ depression measures other than the BDI to address the potential limitations evident in previous studies. Despite the strengths of the current study, several limitations warrant consideration. First, the study's sample was solely comprised of undergraduate students. The demographic profile of the sample was relatively homogenous, as the large majority of participants were Caucasian. However, the experience and presentation of depression varies as a function of culture (e.g., Parker, Cheah, & Roy, 2001). Therefore, the findings in this study may not generalize to culturally diverse populations. Last, and although we have centered the target variables in this study, centering alone may not be sufficient to reduce the threat of multicollinearity (Dalal & Zickar, 2012), and as such the results should be interpreted with caution.

Future research that replicates this study in a sample of clinically depressed participants is needed. A longitudinal study that investigates the predictive power of dysphoria and personality styles on dysfunctional attitudes toward others would elucidate the nature and direction of the relationship among these variables. Specifically, this investigation could ascertain whether dysphoria functions as a risk factor for dysfunctional attitudes, or if dysfunctional attitudes are correlates of depression.

The results of the current study suggest that there is a considerable amount of variation in the extent to which negative attitudes are seen in others, which is not accounted for by the interaction between dysphoria and autonomy or sociotropy. An evaluation of these factors in concert with known risk factors for depression would provide a more comprehensive demonstration of dysphoria, autonomy, and sociotropy as predictors of dysfunctional attitudes seen in others. Last, as the current study suggests that the construct validity of the solitude subscale is questionable, future research is needed to refine the SAS-R, to generate stronger psychometric properties. Whereas the majority of the analyses that involved the solitude subscale produced null findings, analyses of the other two autonomy subscales were significant. This pattern of results supports Clark and Beck's (1991) assertion that the convergent validity of the three autonomy subscales is poor, and likely primarily due to the solitude subscale.

In conclusion, this study investigated the relationship among dysphoria, personality styles, and negative distortions as evidenced by negative attitudes about the self and negative attitudes perceived in others. The findings augment evidence for Beck's cognitive theory. The perception that others hold negative attitudes regarding themselves was stronger for highly autonomous and dysphoric individuals relative to highly sociotropic and dysphoric individuals. While these findings need to be replicated, the present study provides novel insights into the relationship between personality styles and maladaptive attitudes in dysphoria.

REFERENCES

Beck, A. T. (1967). *Depression: Causes and treatment.* Philadelphia, PA: University of Pennsylvania Press.

Beck, A. T. (1983). Cognitive therapy of depression: New perspectives. In P. J. Clayton & J. E. Barrett (Eds.), *Treatment of Depression: Old Controversies and New Approaches* (pp. 265–290). New York, NY: Raven.

Beck, A. T. (2005). The current state of cognitive therapy: A 40–year retrospective. *Archives of General Psychiatry, 62*(9), 953–959. doi: 10.1001/archpsyc.62.9.953

Beck, A. T., Epstein, N., Harrison, R. P., & Emery, G. (1983). *Development of the Sociotropy–Autonomy Scale: A measure of personality factors in psychopathology.* (Unpublished manuscript). Philadelphia: Center for Cognitive Therapy, University of Pennsylvania Medical School.

Beck, A. T., Rush, A. J., Shaw, B. F., & Emery, G. (1979). *Cognitive Therapy of Depression.* New York, NY: Guilford Press.

Beshai, S., Dobson, K. S, & Adel, A. (2012). Cognition and Dysphoria in Egypt and Canada: An Examination of the Cognitive Triad. *Canadian Journal of Behavioural Science, 44*(1), 29–39. doi: 10.1037/a0025744

Blatt, S. J., Quinlan, D. M., Chevron, E. S., McDonald, C., & Zuroff, D. (1982). Dependency and self-criticism: Psychological dimensions of depression. *Journal of Consulting and Clinical Psychology, 50*(1), 113–124. doi: 10.1037/0022-006X.50.1.113

Cane, D. B., Olinger, L. J., Gotlib, I. H., & Kuiper, N. A. (1986). Factor structure of the Dysfunctional Attitude Scale in a student population. *Journal of Clinical Psychology, 42*, 307–309.

Clark, D. A., & Beck, A. T. (1991). Personality factors in dysphoria: A psychometric refinement of Beck's Sociotropy–Autonomy Scale. *Journal of Psychopathology and Behavioral Assessment, 13*(4), 369–388.

Clark, D., Beck, A. T., & Alford, B. A. (1999). *Scientific foundations of cognitive theory and therapy of depression.* New York: John Wiley.

Clark, D. A., Beck, A. T., & Brown, G. K. (1992). Sociotropy, Autonomy, and life event perceptions in dysphoric and nondysphoric individuals. *Cognitive Therapy and Research, 16*(6), 635–652. doi: 10.1007/BF01175404

Coyne, J. C., & Whiffen, V. E. (1995). Issues in personality as diathesis for depression: The case of sociotropy–dependency and autonomy–self-criticism. *Psychological Bulletin, 118*(3), 358–378. doi: 10.1037//0033-2909.118.3.358

Crandell, C. J., & Chambless, D. L. (1986). The validation of an inventory for measuring depressive thoughts: The Crandell Cognitions Inventory. *Behaviour Research and Therapy*, *24*, 403–411.

Dalal, D. K., & Zickar, M. J. (2012). Some common myths about centering predictor variables in moderated multiple regression and polynomial regression. *Organizational Research Methods*, *15*, 339–362.

Devins, G. M., Orme, C. M., Costello, C. G., Binik, Y. M., Frizzell, B., Stam, H. J., & Pullin, W. M. (1988). Measuring depressive symptoms in illness populations: Psychometric properties of the Center for Epidemiologic Studies Depression (CES–D) scale. *Psychology & Health*, *2*, 139–156.

Dobson, K. S., & Dozois, D. J. A. (2008). Introduction: Assessing risk and resilience factors in models of depression. In K. S. Dobson & D. A. Dozois (Eds.), *Risk factors in depression* (pp. 1–16). San Diego, CA: Academic Press. doi:10.1016/B978-0-08-045078-0.00001-0

Dobson, K. S., Pusch, D., Ardo, K., & Murphy, T. (1998). The relationships between sociotropic and autonomous personality styles and depressive realism in dysphoric and nondysphoric university students. *Canadian Journal of Behavioural Science/Revue Canadienne Des Sciences Du Comportement*, *30*(4), 253–265. doi: 10.1037/h0087068

Dobson, K. S., & Shaw, B. F. (1986). Cognitive assessment with major depressive disorders. *Cognitive Therapy and Research*, *10*, 13–29.

Dozois, D. J. A., & Beck, A. T. (2008). Cognitive schemas, beliefs and assumptions. In K. S. Dobson & D. A. Dozois (Eds.), *Risk factors in depression* (pp. 121–143). San Diego, CA: Academic Press. doi: 10.1016/B978-0-08-045078-0.00006-X

Dozois, D. J. A., Covin, R., & Brinker, J. K. (2003). Normative data on cognitive measures of depression. *Journal of Consulting and Clinical Psychology*, *71*, 71–80.

Garber, J., Weiss, B., & Shanley, N. (1993). Cognitions, depressive symptoms, and development in adolescents. *Journal of Abnormal Psychology*, *102*(1), 47–57. doi: 10.1037//0021–843X.102.1.47

Goldberg, J. F., Gerstein, R. K., Wenze, S. J., Welker, T. M., & Beck, A. T. (2008). Dysfunctional attitudes and cognitive schemas in Bipolar manic and unipolar depressed outpatients: Implications for cognitively based psychotherapeutics. *Journal of Nervous & Mental Disease*, *196*(3), 207–210.

Haaga, D. A., Dyck, M. J., & Ernst, D. (1991). Empirical status of cognitive theory of depression. *Psychological Bulletin*, *110*(2), 215–236. doi: 10.1037//0033-2909.110.2.215

Haynes, S. N., Smith, G., & Hunsley, J. (2011). *Scientific foundations of clinical assessment*. New York, NY: Routledge.

Kessler, R. C., Berglund, P., Demler, O., Jin, R., Koretz, D., Merikangas, K. R., ... Wang, P. S. (2003). The epidemiology of major depressive disorder: Results from the National Comorbidity Survey Replication (NCS-R). *JAMA: The Journal of the American Medical Association*, *289*(23), 3095–3105. doi: 10.1001/jama.289.23.3095

Kessler, R. C., Chiu, W. T., Demler, O., & Walters, E. E. (2005). Prevalence, severity, and comorbidity of 12–Month DSM-IV disorders in the National Comorbidity Survey Replication. *Archives of General Psychiatry*, *62*(6), 617–627. doi: 10.1001/archpsyc.62.6.617

Krueger, J., & Clement, R. W. (1994). The truly false consensus effect: An ineradicable and egocentric bias in social perception. *Journal of Personality and Social Psychology*, *67*(4), 596–610. doi: 10.1037//0022-3514.67.4.596

Kuiper, N. A., & MacDonald, M. R. (1983). Schematic processing in depression: The self-based consensus bias. *Cognitive Therapy and Research*, *7*(6), 469–484. doi: 10.1007/BF01172886

Lobitz, W. C., & Post, R. D. (1979). Parameters of self-reinforcement and depression. *Journal of Abnormal Psychology, 88*(1), 33–41. doi: 10.1037/0021-843X.88.1.33

Marks, G., & Miller, N. (1987). Ten years of research on the false consensus effect: An empirical and theoretical review. *Psychological Bulletin, 102,* 72–90.

Morse, J., & Robins, C. (2005). Personality life event congruence effects in late–life depression. *Journal of Affective Disorders, 84*(1), 25–31. doi: 10.1016/j.jad.2004.09.007

Parker, G., Cheah, Y., & Roy, K. (2001). Do the Chinese somatize depression? A cross–cultural study. *Social Psychiatry and Psychiatric Epidemiology, 36*(6), 287–293. doi: 10.1007/s001270170046

Radloff, L. S. (1977). The CES-D scale: A self-report depression scale for research in the general population. *Applied Psychological Measurement, 1*(3), 385–401.

Robins, C. J., Block, P., & Peselow, E. D. (1989). Relations of sociotropic and autonomous personality characteristics to specific symptoms in depressed patients. *Journal of Abnormal Psychology, 98*(1), 86–88. doi: 10.1037//0021-843X.98.1.86

Robins, C. J., Hayes, A. M., Block, P., Kramer, R. J., & Villena, M. (1995). Interpersonal and achievement concerns and the depressive vulnerability and symptom specificity hypotheses: A prospective study. *Cognitive Therapy and Research, 19*(1), 1–20. doi: 10.1007/BF02229673

Ross, C. E., & Mirowsky, J. (1984). Components of depressed mood in married men and women. *American Journal of Epidemiology, 119*(6), 997–1004.

Ross, L., Greene, D., & House, P. (1977). The "false consensus effect": An egocentric bias in social perception and attribution processes. *Journal of Experimental Social Psychology, 13*(3), 279–301. doi: 10.1016/0022-1031(77)90049-X

Sato, T., & McCann, D. (2000). Sociotropy–Autonomy and the Beck Depression Inventory. *European Journal of Psychological Assessment, 16*(1), 66–76. doi: 10.1027//1015-5759.16.1.66

Segal, Z. V., Shaw, B. F., Vella, D. D., & Katz, R. (1992). Cognitive and life stress predictors of relapse in remitted unipolar depressed patients: Test of the congruency hypothesis. *Journal of Abnormal Psychology, 101*(1), 26–36. doi: 10.1037//0021-843X.101.1.26

Simon, G., Goldberg, D., Von Korff, M., & Üstün, T. (2002). Understanding cross–national differences in depression prevalence. *Psychological Medicine, 32*(04). doi: 10.1017/S0033291702005457

Stephens, T., & Joubert, N. (2001). The economic burden of mental health problems in Canada. *Chronic Diseases in Canada, 22,* 18–23.

Tabachnik, N., Crocker, J., & Alloy, L. B. (1983). Depression, social comparison, and the false– consensus effect. *Journal of Personality and Social Psychology, 45,*688–699.

Weissman, A. N. & Beck, A. T. (1978). Development and validation of the Dysfunctional Attitudes Scale: A preliminary investigation. In *Proceedings of the meeting of the American Educational Research Association,* Toronto, ON.

Hope, Anger, and Depression as Mediators for Forgiveness and Social Behavior in Turkish Children

EBRU TAYSI

FERZAN CURUN

FATIH ORCAN

ABSTRACT. This study examined the mediating effects of hope, anger, and depression in the associations between forgiveness and social behavior, in fourth grade students in Turkey. The 352 fourth grade primary school students were involved in the study. The average age was 9.98 and 56.3% were boys. The Enright Forgiveness Inventory for Children (EFI-C), the Beck Anger Inventory for Youth (BANI-Y), the Children Hope Scale (CHS), the Social Behavior Questionnaire (SBQ), and the Children's Depression Inventory (CDI) were used. Results showed that depression mediates the relationship between anger and antisocial behavior and between hope and antisocial behavior. Anger mediates the relationship between hope and depression and between hope and antisocial behavior. Forgiveness was related to anger and hope directly. Implications of this study for child counseling were discussed.

FORGIVENESS IS IMPORTANT FOR THE WELL-BEING of human relations. It is known that forgiveness contribute to adult's physical, mental, and social well-being (Worthington, Berry, & Parrott, 2001). Although there are different definitions of forgiveness, there is an agreement about what forgiveness is among most researches (Wade & Worthington, 2005). According to this common definition, forgiveness involves abandoning negative feelings like anger and these negative emotions being replaced with positive ones such as compassion and love (Holter, Magnuson, Knutson, Knutson-Enright, & Enright, 2008). Forgiveness is explained as a moral virtue and offered unconditionally to the offender who caused the unfair hurt (Enright, 2011).

Enright, Santos, and Al-Mabuk (1989), from a cognitive developmental process, conceptualized forgiveness in the context of age and justice. Their investigation showed that as cognitive abilities increase with age, children develop more abstract thinking regarding forgiveness; different from adolescence, younger children experience forgiveness in order to avoid punishment, gain rewards, and look for approval. Other research revealed that for many children, an apology is the core element for forgiving a wrongdoer (Darby & Schlenker, 1982; Neal, Bassett, & Denham, 2004).

As forgiveness seems important for adult psychology, it may serve as a pathway toward wellbeing in children as well. For that reason, although research has paid much attention to interpersonal forgiveness among adults (e.g., Enright & Fitzgibbons, 2000; McCullough, Pargament, & Thoresen, 2000), an increasing number of studies provide exciting insights into the benefits of forgiveness among children (e.g., Enright & Fitzgibbons; Hui & Chau, 2009). Studies examining forgiveness showed that forgiveness is positively related with hope, and negatively associated with anger and depression among children (Enright & Coyle, 1998; Gassin, 1995). While previous studies have shown the relationships between forgiveness with these variables, there has been no study showing the indirect links among them in children. The purpose of this study is to examine the direct and indirect links between forgiveness and social behavior via hope, anger, and depression among fourth grade students in Turkey. Although Turkish culture involves both patterns of individualism and collectivism (Cukur, de Guzman, & Carlo, 2004), primary and middle school children has collectivist values (Kumru, Carlo, & Edwards, 2004) which emphasize social harmony (Hook, Worthington, & Utsey, 2009). It is expected in this study that children may highly value forgiveness as a relationship repair strategy.

Forgiveness and Hope

Snyder's theory of hope (Snyder, Irving, & Anderson, 1991) defines hope as the perceived ability to effectively create pathways to a goal and effectively implement those pathways to the goals. Specifically, this definition includes three components: goals, pathway thinking, and agency thinking. The first component is clearly operationalized goals, and Snyder (2002) proposes two major types of goals: positive goal outcomes and negative goal outcomes. The second component, pathway thinking, reflects one's ability to formulate routes to reach one's goals. The final component is the motivational one, agency thinking. Agency is the belief that one can use pathways to reach desired goals. High hopers perceive barriers as a challenge so they experience positive emotions. However, low hopers become stuck when faced with barriers, and will experience negative emotions, like depression, rumination, and anger (Snyder et al., 2000; Snyder, 2002; Gilman & Dooley, 2006).

Sandage, Worthington, and Calvert-Minor (2000) has demonstrated two common important components of the definitions of forgiveness and hope proposed by Enright and the Human Development Study Group (1996) and Snyder et al. (1991). The two components that forgiveness and hope have in common are agency and pathways. That is, both forgiveness and hope include beliefs to reach a goal and the ability to initiate and maintain the movement to reach that goal. Reconciliation is the common willpower or agency that links forgiveness and hope. As a highly effective relationship maintenance and repair strategy (Allemand, Amberg, Zimprich, & Fincham, 2007), forgiveness may offer the most direct pathway reaching the goal of reconcile with the offender (Toussaint, Williams, Musick, & Everson-Rose, 2008). As peer relationships are at the core of childhood interactions (Grifford-Smith & Brownell, 2003) forgiveness can be a most appropriate pathway as a conflict resolution (Denham, Neal, Wilson, Pickering, & Boyatzis, 2005) for maintaining peer relationships.

Another explanation of this positive relationship between forgiveness and hope might lay in their buffering effect from rumination and depression. According to Worthington's (2006) biopsychosocial stress and coping theory of forgiveness, the inadequacy in forgiving the other or oneself might lead anger or revenge rumination which can lead depression. Geiger and Kwon (2010) demonstrated that high hope served as a buffer against the depressive effects of rumination by providing a plan to overcome the stress. Moreover, Thompson et al. (2005) demonstrated that forgiveness is negatively correlated with rumination.

Research on forgiveness in children has examined changes in levels of forgiveness and hope through interventions (Hui & Ho, 2004; Freedman & Knupp, 2003; Luskin, Ginzburg, & Thoresen, 2005). Hui and Ho's (2004) research with adolescence aged 16 found no significant differences between experiment and control group in hope but Hui and Chau's (2009) research with children aged 11–12 obtained a significant increase in hope but only in post test one. The link between forgiveness and hope is not entirely well known yet in children. The present study was designed to answer the question firstly whether forgiveness predict hope in fourth grade students.

Forgiveness, Anger, Depression, and Social Behavior

Applying Worthington's (2006) coping theory of forgiveness to children, hurtful events experienced in close relationships are potential stressors and to forgive the offender is an appropriate coping strategy. But if unforgiveness occurs, anger may arise which is an inadequate coping strategy. Additionally, anger could lead to hostility and violent behavior. When rumination occurs regarding a hurtful event, it may generate negative emotions such as depression. With ongoing assaults with anger in other hurtful events, social interactions can be damaged. Eventually, Worthington's (2006) theory focuses on the consequences of "to forgive" and "not to forgive." Forgiveness can offer many benefits such as positive emotions and positive peer interactions.

Some research shows forgiveness will reduce anger and that a decrease in anger causes less depression and more social behavior (Gassin, Enright, & Knutson, 2005; Worthington & Wade, 1999). Moreover, depression symptoms have been shown to occur with antisocial behaviors (Miller-Johnson, Lochman, Coie, Terry, & Hyman 1998). In addition, research has demonstrated that forgiveness generally fosters prosocial behaviors toward the transgressor (Karremans & Van Lange, 2004). Prosocial behavior leads to different types of desirable traits involving positive relationships and communications with peers (Eisenberg & Fabes, 1998).

Hope, Depression, Anger, and Social Behavior

Snyder, Lapointe, Crowson, and Early (1998) proposed that when people encounter continued blockages to their important goals they feel despair and give up these goals, which is similar to depression-related thinking. Recent research has provided adequate evidence that lower hope is associated with greater depressive symptoms in children (Asarnow & Bates, 1988; Kazdin, French, Unis, Esveldt-Dawson, & Sherick, 1983) and depression increased antisocial behavior (Ritakallio et al., 2008), which is expected in the present study as well.

Another negative emotion, anger, can arise in the absence of hope. Although, to the authors' knowledge, not much research has been performed investigating the link between anger and hope, a possible explanation can be speculated involving the frustration–aggression hypothesis as Snyder (1994) proposed. As the basic assumption of the theory proposes, an impediment to goal attainment is likely to arouse anger (Dollard, Doob, Miller, Mowrer, & Sears, 1939). Thus, it is possible to speculate that high hopers and low hopers will differ in experiencing anger when faced with obstacles during goal attainment. As previously mentioned, as high-hopers perceive barriers as a challenge and manage to find alternative routes, they might experience less anger, which might turn to prosocial behavior; whereas, as low hopers become stuck when confronting barriers, they might feel more frustrated, which might lead them to feel anger.

These explanations might be applied to children, which is the focus of the present study. Children who encounter stressful situations need to concentrate on new goals and create alternative pathways to handle the problem (Snyder et al., 1997). This successful accomplishment of goals in the face of obstacles causes positive emotions (Snyder, 1994). Additionally, it is theorized that negative emotions, such as anger or depression, follow unsuccessful goal pursuits in children (Snyder et al., 1997).

Hypothesis

To date, no study has examined the extent to which forgiveness and hope predict negative effects and social behaviors in children. Consistent with the empirical

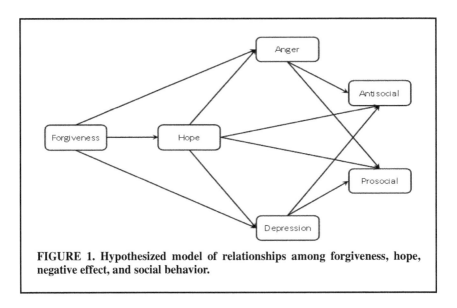

FIGURE 1. Hypothesized model of relationships among forgiveness, hope, negative effect, and social behavior.

studies previously described, we hypothesized that the associations among forgiveness, hope, anger, depression, and social behavior in children could be conceptualized in a model as shown in Figure 1. Although empirical evidences provided for the relationships between these variables (e.g., forgiveness and anger; hope and depression; forgiveness and social behavior), no research has investigated the relationships between forgiveness and social behavior in the light of the impact of hope, anger, and depression in children. The forgiveness–anger–depression–social behavior link has been shown by other studies (e.g., Gassin et al., 2005; Worthington & Wade, 1999). This study, however, is the first to include hope as a mediator in this sequence. The model supposes that a high level of forgiveness and hope will promote prosocial behavior both directly and indirectly through the mediation of less anger and less depression in children.

Method

Participants

The participants were 352 Turkish children (151 girls, 201 boys; *Mage* = 9.98 years, *SD* = 0.14, age range 9–11 years) in the fourth grade. Participants were recruited from among students of different public schools. The sample design was based on a selection of schools in Isparta city in Turkey that represented different socioeconomic levels. In total, eight schools took part in the study. A convenience method was used. Data were completed by the fourth graders in all eight schools. The students were identified from school registers. The students absent from school on the survey day were given the opportunity to participate on the next day. All participants were Turkish-speaking and of Turkish nationality.

Procedure

The children were given the questionnaires individually by one of two assistants educated in the process of testing within the school settings. Questions were read orally to the participants. The interview took nearly 30 minutes. Children voluntarily participated and were informed that there were no good and bad answers. In order to avoid sequencing effects, the measures included in the battery were counterbalanced, resulting in three different sequences of forms. The Enright Forgiveness Inventory for Children (EFI-C), the Children's Hope Scale (CHS), the Beck Anger Inventory for Youth (BANI-Y), the Social Behavior Questionnaire (SBQ), and Children's Depression Inventory (CDI) were administered during the study.

Instruments

The Enright Forgiveness Inventory for Children (EFI-C)

The EFI-C is a version of the Enright Forgiveness Inventory (Enright, 2005) administered to measure forgiveness. The measure consists of 30 items, ranging from 30 to 120. Children define an event in which they were unfairly hurt by a person and give answers concerning their emotional, cognitive, and behavioral responses to the transgressor. Responses to the questions are scored on a 4-point Likert scale: (1) *Yes*, (2) *A little bit yes*, (3) *A little bit no*, and (4) *No*. A high score represents high forgiveness. The measure contains 15 positive items ("Would you be a friend of him or her," "I feel happy toward him") and 15 negative items ("I feel upset toward him," "Do you think [name] is not nice"). Cronbach's alpha coefficient indicates .94 (Enright, Knutson Enright, Holter, Baskin, & Knutson, 2007). Internal consistency with the present sample was good with a Cronbach alpha of .91. The scale was translated into Turkish and back-translated by two bilinguals (Brislin, 1986). Confirmatory factor analysis was conducted and one factor structure was confirmed.

The Children's Hope Scale (CHS)

The CHS was developed by Snyder et al. (1997) and consists of six items including children's agency and pathways. Three items of the scale represent agency thinking (e.g., "I think the things I have done in the past will help me in the future," "I think I am doing pretty well"), and three reflect pathway thinking (e.g., "When I have a problem, I can come up with lots of ways to solve it," "I can think of many ways to get the things in life that are most important to me"). The CHS items are rated using a Likert-type format from 1 (*none of the time*) to 6 (*all of the time*). The score ranges from 6 to 36. A higher score indicates a higher level of hope. The original scale has a median Cronbach alpha of .77 and a one month test-retest correlation of .71. The CHS has been introduced and validated for use with children aged 7 to 14. The scale was adapted into Turkish by Atik and Kemer (2009). Findings regarding the construct validity of the scale are consistent with the original scale's two-factor structure. For the Turkish version, the Cronbach alpha coefficient for the overall scale was .74. Internal consistency with the present sample was good with a Cronbach alpha of .71.

The Beck Anger Inventory for Youth (BANI-Y)

The BANI-Y (Beck, Beck, & Jolly, 2001) intends to measure child anger affect and cognitions. The BANI-Y contains 20 questions which are scored using a 0 *(never)* to 3 *(always)* scale. Children and adolescents describe how frequently the statement has been true for them during the past two weeks, including today. Scale items are: "I think people try to cheat me," "People make me mad," "I think people bother me." The BANI-Y has been developed for use with children and adolescents aged between seven and 14 years. The inventories can be administered individually or in a group. The Cronbach alpha of internal consistency is stated as .91 in the manual. The Cronbach alpha for this sample was .83. Parallel back translation procedure (Brislin, 1986) was used for this scale. Confirmatory factor analysis was conducted and one factor structure was confirmed.

The Social Behavior Questionnaire (SBQ)

This questionnaire was developed by Warden and Mackinnon (2003) to reflect the definition of prosocial and antisocial child behaviors developed by Warden and Christie (1997). The SBQ comprises 12 items including prosocial behaviors (four items) ("Offered to share your things with another child"), relational antisocial (four items) ("Tried to stop your friends being friends with another child you didn't like"), and physical antisocial (four items) ("Broken or damaged another child's things, meaning to upset them") behaviors. The SBQ is administered to children aged between nine and ten years. Each item represents a specific and typical example of a child's experience. Each item is rated using a Likert-type format from 1 *(something you never do)* to 5 *(something you always do)*. In the present study, relational antisocial and physical antisocial subscales were included as one factor named as antisocial subscale. Parallel back translation procedure (Brislin, 1986) was used for this scale. The Cronbach alpha reliability coefficient for each of the three subscales is .80 or above. In this study, the Cronbach alpha of internal consistency for prosocial and antisocial subscales were .71 and .70 respectively. Confirmatory factor analysis was conducted and three-factor structure was confirmed.

The Children's Depression Inventory (CDI)

The Children's Depression Inventory was developed by Kovacs (1992) for children and adolescents aged six to 17 years. The scale adapted into Turkish by Oy (1991). The CDI has 27 items evaluating cognitive, affective, and behavioral symptoms of depression in youths. Scale items include: Each item is scored on a 3-point Likert scale: 0 (*never*) to 2 (*always*). Row scores converted to T-scores and the total depression score is obtained from summing each score. The Cronbach alpha of internal consistency is .88. Internal consistency in the present sample was good with a Cronbach alpha of .77.

Results

Data analyses were conducted using Mplus 5.1 (Muthén & Muthén, 2008). The hypothesized model was updated to obtain the final model and is shown in Figure 1. The hypothesized model was run first; however, there were some parameter estimates that were nonsignificant, which were subsequently removed from the model. Then, due to a lack of model-data fit, meaningful parameters were added to the modified hypothesized model, as suggested by the modification indices of Mplus 5.1. Subsequently, the final model was reached, as shown in Figure 2.

Descriptive Statistics and Correlations

Table 1 summarizes the descriptive statistics for the items. For example, the mean of the independent variable forgiveness was 10.74 with a standard deviation of 19.06. Table 2 indicates the inter-correlations among the variables. Some of the items significantly correlate with each other while others do not. For example, forgiveness significantly correlated with anger, hope, depression, and

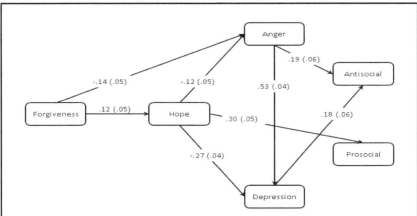

FIGURE 2. Model of obtained relationships (in standardized values) among forgiveness, hope, negative effect, and social behavior. All the paths were significant at .05 alpha level (i.e., smaller than .05).

TABLE 1. Means and Standard Deviations for Forgiveness, Anger, Hope, Depression, and Social Behavior (Prosocial and Antisocial)

	Minimum	Maximum	Mean	Standard Deviation
Forgiveness	24	96	10.74	19.06
Anger	0	51	14.39	8.51
Hope	9	36	26.49	5.38
Depression	0	31	11.20	6.27
Prosocial	6	20	16.53	2.70
Antisocial	8	23	9.78	2.43

antisocial behavior. The values of the correlations were −.115, .125, −.117, and −.134, respectively.

Modeling Strategy

The model-data fit indices indicated good results for the final model. The model chi-square value is 12.41 with degrees of freedom of 7 (p-value = .088). The p-value of the model was .088, not significant at a .05 alpha-level. That is, the chi-square value supported the final model. The value of the comparative fit index (CFI) was .979, which indicated good model-data fit, based on Hu and Bentler's (1999) cut off criteria. Hu and Bentler's recommendation for cut-off points are as follow: The root mean square error of approximation (RMSEA) shows a good fit for lower than .06, the comparative fit index (CFI) values are greater than .95 (or .90), the standardized root mean square residual (SRMR) is lower than .08 (or .06). Based on Hu and Bentler, the present research's RMSEA and SRMR indicated a good model-data fit with values of .047 and .032, respectively.

TABLE 2. Correlations Among Forgiveness, Anger, Hope, Depression, and Social Behavior (Prosocial and Antisocial)

	Forgiveness	Anger	Hope	Depression	Prosocial	Antisocial
Forgiveness	1.000					
Anger	−.155**	1.00				
Hope	.125*	−.145**	1.00			
Depression	−.117*	.565**	−.340**	1.000		
Prosocial	−.020	.060	.295**	−.098	1.000	
Antisocial	−.134*	.298**	−.145**	.296**	−.086	−.323**

*$p \leq .05$. **$p \leq .01$.

TABLE 3. Significant Standardized Indirect Effects for the Mediations

Indirect Effects	Value
Anger → Depression → Antisocial	.10(.03)*
Hope → Depression → Antisocial	−.05(.02)*
Hope → Anger → Depression	−.06(.03)*

*$p \leq .05$.

All the direct effects included in the model (as shown in Figure 2) were significant. The values of the standardized direct effects are presented in Figure 2. For example, there was a significant direct effect from *forgiveness* to *hope* with a size of .12, with a standard error of the estimate.05. In addition, there were some negative direct effects among some of the variables, as can be seen in Figure 2. For example, the direct effect from *hope* to *depression* was −.27, with a standard error of .04. Although a significant direct effect between *forgiveness* and *depression* was hypothesized, the independent variable (i.e., *forgiveness*) was not significantly related to *depression*, but is significantly related to *hope* and *anger*. This suggests that a one unit increase in *forgiveness* is related to .12 unit increases in *hope* and .14 decreases in *anger*.

One aim of the current study was to estimate the significant mediator effect among any of the data variables. The Mplus *Model Indirect* function was used to estimate significant indirect effects. The indirect function is simply multiplication of associated direct effects, while the standard error was calculated based on Delta method (see Mplus User's Guide for more information). The model exposed three significant indirect effects, as shown in Table 3. The values of the indirect effects were relatively small compared to the direct effects in the model; however, all the indirect effects as reported in Table 3 were significant at a .05 error rate.

Discussion

This research, examined the potential mediators (hope, anger, and depression) between forgiveness and social behavior. Although the associations regarding forgiveness were not confirmed, some expected mediations were confirmed. Depression mediated anger and antisocial behavior and hope and antisocial behavior. Anger mediated the relationship between hope and depression and hope and antisocial behavior. The mediating role of depression between anger and antisocial behavior partially supports Worthington's (2006) biopsychosocial stress and coping theory of forgiveness in fourth grade children. The present study showed that without the effect of unforgiveness, anger caused depression and antisocial behavior. After a hurtful event, anger occurred first, depression and antisocial behavior followed, respectively. Additionally, forgiveness and anger showed a negative correlation which was consistent with this theory. This association between forgiveness and anger was supported by other research (Enright et al., 2007; Gassin et al., 2005; Holter et al., 2008).

Additionally, depression was found as a mediator between hope and antisocial behavior. This result is consistent with our hypothesis that a low level of hope would increase depression and a high level of depression would raise antisocial behavior among fourth grade children. The relationship between hope and depression is an expected finding and consistent with previous research (Asarnow & Bates, 1988; Kazdin et al., 1983). Consistent with this finding regarding depression and antisocial behavior, Ritakallio et al. (2008) showed in a follow up research that self-report depressive symptoms predicted antisocial behavior in a two-year period for females, whereas depressive symptoms had a protective function against subsequent antisocial behavior for males. Moreover, researchers generally emphasize the co-occurrence or co-morbidity of depression and antisocial behavior in adolescents (i.e., O'Connor, McQuire, Reiss, Hetherington, & Plomin, 1998; Ritakallio et al.). It seems that more research is needed to inspect the dynamics of pure depression or pure antisocial behavior from the co-occurrence of these concepts in children or in adolescents.

In the present study, anger mediated the relationship between hope and antisocial behavior. This finding confirmed our hypothesis that those lower levels of hope would be associated with higher levels of anger, which can lead to antisocial behavior. We based this idea on the frustration–aggression hypothesis. As the basic assumption of the theory proposes that an impediment to goal attainment is likely to arouse anger, we speculated that high-hopers would perceive barriers as a challenge and manage to find alternative routes, and they might experience less anger; whereas, low hopers would become stuck when confronting barriers and feel more frustrated, which might lead them to feel anger that would lead them to antisocial behaviors (Dollard et al., 1939). Anger also mediated the relationship between hope and depression. This mediation was an expected finding as well. Different theoretical approaches such as psychoanalysis and Gestalt therapy have been focused on the association between anger and depression (Mohr, Shoham-Salomon, Engle, & Beutler, 1991) and several empirical findings have shown this link, especially anger rumination and depression (e.g., Worthington, 2006; Geiger & Kwon, 2010). Thus, in this study anger rumination might lead to higher levels of depression, which is related to lower levels of hope.

The hypothesis that we expected that forgiveness would predict hope in fourth grade children, was not supported. This result is somewhat consistent with previous research (e.g., Hui & Ho, 2004; Hui & Chau, 2009), which was conducted in a collectivist society (China). In these studies no significant difference was found in hope after forgiveness intervention. This finding may support the notion that collectivist cultural settings value forgiveness to maintain social harmony rather than inner well-being (Sandage & Wiens, 2001). However, two forgiveness intervention studies (Al-Mabuk, Enright, & Cardis, 1995; Luskin et al., 2005) with adolescence showed an increase in hope but in these studies different hope scale was used. In addition, this result could be explained by measuring these two variables at different levels of analysis. That is, state forgiveness did not generate dispositional hope in fourth grade children. In addition, forgiveness and hope do not share any agency among fourth grade children as the study by Sandage et al. (2000) stated.

However, the present study showed that forgiveness and hope had a low but a significant correlation. This finding may indicate that this positive link could be higher if the variables measured at similar levels of analysis in fourth grade children. This result is not consistent with the findings in adults (Sandage et al., 2000; Snyder, Yamhure, & Heinze, 2000). There are a few limitations that bear remark: First, future research could replicate this study by considering the link between forgiveness and hope, measured at the same level of analysis; that is, both variables could be measured at the dispositional level, which could say much more about the link between these two variables. Moreover, as mentioned earlier, they can investigate their relationships between positive and negative affectivity. Second, although this research was focused on forgiveness in fourth grade children, the results of the present study cannot be generalized to all children in Turkey. In order to gain a strong notion about the process of forgiveness during childhood, children from different cities or regions of Turkey and different age groups should be recruited in future research. Third, although a structural model was used to show the links among the variables investigated, the data are correlational and cannot be interpreted as a sign of causality. A longitudinal study could be used to explore the causal links among these variables. Lastly, this study is performed in Turkey, which involves both the patterns of individualism and collectivism (Cukur et al., 2004). However, this study did not focus on cultural implications of the concept of forgiveness but instead examined the predictive effect of forgiveness in children in Turkey. Future research on forgiveness in Turkish setting may focus on cultural implications.

Despite these limitations, the present study is the first that investigates the role of forgiveness in mental health variables and social behavior in Turkish fourth grade children. Forgiveness is given significant attention in psychotherapy (e.g., Al-Mabuk et al., 1995) and education (Enright et al., 2007). However, forgiveness interventions need more empirical data on child forgiveness. The present study offers empirical information on how forgiveness predicts mental health variables and social behavior in children.

FUNDING

This research was supported by grant number 110K429 from the Scientific and Technological Research Council of Turkey awarded to the first author.

REFERENCES

Allemand, M., Amberg, I., Zimprich, D., & Fincham, F. D. (2007). Trait forgiveness, relationship satisfaction, and episodic forgiveness. *Journal of Social and Clinical Psychology*, *26*, 199–217.

Al-Mabuk, R. H., Enright, R. D., & Cardis, P. A. (1995). Forgiveness education with parentally love-deprived late adolescents. *Journal of Moral Education*, *24*, 427–444.

Asarnow, J. R., & Bates, S. (1988). Depression in child psychiatric inpatients: Cognitive and attributional patterns. *Journal of Abnormal Child Psychology*, *16*, 601–615.

Atik, G., & Kemer, G. (2009). Çocuklarda Umut Ölçeği'nin psikometrik özellikleri: Geçerlik ve güvenirlik çalışması [Psychometric properties of Children's Hope Scale: Validity and reliability study]. *Elementary Education Online*, *8*, 379–390.

Beck, S., Beck, A. T. & Jolly, J. (2001). *Beck Youth Inventory*. New York, NY: Psychological Corporation.

Brislin, R. W. (1986). The wording and translation of research instruments. In W. Lonner & J. Berry (Eds.), *Field methods in cross-cultural research* (pp. 137–164). Beverly Hills, CA: Sage.

Cukur, C. S., de Guzman, M. R. T., & Carlo, G. (2004). Religiosity, values and horizontal and vertical individualism–collectivism: A study of Turkey, the United States and the Philippines. *Journal of Social Psychology*, *144*, 613–63.

Darby, B. W., & Schlenker, B. R. (1982). Children's reactions to transgressions: Effects of the actor's apology, reputation, and remorse. *British Journal of Social Psychology*, *28*, 353–364.

Denham, S., Neal, K., Wilson, B., Pickering, S., & Boyatzis, C. (2005). Emotional development and forgiveness in children: Emerging evidence. In E. L. Worthington, Jr. (Ed.), *Handbook of forgiveness* (pp. 127–142). New York, NY: Routledge.

Dollard, J., Doob, L., Miller, N., Mowrer, O., & Sears, R. (1939). *Frustration and aggression*. New Haven, CT: Yale University Press.

Eisenberg, N., & Fabes, R. A. (1998). Prosocial development. In W. Damon (Series Ed.) & N. Eisenberg (Vol. Ed.), *Handbook of child psychology, vol. 3. Social, emotional, and personality development* (5th ed.) (pp. 701–778). New York, NY: Wiley.

Enright, R. (2005). *Enright Forgiveness Inventory and manual*. Redwood City, CA: Mind Garden.

Enright, R. D. (2011, February). *Psychological science of forgiveness: Implications for psychotherapy and education*. Paper presented at the Conference, Neuroscience and Moral Action: Neurological Conditions of Affectivity, Decisions, and Virtue, Rome, Italy.

Enright, R. D., & Coyle, C. T. (1998). Researching the process model of forgiveness within psychological interventions. In E. L. Worthington Jr. (Ed.), *Dimensions of forgiveness:*

Psychological research and theological perspectives (pp. 139–161). Philadelphia, PA: Templeton Foundation Press.

Enright, R. D., & Fitzgibbons, R. P. (2000). *Helping clients forgive: An empirical guide for resolving anger and restoring hope.* Washington, DC: American Psychological Association.

Enright, R. D., & The Human Development Study Group (1996). Counseling within the forgiveness triad: On forgiving, receiving forgiveness, and self-forgiveness. *Counseling and Values, 40*, 107–146.

Enright, R. D., Knutson Enright, J. A., Holter, A. C., Baskin, T., & Knutson, C. (2007). Waging peace through forgiveness in Belfast, Northern Ireland, II: educational programmes for mental health improvement of children. *Journal of Research in Education, Fall*, 63–78.

Enright, R. D., Santos, M. J., & Al-Mabuk, R. (1989). The adolescent as forgiver. *Journal of Adolescence, 12*, 99–110.

Freedman, S. R., & Knupp, A. (2003). The impact of forgiveness on adolescent adjustment to parental divorce. *Journal of Divorce & Remarriage, 39*, 135–165.

Gassin, E. A. (1995). *Social cognition and forgiveness in adolescent romance: An intervention study.* Unpublished doctoral dissertation, University of Wisconsin, Madison.

Gassin, E. A., Enright, R. D., & Knutson, J. A. (2005). Bringing peace to the central city: Forgiveness education in Milwaukee. *Theory Into Practice, 44*(4), 319–328.

Geiger, K. A., & Kwon, P. (2010). Rumination and depressive symptoms: Evidence for the moderating role of hope. *Personality and Individual Differences, 49*, 391–395.

Gilman, R., & Dooley, J. (2006). Relative levels of hope and their relationship with academic and psychological indicators among adolescents. *Journal of Social and Clinical Psychology, 25*(2), 166–178.

Grifford-Smith, M., & Brownell, C. (2003). Chilhood peer relationships: social acceptance, friendships, and peer networks. *Journal of School Psychology, 41*, 235–284.

Holter, A. C., Magnuson, C. M., Knutson, C., Knutson-Enright, J., & Enright, R. D. (2008). The forgiving child: The impact of forgiveness education on excessive anger for elementary-aged children in Milwaukee's central city. *Journal of Research in Education, 18*, 82–93.

Hook, J. N., Worthington, E. L., Jr., & Utsey, S. O. (2009). Collectivism, forgiveness, and social harmony. *The Counseling Psychologist, 37*, 786–820.

Hu, L. T., & Bentler, P. M. (1999). Cutoff criteria for fit indexes in covariance structure analysis: Conventional criteria versus new alternatives. *Structural Equation Modeling, 6*, 1–55.

Hui, E. K. P., & Chau, T. S. (2009). The impact of a forgiveness intervention with Hong Kong Chinese children hurt in interpersonal relationships. *British Journal of Guidance and Counselling, 37*, 141–156.

Hui, E. K. P., & Ho, D. K. Y. (2004) Forgiveness in the context of developmental guidance: implementation and evaluation. *British Journal of Guidance & Counseling, 32*, 477–492.

Karremans, J. C., & Van Lange, P. A. M. (2004). Back to caring after being hurt: The role of forgiveness. *European Journal of Social Psychology, 34*, 207–227.

Kazdin, A. E., French, N. H., Unis, A. S., Esveldt-Dawson, K., & Sherick, R. B. (1983). Hopelessness, depression, and suicidal intent among psychiatrically disturbed inpatient children. *Journal of Consulting and Clinical Psychology, 51*, 504–510.

Kovacs, M. (1992). *Children's Depression Inventory, CDI.* Toronto: Multi-Health Systems, Inc.

Kumru, A., Carlo, G., & Edwards, C. P. (2004). Olumlu sosyal davranışların ilişkisel, kültürel, bilişsel ve duyuşsal bazı değişkenlerle ilişkisi [Relational, cultural, cognitive, and affective predictors of prosocial behaviors]. *Türk Psikoloji Dergisi, 19*, 109–129.

Luskin, F. M., Ginzburg, K., & Thoresen, C. E. (2005). The efficacy of forgiveness intervention in college age adults: Randomized controlled study. *Humboldt Journal of Social Relations, 29,* 163–184.

McCullough, M. E., Pargament, K. I., & Thoresen, C. E. (2000). The psychology of forgiveness: History, conceptual issues, and overview. In M. E. McCullough, K. I. Pargament, & C. E. Thoresen (Eds.), *Forgiveness: Theory, research, and practice* (pp. 1–14). New York, NY: Guilford Press.

Miller-Johnson, S., Lochman, J. E., Coie, J. D., Terry, R., & Hyman, C. (1998). Comorbidity of conduct and depressive symptoms at sixth grade: substance abuse outcomes across adolescents. *Journal of Abnormal Child Psychology, 26,* 221–232.

Mohr, D., Shoham-Salomon, V., Engle, D., & Beutler, L. (1991). The expression of anger in psychotherapy for depression: Its role and measurement. *Psychotherapy Research, 1,* 124–134.

Muthén, L. K., & Muthén, B. O. (2008). *Mplus user's guide* (6th Ed.). Los Angeles, CA: Muthén & Muthén.

Neal, K., Bassett, H. H., & Denham, S. A. (2004, April). *Affective processes and children's propensity to forgive.* Paper presented at the biennial meeting of the Conference on Human Development, Washington, DC.

O'Connor, T. G., McGuire, S., Reiss, D., Hetherington, E. M., & Plomin, R. (1998). Co-ocurrence of depressive symptoms and antisocial behavior in adolescence: A common genetic liability. *Journal of Abnormal Psychology, 107,* 27–37.

Oy, B. (1991). Çocuklar için depresyon ölçeği: Geçerlik ve güvenirlik çalışması [Depression rating scale for children: Validity and reliability study]. *Turkish Journal of Psychiatry, 2,* 132–137.

Ritakallio, M., Koivisto, A.M., von der Pahlen, B., Pelkonen, M., Marttunen, M., & Kaltiala-Heino, R. (2008). Continuity, comorbidity and longitudinal associations between depression and antisocial behaviour in middle adolescence: A 2–year prospective follow-up study. *Journal of Adolescence, 31,* 355–370.

Sandage, S., & Wiens, T. (2001). Contextualizing models of humility and forgiveness: A reply to Gassin. *Journal of Psychology and Theology, 29,* 201–211.

Sandage, S., Worthington, E., & Calvert-Minor, D. (2000). *Hope and forgiveness: Initial correlations, directions for future research, and an intervention with couples.* Paper presented at the meeting of the American Psychological Association, Washington, DC.

Snyder, C. R. (1994). *The psychology of hope.* New York, NY: A division of Simon & Schuster Inc.

Snyder, C. R. (2002). Hope theory: Rainbows in the mind. *Psychological Inquiry, 13,* 249–275.

Snyder, C. R., Hoza, B., Pelham, W. E., Rapoff, M., Ware, L., Danovsky, M., ... Stahl, K. J. (1997). The development and validation of the Children's Hope Scale. *Journal of Pediatric Psychology, 22,* 399–421.

Snyder, C. R., Ilardi, S. S., Cheavens, J., Michael, T., Yamhure, L., & Sympson, S. (2000). The role of hope in cognitive-behavior therapies. *Cognitive Therapy and Research, 24,* 747–762.

Snyder, C. R., Irving L., & Anderson J. (1991). Hope and health: Measuring the will and the ways. In Snyder C. R., & Forsyth D. R. (Eds.), *Handbook of social and clinical psychology* (pp. 285–305). Elmsford, NY: Pergamon.

Snyder, C. R., Lapointe, A. B., Crowson, J. J., & Early, S. (1998). Preferences of high- and low- hope people for self-referential input. *Cognition and Emotion, 12,* 807–823.

Snyder, C. R., Yamhure, L. C., & Heinze, L. (2000). *The tranquility trilogy: High forgiveness, high hope, and low hostility.* Paper presented at the 108th annual convention of the American Psychological Association, Washington, DC.

Thompson, L. Y., Snyder, C. R., Hoffman, L., Michael, S. T., Rasmussen, H. N., Billings, L. S., . . . Roberts, D. E. (2005). Dispositional forgiveness of self, others, and situations. *Journal of Personality, 73*, 313–359.

Toussaint, L. L., Williams, D. R., Musick, M. A., & Everson-Rose, S. A. (2008). Why forgiveness may protect against depression: Hopelessness as an explanatory mechanism. *Personality and Mental Health, 2*, 89–103.

Wade, N. G., & Worthington, E. L. Jr. (2005). In search of a common core: A content analysis of interventions to promote forgiveness. *Psychotherapy: Theory, Research, Practice, Training, 42*, 160–177.

Warden, D., & Christie, D. (1997). *Teaching social behaviour.* London: David Fulton.

Warden, D., & Mackinnon, S. (2003). Prosocial children, bullies, and victims: An investigation of their sociometric status, empathy, and social problem-solving strategies. *British Journal of Developmental Psychology, 21*, 367–385.

Worthington, E. L., Jr. (2006). *Forgiveness and reconciliation: Theory and application.* New York, NY: Brunner-Routledge.

Worthington, E. L., Jr., Berry, J. W., & Parrott, L., III. (2001). Unforgiveness, forgiveness, religion, and health. In T. G. Plante & A. Sherman (Eds.), *Faith and Health: Psychological Perspectives* (pp. 107–138). New York, NY: Guilford.

Worthington, E. L. Jr., & Wade, N. G. (1999). The social psychology of unforgiveness and forgiveness and implications for clinical practice. *Journal of Social and Clinical Psychology, 18*, 385–418.

Hostility/Anger as a Mediator Between College Students' Emotion Regulation Abilities and Symptoms of Depression, Social Anxiety, and Generalized Anxiety

KIA ASBERG

ABSTRACT. Internalizing problems are common among college students and have been linked consistently to deficits in emotion regulation (ER). Also, hostility/anger (animosity toward others, phenomenological aspect of anger) is an important feature of internalizing problems, but has received limited attention as a mediator between ER and outcomes. Results ($N = 160$) indicated that although college students' ER abilities corresponded with all three types of internalizing symptoms, hostility/anger mediated fully the relationship for symptoms of depression and social anxiety, but not generalized anxiety (GAD). The stronger interpersonal aspect inherent in depression and social anxiety relative to GAD may in part explain findings, but findings must be viewed in lieu of limitations, which include self-report, a non-clinical sample, and a cross-sectional design. Overall, hostility/anger may be important to address in interventions and programs aimed at reducing internalizing problems, especially among those who demonstrate ER deficits and are prone to depression and social anxiety.

APPROXIMATELY ONE IN THREE COLLEGE STUDENTS have experienced depressive symptoms that interfered with their functioning in the past year (see Eiser, 2011, for a review), according to the American College Health Association. Further, it is well established that depression and anxiety disorders commonly co-occur (Kendler, Prescott, Myers, & Neale, 2003; Mineka, Watson, & Clark, 1998) and that symptoms of depression, generalized anxiety (GAD), and social anxiety often overlap in non-clinical undergraduate samples (e.g., Weeks, Rodebaugh, Heimberg, Norton, & Jakatdar, 2009). Specifically, depression and social anxiety share features of cognitive distortions pertaining to interpersonal situations (Johnson, Johnson, & Petzel, 1992) and submissiveness (Weeks et al., 2009), while

GAD and social anxiety share intolerance for uncertainty (Boelen & Reijntjes, 2009) and a tendency to worry extensively (Starcevic et al., 2007). Both depression (Nolen-Hoeksema, 2000) and GAD symptoms (Fresco, Frankel, Mennin, Turk, & Heimberg, 2002; Yook, Kim, Suh, & Lee, 2010) have been linked also to rumination.

One of the most consistent findings among individuals with symptoms of depression, GAD, or social anxiety, however, is a more general deficit in *emotion regulation* (e.g., ER; Aldao, Nolen-Hoeksema, & Schweizer, 2010; Gross & Munoz, 1995; John & Gross, 2007; Mennin, Heimberg, Turk, & Fresco, 2005; Salovey, Stroud, Woolery, & Epel, 2002; Werner, Goldin, Ball, Heimberg, & Gross, 2011), which has sparked a call for more unified approaches to treating these syndromes (e.g., Barlow, 2002; 2008; Barlow, Allen, & Choate, 2004; Moses & Barlow, 2006; Trosper, Buzzella, Bennett, & Ehrenreich, 2009). It has been proposed also that efforts to elucidate commonalities among internalizing syndromes include investigations of context and mechanisms by which ER deficits and abilities contribute to problems (e.g., Aldao et al., 2010; Berking et al., 2012).

Emotion Regulation

The concept of ER has been defined as "the use of strategies that individuals employ to modify the course and expression of emotional experiences" (Dennis, 2007, p. 200). As an individual process, then, ER refers to changes in any given emotion, including changes in the valence, intensity, and duration of the emotion (Cole, Martin, & Dennis, 2004) or any effort of a person that involves when and how his or her emotions are experienced (Sloan & Kring, 2007). Specifically, Gross (2002) suggested that ER can occur at any point in the process by which emotions are generated. Although similar to coping in some regards, ER is different in that it entails regulation of both positive and negative affective states (e.g., John & Gross, 2007; see also Watson & Sinha, 2008, for a review). Also, Bridges, Denham, and Ganiban (2004) suggested that "adaptive [ER] must involve initiation and maintenance of emotion states, both positive and negative, as well as the ability to reduce heightened levels of negativity" (p. 344). In other words, ER is any attempt to regulate an emotion, regardless of a particular strategy (Gross & Thompson, 2007; Hamilton et al., 2009; Trosper et al., 2009) or one's *perceived ability* to act effectively (e.g., Tull, Barrett, McMillan, & Roemer, 2007) by engaging in ER.

Although many mental health issues can be linked to problems with affective control, internalizing problems such as depression (Campbell-Sills, Barlow, Brown, & Hofmann, 2006) and anxiety (Mennin, McLaughlan, & Flanagan, 2009) are linked more closely to ER difficulties relative to externalizing disorders (Aldao et al., 2010). For example, depressed college students show less adaptive patterns of ER relative to non-depressed students (Rude & McCarthy, 2003), including more rumination (Nolen-Hoeksema, Wisco, & Lyubomirsky, 2008), less use of reappraisal, and more use of expressive suppression (Joormann & Gotlib, 2010).

Likewise, formerly depressed individuals endorse lower levels of negative mood regulation (NMR) expectancies and higher levels of emotion avoidance relative to never-depressed adults (Brockmeyer et al., 2012), suggesting multiple problems with ER in those at risk for depression. Also, a recent empirical investigation demonstrated that college students who are vulnerable to depression based on their previous history *spontaneously* use maladaptive ER patterns (i.e., suppress emotions) even when *not* depressed (Ehring, Tuschen-Caffier, Schnülle, Fischer, & Gross, 2010), which may increase risk for relapse. Relative to non-vulnerable controls, however, depression prone college students are equally successful in using functional ER skills when instructed to do so (Ehring et al.).

Similarly, GAD is "characterized by significant deficits in emotional experience and regulation" (Mennin et al., 2009, p. 866), such as the use of worry to prevent actual processing of fear-related stimuli (Borkovec, 1994; see also Newman & Llera, 2011, for a review), difficulty accessing appropriate ER skills, and "poor ability to engage in goal-pursuit behavior" under stress (Mennin et al. p. 867). Further, a growing body of evidence suggest that ER through avoidance (i.e., cognitive avoidance of emotional content and other feared stimuli) is not only a key factor in the maintenance of GAD (Borkovec, Alcaine, & Behar, 2004), but also observed in individuals with depression (Ottenbreit & Dobson, 2004; Rude & McCarthy, 2003) and social anxiety (Wong & Moulds, 2010). Also, for regulation of social anxiety, suppression is less effective relative to reappraisal and acceptance (for physiological symptoms), with reappraisal outperforming both acceptance and suppression in terms of subjective feelings of anxiety (Hofmann, Heering, Sawyer, & Asnaani, 2009). In addition, poor ER abilities may present additional challenges, especially in combination with neuroticism, such that college students "who are prone to both experience aversive mood states *and* have diminished capacity to effectively repair such mood states may be more apt to utilize risky behaviors in response to negative affect" (Auerbach, Abela, & Ringo-Ho, 2007, p. 2189).

Overall, ER deficits may be viewed as a vulnerability for negative affective states among college students, but recent research has sought to identify mediators between such deficits and outcomes.

Hostility/Anger and Adjustment

As noted, one variable to consider in the relationship between ER and outcomes is hostility/anger, which combines the attitudinal hostility construct with the cognitive and phenomenological aspect of anger. Specifically, hostility/anger is conceptualized as *hostile attitudes* (e.g., animosity toward others; Ingram, Trenary, Odom, Berry, & Nelson, 2007; cynicism, mistrust; Eckhardt, Norlander, & Deffenbacher, 2004) in combination with the closely related construct of *anger experience* (Sanz, García-Vera, & Magán, 2010). For example, the anger component of hostility/anger consists of *cognitive* (angry beliefs) and *phenomenological* (labeling of subjective experience) aspects of anger experience, rather than behavioral or physiological aspects (see Eckhardt et al., 2004). In previous studies, hostility (Mao, Bardwell, Major, & Dimsdale, 2003) and hostility/anger (Stewart, Fitzgerald, & Kamarck, 2010) have been linked to depression, while anger experience is related to GAD and social anxiety disorder, even after controlling for depression (Hawkins & Cougle, 2011).

In general, most studies confirm the relationship between hostility and related constructs and depression (Heponiemi et al., 2006; Mao et al., 2003; Rude, Chrisman, Burton Denmark, & Maestas, 2012; Stewart et al., 2010) and anxiety (Vandervort, 1995). In addition, social anxiety correlates positively with hostile feelings toward others, even after controlling for depression (DeWall, Buckner, Lambert, Cohen, & Fincham, 2010). Also, hostility in childhood predicts poorer emotional stability (Hampson, Andrews, Barckley, & Peterson, 2007). For example, hostile/angry individuals may be more vulnerable to stress and negative affect (Weiss et al., 2005), and college students at high risk for depression demonstrate higher hostility relative to their low risk counterparts (Ingram et al., 2007). Furthermore, a recent study by the Center for Collegiate Mental Health (2010) suggested that hostility/anger correlated significantly with depressive symptoms ($r = .50$) on the BDI-II. In fact, hostility can be a prominent way in which depression manifests itself and some studies have suggested that "depressive hostility" is comprised of poor assertiveness, a tendency to suppress [phenomenological] anger, and experience of depression (Maier et al., 2009).

One possible explanation for why hostile/angry individuals may experience more distress (relative to non-hostile individuals) is because of their proneness to "reciprocal hostility and social isolation" (Prkachin & Silverman, 2002, p. 33). Hostility/anger may also contribute to depression by ways of faulty interpretation of others' behavior in interpersonal situations (see Ingram et al., 2007, for a review). Specifically, "heightened levels of anger and hostility may create problematic interactions that, if not creating stress, at least set the stage for stress" (Ingram et al., 2007, p. 89). It may also be that hostility/anger directly promotes negative affect, which in turn leads to unhealthy coping behaviors (Whalen, Jamner, Henker, & Delfino, 2001) that are ineffective in resolving the negative affective state and instead may perpetuate it. Some contend that the reverse is also true, such that life satisfaction, depression, and perceived stress are significant predictors of hostility (Hamdan-Mansour, 2010), highlighting the complex relationship between hostility and depression. Overall, the interplay among ER abilities, hostility/anger, and symptoms of depression, social anxiety, and GAD warrant further study.

Present Study

Internalizing problems are common among college students (e.g., Eiser, 2011) and the identification of predictors and ameliorating factors is important.

Previous studies have linked ER abilities to internalizing problems (Aldao et al., 2010; Barlow, 2002), including symptoms of depression (Rude & McCarthy, 2003), generalized anxiety (Mennin et al., 2005; Roemer, Lee, Salters-Pedneault, Erisman, Orsillo, & Mennin, 2009), and social anxiety (Mennin et al., 2009). Additionally, hostility and closely related constructs (i.e., cognitive aspects of anger) are related also to symptoms of depression (Mao et al., 2003; W. D. Scott, Ingram, & Shadel, 2003; Stewart et al., 2010), social anxiety (DeWall et al., 2010; Gilbert & Miles, 2000), and GAD (Hawkins & Cougle, 2011). To our knowledge, however, few studies have examined hostility/anger as a mediator between college students' perceived ER abilities and their internalizing symptoms.

Rationale for Framework

The temporal order of variables, that is, the rationale for using hostility/anger as a mediator, is based on the assumptions that a) hostility/anger must precede the outcome of interest, and b) deficits in managing one's emotions in response to environmental stressors may lead to internalizing problems and/or the experience of hostility/anger. With regards to the first assumption, recent path analytic modeling has suggested that "the cognitive aspects of hostility/anger precede and independently predict future increases in depressive symptoms, but not vice versa" (Stewart et al., 2010, p. 263). Also, main theorists argue that anxiety and anger share genetic underpinnings such that stress sensitivity can produce anxiety *or* anger in an individual, depending on his/her ability to master the environment (Barlow, 2002). In other words, ER *precede* outcomes pertaining to anger (or, for our purposes, hostility/anger) and anxiety, respectively. Studies confirming this temporal relationship between ER and hostility/anger are scarce, however, although tests of alternative paths using the related construct of coping suggested that hostility was a more robust *mediator* between coping and depression outcomes than it was a predictor of coping (Mao et al., 2003).

Based on previous research and the prevalence of mental health concerns among college students, especially depression and anxiety, evaluating the extent to which college students' beliefs about their ER abilities and anger/hostility, respectively, contribute to internalizing symptoms is an important goal of this study.

Method

Participants

Participants ($N = 160$: 72% women) were recruited from undergraduate courses at a university in the southeastern United States. Ages of participants ranged from 18 to 26-years, with a mean age of 18.6 years ($SD = 1.71$). The overall sample population, although representative of the university at large, was overwhelmingly Caucasian (90%), followed by African-American (4.5%),

Hispanic/Latin (2.5%), Asian-American (2%), and approximately 1% of participants indicated "Other" racial or ethnic background. Of the total sample, 72% of participants were in their freshman year of study, 13% were sophomores, 11% were juniors, and 4% were seniors.

Measures

Participants completed a demographics form and measures of *psychological adjustment*, (CCAPS-62; Center for Collegiate Mental Health, 2010) and *emotion regulation* (TEARS; Hamilton et al., 2009). Specifically, the Counseling Center Assessment of Psychological Symptoms-62 (CCAPS-62) is a widely used tool designed to assess psychological symptoms in college-age individuals (Locke et al., 2011). Initial pilot testing of the CCAPS began in 2001, and the CCAPS-62 has undergone a variety of modifications over the past decade. The most recent normative data ($N = 19{,}247$) and psychometrics of the 62-item scale are from 2009 (published in 2010), and based on college students seeking counseling. The CCAPS-62 uses a 5-point Likert-type scale to assess several dimensions of psychological and social functioning. Each item is rated from 0 (*not at all like me*) to 4 (*extremely like me*). For the present study, subscales for symptoms of depression, GAD, social anxiety, and hostility/anger were used.

Depressive Symptoms. The depressive symptoms subscale (12 items) of the CCAPS has demonstrated a .71 correlation with the Beck Depression Inventory (BDI-II) and taps a variety of depressive symptoms. Items such as; "I feel sad all the time" and "I feel worthless" are rated on the aforementioned Likert-scale (0 to 4). The Depression subscale has a Cronbach alpha of .90 and the test-retest reliability was reported as .88 (one week) and .92 (two week) previously. For the present study, Cronbach alpha was .76.

Generalized Anxiety Symptoms. The GAD symptom subscale (9 items) includes items pertaining to anxiety and generalized worry, such as "There are many things I am afraid of." The GAD subscale has shown a .64 correlation with the Beck Anxiety Inventory (BAI). This subscale has a Cronbach alpha of .84 and test-retest reliability was .84 at both one week and two week follow-up in a previous study. In the current study, Cronbach alpha was .83.

Social Anxiety Symptoms. The social anxiety symptom subscale (7 items) asks participants to endorse how much they agree with statements such as "I become anxious when I have to speak in front of audiences." This subscale has a Cronbach alpha of .82 and demonstrated a .73 correlation with the Social Phobia Diagnostic Questionnaire previously. Test-retest reliability coefficients were reported as .88 (one week) and .86 (two week) previously. In the present study, Cronbach alpha was .76.

Hostility/Anger. The Hostility/anger subscale (7 items) of the CCAPS-62 consists of statements such as "I feel irritable," "I get angry easily." This subscale shows a moderate correlation with the Trait Anger subscale of the STAXI-2 ($r = .57$) and demonstrated a Cronbach alpha of .86, with test-retest reliability of .87

(one week) and .83 (two week) previously. In the present study, Cronbach alpha was .85.

Emotion Regulation. The Emotion Amplification and Reduction Scales (TEARS; Hamilton et al., 2009) is an 18-item measure specifically designed to "assess perceived ability to change the trajectory of an emotional response" (Hamilton et al., 2009, p. 255). The TEARS asks individuals the extent to which they feel they are able to regulate their emotions by reducing (ER-Reduction; 9 items) or amplifying (ER-Amplification; 9 items) them, but does not specifically assess strategies used to do so. For example, items such as "I can stop an emotion before it overwhelms me," "I can choose to remain calm in almost any situation" (ER-reduction) are rated on a 4-point Likert-type scale ranging from 1 (*Not at all true for me*) to 4 (*Very true for me*). The ER-Reduction subscale was related to lower negative affect (PANAS scores) and fewer depressive symptoms (BDI scores), as indicated by correlations of $-.37$ ($p < .01$) and $-.20$ ($p < .01$), respectively, while the ER-amplification subscale was largely unrelated to scores on the Beck Depression Inventory in the original study ($r = .03$). Thus, only the ER-reduction subscale, with an alpha of .87 previously, was the focus of the present study. Cronbach alpha for the current study was .91.

Finally, it should be noted that the TEARS does not specifically tap emotional *dysregulation*, but rather it measures an individual's *perceived ability* to select an emotional response, prevent an emotional response, shorten its duration, stop or soften it, and reduce emotional arousal, i.e., "the process of emotion regulation" (Hamilton et al., 2009, p. 261).

Procedure

Participants were recruited from various undergraduate courses at university in the southeastern United States. After a brief introduction of the study, including an overview of confidentiality, risks and benefits, and the voluntary nature of participation, students were asked to read and sign the consent form. Next, participants completed the survey packet in classrooms on campus. Upon completion of the survey, they were awarded with extra credit or points toward a research participation component of their course grade. Finally, participants were debriefed and provided contact information for the experimenters as well as for the counseling center on campus in the event they experienced any lasting distress as a result of their participation.

Results

First, means and standard deviations were calculated for the study measures and demographic variables. Group differences between women ($n = 115$) and men ($n = 45$) were also examined. Women and men did not differ significantly on symptoms of depression, GAD, social anxiety, or hostility/anger, but men endorsed

TABLE 1. Means, Standard Deviations, and Possible Range of Scores for Study Measures (Overall Sample)

Variable	M (SD)	Treatment seeking M	N	Possible range
TEARS – ER Reduction	23.41 (6.71)	n/a	159	(9–36)
CCAPS Hostility/anger	5.27 (5.22)	7.07	159	(0–28)
CCAPS Depression	10.33 (8.89)	18.84	159	(0–48)
CCAPS Social Anxiety	11.12 (5.91)	12.53	159	(0–28)
CCAPS GAD	9.96 (6.94)	14.04	159	(0–36)
Gender Differences on Continuous Variables				
Variable	Men ($n = 45$) M (SD)	Women ($n = 115$) M (SD)	t	p
TEARS – ER Reduction	26.76 (6.51)	22.10 (6.35)	4.13	.001
CCAPS Hostility/anger	6.22 (5.01)	4.90 (5.26)	1.45	.15
CCAPS Depression	11.20 (8.13)	9.99 (9.19)	.77	.44
CCAPS Social Anxiety	10.96 (6.95)	11.18 (5.48)	−.20	.84
CCAPS GAD	9.13 (5.25)	10.27 (7.48)	−1.08	.28
Age	18.64 (1.17)	18.65 (1.27)	.04	.97
Gender Differences on Categorical Demographic Variables				
Variable	Men ($n = 45$) %	Women ($n = 115$) %	χ^2	p
White (%)	93.3	88.5	.83	.36
Black (%)	6.7	3.5	.74	.39
Hispanic (%)	0	3.5	1.63	.20
Asian (%)	0	3.5	1.63	.20
Other (%)	0	1	.40	.53
Freshman (%)	69.0	73.0	.28	.60
Sophomore (%)	13.3	12.3	.04	.84
Junior (%)	13.3	10.2	.27	.60
Senior (%)	4.4	4.5	.08	.77

slightly more confidence in their ER-reduction abilities ($M = 26.76$, $SD = 6.51$) compared to women ($M = 22.10$, $SD = 6.35$), $p = .001$. The average age of the women ($M = 18.65$; $SD = 1.27$) did not differ from the average age of men ($M = 18.64$; $SD = 1.17$) in this sample, $t = .04$, $p = .97$. Women and men also did not differ on race/ethnicity variables or on year in school (i.e., likelihood of endorsing a particular race, ethnicity, or year in school). See Table 1 for means, standard deviations, and tests of group differences. Next, a correlation matrix was examined for bivariate relationships between variables. All correlations were significant ($p < .01$), such that ER-reduction abilities were inversely related to internalizing symptoms (i.e., depression, social anxiety, and GAD) and hostility/anger was positively related to internalizing symptoms (Table 2).

TABLE 2. Bivariate Relationships Between Study Variables for the Overall Sample

Variables ($N = 160$)	1	2	3	4	5
1. TEARS ER-reduction	1				
2. CCAPS Hostility/Anger	−.28**	1			
3. CCAPS Depression	−.26**	.55**	1		
4. CCAPS Social Anxiety	−.21**	.30**	.44**	1	
5. CCAPS GAD symptoms	−.37**	.56**	.71**	.39**	1

Note. **$p < .01$.

Statistical Plan for Mediation Analyses

Next, to explore hostility/anger as a mediator in the relationship between perceived ER abilities (TEARS: ER-reduction subscale) and internalizing symptoms (CCAPS-62: depression, GAD, social anxiety subscales), regression equations were examined in the context of Baron and Kenny's (1986) guidelines for mediation. The three conditions for testing mediation include 1) a significant relationship between the independent variable (IV) and the proposed mediator (Hostility/anger), 2) a significant relationship between the IV and the dependent variable (DV), and 3) a significant relationship between the proposed mediator and the DV. Finally, when the IV and mediator are entered together to predict the DV (i.e., symptoms of depression, social anxiety, or GAD), the effect of the IV on the DV should no longer be significant.

Further, Sobel tests (more conservative than bootstrapping) were used to examine indirect effects of the predictor (ER) on the DV after accounting for the effects of the mediator (hostility/anger) (Preacher & Hayes, 2004). This helps determine "whether or not the total effect of IV on the DV is significantly reduced upon the addition of a mediator to the model" (Preacher & Hayes, 2004, p. 720). Mediation is inferred when the link between the IV and DV is accounted for by the hypothesized mediator (MacKinnon, Fairchild, & Fritz, 2007). Each mediation analysis will be discussed next. (Also see Tables 3–5).

Hostility/Anger as a Mediator Between ER and Depressive Symptoms. To examine hostility/anger as a mediator between ER abilities and depressive symptoms, four separate regression equations were examined. First, perceived ER abilities pertaining to reduction of emotions predicted significantly depressive symptoms, $F(1, 158) = 10.86$, $p < .001$. Next, ER abilities predicted also the proposed mediator of hostility/anger, $F(1, 158) = 13.08$, $p < .001$. Specifically, a decrease in the perceived ability to down-regulate, reduce, or soften emotions (ER-reduction) was related significantly to more depressive symptoms (CCAPS-depression) and more hostility/anger (CCAPS-hostility/anger). Third,

TABLE 3. Regression Equation for the Prediction of Depressive Symptoms

Step of Analysis/Variable	Beta	t	p
1. ER predicting Symptoms: $R^2 = .06$			
ER-Reduction	−.25	−3.30	.001
2. ER predicting Hostility/Anger: $R^2 = .08$			
ER-Reduction	−.28	−3.62	.001
3. Hostility/Anger predicting Symptoms): $R^2 = .30$			
Hostility/Anger	.55	8.20	.001
4. ER and Hostility/Anger predicting Symptoms: $R^2 = .30$			
Block 1			
ER-Reduction	−.25	−3.30	.001
Block 2			
ER-Reduction	−.11	−1.61	.110
Hostility/Anger	.52	7.47	.001

Note. Overall model significant with $F(2,157) = 35.23, p < .001$.

the proposed mediator (CCAPS-hostility/anger) predicted the dependent variable (CCAPS-depression) as indicated by $F(1, 158) = 67.20, p < .001$, suggesting that higher levels of hostility was related to more depressive symptoms. For the fourth and final regression equation, ER-reduction was entered by itself in block 1 ($p < .001$), followed by ER-reduction and hostility/anger together

TABLE 4. Regression Equation for the Prediction of Social Anxiety Symptoms

Step of Analysis/Variable	Beta	t	p
1. ER predicting Symptoms: $R^2 = .04$			
ER-Reduction	−.22	−2.78	.008
2. ER predicting Hostility/Anger: $R^2 = .08$			
ER-Reduction	−.28	−3.60	.001
3. Hostility/Anger predicting Symptoms: $R^2 = .09$			
Hostility/Anger	.30	3.99	.001
4. ER and Hostility predicting Symptoms: $R^2 = .10$			
Block 1			
ER-Reduction	−.22	−2.78	.006
Block 2			
ER-Reduction	−.14	−1.80	.073
Hostility/Anger	.26	3.35	.001

Note. Overall model significant with $F(2, 156) = 9.70, p < .001$.

TABLE 5. Regression Equation for the Prediction of Generalized Anxiety Symptoms

Step of Analysis/Variable	Beta	t	p
1. ER predicting Symptoms: $R^2 = .14$			
ER-Reduction	−.37	−5.06	.001
2. ER predicting Hostility/Anger: $R^2 = .08$			
ER-Reduction	−.28	−3.62	.001
3. Hostility/Anger predicting Symptoms: $R^2 = .31$			
Hostility/Anger	.56	8.42	.001
4. ER and Hostility predicting Symptoms: $R^2 = .36$			
Block 1			
ER-Reduction	−.37	−5.06	.001
Block 2			
ER-Reduction	−.24	−3.62	.001
Hostility/Anger	.49	7.42	.001

Note. Overall model significant with $F(2, 156) = 44.73, p < .001$.

(block 2). The overall model was significant, $F(2,157) = 35.23, p < .001$, but only hostility/anger contributed significantly to the prediction of depressive symptoms. In other words, ER-reduction was no longer related significantly to depressive symptoms ($p = .11$) after accounting for hostility/anger, indicating full mediation. The Sobel test ($z = -3.24, p < .001$) confirmed that the effect of ER-reduction on depression was significantly diminished. Thus, hostility/anger mediates fully the relationship between ER-reduction abilities and depressive symptoms.

Hostility/Anger as a Mediator Between ER and Social Anxiety Symptoms. Next, hostility/anger was examined as a mediator between ER-reduction abilities and social anxiety symptoms. First, consistent with Baron and Kenny's guidelines, ER-reduction abilities predicted significantly symptoms of social anxiety [$F(1, 157) = 7.71, p < .01$] and predicted also the proposed mediator (hostility/anger) [$F(1, 158) = 13.08, p < .001$]. In other words, as ER-reduction abilities decreased, symptoms of social anxiety and hostility/anger increased. Next, hostility/anger predicted social anxiety [$F(1, 157) = 15.92, p < .001$] such that when hostility/anger scores increased, so did participants' symptoms of social anxiety. Finally, ER-reduction was entered by itself (block 1) followed by ER-reduction and hostility/anger together (block 2) as predictors of social anxiety symptoms. The overall equation was significant, $F(2, 156) = 9.70, p < .001$, but only hostility/anger contributed significantly to the model ($p < .01$), while ER-reduction was no longer a significant predictor of social anxiety symptoms ($p = .073$) after hostility/anger was accounted for. A Sobel test ($z = -2.45, p < .001$) confirmed hostility/anger as a mediator between ER-reduction abilities and social anxiety symptoms.

Hostility/Anger as a Mediator Between ER and GAD Symptoms. Next, hostility/anger was examined as a mediator between ER-reduction abilities and GAD symptoms. For this series of regression equations, ER-reduction predicted GAD symptoms $F(1, 158) = 25.56$, $p < .001$ and predicted also hostility/anger $F(1, 158) = 13.08$, $p < .001$. In addition, hostility/anger predicted GAD symptoms, $F(1,157) = 70.85$, $p < .001$, satisfying the three initial conditions for mediation suggested by Baron and Kenny (1986). In the fourth and final regression equation, ER-reduction was entered by itself in block 1, followed by both ER-reduction and hostility/anger in block 2. Results indicated that the overall model predicted significantly GAD symptoms, $F(2, 156) = 44.73$, $p < .001$. The prediction of GAD symptoms by ER-reduction was slightly reduced, but still significant ($p < .001$) after accounting for hostility/anger. Thus, hostility/anger does not fully mediate the relationship between ER-reduction abilities and GAD symptoms.

Overall, although ER deficits were positively associated with symptoms of depression and social anxiety in this sample, the relationship between ER and these outcomes was no longer significant after accounting for participants' hostility/anger scores. Thus, hostility/anger fully mediated the relationship between ER deficits and symptoms of depression and social anxiety, respectively. In contrast, the relationship between ER and GAD was reduced but remained significant even after hostility/anger was added to the model, suggesting partial mediation.

Discussion

Internalizing disorders, which are prevalent on college campuses, have been linked consistently to deficits in ER. Also, hostility/anger (i.e., animosity toward others, labeling of subjective anger experience) is an important—possibly perpetuating and debilitating—feature among some individuals with symptoms of depression and anxiety. Findings indicated that although college students' ER abilities correspond with their internalizing symptoms, hostility/anger should also be examined as a potential contributing factor to such problems. Specifically, assessing hostility/anger in college students who endorse fewer ER abilities pertaining to *reduction* (i.e., prevention, shortening, softening) of emotions may be of particular importance in terms of predicting their internalizing symptoms.

The finding that hostility/anger was related robustly to symptoms of depression and social anxiety, and fully mediated the relationship between ER and these symptoms, is not surprising. Hostility or anger is linked commonly to internalizing problems (Bridewell & Chang, 1997; DeWall et al., 2010) and may be one way in which depression manifests itself in college students (see Ingram et al., 2007, for a review), thereby contributing to social alienation and reciprocal hostility (Prkachin & Silverman, 2002). By definition, there is also a strong interpersonal dimension to social anxiety (Alden, 2001) in that socially anxious individuals experience pervasive fears about being negatively evaluated by others (e.g., Clark, 2001), which could contribute to their hostile feelings (DeWall et al., 2010). Individuals with social anxiety, especially generalized social phobia, may exhibit also social skills deficits (e.g., Beidel, Rao, Scharfstein, Wong, & Alfano, 2010; Wong, Sarver, & Beidel, 2012), and this could be an appropriate target for intervention.

In contrast, hostility/anger did not fully mediate the relationship between ER abilities and GAD symptoms in this sample of college students. This may suggest that the potential for finding a mediating effect of hostility/anger may depend on the type of cognitive distortion that is being assessed. For example, although depression, GAD, and social anxiety all share aspects of ER deficits and hostility/anger, depression and social anxiety share more closely distortions of *interpersonal deficits*, specifically. Evidence for such interpersonal problems in both depression and social anxiety has mounted over the past two decades. For example, in their study of college students, Johnson and colleagues (1992) concluded that "socially anxious people and depressed people appear to share similar negative expectancies regarding their interpersonal abilities" (p. 182). Also, socially anxious individuals report lower self-efficacy in implementing adaptive strategies in response to an anxiety provoking situation compared to non-anxious individuals (Werner et al., 2011). In other words, it may be that hostility/anger is simply another aspect of 'interpersonal difficulties' commonly experienced by college students who are depressed or socially anxious. In fact, Prkachin and Silverman (2002) suggested that interpersonal situations contain an inherent threat which hostile individuals fail to diffuse, which increases interpersonal stress, discomfort, and the risk of alienation, "which are related to depression and social anxiety" (p. 37). Overall, findings highlight the need for assessing hostility/anger in college students, especially those who are prone to depression and social anxiety.

Also, it may be that ER abilities are especially important (relative to hostility/anger) in predicting college students' GAD symptoms. A hallmark feature of GAD is the difficulty controlling worries, which may be related to college students' perceived ability to regulate their emotions. It may also be important to assess other nuances of hostility/anger, or related concepts, such as irritability, which is predictive of GAD symptoms (Stringaris, Cohen, Pine, & Leibenluft, 2009). It should be noted that individuals with GAD also experience significant impairment in interpersonal relationships and decreases in quality of life (see Mogotsi, Kaminer, & Stein, 2000, for a review). Future studies may want to examine hostility/anger in the context of other types of interpersonal problems, ER, and internalizing symptoms, as well as utilize other predictors that may influence ER abilities, deficits, and hostility/anger (e.g., mindfulness; Borders, Earleywine, & Jajodia, 2010) to assess whether or not hostility/anger remains a robust predictor.

Limitations. Findings should be interpreted with caution given the use of a non-clinical sample of undergraduate students. Replication of findings in clinical samples or among college students who demonstrate elevated levels of symptomatology would certainly strengthen the generalizability of our findings. Similarly, we agree with Eisner, Johnson, and Carver (2009) who noted that tendencies observed in non-clinical samples can provide *preliminary* support for similarities (e.g., use of maladaptive regulatory responses to affect) among internalizing syndromes, but additional research using clinical samples is needed for more robust conclusions to be drawn. Our position is also similar to that of DeWall and colleagues (2010), who suggested that relationships among internalizing symptoms and hostility found among undergraduate students would likely be even more robust in clinical samples. Also, a larger sample would allow for comparisons between those with elevated scores on internalizing subscales and those with no such elevations, as well as more sophisticated analyses, such as path analytic modeling. It is important to note, however, that subclinical levels of depression (ACHA, 2011; Scott et al., 2003), GAD (e.g., prolonged worry; Scott et al., 2010), and social anxiety (DeWall et al., 2010; Russell & Shaw, 2009) have the potential to disrupt an individual's functioning and should not be taken lightly. Also, young adults who have "difficulty in regulating emotion may be especially at the mercy of negative life events that initiate a cascade into emotional disorders" (Hamilton et al., 2009, p. 261), suggesting that identification of protective factors is important.

Another limitation of the present study is the reliance on self-report measures. Future studies on ER and its effect on negative mood states (e.g., depression) may be strengthened by the utilization of physiological measures of affect and also behavioral observations of actual strategies (Ehring et al., 2010; Hamilton et al., 2009) and skills deficits (e.g., Beidel et al., 2010). Along the same lines, the present study explored specifically perceptions of an individual's *adaptive* ER abilities, that is, the ability to reduce or soften emotions as needed, regardless of the strategy used to do so. Future studies should examine hostility/anger as a mediator between *maladaptive* ER strategies and outcomes. For example, a previous review noted that "presence of a maladaptive emotion-regulation strategy is more deleterious than the relative absence of particularly adaptive emotion-regulation strategies" (Aldao et al., 2010, p. 231).

Findings should also be interpreted in lieu of a fairly small sample size ($N = 160$), however, the relationship between social anxiety symptoms and hostility tends to remain robust even in smaller samples ($N = 84$; DeWall et al., 2010). Also, the size of our sample and the uneven gender distribution (72% of participants were women) did not allow for more specific assessment of group differences, thus it is possible that the hostility/anger construct could manifest itself differently in men and women. For example, studies argue that men may engage in more overt hostility (Storch, Bagner, Geffken, & Baumeister, 2004) and "cynical hostility" (Yan et al., 2003) relative to women, while women show more "angry hostility" compared to men (Costa, Terracciano, & McCrae, 2001). In contrast, a recent study suggested that men and women in college were no different on measures of hostility (Jordanian students: Hamdan-Mansour, 2010), which is in line with our findings of participants' overall scores on the hostility/anger scale. Likewise, men and women in our study did not differ on symptomatology. This is similar to Lindsey, Fabiano, and Stark (2009) and may be attributable to the non-clinical nature of our sample. Future studies should aim to include a more equal number of men and women from diverse backgrounds to allow for generalizations and examination of ethnic and racial differences in the predictive properties of hostility that have been suggested previously (Maier et al., 2009).

Moreover, the present study assessed hostility/anger as a broad, unified concept with mostly cognitive aspects, which precludes us from drawing conclusions about specific nuances or expressed hostility/anger. For example, a previous multi-measure study of hostility/anger in a diverse sample suggested that "assertive anger expression . . . is a potentially adaptive expressive dimension of hostility, with a lack of assertiveness associated with depression" (Maier et al., 2009, p. 1218). It is also important to note that previous studies linked cognitive hostility (i.e., a mixture of resentment and suspicion), but not behavioral hostility, to risk of suicide after controlling for baseline depressed mood (Lemogne et al., 2011). Future studies may examine different types of hostility/anger in relation to ER and affective symptoms. Also, we agree with Rivers, Brackett, Katulak, and Salovey (2007) who highlighted the importance of assessing ER processes and effectiveness of strategies in relation to *discrete* emotions, such as anger and sadness. Given that we did not assess strategies or ability to regulate specific emotions, but rather the general ability to reduce an emotion (presumably, but not necessarily, a negative one) we are unable to make inferences regarding effectiveness.

Further, the cross sectional design and the fact that we did not address other plausible relationships among variables present additional limitations. For example, it is possible that ER would function as a mediator between hostility/anger and outcomes, or that internalizing symptoms predict an individual's hostility/anger scores. In other words, findings are discussed as consistent with research that links hostility to outcomes (path analytic modeling; Stewart et al., 2010) and suggest that the construct is most appropriate as a mediator (Mao et al., 2003), but future research may want to examine other relationships. For example, Trew and Alden (2009) found that "brooding" fully mediated the relationship between social anxiety and trait anger and also mediated partially the relationship between social anxiety and outward anger expression.

It is also possible that other variables not assessed in this study can help determine under what conditions hostility/anger best explains the relationship between a "known" predictor and outcomes. For example, Sprague, Verona, Kalkhoff, and Kilmer (2011) found that experiences of anger and hostility mediated the relationship between perceived stress and aggressive behavior among individuals low, but not high, in executive function abilities. Also, the degree to which individuals experience reciprocal hostility may also influence internalizing symptoms (Prkachin & Silverman, 2002) and could be examined in future studies.

Clinical Implications

Findings of the present study pointed to the link between ER abilities and symptoms of depression, GAD, and social anxiety, but suggested also that college students' hostile feelings and phenomenological anger experiences may better explain adjustment outcomes. It may be important, then, to examine college students' perceptions of their ability to regulate emotions (in terms of preventing, softening, reducing, and shortening emotion) as well as the level of hostility/anger. Moreover, it may be helpful to assess more specific nuances of ER deficits and actual strategies. For example, the maladaptive ER strategy of rumination has been linked to increases in hostility (Borders et al., 2010), anger (Martin & Dahlen, 2005), and depression and anxiety (McLaughlin & Nolen-Hoeksema, 2011). Also, Anestis, Anestis, Selby, and Joiner (2009) found that anger rumination predicted hostility, physical and verbal aggression, but not anger, in their sample of college students. Given that the present study did not assess rumination, specifically, it is possible that within the construct of hostility/anger lies a tendency to ruminate which would better explain internalizing symptoms. The nature of such rumination (e.g., anger, depressive thoughts) may be important to assess as well. From a clinical perspective, cognitive behavioral interventions (e.g., Conradi, de Jonge, & Ormel, 2008) and mindfulness based interventions (Borders et al., 2010) that are effective in reducing rumination may also be effective in reducing hostility/anger. Also, teaching mood regulation skills, improving ER expectancies, and reducing avoidance of emotion can be potentially relevant in reducing the risk for internalizing problems (Brockmeyer et al., 2012; Feldman, Harley, Kerrigan, Jacobo, & Fava, 2009; Fergus, Bardeen, & Orcutt, 2013; Park, Edmondson, & Lee, 2012). Overall, given that hostility/anger is related to negative outcomes beyond internalizing symptoms, including a lesser likelihood of gaining permanent employment (Virtanen et al., 2005), such feelings may be worth addressing in therapy or contexts that aim to enhance college students' interpersonal skills and self-efficacy in interpersonal situations for the goal of improving their psychological adjustment.

REFERENCES

Aldao, A., Nolen-Hoeksema, S., & Schweizer, S. (2010). Emotion-regulation strategies across psychopathology: A meta-analytic review. *Clinical Psychology Review, 30,* 217–237. doi:10.1016/j.cpr.2009.11.004

American College Health Association. (2011). *American College Health Association-National College Health Assessment II: Reference Group Executive Summary Spring 2011.* Hannover, MD: ACHA.

Alden, L. E. (2001). Interpersonal perspectives on social phobia. In W. R. Crozier & L. E. Alden (Eds.), *International Handbook of Social Anxiety* (pp. 405–430). Chichester, England: John Wiley & Sons.

Anestis, M. D., Anestis, J. C., Selby, E. A., & Joiner, T. E. (2009). Anger rumination across forms of aggression. *Personality and Individual Differences, 46,* 192–196. doi:10.1016/j.paid.2008.09.026

Auerbach, J. P., Abela, J. R. Z., & Ringo-Ho, M. H. (2007). Responding to symptoms of depression and anxiety: Emotion regulation, neuroticism, and engagement in risky behaviors. *Behaviour Research and Therapy, 45,* 2182–2191. doi:10.1016/j.brat.2006.11.002

Barlow, D. H. (2002). *Anxiety and its disorders: The nature and treatment of anxiety and panic* (2nd ed). New York, NY: Guilford Press.

Barlow, D. H. (2008). *Clinical handbook of psychological disorders: A step-by-step treatment manual* (4th ed.). New York, NY: Guilford Press.

Barlow, D. H., Allen, L. B., & Choate, M. L. (2004). Toward a unified treatment for emotional disorders. *Behavior Therapy, 35,* 205–230. doi:10.1016/S0005-7894(04)80036-4

Baron, R. M., & Kenny, D. A. (1986). Moderator-mediator variables distinction in social psychological research: Conceptual, strategic, and statistical considerations. *Journal of Personality and Social Psychology, 51,* 1173–1182.

Beidel, D. C., Rao, P. A., Scharfstein, L., Wong, N., & Alfano, C. A. (2010). Social skills and social phobia: An investigation of DSM-IV subtypes. *Behaviour Research and Therapy, 48,* 992–1001. doi:10.1016/j.brat.2010.06.005

Berking, M., Poppe, C., Luhmann, M., Wupperman, P., Jaggi, V., & Seifritz, E. (2012). Is the association between various emotion-regulation skills and mental health mediated by the ability to modify emotions? Results from two cross-sectional studies. *Journal of Behavior Therapy and Experimental Psychiatry, 43,* 931–937. doi: 10.1016/j.jbtep.2011.09.009

Boelen, P. A., & Reijntjes, A. (2009). Intolerance of uncertainty and social anxiety. *Journal of Anxiety Disorders, 23,* 130–135. doi:10.1016/j.janxdis.2008.04.007

Borders, A., Earleywine, M., & Jajodia, A. (2010). Could mindfulness decrease anger, hostility and aggression by decreasing rumination? *Aggressive Behavior, 36,* 28–44. doi: 10.1002/ab.20327

Borkovec, T. D. (1994). The nature, functions, and origins of worry. In G. C. L. Dave y & F. Tallis (Eds.), *Worrying: Perspectives on theory, assessment and treatment* (pp. 5–33). London, England: John Wiley & Sons.

Borkovec, T. D., Alcaine, O., & Behar, E. (2004). Avoidance theory of worry and generalized anxiety disorder. In R. G. Heimberg, C. L. Turk, & D. S. Mennin (Eds.), *Generalized anxiety disorder: Advances in research and practice* (pp. 77–108). New York: Guilford.

Bridewell, W. B. & Chang, E. C. (1997). Distinguishing between anxiety, depression, and hostility: Relations to anger-in, anger-out, and anger control. *Personality and Individual Differences, 22,* 587–590. doi:10.1016/S0191-8869(96)00224-3

Bridges, L. J., Denham, S. A., & Ganiban, J. M. (2004). Definitional issues in emotion regulation research. *Child Development, 75,* 340–345. doi:10.1111/j.1467-8624.2004.00675.x

Brockmeyer, T., Grosse Holtforth, M., Pfeiffer, N., Backenstrass, M., Friederich, H., & Bents, H. (2012). Mood regulation expectancies and emotion avoidance in depression vulnerability. *Personality and Individual Differences*, *53*, 351–354. doi:10.1016/j.paid.2012.03.018

Campbell-Sills, L., Barlow, D. H., Brown, T. A., & Hofmann, S. G. (2006). Acceptability and suppression of negative emotion in anxiety and mood disorders. *Emotion*, *6*, 587–595. doi:10.1037/1528-3542.6.4.587

Center for Collegiate Mental Health. (2010). *CCAPS 2010 User Manual*. University Park, PA: Penn State University Press.

Clark, D. M. (2001). A cognitive perspective on social phobia. In W. R. Crozier & L. E. Alden (Eds.), *International Handbook of Social Anxiety* (pp. 405–430). Chichester, England: John Wiley & Sons.

Cole, P. M., Martin, S. E., & Dennis, T. A. (2004). Emotion regulation as a scientific construct: Methodological challenges and directions for child development research. *Child Development*, *75*, 317–333. doi:10.1111/j.1467-8624.2004.00673.x

Conradi, H. J., de Jonge, P., & Ormel, J. (2008). Cognitive behavioral therapy v. usual care in recurrent depression. *British Journal of Psychiatry*, *193*, 505–506. doi:10.1192/bjp.bp.107.042937

Costa, P. T., Jr., Terracciano, A., & McCrae, R. R. (2001). Gender differences in personality traits across cultures: Robust and surprising findings. *Journal of Personality and Social Psychology*, *81*, 322–331. doi:10.1037/0022-3514.81.2.322

Dennis, T. A. (2007). Interactions between emotion regulation strategies and affective style: Implications for trait anxiety versus depressed mood. *Motivation and Emotion*, *31*, 200–207. doi:10.1007/s11031-007-9069-6

DeWall, C. N., Buckner, J. D., Lambert, N. M., Cohen, A. S., & Fincham, F. D. (2010). Bracing for the worst, but behaving the best: Social anxiety, hostility, and behavioral aggression. *Journal of Anxiety Disorders*, *24*, 260–268. doi:10.1016/j.janxdis.2009.12.002

Eckhardt, C., Norlander, B., & Deffenbacher, J. (2004). The assessment of anger and hostility: A critical review. *Aggression and Violent Behavior*, *9*, 17–43. doi:10.1016/S1359-1789(02)00116-7

Ehring, T., Tuschen-Caffier, B., Schnülle, J., Fischer, S., & Gross, J. J. (2010). Emotion regulation and vulnerability to depression: Spontaneous versus instructed use of emotion suppression and reappraisal. *Emotion*, *10*, 563–572. doi:10.1037/a0019010

Eiser, A. (2011, September). The crisis on campus. *The Monitor on Psychology*, 42. Retrieved from http://www.apa.org/monitor/2011/09/crisis-campus.aspx

Eisner, L. R., Johnson, S. L., & Carver, C. S. (2009). Positive affect regulation in anxiety disorders. *Journal of Anxiety Disorders*, *23*, 645–649. doi:10.1016/j.janxdis.2009.02.001

Feldman, G., Harley, R., Kerrigan, M., Jacobo, M., & Fava, M. (2009). Change in emotional processing during a dialectical behavior therapy-based skills group for major depressive disorder. *Behaviour Research and Therapy*, *47*, 316–321. http://dx.doi.org/10.1016/j.brat.2009.01.005.

Fergus, T. A., Bardeen, J. R., & Orcutt, H. K. (2013). Experiential avoidance and negative emotional experiences: The moderating role of expectancies about emotion regulation strategies. *Cognitive Therapy and Research*, *37*(2), 352–362. doi: 10.1007/s10608-012-9469-0

Fresco, D. M., Frankel, A. N., Mennin, D. S., Turk, C. L., & Heimberg, R. G. (2002). Distinct and overlapping features of rumination and worry: The relationship of cognitive production to negative affective states. *Cognitive Therapy and Research*, *26*, 179–188.

Gilbert, P., & Miles, J. N. V. (2000). Sensitivity to social put-down: Its relationship to perceptions of social rank, shame, social anxiety, depression, anger and self-other blame. *Personality and Individual Differences*, *29*, 757–774. doi:10.1016/S0191-8869(99)00230-5

Gross, J. J. (2002). Emotion regulation: Affective, cognitive, and social consequences. *Psychophysiology, 39*, 281–291. doi:10.1017/S0048577201393198

Gross, J. J., & Munoz, R. F. (1995). Emotion regulation and mental health. *Clinical Psychology: Science and Practice, 2*, 151–164. doi:10.1111/j.1468-2850.1995.tb00036.x

Gross, J. J., & Thompson, R. A. (2007). Emotion regulation: Conceptual foundations. In J. J. Gross (Ed.), *Handbook of emotion regulation.* New York, NY: Guilford Press.

Hamdan-Mansour, A. M. (2010). Predictors of hostility among university students in Jordan. *Scandinavian Journal of Caring Sciences, 24*, 125–130. doi:10.1111/j.1471-6712.2009.00695.x

Hamilton, N. A., Karoly, P., Gallagher, M., Stevens, N., Karlson, C., & McCurdy, D. (2009). The assessment of emotion regulation in cognitive context: The emotion amplification and reduction scales (TEARS). *Cognitive Therapy Research, 33*, 255–263. doi:10.1007/s10608-007-9163-9

Hampson, S. E., Andrews, J. A., Barckley, M., & Peterson, M. (2007). Trait stability and continuity in childhood: Relating sociability and hostility to the Five-Factor model of personality. *Journal of Research in Personality, 41*, 507–523. doi:10.1016/j.jrp.2006.06.003

Hawkins, K. A., & Cougle, J. R. (2011). Anger problems across the anxiety disorders: Findings from a population-based study. *Depression and Anxiety, 28*, 145–152. doi:10.1111/j.1471-6712.2009.00695.x

Heponiemi, T., Elovainio, M., Kivimäki, M., Pulkki, L., Puttonen, S., & Keltikangas-Järvinen, L. (2006). The longitudinal effects of social support and hostility on depressive tendencies. *Social Science and Medicine, 63*, 1374–1382. doi:10.1016/j.socscimed.2006.03.036

Hofmann, S. G., Heering, S., Sawyer, A. T., & Asnaani, A. (2009). How to handle anxiety: The effects of reappraisal, acceptance, and suppression strategies on anxious arousal. *Behaviour Research and Therapy, 47*, 389–394. doi:10.1016/j.brat.2009.02.010

Ingram, R. E., Trenary, L., Odom, M., Berry, L., Nelson, Tyler. (2007). Cognitive, affective and social mechanisms in depression risk: Cognition, hostility, and coping style. *Cognition and Emotion, 21*, 78–94. doi:10.1080/02699930600950778

John, O. P., & Gross, J. J., (2007). Individual differences in emotion regulation. In J. J. Gross (Ed.), *Handbook of emotion regulation* (pp. 351–372). New York, NY: Guilford Press.

Johnson, K. A., Johnson, J. E., & Petzel, T. P. (1992). Social anxiety, depression, and distorted cognitions in college students. *Journal of Social and Clinical Psychology, 11*, 181–195. doi:10.1521/jscp.1992.11.2.181

Joormann, J., & Gotlib, I. H. (2010). Emotion regulation in depression: Relation to cognitive inhibition. *Cognition and Emotion, 24*, 281–298. doi:10.1080/02699930903407948

Kendler, K. S., Prescott, C. A., Myers, J., & Neale, M. C. (2003). The structure of genetic and environmental risk factors for common psychiatric and substance use disorders in men and women. *Archives of General Psychiatry, 60*, 929–937. doi:10.1001/archpsyc.60.9.929

Lemogne, C., Fossati, P., Limosin, F., Nabi, H., Encrenaz, G., Bonenfant, S., & Consoli, S. M. (2011). Cognitive hostility and suicide. *Acta Psychiatrica Scandinavica, 124*, 62–69. doi: 10.1111/j.1600-0447.2010.01658.x

Lindsey, B. J., Fabiano, P., & Stark, C. (2009). The prevalence and correlates of depression among college students. *College Student Journal, 43*, 999–1014.

Locke, B. D., Soet Buzolitz, J., Lei P. W., Boswell, J. F., McAleavey, A. A., Sevig, T. D., ...Hayes, J. A. (2011). Development of the Counseling Center Assessment of Psychological Symptoms-62. *Journal of Counseling Psychology, 58*, 97–109. doi:10.1037/a002128297

MacKinnon, D. P., Fairchild, A. J., & Fritz, M. S. (2007). Mediation analysis. *Annual Review of Psychology, 58*, 593–614. doi:10.1146/annurev.psych.58.110405.085542

Maier, K. J., Goble, L. A., Neumann, S. A., Giggey, P. P., Suarez, E. C., & Waldstein, S. R. (2009). Dimensions across measures of dispositional hostility, expressive style, and depression show some variation by race/ethnicity and gender in young adults. *Journal of Social and Clinical Psychology*, *28*, 1199–1225. doi:10.1521/jscp.2009.28.10.1199

Mao, W., Bardwell, W. A., Major, J. M., & Dimsdale, J. E. (2003). Coping strategies, hostility, and depressive symptoms: A path model. *International Journal of Behavioral Medicine*, *10*, 331–342. doi:10.1207/S15327558IJBM1004_4

Martin, R. C., & Dahlen, E. R. (2005). Cognitive emotion regulation in the prediction of depression, anxiety, stress, and anger. *Personality and Individual Differences*, *39*, 1249–1260. doi:10.1207/S15327558IJBM1004_4

McLaughlin, K. A., & Nolen-Hoeksema, S. (2011). Rumination as a transdiagnostic factor in depression and anxiety. *Behaviour Research and Therapy*, *49*, 186–193. doi:10.1016/j.brat.2010.12.006

Mennin, D. S., Heimberg, R. G., Turk, C. L., & Fresco, D. M. (2005). Preliminary evidence for an emotion regulation deficit model of generalized anxiety disorder. *Behaviour Research and Therapy*, *43*, 1281–1310. doi:10.1016/j.brat.2004.08.008

Mennin, D. S., McLaughlan, K. A., & Flanagan, T. J. (2009). Emotion regulation deficits in generalized anxiety disorder, social anxiety disorder, and their co-occurrence. *Journal of Anxiety Disorders*, *23*, 866–871. doi:10.1016/j.janxdis.2009.04.006

Mineka, S., Watson, D., & Clark, L. A. (1998). Comorbidity of anxiety and unipolar mood disorders. *Annual Review of Psychology*, *49*, 377–412. doi:10.1146/annurev.psych.49.1.377

Mogotsi, M., Kaminer, D., & Stein, D. J. (2000). Quality of life in the anxiety disorders. *Harvard Review of Psychiatry*, *8*, 273–282. doi:10.1093/hrp/8.6.273

Moses, E. B., & Barlow, D. H. (2006). A new unified treatment approach for emotional disorders based on emotion science. *Current Directions in Psychological Science*, *15*, 146–150. doi:10.1111/j.0963-7214.2006.00425.x

Newman, M. G., & Llera, S. J. (2011). A novel theory of experiential avoidance in generalized anxiety disorder: A review and synthesis of research supporting a contrast avoidance model of worry. *Clinical Psychology Review*, *31*, 371–382. doi:10.1016/j.cpr.2011.01.008

Nolen-Hoeksema, S. (2000). The role of rumination in depressive disorders and mixed anxiety/depressive symptoms. *Journal of Abnormal Psychology*, *109*, 504–511. doi:10.1037/0021-843X.109.3.504

Nolen-Hoeksema, S., Wisco, B. E., & Lyubomirsky, S. (2008). Rethinking rumination. *Perspectives on Psychological Science*, *3*, 400–424. doi:10.1111/j.1745-6924.2008.00088.x

Ottenbreit, N. D., & Dobson, K. S. (2004). Avoidance and depression: The construction of the cognitive-behavioral avoidance scale. *Behaviour Research and Therapy*, *42*, 293–313. doi:10.1016/S0005-7967(03)00140-2

Park, C. L., Edmondson, D., & Lee, J. (2012). Development of self-regulation abilities as predictors of psychological adjustment across the first year of college. *Journal of Adult Development*, *19*, 40–49. doi:10.1007/s10804-011-9133-z

Preacher, K. J., & Hayes, A. F. (2004). SPSS and SAS procedures for estimating indirect effects in simple mediation models. *Behavior Research Methods, Instruments, and Computers*, *36*, 717–731. doi:10.3758/BF03206553

Prkachin, K. M., & Silverman, B. E. (2002). Hostility and facial expressions in young men and women: Is social regulation more important than negative affect? *Health Psychology*, *21*, 33–39. doi:10.1037/0278-6133.21.1.33

Rivers, S. E., Brackett, M. A., Katulak, N. A., & Salovey, P. (2007). Regulating anger and sadness: An exploration of discrete emotions in emotion regulation. *Journal of Happiness Studies*, *8*, 393–427. doi:10.1007/s10902-006-9017-2

Roemer, L., Lee, J. K., Salters-Pedneault, K., Erisman, S. M., Orsillo, S. M., & Mennin, D. S. (2009). Mindfulness and emotion regulation difficulties in generalized anxiety disorder: Preliminary evidence for independent and overlapping contributions. *Behavior Therapy, 40*, 142–156. doi:10.1016/j.beth.2008.04.001

Rude, S. S., Chrisman, J. G., Burton Denmark, A., & Maestas, K. L. (2012). Expression of direct anger and hostility predict depression symptoms in formerly depressed women. *Canadian Journal of Behavioural Science, 44*, 200–209. doi: 10.1037/a0027496

Rude, S. S., & McCarthy, C. T. (2003). Emotional functioning in depressed and depression-vulnerable college students. *Cognition and Emotion, 17*, 799–806. doi:10.1080/02699930302283

Russell, G., & Shaw, S. (2009). A study to investigate the prevalence of social anxiety in a sample of higher education students in the United Kingdom. *Journal of Mental Health, 18*, 198–206. doi:10.1080/09638230802522494

Salovey, P., Stroud, L. R., Woolery, A., & Epel, E. S. (2002). Perceived emotional intelligence, stress reactivity, and symptom reports: Further explorations using the Trait Meta-Mood Scale. *Psychology and Health, 17*, 611–627. doi:10.1080/08870440290025812

Sanz, J., García-Vera, M. P., & Magán, I. (2010). Anger and hostility from the perspective of the Big Five personality model. *Scandinavian Journal of Psychology, 51*, 262–270. doi:10.1111/j.1467-9450.2009.00771.x

Wong, N., Sarver, D. E., & Beidel, D. (2012). Quality of life impairments among adults with social phobia: The impact of subtype. *Journal of Anxiety Disorders, 26*, 50–57. doi:10.1016/j.janxdis.2011.08.012

Scott, S. L., Marino Carper, T., Middleton, M., White, R., Renk, K., & Grills-Taquechel, A. (2010). Relationships among locus of control, coping behaviors, and levels of worry following exposure to hurricanes. *Journal of Loss and Trauma, 15*, 123–137. doi:10.1080/15325020902925985

Scott, W. D., Ingram, R. E., & Shadel, W. G. (2003). Hostile and sad mood profiles in dysphoria: Evidence for cognitive specificity. *Journal of Social and Clinical Psychology, 22*, 233–253. doi:10.1521/jscp.22.3.233.22892

Sloan, D. M., & Kring, A. M. (2007). Measuring changes in emotion during psychotherapy: Conceptual and methodological issues. *Clinical Psychology: Science and Practice, 14*, 307–322. doi:10.1111/j.1468-2850.2007.00092.x

Sprague, J., Verona, E., Kalkhoff, W., & Kilmer, A. (2011). Moderators and mediators in the stress-aggression relationship: Executive functioning and anger. *Emotion, 11*, 61–73. doi:10.1037/a0021788

Starcevic, V., Berle, D., Milicevic, D., Hannan, A., Lamplugh, C., & Eslick, G. D. (2007). Pathological worry, anxiety disorders and the impact of co-occurrence with depressive and other anxiety disorders. *Journal of Anxiety Disorders, 21*, 1016–1027. doi:10.1016/j.janxdis.2006.10.015

Stewart, J. C., Fitzgerald, G. J., & Kamarck, T. W. (2010). Hostility now, depression later? Longitudinal associations among emotional risk factors for coronary artery disease. *Annals of Behavioral Medicine, 39*, 258–266. doi:10.1007/s12160-010-9185-5

Storch, E. A., Bagner, D. M., Geffken, G. R., & Baumeister, A. L. (2004). Association between overt and relational aggression and psychosocial adjustment in undergraduate college students. *Violence and Victimization, 19*, 689–700. doi:10.1891/vivi.19.6.689.66342

Stringaris, A., Cohen, P., Pine, D. S., & Leibenluft, E. (2009). Adult outcomes of youth irritability: A 20-year prospective community-based study. *The American Journal of Psychiatry, 166*, 1048–1054. doi:10.1176/appi.ajp.2009.08121849

Trew, J. L., & Alden, L. E. (2009). Predicting anger in social anxiety: The mediating role of rumination. *Behaviour Research and Therapy, 47*, 1079–1084. doi:10.1016/j.brat.2009.07.019

Trosper, S. E., Buzzella, B. A., Bennett, S. M. & Ehrenreich, J. T. (2009). Emotion regulation in youth with emotional disorders: Implications for a unified treatment approach. *Clinical Child and Family Psychology Review*, *12*, 234–254. doi:10.1007/s10567-009-0043-6

Tull, M. T., Barrett, H. M., McMillan, E. S., & Roemer, L. (2007). A preliminary investigation of the relationship between emotion regulation difficulties and posttraumatic stress symptoms. *Behavior Therapy*, *38*, 303–313. doi:10.1016/j.beth.2006.10.001

Vandervort, D. J. (1995). Depression, anxiety, hostility and physical health. *Current Psychology: A Journal for Diverse Perspectives on Diverse Psychological Issues*, *14*, 69–82. doi:10.1007/BF02686875

Virtanen, M., Kivimäki, M., Elovainio, M., Vahtera, J., Kokko, K., & Pulkkinen, L. (2005). Mental health and hostility as predictors of temporary employment: Evidence from two prospective studies. *Social Science and Medicine*, *61*, 2084–2095. doi:10.1016/j.socscimed.2005.04.028

Watson, D. C., & Sinha, B. (2008). Emotion regulation, coping, and psychological symptoms. *International Journal of Stress Management*, *15*, 222–234. doi:10.1037/1072-5245.15.3.222

Whalen, C. K., Jamner, L. D., Henker, B., & Delfino, R. J. (2001). Smoking and moods in adolescents with depressive and aggressive dispositions: Evidence from surveys and electronic diaries. *Health Psychology*, *20*, 99–111. doi:10.1037/0278-6133.20.2.99

Weeks, J. W., Rodebaugh, T. L., Heimberg, R. G., Norton, P. J., & Jakatdar, T. A. (2009). "To avoid evaluation, withdraw": Fears of evaluation and depressive cognitions lead to social anxiety and submissive withdrawal. *Cognitive Therapy Research*, *33*, 375–389. doi:10.1007/s10608-008-9203-0

Weiss, J. W., Mouttapa, M., Chou, C. P., Nezami, E., Anderson Johnson, C., Palmer, P. H., ... Unger, J. B. (2005). Hostility, depressive symptoms, and smoking in early adolescence. *Journal of Adolescence*, *28*, 49–62. doi:10.1016/j.adolescence.2004.03.009

Werner, K. H., Goldin, P. R., Ball, T. M., Heimberg, R. G., & Gross, J. J. (2011). Assessing emotion regulation in social anxiety disorder: The emotion regulation interview. *Journal of Psychopathology and Behavioral Assessment*, *33*, 346–354. doi:10.1007/s10862-011-9225-x

Wong, Q. J. J., & Moulds, M. L. (2010). Do socially anxious individuals hold positive metacognitive beliefs about rumination? *Behaviour Change*, *27*, 69–83. doi:10.1375/bech.27.2.69

Yan, L. L., Liu, K., Matthews, K. A., Daviglus, M. L., Ferguson, T. F., & Kiefe, C. I. (2003). Psychosocial factors and risk of hypertension: The coronary artery risk development in young adults study. *Journal of the American Medical Association*, *290*, 2138–2148. doi:10.1001/jama.290.16.2138

Yook, K., Kim, K. H., Suh, S. Y., & Lee, K. S. (2010). Intolerance of uncertainty, worry, and rumination in major depressive disorder and generalized anxiety disorder. *Journal of Anxiety Disorders*, *24*, 623–628. doi:10.1016/j.janxdis.2010.04.003

Social Hierarchy and Depression:
The Role of Emotion Suppression

CARRIE A. LANGNER

ELISSA S. EPEL

KAREN A. MATTHEWS

JUDITH T. MOSKOWITZ

NANCY E. ADLER

ABSTRACT. Position in the social hierarchy is a major determinant of health outcomes. We examined the associations between aspects of social hierarchy and depressive symptoms with a specific focus on one potential psychological mechanism: emotion suppression. Suppressing negative emotion has mental health costs, but individuals with low social power and low social status may use these strategies to avoid conflict. Study 1 assessed perceived social power, tendency to suppress negative emotion, and depressive symptoms in a community sample of women. Low social power was related to greater depressive symptoms, and this relationship was partially mediated by emotion suppression. Study 2 examined education as a proxy for social hierarchy position, anger suppression, and depressive symptoms in a national, longitudinal cohort study (The Coronary Artery Risk Development in Young Adults [CARDIA] study; Cutter et al., 1991). Much as in Study 1, low education levels were correlated with greater depressive symptoms, and this relationship was partially mediated by anger suppression. Further, suppression mediated the relationship between low education and subsequent depression up to 15 years later. These findings support the theory that social hierarchy affects mental health in part through a process of emotion suppression.

WHY DO INDIVIDUALS with low social status experience poor health outcomes? In addition to a lack of resources, the psychological experience of low status itself appears to affect health (Adler, Epel, Castellazzo, & Ickovics, 2000). Past research suggests that the relationship between low socioeconomic status (SES) and poor health may be mediated by cognitive-emotional factors (Gallo & Matthews, 2003). Researchers have focused on effects of negative affect as well as lack of positive emotion (Cohen & Pressman, 2006; Salovey, Rothman, Detweiler, & Steward, 2000). However, it may be that it is not only the experience of negative emotion or lack of positive emotion that influences health but also the need to suppress the expression of emotion—particularly negative emotion—that is health-damaging. No studies have examined emotion suppression as a mediator of the relationship between social hierarchy and mental health. We hypothesized that people with low positions in the social hierarchy may feel pressured to suppress outward expression of negative emotion, which harms long-term emotional health, resulting in depressive symptoms. We tested this hypothesis in two samples by first establishing a relationship between an index of social hierarchy position and depressive symptoms and by then examining the extent to which this association was mediated by emotion suppression.

Adverse Consequences of Emotion Suppression

There are different ways of coping with threats, including threats related to one's position in the social hierarchy (Folkman, Lazarus, Dunkel-Schetter, De-Longis, & Gruen, 1986). Emotion suppression is a coping strategy for regulating negative emotions that suppresses the outward expression of a negative emotional experience (see Gross & Levenson, 1997). In the short term, emotion suppression can be socially advantageous to those at the bottom of a hierarchy by decreasing conflict with individuals who control resources and outcomes. However, emotion suppression does not reduce the internal experience of negative emotion (Gross & Levenson, 1997; John & Gross, 2004), and its use requires high cognitive effort and is related to decreased positive affect (Gross, 2002). Additionally, the tendency to suppress the expression of emotions reduces opportunities for social support and closeness to others (Srivastava, Tamir, McGonigal, John, & Gross, 2009). Perhaps due to corresponding elevated negative emotion, decreased positive emotion, and impaired social relationships, the use of emotion suppression strategies is consistently associated with depression (Bromberger & Matthews, 1996; McDaniel & Richards, 1990; Nolen-Hoeksema, 1987; Riley, Treiber, & Woods, 1989; Thomas & Atakan, 1993).

Indices of Social Hierarchy and Depression

The constructs of social power and social status capture different aspects of social hierarchy. Social power reflects control relative to others over valued outcomes (Fiske & Berdhal, 2007), whereas social status reflects one's perceived prominence within a social group (Anderson, John, Keltner, & Kring, 2001). Socioeconomic status (education, occupation, and income) provides social resources and influences one's standing within a social group (Adler et al., 2000; Berger, Cohen, & Zelditch, 1972). Social status may serve as a source of social power (Fiske & Berdahl, 2007) perhaps via allocation of resources (Keltner, Gruenfeld, & Anderson, 2003). Past research on social hierarchy, reviewed below, indicates that low social status and low social power are associated with negative emotion and depressive symptoms.

Low SES has been linked to depressive symptoms (Dohrenwend et al., 1992), and longitudinal research suggests that the prevalence and persistence of depressive symptoms are predicted by early life socioeconomic disadvantage (Danese et al., 2009; Wheaton, 1978). Looking at psychological distress more generally, lower SES predicts distress within all major American ethnic groups (Centers for Disease Control and Prevention [CDC], 2004). In addition to affecting material resources available to individuals, SES appears to affect mental and physical health through subjective perceptions of lower relative status (Adler et al., 2000; Adler et al., 2008; Goodman et al., 2001; Leu et al., 2008; Singh-Manoux, Adler, & Marmot, 2003).

The relationship between social power and depression has not been documented as extensively as that between SES and depression. However, social power may be particularly relevant to the interpersonal processes related to depression because it is instantiated within personal relationships. Past studies of social power indicate that perceiving oneself as having less power than others is associated with low positive emotional experience (Berdahl & Martorana, 2006). Interactions with a powerful partner, whether within a long-term intimate relationship or a new acquaintanceship, are associated with negative emotions (Langner & Keltner, 2008). Within marital relationships, having lower social power than one's partner is associated with greater depressive symptoms (Mirowsky, 1985).

A Theory of Emotion Suppression as a Mediator of the Hierarchy-Depression Relationship

The experience of low social power and status unfolds in a social environment that may increase the need to suppress or inhibit one's experience to the extent that others with more power can punish and threaten those below them (Keltner et al., 2003). Those with low social power and status are not sanctioned to express certain types of negative emotions (e.g., anger), which are seen as inappropriate when displayed by low status individuals (Tiedens, Ellsworth, & Mesquita, 2000). Other aspects of inhibition, such as hiding one's attitudes (Bradberry, 2006; Eaker, Sullivan, Kelly-Hayes, D'Agostino, & Benjamin, 2007; Frank & Thomas, 2003; Krieger, 1990) or behavioral constriction (Tiedens & Fragale, 2003), may also play a mediating role in the relationship between social hierarchy and health. We focus here on emotion suppression because it may be especially potent in relation to depression, an affective disorder.

There is some evidence that individuals with lower social status and power are more likely to suppress the expression of emotion. Social groups who have traditionally experienced less social power and status are more likely to use suppression strategies. For example, compared to European Americans, people of color more frequently use emotion suppression as an emotion regulation strategy (Gross & John, 2003). Further, facial muscle actions associated with the suppression of emotion expressions are more common among individuals with low status compared to those with high status (Keltner, Young, Heerey, Oemig, & Monarch, 1998). Similarly, a cluster of symptoms related to lower status that are more common in women (e.g., low instrumentality, rumination, anger suppression) create vulnerability to depression (Bromberger & Matthews, 1996). The process of silencing the self in order to maintain harmony within a relationship is a proposed mechanism for the prevalence of depression among women (Jack & Dill, 1992). These gender-typed processes may be, at least in part, a function of low social power and status. Self-silencing is associated with depression across men and women and multiple American ethnic groups (Gratch, Bassett, & Attra, 2006).

We theorize that individuals with low SES will more frequently be engaged in relationships in which they have low social power, which pressures them to suppress their expression of emotion. This is particularly true in work relationships, but may also occur in other social interactions. Individuals with low social status may be more likely to have low social power in a greater number of their interpersonal relationships (for example, an individual with a low level of education filling a subordinate role in the workplace and having low power within a marital relationship due to low income). An individual with less control over outcomes may have a greater need to avoid interpersonal conflict and thereby choose to suppress the expression of negative emotions.

One previous study has examined social status in relation to emotion suppression and depression (Allan & Gilbert, 2002). This study demonstrated that anger suppression was employed significantly more often in imagined interactions with a higher status person than with a lower status person. Further, greater anger suppression was associated with higher depressive symptoms. While this research did not explore the role of emotion suppression as a *mediator* of the relationship between social hierarchy and depression, the findings are supportive of this idea.

In sum, we argue that social pressure to be polite and deferential to people with greater status and power results in more emotion suppression among those who occupy low positions within a social hierarchy. This behavioral pattern of suppression may account in part for why they experience more depressive symptoms. By linking research on social power and health disparities with the literature on emotion suppression, we hypothesize that social hierarchy variables (social power, education) will be associated with depressive symptoms and that emotion suppression will partially mediate this relationship. While other studies have examined various aspects of this process, this is the first study to examine emotion suppression as a mediator of the relationship between social hierarchy and mental health.

We tested the proposed theory in a set of secondary data analyses on two datasets. In Study 1, we measured self-reported social power as an index of social hierarchy position, assessing the relationship between an individual's control over outcomes in interpersonal relationships, the tendency to suppress emotion expression, and depressive symptoms. In Study 2, we examined these relationships in a longitudinal, population-based sample with a more diverse education distribution, utilizing an education measure as the index of social hierarchy position.

Study 1

First, we tested our theory of social hierarchy, emotion suppression, and depression in a community sample of women. We examined social power as the operationalization of social hierarchy position in relation to emotion suppression tendencies and depressive symptoms. In this study, we extended past research by examining the relationship between social power and depression and then by testing our hypothesis of emotion suppression as a partial mediator.

Method

Participants

Sixty-nine women, all healthy mothers of young children, participated in a broader study of stress and coping. Forty-five of the women had a child with a serious chronic medical condition, and the rest had healthy children. The women ranged in age from 19 to 50 years ($M = 38.46$ years, $SD = 6.11$ years). Educational background ranged from 12 to 20 years of schooling, and on average, participants had completed about 3 years of college or training past high school ($M = 14.96$, $SD = 1.93$). Participants reported the following ethnic backgrounds: 59% Caucasian, 13% Black, 12% Asian, 10% Hispanic, and 6% other.

Procedure

Participants were recruited through their child's health care professional in San Francisco Bay Area clinics or by public postings. Laboratory sessions took place at the Oakland Children's Hospital Pediatric Clinical Research Center (see Epel et al., 2004). Participants filled out a questionnaire battery at home and returned it to the clinic. This included demographics, social power scale, ways of coping, and depressive symptoms.

Measures

Our measures of social power, emotion suppression, and depression were as follows.

Social power. Social power was measured with the 8-item capacity for power scale (e.g., "I think I have a great deal of power," "If I want to, I get to make the decisions"; Anderson & Galinsky, 2006). Past research demonstrated that scores on this scale are associated with social standing within hierarchies and occupation of powerful roles (Anderson & Galinsky, 2006). Participants rated the degree to which they experienced social power across their interpersonal relationships. Response options ranged from 1 (*disagree strongly*) to 7 (*agree strongly*) with higher scores indicating a greater sense of social power. The sample in the current study rated their capacity for social power above the midpoint ($M = 5.28$, $SD = 0.75$) and the items demonstrated acceptable reliability ($\alpha = .83$).

Emotion suppression. We created a measure of emotion suppression by forming a composite of two items from the Self-Controlling subscale of the Ways of Coping scale (Folkman & Lazarus, 1988) that measure the suppression of emotion and negative experience in the presence of others: "You tried to keep your feelings to yourself"; "You kept others from knowing how bad things were." Participants rated each item on a 4-point scale assessing how often they use the strategy (0: not used, 1: used somewhat, 2: used quite a bit, 3: used a great deal). On average, the participants in this sample scored below the midpoint ($M = 0.92$, $SD = 0.77$). The two items demonstrated acceptable internal reliability ($\alpha = .72$).

Depression. The Center for Epidemiologic Studies Depression Scale (CES-D), a 20-item self-report measure, was developed at the National Institute for Mental Health to measure depressive symptomatology and demonstrated high internal reliability and validity in prior research (e.g., correlated with clinical ratings of depression; Radloff, 1977). Participants rated the presence of depressive symptoms during the last 2 weeks (0: rarely; 3: most of the time; $M = 13.88$, $SD = 10.13$; $\alpha = .91$). Total scores can range from 0 to 60 on the CES-D, and a symptom threshold of 16 or above has been designated as clinically significant depressive symptoms (Weissman, Sholomskas, Pottenger, Prusoff, & Locke, 1977). In this sample, 31.9% scored above this threshold, indicating at least mild depressive symptoms.

Results

Before testing the mediational models, we examined the relationships between the primary variables and demographic variables (see Table 1). Ethnic background was coded as White (1) and Other (0) because there were not enough participants in any one ethnic minority category to provide statistical power for two-way comparisons. Social power was not significantly related to age, ethnic background, or education. Emotion suppression was not significantly related to age, ethnic background, or education. Depression was significantly related to education, but was not related to age or ethnic background.

As would be expected, the mothers of children with chronic conditions experienced a greater degree of depressive symptoms, $t(67) = 3.46$, $p < .01$, $r = .38$.

TABLE 1. Interrelationships Between Primary Variables and Demographic Variables in Study 1

Variable	Suppression	Depression	Age	Education	Ethnicity[a]
Social power	−.35*	−.25*	−.11	.02	.15
Suppression		.39*	−.13	−.04	−.13
Depression			.08	−.36*	−.10
Age				.33*	.09
Education					.11

[a]Ethnic groups coded as White (1) and Other (0) due to small sample size.
*$p < .05$.

However, there were no differences in mean social power, $t(67) = -1.65$, ns, or emotion suppression, $t(67) = 1.53$, ns, between mothers with healthy children and mothers with chronically ill children. Further, the hypothesized relationships between independent and dependent variables demonstrated the same pattern across groups; given that the subsamples were small, only analyses for the whole sample are presented.

Following Baron and Kenny (1986), a series of simultaneous regressions were performed to test for statistical mediation. All hypothesis testing was directional and therefore tested at the one-tailed significance level. Emotion suppression was examined as a mediator of the relationship between social power and depression (see Figure 1). First, emotion suppression was regressed onto social power (ß = −0.35, $p < .01$). Second, depression scores (CES-D) were regressed on to social power (ß = −0.25, $p < .05$). Third, depression scores were regressed on to emotion suppression, controlling for social power (ß = 0.35, $p < .01$). Lastly, the

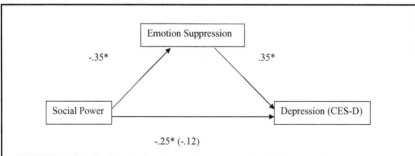

FIGURE 1. Mediational role of emotion suppression in the relationship between social power and depressive symptoms (Study 1).

relationship between social power and depression was assessed after controlling for emotion suppression ($ß = -0.12$, *ns*).

The results indicate that the relationship between social power and depression was reduced when emotion suppression was included in the model; however, the relationship did not drop to zero. A Sobel test of the variance explained by the mediator was statistically significant ($z = -2.38$, $p < .01$), indicating that the relationship between social power and depression is partially mediated by emotion suppression.[1] The same pattern of results and significance held when controlling for education, ethnicity, and age.

Discussion

Study 1 provided evidence that emotion suppression partially mediates the relationship between social power and depressive symptoms. This initial evidence is a first step in documenting the role of emotion suppression in health disparities. The current work adds support to the approach/inhibition theory of social power (Keltner et al., 2003). Considering emotion suppression as a specific type of behavioral inhibition, we demonstrated that individuals with low social power are more likely to report inhibiting emotionally expressive behavior. The current work connects the approach/inhibition theory to the field of health disparities by suggesting that in addition to negative emotional experience consequences of power, inhibition of emotion expression plays a role in mediating the relationship between power and depressive symptoms.

Education was not significantly correlated with social power or emotion suppression in this sample. Study 1 had a small sample, and unfortunately there was not a large range of educational levels (the vast majority were college-educated). In addition to the restricted range, the lack of correlation may have been due to the fact that a majority of our sample were women who were caring for children with a chronic health condition. This caretaking role might decrease social power due to a reduction in time spent within the public sphere regardless of education level. It is possible that the demands of this role countered any potential social power boost from high education. In contrast, some women may experience increased social power if their caregiving role leads them to advocate on behalf of their children. Future research might examine the possibility that the strength of the link between SES and power varies with the number and type of social roles individuals enact in their daily lives.

The research design in Study 1 was cross-sectional, so it was not possible to establish whether reported social hierarchy position and emotion suppression preceded or followed from depressive symptoms. Examining longitudinal relationships between social hierarchy, emotion suppression, and depression could help address this ambiguity. Study 2 addresses these limitations and also tests our hypotheses in a sample with gender, ethnic, and educational diversity.

Study 2

Study 2 utilized data from The Coronary Artery Risk Development in Young Adults (CARDIA) study (see Cutter et al., 1991). This longitudinal study was conducted by the National Heart, Lung, and Blood Institute to examine how heart disease risk develops in young adults. Taking advantage of the measures included in this longitudinal dataset, we examined education level as the indicator of social hierarchy position and a specific type of emotion suppression: anger suppression. Education level is one of the most commonly used indicators of socioeconomic position used in health research (Liberatos, Link, & Kelsey, 1988). Anger may be a particularly important emotion for the study of social hierarchy and suppression as this is an emotion in which expression is deemed appropriate only for those with high social power (Tiedens et al., 2000). In this study, we tested whether education level was related to subsequent level of depressive symptoms and whether this relationship was mediated in part by anger suppression.

Method

The study included African American and European American men and women in four regions of the United States and was stratified on race, gender, and education. The study began with participants aged 18–30 years and included six follow-up examinations. Within this sample, we examined participants with complete data for the variables of interest (Time 1 education measured 1985–1986, Time 2 anger suppression measured 1990–1991, and Time 3 depressive symptoms were reported in 1995–1996). We also explored depressive symptoms at two later measurement time points (2000–2001 and 2005–2006).

Participants

A total of 5,115 participants were recruited in 1985–1986 (Time 1) and were followed over time. Of the original sample, 4,352 participants participated in the 5-year follow-up in 1990–1991 (Time 2), and 3,950 participated in the 10-year follow-up in 1995–1996 (Time 3). Our subsample with complete data across all of the three primary time points was composed of 3,644 participants (55.6% women, 47.1% African American). An assessment of attrition over time indicated that in comparison with the Time 1 sample (54.5% women, 48.4% African American), the remaining sample at Time 2 contained a slightly greater proportion of women (55.1%) and a similar ethnic distribution (48.5% African American), and the sample at Time 3 contained a slightly greater proportion of women (55.3%) and similar ethnic distribution (48.5% African American).

Follow-up samples in 2000–2001 and 2005–2006 included 3,672 participants and 3,549 participants, respectively. In comparison with Time 1, the 15-year follow-up sample (2000–2001) contained a slightly greater proportion of women (55.7%) and a slightly smaller proportion of African American participants

(46.9%). In comparison with Time 1, the 20-year follow-up sample (2005–2006) contained a slightly greater proportion of women (56.7%) and a slightly smaller proportion of African American participants (46.1%).

Measures

Our measures of SES, emotion suppression, and depressive symptoms were as follows.

Socioeconomic status. Education level was measured at baseline, prior to our hypothesized mediator. Participants reported the number of years of schooling they had completed, ranging from 1 to 20 (1–6: elementary school grades, 9–12: high school, 13–16: college, 17–20: graduate school). On average, participants had completed 1–2 years of college ($M = 13.95$, $SD = 2.26$). The lowest score in the sample was for seventh grade (7) and the highest was for 4 or more years of graduate school (20). Participants who did not participate at Time 2 and Time 3 had less education ($M = 13.24$, $M = 13.52$, respectively) than the original sample. Although there were some small increases in education level from Time 1 to Time 2 ($M = 14.37$) in the retained sample, using Time 2 education in place of Time 1 education produced the same pattern and significance of results. In order to test mediation, we use Time 1 education as the predictor as it preceded the mediator.

Emotion suppression. Several items from the "Anger-In" subscale of Spielberger's (1985) State, Trait, Expression of Anger Inventory were administered in the 1990 CARDIA survey administration (Cutter et al., 1991). Prior research indicated a relationship between scores on the anger-in scale and internalizing responses to hypothetical anger scenarios (Spielberger, 1988). The instructions for the scale were "Here is a list of things people do when they get angry, irritated, or annoyed. Please check whether, when you are really angry or annoyed, you are likely, somewhat likely or not too likely to do the following things." Two scale items ("Try to act as though nothing much happened," "Keep it to yourself"; 3: not too likely, 2: somewhat likely, 1: very likely) were averaged to form a composite measure of anger suppression ($M = 2.14$, $SD = .64$; $\alpha = .67$). A third item ("Apologize even though you are right") was not included because it had low face validity as a measure of emotion suppression. Apologizing to avoid conflict is a behavior that extends beyond suppressing the visible manifestations of an experienced emotion. Further, the item demonstrated a lower item-total correlation ($r = .25$ vs. $r = .47$ and $r = .49$ for the two retained items) and would have reduced the overall scale reliability ($\alpha = .59$). Mean scale scores are reverse-scored for analyses so that larger numbers reflect a greater tendency to suppress anger.

Depressive symptoms. The CES-D (Radloff, 1977), described in relation to Study 1, was also used in the CARDIA study (Cutter et al., 1991). At the Time 3 (10-year follow-up) measurement (1995–1996), 21.7% of the sample scored above the threshold (total score greater than 16) indicating at least mild depressive symptoms ($M = 10.65$, $SD = 8.19$; $\alpha = .89$). At the 15-year follow-up measurement (2000–2001), 17% scored above the threshold indicating at least mild depressive symptoms ($M = 9.07$, $SD = 7.78$; $\alpha = .88$). At the 20-year follow-up measurement (2005–2006), 17.7% scored above the threshold indicating at least mild depressive symptoms ($M = 9.27$, $SD = 7.87$; $\alpha = .88$).

Results

Before testing the mediational models, we examined the relationships between the primary variables and demographic variables (age, sex, race; see Table 2). Education levels were higher among European American than among African American participants and for older participants in comparison with younger participants. Emotion suppression was significantly greater among African American participants, men, and older participants. Depressive symptom mean scores were higher among African American participants and women. Despite these significant relationships between some of the demographic variables and our primary variables, controlling for age, race, and gender did not alter the pattern or significance of results from hypothesis testing reported below.

Following the mediation approach used in Study 1, a series of simultaneous regressions were performed to test for statistical mediation (Baron & Kenny,

TABLE 2. Interrelationships Between Primary Variables and Demographic Variables in Study 2

		Demographic variables			
	Age	Race		Sex	
Primary variables		African American (1)	European American (2)	Male (1)	Female (2)
Education					
Effect (r)	.31*		.34*		−.01
Mean		13.13	14.68	13.96	13.94
SD		1.86	2.32	2.38	2.15
Suppression					
Effect (r)	−.05*		−.14*		−.13*
Mean		2.05	2.22	2.05	2.21
SD		.63	.63	.63	.63
Depression					
Effect (r)	−.02		−.19*		.09*
Mean		12.26	9.22	9.87	11.27
SD		8.95	7.16	7.31	8.78

*$p < .05$.

1986). All hypothesis testing was directional and therefore tested at the one-tailed significance level. In order to test for changes in depressive symptoms over time, depressive symptoms levels at Time 2 (depressive symptom measurement concurrent with the measurement of the mediator) were included as a control variable in each step. First, anger suppression was regressed onto education ($\beta = -.09$, $p < .01$). Second, mean depressive symptom levels (CES-D) were regressed on to education ($\beta = -.11$, $p < .001$). Third, mean depressive symptom levels were regressed on to anger suppression, controlling for education ($\beta = .04$, $p < .05$). Lastly, the relationship between education and depressive symptoms was assessed after controlling for anger suppression ($\beta = -.10$, $p < .001$; see Figure 2).

The results indicate that although the relationship between education and depressive symptoms was reduced when anger suppression was included in the model, the change in the size of the relationship is small. However, a Sobel test revealed that significant variance was explained by the mediator ($z = -2.37$, $p < .05$), indicating that the effect of education on depressive symptom levels is partially mediated by anger suppression.

Further, the same pattern of results and significance was obtained when examining depressive symptoms measured years later. Anger suppression partially mediated the relationship between education and mean depressive symptom levels at Year 15 (2000–2001; $z = -2.80$, $p < .001$) and between education and mean depressive symptom levels at Year 20 (2005–2006; $z = -2.82$, $p < .001$).

The mediation hypothesis was tested separately in the four Ethnicity × Sex subgroups; the pattern was significant for African American women ($z = -3.09$, $p < .01$), European American women ($z = -2.79, p < .01$), and African American men ($z = -1.69, p < .05$). There was not a significant mediation effect for European American men ($z = 0.84, p > .10$).

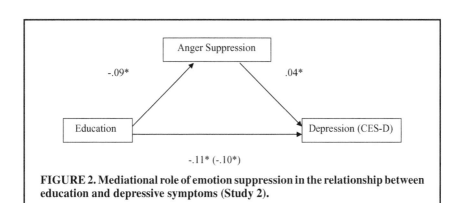

FIGURE 2. Mediational role of emotion suppression in the relationship between education and depressive symptoms (Study 2).

Discussion

In sum, anger suppression partially mediated the relationship between education and depressive symptoms at 10-, 15-, and 20-year follow-ups. For the most part, the pattern of results was consistent across gender and ethnic groups. This replicates the pattern of results found in Study 1, but with a measure of education as the proxy for social hierarchy position.

While the second study had some longitudinal features, we lacked multiple time measurements for some of our variables (e.g., anger suppression). Therefore, we could not analyze changes in anger suppression over time in addition to changes in depression over time in order to more fully understand the temporal ordering of these relationships. In a longitudinal dataset designed to test these particular relationships, multifaceted measures of social status and emotion suppression could be administered at multiple time points.

GENERAL DISCUSSION

The proposed model was supported in two samples, garnering initial evidence for the theory-based prediction that emotion suppression would partially mediate the relationship between indicators of social hierarchy and depressive symptoms. Further, within Study 2 the small but consistent mediation effect of emotion suppression was replicated at 10-, 15-, and 20-year time-lagged measures of depressive symptoms. To our knowledge, these are the first studies to examine emotion suppression as a pathway by which social hierarchy variables affect mental health. These findings lend support to the idea that those on the lower end of a social hierarchy are more likely to use emotion suppression strategies, providing evidence of a relationship between direct measures of social power and status (vs. indirect measures such as race and gender) and emotion suppression. Further, these data indicate that chronic emotion suppression is one factor contributing to the disproportionate experience of depression among those with lower social power and status. This initial evidence is a first step in documenting the role of emotion suppression in health disparities.

The current investigation examined two aspects of social hierarchy: self-reported social power and education level. We theorized that social hierarchy position will affect depression through emotion suppression processes. We found support for the model using two aspects of social hierarchy: social power and education level. The current studies were limited with regard to examining multiple aspects of hierarchy simultaneously. In Study 1's small sample, the education measure had restricted range, which hampered our ability to use it as a proxy for social hierarchy position in our proposed model. In Study 2, SES was the only aspect of social hierarchy that was measured. Ideally, the CARDIA data (Cutter et al., 1991; Study 2) would have included a measure of social power in addition to assessing SES. Multiple aspects of social hierarchy are interrelated and may have varying degrees of effect on emotion suppression and depressive symptoms. Further research could assess multiple measures of social hierarchy position in a large sample, testing whether our findings translate to other hierarchy-related phenomena (e.g., peer-nominated social status, role-based social power). While education is likely to be the best predictor of health compared to other SES parameters (Winkelby, Jatulis, Frank, & Formann, 1992), future research might examine multiple measures of social hierarchy simultaneously to assess their relative contributions to emotion suppression and health.

It will also be important to test this theory with other measures of emotion suppression. The items used in both studies have good face validity and acceptable reliability and are a first step. However, one scale was specific to anger suppression, and each scale had a limited number of items. It would have been preferable to use a more extensively validated scale of emotion suppression with a greater number of items (e.g., Gross & John, 2003). While epidemiological datasets have the advantage of large, representative samples, they often have the disadvantage of shortened scales due to space constraints, and with secondary data analyses the measures have not necessarily been designed to test the specific hypotheses. Moving beyond self-reported emotion suppression, future research could examine the nonverbal and physiological markers of emotion suppression following changes in social status or social power. More reliable measures of emotion suppression would help indicate whether the small effect sizes found in Study 2 are consistent effects or the effect sizes were constrained by the reliability of the available measures.

Experimental data could provide complementary evidence for the effects of low social hierarchy positions on emotion suppression and subsequent depressive symptoms. Although we found support for the theorized relationships in a longitudinal dataset, an experimental design could isolate the causal direction between hierarchy and emotion suppression. Researchers are beginning to examine the extent to which engagement in emotion regulation is deliberate or automatic (Mauss, Bunge, & Gross, 2007), and experimental work might test the effects of social status and power manipulations on automatic emotion suppression.

Additional studies might examine the suppression of both positive and negative emotions to compare the effects of these aspects of emotion suppression. It may be that people with low positions in a social hierarchy are most often suppressing negative emotions (e.g., anger at a boss) and only occasionally suppressing positive emotion (e.g., amusement at a highly educated acquaintance's gaffe). Alternatively, emotion suppression may be difficult to enact selectively based upon emotional valence, and therefore chronic use of emotion suppression strategies might lead to a broader inhibitory disposition (Gross & John, 2003).

These findings can be linked to recent work on the embodiment of social hierarchy position. Differential nonverbal markers of SES are distinct enough that observers can guess the SES level of strangers (Kraus & Keltner, 2009). Individuals with low SES display "engagement" (nonverbal markers of attention to one's partner such as gaze) in contrast with a disinhibited lack of engagement displayed by those with high SES. An emotionally "controlled" appearance resulting from emotion suppression may be another nonverbal signal of an individual's social power or status. The embodiment of social hierarchy position has implications for physiological and behavioral facets. Carney, Cuddy, and Yap (2010) found that posing in a position of low power was associated with decreased testosterone, increased cortisol, and decreased feelings of power and tolerance of risk. This suggests that an individual with low social standing who suppresses emotions might experience physiological reactions that in turn lead the individual to feel less powerful, perhaps perpetuating a cycle that maintains the stability of a hierarchy.

Future research should address the boundary conditions of the current model. Cultural differences in the meaning and evaluation of emotion suppression strategies may mean that the effects of emotion suppression are not as deleterious in some cultures (e.g., East Asian cultures; see Butler, Lee, & Gross, 2007). In cultures where hierarchy is valued and individuals employing emotion suppression strategies are still able to be socially responsive, emotion suppression may not have as strong an association with depression and may not play a mediating role in the relationship between social hierarchy and health. The current samples are from a Western culture (United States) where egalitarianism and self-expression are valued and emotion suppression is less likely to feel comfortable.

We propose emotion suppression as one pathway from social hierarchy to depression. Other pathways that would be interesting to investigate in relation to emotion suppression include postural constriction, attitude expression, rumination, and social support. For example, emotion suppression makes interpersonal interactions more stressful (Butler et al., 2003) and affects the quality of social relationships (Srivastava et al., 2009), suggesting that the chronic use of emotion suppression could contribute to and exacerbate depressive symptoms due to a reduction in social support. Additionally, mediating processes that may run in the opposite direction could be investigated simultaneously (e.g., self-control associated with high education and good health; Moffitt et al., 2011).[2] It remains to be seen what the relative contribution of emotion suppression is to the hierarchy-health relationship in comparison with other mediating processes.

In conclusion, these findings offer preliminary support for the theory that low social hierarchy position promotes depression, in part through emotion suppression. These findings have implications for our understanding of how perceptions of social status and social power may affect mental health, and in turn, possibly physical health. The plethora of research findings demonstrating a relationship between social stratification and health may be partly explained by emotion suppression, a hypothesis that is testable both in experimental studies and in population health studies.

ACKNOWLEDGMENTS

The authors thank the UCSF Health Psychology postdoctoral research group for their feedback on this research. C.L. was supported by an NIH Ruth L. Kirschstein National Research Service Award (T32 MH019391-15) at UCSF and an NIH Loan Repayment Program award (1 L60 MD002064-01). E.E. was supported by an NIMH K08 award (MH64110-01A1). The authors also thank the Oakland Children's Hospital-UCSF PCRC NIH MO1 RR01271. The work on the second study in this manuscript was partially supported by contracts: University of Alabama at Birmingham, Coordinating Center, N01-HC-95095; University of Alabama at Birmingham, Field Center, N01-HC-48047; University of Minnesota, Field Center and Diet Reading Center (Year 20 Exam), N01-HC-48048; Northwestern University, Field Center, N01-HC-48049; Kaiser Foundation Research Institute, N01-HC-48050; University of California, Irvine, Echocardiography Reading Center (Year 5 & 10), N01-HC-45134; Harbor-UCLA Research Education Institute, Computed Tomography Reading Center (Year 15 Exam), N01-HC-05187; Wake Forest University (Year 20 Exam), N01-HC-45205; New England Medical Center (Year 20 Exam), N01-HC-45204 from the National Heart, Lung and Blood Institute.

NOTES

1. Analyses using bootstrapping, an alternative approach to mediation testing appropriate for small samples (Preacher & Hayes, 2004), replicated the findings in pattern and significance (with bootstrap samples set at 3,000).

2. We thank an anonymous reviewer for the idea that self-regulation could be a possible conflicting process in mediating the relationship between status and emotion suppression, in part accounting for the small effect size.

REFERENCES

Adler, N., Epel, E., Castellazzo, G., & Ickovics, J. R. (2000). Relationship of subjective and objective status with psychological and physiological functioning: Preliminary data in healthy white women. *Health Psychology, 19*(6), 586–592.

Adler, N., Singh-Manoux, A., Schwartz, J., Stewart, J., Matthews, K., & Marmot, M. G. (2008). Social status and health: A comparison of British civil servants in Whitehall-II with European- and African-Americans in CARDIA. *Social Science & Medicine, 66*(5), 1034–1045.

Allan, S., & Gilbert, P. (2002). Anger and anger expression in relation to perceptions of social rank, entrapment, and depressive symptoms. *Personality and Individual Differences, 32*, 551–565.

Anderson, C., & Galinsky, A. D. (2006). Power, optimism, and risk-taking. *European Journal of Social Psychology, 36*, 511–536.

Anderson, C., John, O. P., Keltner, D., & Kring, A. M. (2001). Who attains social status? Effects of personality traits and physical attractiveness in social groups. *Journal of Personality and Social Psychology, 81*, 116–132.

Baron, R. M., & Kenny, D. A. (1986). The moderator-mediator variable distinction in social psychological research: Conceptual, strategic, and statistical considerations. *Journal of Personality and Social Psychology, 51*(6), 1173–1182.

Berdahl, J. L., & Martorana, P. (2006). Effects of power on influence, expression, and emotion during a controversial discussion. *European Journal of Social Psychology: Special Issue on Social Power and Group Processes, 36*, 497–509.

Berger, J., Cohen, B. P., & Zelditch, M. (1972). Status characteristics and social interaction. *American Sociological Review, 37*, 241–255.

Bradberry, M. P. (2006). Self-silencing behavior and its relation to depressive symptoms in Mexican and Mexican American women. *Dissertation Abstracts International, 66*, 6914.

Bromberger, J. T., & Matthews, K. A. (1996). A "feminine" model of vulnerability to depressive symptoms: A longitudinal investigation of middle-aged women. *Journal of Personality & Social Psychology, 70*(3), 591–598.

Butler, E. A., Egloff, B., Wilhelm, F. H., Smith, N. C., Erickson, E. A., & Gross, J. J. (2003). The social consequences of expressive suppression. *Emotion, 3*, 48–67.

Butler, E. A., Lee, T. L., & Gross, J. J. (2007). Emotion regulation and culture: Are the social consequences of emotion suppression culture-specific? *Emotion, 7*(1), 30–48.

Carney, D. R., Cuddy, A. J., & Yap, A. J. (2010). Power posing: Brief nonverbal displays affect neuroendocrine levels and risk tolerance. *Psychological Science, 21*(10), 1363–1368.

Centers for Disease Control and Prevention (CDC). (2004). Self-reported frequent mental distress among adults: United States, 1993–2001. *Morbidity and Mortality Weekly Report, 53*(41), 963–966.

Cohen, S., & Pressman, S. D. (2006). Positive affect and health. *Current Directions in Psychological Science, 15*, 122–125.

Cutter, G. R., Burke, G. L., Dyer, A. R., Friedman, G. D., Hilner, J. E., Hughes, G. H., … Wagenknecht, L. E. (1991). Cardiovascular risk factors in young adults: The CARDIA baseline monograph (Supplement 1). *Controlled Clinical Trials*, 1S–77S.

Danese, A., Moffitt, T. E., Harrington, H., Milne, B. J., Polanczyk, G., Pariante, C. M., … & Caspi, A. (2009). Adverse childhood experiences and adult risk factors for age-related disease: Depression, inflammation, and clustering of metabolic risk markers. *Archives of Pediatric & Adolescent Medicine, 163*(12), 1135–1143.

Dohrenwend, B. P., Levav, I., Shrout, P., Schwartz, S., Naveh, G., Link, B., . . . & Atueve, A. (1992). Socioeconomic status and psychiatric disorders: The causation-selection issue. *Science*, *255*, 946–952.

Eaker, E. D., Sullivan, L. M., Kelly-Hayes, M., D'Agostino, R. B., & Benjamin, E. J. (2007). Marital status, marital strain, and risk of coronary heart disease or total mortality: The Framingham offspring study. *Psychosomatic Medicine*, *69*(6), 509–513.

Epel, E. S., Blackburn, E. H., Lin, J., Dhabhar, F. S., Adler, N. E., Morrow, J. D., & Cawthon, R. M. (2004). Accelerated telomere shortening in response to life stress. *Proceedings of the National Academy of Sciences, USA*, *101*, 17312–17315.

Fiske, S. T., & Berdahl, J. L. (2007). Social power. In A. Kruglanski & E. T. Higgins (Eds.), *Social psychology: A handbook of basic principles* (pp. 678–692). New York and London: Guilford Press.

Folkman, S., & Lazarus, R. S. (1988). *The Ways of Coping Questionnaire*. Palo Alto, CA: Consulting Psychologists Press.

Folkman, S., Lazarus, R. S., Dunkel-Schetter, C., DeLongis, A., & Gruen, R. (1986). The dynamics of a stressful encounter: Cognitive appraisal, coping and encounter outcomes. *Journal of Personality and Social Psychology*, *50*, 992–1003.

Frank, J. B., & Thomas, C. D. (2003). Externalizing self-perceptions, self-silencing, and the prediction of eating pathology. *Canadian Journal of Behavioural Science*, *35*(3), 210–228.

Gallo, L. C., & Matthews, K. A. (2003). Understanding the association between socioeconomic status and physical health: Do negative emotions play a role? *Psychological Bulletin*, *129*(1), 10–51.

Goodman, E., Adler, N. E., Kawachi, I., Frazier, A. L., Huang, B., & Colditz, G. A. (2001). Adolescents' perceptions of social status: Development and evaluation of a new indicator. *Pediatrics*, *108*(2), 1–8.

Gratch, L. V., Bassett, M. E., & Attra, S. L. (2006). The relationship of gender and ethnicity to self-silencing and depression among college students. *Psychology of Women Quarterly*, *19*(4), 509–515

Gross, J. J. (2002). Emotion regulation: Affective, cognitive, and social consequences. *Psychophysiology*, *39*, 281–291.

Gross, J. J., & John, O. P. (2003). Individual differences in two emotion regulation processes: Implications for affect, relationships, and well-being. *Journal of Personality & Social Psychology*, *85*(2), 348–362.

Gross, J. J., & Levenson, R. W. (1997). Hiding feelings: The acute effects of inhibiting negative and positive emotion. *Journal of Abnormal Psychology*, *106*, 95–103.

Jack, D. C., & Dill, D. (1992). The Silencing the Self Scale: Schemas of intimacy associated with depression in women. *Psychology of Women Quarterly*, *16*, 97–106.

John, O. P., & Gross, J. J. (2004). Healthy and unhealthy emotion regulation: Personality processes, individual differences, and life span development. *Journal of Personality*, *72*, 1301–1333.

Keltner, D., Gruenfeld, D. H., & Anderson, C. (2003). Power, approach and inhibition. *Psychological Review*, *110*(2), 265–284.

Keltner, D., Young, R. C., Heerey, E. A., Oemig, C., & Monarch, N. D. (1998). Teasing in hierarchical and intimate relations. *Journal of Personality and Social Psychology*, *75*, 1231–1247.

Kraus, M. W., & Keltner, D. (2009). Signs of socioeconomic status: A thin-slicing approach. *Psychological Science*, *20*(1), 99–106.

Krieger, N. (1990). Racial and gender discrimination: Risk factors for high blood pressure? *Social Science & Medicine*, *30*(12), 1273–1281.

Langner, C. A., & Keltner, D. (2008). Social power and emotional experience: Actor and partner effects within dyadic interactions. *Journal of Experimental Social Psychology*, *44*, 848–856.

Leu, J., Yen, I. H., Gansky, S. A., Walton, E., Adler, N. E., & Takeuchi, D. T. (2008). The association between subjective social status and mental health among Asian immigrants: Investigating the influence of age at immigration. *Social Science & Medicine*, *66*(5), 1152–1164.

Liberatos, P., Link, B. G., & Kelsey, J. L. (1988). The measurement of social class in epidemiology. *Epidemiologic Reviews*, *10*, 87–121.

Mauss, I. B., Bunge, S. A., & Gross, J. J. (2007). Automatic emotion regulation. *Social and Personality Psychology Compass*, *1*, 146–167.

McDaniel, D. M., & Richards, C. S. (1990). Coping with dysphoria: Gender differences in college students. *Journal of Clinical Psychology*, *46*, 896–899.

Mirowsky, J. (1985). Depression and marital power: An equity model. *American Journal of Sociology*, *91*(3), 557–592.

Moffitt, T. E., Arseneault, L., Belsky, D., Dickson, N., Hancox, R. J., Harrington, H., . . . & Caspi, A. (2011). A gradient of childhood self-control predicts health, wealth, and public safety. *Proceedings of the National Academy of Sciences, USA*, *108*(7), 2693–2698.

Nolen-Hoeksema, S. (1987). Sex differences in unipolar depression: Evidence and theory. *Psychological Bulletin*, *101*, 259–282.

Preacher, K. J., & Hayes, A. F. (2004). SPSS and SAS procedures for estimating indirect effects in simple mediation models. *Behavior Research Methods, Instruments, & Computers*, *36*(4), 717–731.

Radloff, L. S. (1977). The CES-D Scale: A self-report depression scale for research in the general population. *Journal of Applied Psychological Measurement*, *1*, 385–401.

Riley, W. T., Treiber, F. A., & Woods, M. G. (1989). Anger and hostility in depression. *Journal of Nervous and Mental Disease*, *177*, 668–674.

Salovey, P., Rothman, A. J., Detweiler, J. B., & Steward, W. T. (2000). Emotional states and physical health. *American Psychologist*, *55*(1), 110–121.

Singh-Manoux, A., Adler, N. E., & Marmot, M. G. (2003). Subjective social status: Its determinants and its association with measures of ill-health in the Whitehall II study. *Social Science & Medicine*, *56*(6), 1321–1333.

Spielberger, C. D. (1985). Assessment of state and trait anxiety: Conceptual and methodological issues. *Southern Psychologist*, *2*(4), 6–16.

Spielberger, C. D. (1988). *Manual for the State-Trait Anger Expression Inventory (STAXI)*. Odessa, FL: Psychological Assessment Resources.

Srivastava, S., Tamir, M., McGonigal, K. M., John, O. P., & Gross, J. J. (2009). The social costs of emotion suppression: A prospective study of the transition to college. *Journal of Personality and Social Psychology*, *96*(4), 883–897.

Thomas, S. P., & Atakan, S. (1993). Trait anger, anger expression, stress, and health status of American and Turkish midlife women. *Health Care for Women International*, *14*, 129–143.

Tiedens, L. Z., Ellsworth, P. C., & Mesquita, B. (2000). Stereotypes about sentiments and status: Emotional expectations for high- and low-status group members. *Personality & Social Psychology Bulletin*, *26*(5), 560–574.

Tiedens, L. Z., & Fragale, A. (2003). Power moves: Complementarity in dominant and submissive nonverbal behavior. *Journal of Personality and Social Psychology*, *84*(3) 558–568.

Weissman, M. M., Sholomskas, D., Pottenger, M., Prusoff, B. A., & Locke, B. Z. (1977). Assessing depressive symptoms in five psychiatric populations: A validation study. *American Journal of Epidemiology*, *106*, 203–214.

Wheaton, B. (1978). The sociogenesis of psychological disorder: Reexamining the causal issues with longitudinal data. *American Sociological Review*, *43*, 383–403.

Winkelby, M. A., Jatulis, D. E., Frank, E., & Formann, S. P. (1992). Socioeconomic status and health: How education, income, and occupation contribute to risk factors for cardiovascular disease. *American Journal of Public Health*, *82*, 816–820.

Negatively Biased Emotion Perception in Depression as a Contributing Factor to Psychological Aggression Perpetration: A Preliminary Study

AMY D. MARSHALL
LAUREN M. SIPPEL

EMILY L. BELLEAU

ABSTRACT. Based on research linking depressive symptoms and intimate partner aggression perpetration with negatively biased perception of social stimuli, the present authors examined biased perception of emotional expressions as a mechanism in the frequently observed relationship between depression and psychological aggression perpetration. In all, 30 university students made valence ratings (negative to positive) of emotional facial expressions and completed measures of depressive symptoms and psychological aggression perpetration. As expected, depressive symptoms were positively associated with psychological aggression perpetration in an individual's current relationship, and this relationship was mediated by ratings of negative emotional expressions. These findings suggest that negatively biased perception of emotional expressions within the context of elevated depressive symptoms may represent an early stage of information processing that leads to aggressive relationship behaviors.

DEPRESSION IS CONSIDERED THE MOST pervasive and burdensome of all psychiatric disorders (Murray & Lopez, 1996). Prevalence rates for current and lifetime diagnoses of major depressive disorder have been estimated at 6.6% and 16.2%, respectively (Kessler et al., 2003). Moreover, community surveys suggest that subsyndromal depressive symptoms may currently affect as much as 20% of the general population (Kessler, Avenevoli, & Merikangas, 2001). In addition to a variety of physical health and employment consequences (Greenberg, Kessler, Nells, Finkelstein, & Berndt, 1996), individuals suffering from depressive symptoms often experience serious social and relationship difficulties (Wade & Cairney, 2000).

Depressive symptoms are associated with a wide range of interpersonal problems (Youngren & Lewinsohn, 1980). Couples in which one partner experiences elevated depressive symptoms demonstrate negative communication styles, including elevated verbal and nonverbal negative behaviors and lack of affectionate behaviors (Gotlib & Hooley, 1988; McCabe & Gotlib, 1993). Depressed partners, in particular, demonstrate high levels of tension, hostility, and criticism during problem-solving tasks (Gotlib & Beach, 1995), as well as diminished cooperation (Joiner, 2002), low assertiveness, and negative attributions for their partner's behavior (Gotlib & Whiffen, 1989). Evidence also indicates that elevated depressive symptoms are associated with increased perpetration of psychological aggression (i.e., coercive or aversive acts directed at the recipients' sense of self and intended to produce emotional harm or threat of harm; Murphy & Cascardi, 1999) in their intimate relationships (Kim & Capaldi, 2004).

Development of a clearer understanding of the association between depressive symptoms and psychological aggression perpetration is important for a number of reasons. First, psychological aggression is extremely pervasive, with reported rates of at least 74% of individuals in a nationally representative sample (Straus & Sweet, 1992), and the experience of psychological aggression leads to a host of negative physical and mental health consequences for both men and women (Coker, Smith, McKeown, & King, 2000; Straight, Harper, & Arias, 2003). Second, comparable rates of psychological aggression perpetration have been found across genders (Straus & Sweet, 1992), and the association between depressive symptoms and psychological aggression perpetration exists across genders (Kim & Capaldi, 2004), suggesting that a generalized mechanism may be responsible. Finally, the association between depressive symptoms and psychological aggression perpetration may represent the beginning of a cascade of negative consequences. Among a sample selected based on high risk for externalizing disorders, depressive symptoms in late adolescence have been found to be longitudinally associated with psychological aggression perpetration in young adulthood (Kim & Capaldi, 2004). In addition, premarital psychological aggression perpetration is a strong risk factor for the perpetration of physical aggression during marriage (Murphy & O'Leary, 1989). In the current study, which is based in a social information-processing framework (McFall, 1982), we examine biased perception of emotional expressions as a potential explanatory factor for the association between depressive symptoms and psychological aggression perpetration among a relatively low-risk sample of late adolescence men and women.

Several studies have found that individuals with elevated depressive symptoms have a negatively biased perception of social stimuli such as facial expressions of emotions. Consistent with the mood congruency principle (Bower, 1981) and the negative potentiation hypothesis (Beck, 1967), individuals experiencing elevated depressive symptoms have been found to selectively attend to negative social stimuli and have a negatively biased perception of negative social stimuli (Gur et al., 1992; Kellough, Beevers, Ellis, & Wells, 2008; Krompinger & Simons, 2009). Consistent with the positive attenuation hypothesis, these individuals also demonstrate diminished attention toward positive stimuli and perceive less positive affect in positive social stimuli (Cavanagh & Geisler, 2006; Hale, Jansen, Bouhuys, & van den Hoofdakker, 1998). It appears that individuals with elevated depressive symptoms experience these cognitive patterns simultaneously (Bylsma, Morris, & Rottenberg, 2008; Gur et al., 1992; Kellough et al., 2008). In the context of intimate relationships, particularly during episodes of conflict in which negative emotions (e.g., anger, sadness, disgust) are expressed, an overly negative perception of such emotions may be particularly likely to lead to elevated conflict and the use of psychological aggression.

Biased perception of emotional expressions has not previously been associated with the perpetration of psychological aggression, but two studies have found that emotion recognition deficits are associated with the perpetration of physical aggression in intimate relationships. Babcock, Green, and Webb (2008) found that violent husbands made more errors in the categorical recognition of neutral facial expressions than did nonviolent husbands, suggesting biased perception of these expressions. Unfortunately, the direction of this bias (i.e., whether violent husbands were more likely to choose positively or negatively valanced expressions when the displayed expression was neutral) was not reported. Marshall and Holtzworth-Munroe (2010), however, examined husbands' perception of their wives' expressions of happiness and fear and found that husbands' physical aggression perpetration was associated with misperceiving their wives' expressions of happiness as each negatively valanced emotion (i.e., anger, disgust, sadness, and fear) but not neutral, suggesting a negatively biased perception of emotional expressions.

In the current study, we examined biased perception of emotional expressions as a potential mechanism accounting for the expected relationship between depressive symptoms and use of psychological aggression in one's intimate relationship. Given the high prevalence rates of both subsyndromal depression (Kessler et al., 2001) and psychological aggression perpetration (Straus & Sweet, 1992), as well as research suggesting that depression may initiate a cascade of negative consequences among late adolescents (Kim & Capaldi, 2004), we examined these relationships among a relatively low-risk sample of late adolescence college students. In addition, based on research indicating that depressive disorders are not taxometric (Ruscio & Ruscio, 2000), we examined depressive symptoms dimensionally among this nonclinical sample. We focused on the perception of anger, disgust, and sad expressions given the relevance of these emotions to relationship conflicts (i.e., events during which psychological aggression is most likely to be used). Finally, to accurately characterize the generality of the negative potentiation hypothesis and to represent contemporary conceptualizations of emotion (LeDoux, 1996; Russell, 2003), we asked participants to rate emotional expressions on a valence dimension ranging from negative to positive. We hypothesized the following: (a) Participants' depressive symptoms will be positively correlated with the degree of their use of psychological aggression in their current relationship, (b) depressive symptoms will be associated with rating negatively valanced emotional expressions (i.e., anger, disgust, sadness) as more negative, (c) degree of psychological aggression perpetration will be associated with rating negatively valanced emotional expressions as more negative, and (d) ratings of negatively valanced emotional expressions will mediate the expected relationship between depressive symptoms and psychological aggression perpetration.

Method

Participants

Participants were 30 undergraduate participants (70% female) who reported currently being in an intimate relationship. We recruited them through an introductory psychology course at a large university in the Northeastern United States. Participants' mean age was 19.18 years ($SD = 1.47$ years). Most participants self-identified as Caucasian (96%). No participants reported having children, and 4.5% of participants indicated that they live with their current partner. Prior to becoming a college student, 50% of the sample lived in a rural area, and 50% of the sample lived in an urban area.

Measures and Materials

Beck Depression Inventory, Second Edition (BDI-II; Beck, Steer, & Brown, 1996). The BDI-II consists of 21 items for evaluating depressive symptoms experienced in the previous 2 weeks among clinical and nonclinical samples. Each item includes four self-report statements scored on a scale from 0 to 3. Items are summed to yield a total score with higher scores indicative of more severe depressive symptoms. The BDI-II has demonstrated good test–retest reliability and convergent validity with other measures of depression among clinical and nonclinical adult and adolescent samples (Beck, Steer, & Garbin, 1988; Osman, Barrios, Gutierrez, Williams, & Bailey, 2008). In the current sample, the internal consistency reliability coefficient was .82.

Revised Conflict Tactics Scale (CTS2; Straus, Hamby, & Boney-McCoy, 1996). The CTS2 is the most widely used self-report measure of partner aggression. The psychological aggression subscale includes eight items ranging from *insulted or swore at my partner* to *threatened to hit or throw something at my partner*. For each listed behavior, participants indicate how many times they or their partner had engaged in the behavior during the past year. Given that we did not expect many participants to be in their current relationship for the full year, we modified the response format to ask participants how many times each behavior occurred in their current relationship. We then dichotomized responses to reflect whether the behavior had or had not occurred and summed the number of positively endorsed items to yield a total score ranging from 0 to 8, indicating the number of different types of psychologically aggressive acts participants engaged in towards their current partner. This method of summarizing partner aggression data has been found to have more desirable psychometric properties than frequency scores, including greater reliability than methods that can be biased by memory limitations when attempting to report behavior frequencies (Moffitt et al., 1997). The CTS2 has demonstrated factorial validity (Connelly, Newton, & Aarons, 2005), and the CTS2 psychological aggression subscale has good internal consistency and test–retest reliability among a variety of samples (O'Leary & Williams, 2006; Straus, 2004; Vega & O'Leary, 2007), as well as convergent validity across a wide range of measures (Schumacher, Slep, & Heyman, 2001; Straus, 2004). In the current sample, the internal consistency reliability coefficient was .75.

Emotional expressions stimuli. Posed static emotional expressions stimuli were developed through the recruitment of untrained actors from the community. Actors consisted of 26 Caucasian, African American, and Asian men and women of various ages, ranging from 19 to 62 years. Emotional expressions stimuli from 19 actors were developed by Marshall and Holtzworth-Munroe (2010). Identical procedures were used to develop emotional expressions stimuli for the additional 7 actors. That is, instructions for eliciting emotional expressions were developed according to the Facial Affect Coding System (FACS; Ekman & Friesen, 1978) and using the minimum muscular movements for each emotion recommended by Parke and Waters (1996). Actors were informed of the target emotion (i.e., fear, sadness, anger, disgust, happiness, or surprise), and the expression was demonstrated; then they were coached to move each muscle included in the target expression. To make the stimuli representative of naturalistic expressions, expressions were obtained at four intensity levels. Actors began by displaying the highest intensity expression, then slowly relaxed their facial muscles while photographs were taken. This process was repeated until four separate intensity levels were obtained, each judged by the first author to provide an accurate portrayal of the target emotion according to the FACS. One photograph of each actor displaying a neutral expression (i.e., no visible muscular movements) was also taken. Photographs were transformed to gray scale, cropped around the face, and increased in brightness, if necessary. The total stimulus set included 650 photos.

Procedures

Participants were asked to view a series of photographs of emotional expressions on a computer and rate the valence of each photograph on a Likert scale ranging from *negative* (1) to *positive* (9). Photographs were displayed one at a time, with the scale shown on the computer screen below the photograph. To decrease participant fatigue, each participant rated half of the total set of 650 photographs, including the full set of photographs from 13 different actors (approximately half were female). After rating the facial affect stimuli, participants completed self-report measures on a computer.

Results

Descriptive Statistics

Of the sample, 23 participants (77%) reported having engaged in psychological aggression during their current relationship, and the individuals' acts ranged among one to six types of psychologically aggressive acts ($M = 2.20$, $SD = 1.85$). BDI-II depression scores ranged from 0 to 27, with a mean of 8.89 ($SD = 6.4$), indicating that most participants were currently experiencing minimal depressive symptoms, but some participants reported moderate to severe depressive symptoms. As expected, expressions of happiness were rated as the most positively valanced ($M = 6.81, SD = 0.99$), and all negatively valanced emotional expressions were rated as such. Expressions of anger were rated as most negative ($M = 3.01, SD = 0.95$), followed by sadness ($M = 3.15, SD = 0.87$), and disgust ($M = 3.36, SD = 0.96$). Unexpectedly, neutral expressions ($M = 3.71, SD = 0.87$) were rated somewhat more negatively than expressions of fear ($M = 3.89, SD = 0.85$). Expressions of surprise ($M = 4.79, SD = 0.81$) were also rated somewhat negatively. For both conceptual purposes and to ensure that negatively valanced expressions were truly viewed as negative, we computed a negative-emotions composite score comprised of average ratings of anger, sadness, and disgust. This composite score had a mean valence rating of 3.17 ($SD = 0.89$).

Associations Among Study Variables

Bivariate correlations among study variables are displayed in Table 1. As predicted, depressive symptoms were significantly correlated with psychological aggression perpetration ($r = .37, p < .05$). In addition, depressive symptoms were significantly correlated with participant ratings of the negative emotions composite variable ($r = -.36, p < .05$). Across individual emotions, depressive symptoms were most strongly correlated with ratings of sad expressions ($r = -.44, p < .05$). Also as predicted, psychological aggression perpetration was significantly correlated with participant ratings of the negative emotions composite variable ($r = -.40, p < .05$). Across individual emotions, psychological aggression also was most strongly correlated with ratings of sad expressions ($r = -.44, p < .05$).

TABLE 1. Intercorrelations Among Study Variables

Variable	1	2	3	4	5	6	7	8	9
1. Depressive symptoms	—								
2. Psychological aggression	.37*	—							
3. Ratings of negative emotions	-.36*	-.40*	—						
4. Ratings of angry expressions	-.31†	-.36†	.98***	—					
5. Ratings of disgust expressions	-.31	-.35†	.95***	.90***	—				
6. Ratings of sad expressions	-.44*	.44*	.95***	.92***	.84***	—			
7. Ratings of fearful expressions	-.20	-.19	.79***	.77***	.77***	.75***	—		
8. Ratings of surprise expressions	.01	-.04	.34†	.27	.36†	.36*	.55**	—	
9. Ratings of neutral expressions	-.17	-.12	.37*	.31†	.28	.51**	.15	.52**	—
10. Ratings of happy expressions	.20	.34†	-.33	-.38*	-.30	-.27	-.19	.52*	.48*

Note. Negative emotions composite variable includes ratings of angry, disgust, and sad expressions.
†$p < .10$, *$p < .05$, **$p < .01$, ***$p < .001$, all two-tailed.

TABLE 2. Mediating Effect of Ratings of Negative Emotions on the Relationship Between Depressive Symptoms and Psychological Aggression Perpetration

Effect	Unstandardized b	SE	Standardized β	t
Depressive symptoms on ratings of negative emotions	−0.05	0.02	−0.36	−2.07*
Ratings of negative emotions on psychological aggression	−0.82	0.36	−0.40	−2.29*
Depressive symptoms on psychological aggression	0.11	0.05	0.37	2.14*
Depressive symptoms on psychological aggression, accounting for ratings of negative emotions	0.08	0.05	0.27	1.45

*$p < .05$, two-tailed.

Mediating Effect of Ratings of Negative Emotional Expressions on the Relationship Between Depressive Symptoms and Psychological Aggression Perpetration

To test the hypothesis that participants' ratings of negative emotional expressions will mediate the relationship between depressive symptoms and psychological aggression perpetration, we conducted mediation analyses, including Preacher and Hayes' (2004) procedures for conducting a bootstrap analysis of the sampling distribution of the indirect effect. As displayed in Table 2, the direct effect of depressive symptoms on ratings of negative emotions was statistically significant ($\beta = -0.36$, $p < .05$), the direct effect of ratings of negative emotions on psychological aggression perpetration was statistically significant ($\beta = -0.40$, $p < .05$), and the direct effect of depressive symptoms on psychological aggression perpetration was statistically significant ($\beta = 0.37, p < .05$). In addition, the effect of depressive symptoms on psychological aggression perpetration was reduced to nonsignificance when accounting for the effect of ratings of negative emotions ($\beta = 0.27$, ns). Results of the bootstrap analysis indicate that mediation was present ($M = 0.03$, $SE = 0.02$; 95% $CI = 0.001$–0.091).[1]

Discussion

In the current investigation, we examined whether biased perception of emotional expressions serves as an explanatory mechanism in the expected relationship between depressive symptoms and psychological aggression perpetration. As hypothesized, negatively biased ratings of facial expressions of anger, sadness, and disgust mediated the relationship between depressive symptoms and psychological aggression perpetration. This finding integrates prior research demonstrating biased perception of emotional expressions in depression with research demonstrating a relationship between biased perception of emotional expressions and relationship aggression to provide a more comprehensive account of how depressive symptoms may lead to negative relationship consequences such as the use of psychological aggression. Indeed, this is the first known study to demonstrate an association between biased perception of emotional expressions and psychological aggression perpetration. From a social information-processing perspective (McFall, 1982), these results suggest that biased perception of emotional expressions may be an early step in a series of information-processing stages that lead to negative relationship behaviors. For example, biased perception of emotional expressions may contribute to the negative attributions for partners' behavior that have previously been documented among individuals with elevated depressive symptoms (Gotlib & Whiffen, 1989), as well as linked to the perpetration of psychological aggression (Schumacher et al., 2001). The current study provides a foundation upon which to examine such process questions.

The current study result indicating that depressive symptoms were associated with greater perpetration of psychological aggression in one's current relationship is consistent with extensive research documenting negative social and relationship consequences of depression (Gotlib & Beach, 1995; Youngren & Lewinsohn, 1980) and extends the only known prior investigation of this specific phenomenon (Kim & Capaldi, 2004) to a relatively low-risk sample. This extension demonstrates that variability within a relatively mild range of depressive symptoms can have serious consequences for intimate relationships. Moreover, the elevated risk for psychological aggression perpetration among individuals experiencing depressive symptoms may represent the beginning of a cascade of negative relationship behaviors, including physical aggression perpetration, as young adults begin to enter long-term committed relationships. Thus, in addition to demonstrating the utility of a dimensional conceptualization of depression, this research indicates that preventive interventions may be beneficial to individuals experiencing mild to moderate depressive symptoms who may not otherwise be seen in clinical settings.

Participants' depressive symptoms were negatively associated with a composite variable representing valence ratings (from negative to positive) of anger, sad, and disgust expressions and were independently associated with ratings of sad emotional expressions. These results extend prior research supporting the negative potentiation hypothesis (Gur et al., 1992; Kellough et al., 2008; Krompinger & Simons, 2009), which proposes that individuals with elevated depressive symptoms exhibit a negative bias in perceiving emotional stimuli. In contrast, depressive symptoms were not associated with rating positive (i.e., happy) emotional expressions as less positive, thus failing to support the positive attenuation hypothesis. Together, these results may suggest that the negative potentiation hypothesis yields a stronger effect size than the positive attenuation hypothesis and that we were not able to identify an existing association between depressive symptoms and ratings of positive expressions given the limited power of the current study. Alternatively, this pattern of results may be specific to the unique aspects of the current sample. That is, this sample of college students reported less severe symptoms of depression than those reported by other samples; thus, they may not have been experiencing particular aspects of depression such as anhedonia, which, based on the mood congruency principle, is theorized to be the cause of positive attenuation of perceptions of social stimuli.

The current study is the first known study to demonstrate an association between biased perception of emotional expressions and perpetration of psychological aggression. This research builds upon two prior studies demonstrating associations between emotion recognition skills and physical aggression perpetration (Babcock et al., 2008; Marshall & Holtworth-Munroe, 2010) and indicates that biased perception of emotions may be implicated in a wide range of negative relationship behaviors. Within the context of cognitive-behavioral social skills training, treatment providers have begun to teach violent husbands to accurately label emotional expressions as a means of improving their skills for managing conflict in their relationships and preventing future violence (Babcock & La Taillade, 2000). Although such therapy techniques have not yet been tested, they may also be applicable to therapy for distressed couples who engage in psychological aggression.

Some limitations of the current study warrant discussion. Importantly, the sample size is small, thus limiting confidence in the generalizability of the study results. More specifically, the small sample size prohibited us from exploring possible gender differences in relationships among study variables. Although we do not have reason to propose gender differences given that prior literature has documented similar effects of depressive symptoms on psychological aggression perpetration (Straus & Sweet, 1992) and perception of emotional stimuli (Kellough et al., 2008) across genders, the current sample largely comprised women, and thus the questionable generalizability of the current results is particularly salient when attempting to generalize to men. A second limitation is the fact that we did not obtain independent partner reports of psychological aggression. It may be that the experience of elevated depressive symptoms alters the perception and thus reporting of aggression perpetration in one's relationship. Finally, we did not use a standardized set of emotional expression stimuli. However, these stimuli have been used previously and yielded results as expected (Marshall & Holtworth-Munroe, 2010). In addition, emotional expressions were rated in terms of valence as expected. That is, expressions of happiness were rated as positively valanced, and expressions of anger, sadness, disgust, fear, and surprise were rated as negatively valanced. The only unexpected result was the finding that participants rated neutral expressions as negative and more negative than expressions of fear. This finding may be due to the neutral stimuli being invalid or due to the fear stimuli's being invalid, as suggested by prior research indicating that expressions of fear are the least accurately identified of the basic emotions (Calvo & Lundqvist, 2008; Lederman et al., 2007). In any case, the neutral and fear stimuli were not used in the primary analyses, and thus they should not have biased the current study results. Given these potential limitations, the current study results should be considered extremely preliminary.

Despite these limitations, the current study has a number of strengths. First, the emotional expression stimuli were developed without the use of morphing techniques, and yet they represent emotions expressed at lower intensity levels than the prototypical facial expressions utilized in many other studies. Because low-intensity emotional expressions are more representative of the expressions encountered in everyday life and at the beginning of a conflict episode, these stimuli are likely more externally valid (Russell, 2003). In addition, these stimuli were effectively used with a valence rating system, consistent with prior studies indicating that categorical emotions can be rated along a valence dimension in a valid manner (Dunn, Dalgleish, Lawrence, Cusack, & Ogilvie, 2004). Second, we identified a substantial mediation effect, despite the presence of low power and use of a relatively low-risk sample. Thus, the relationships identified may be present among a wide range of populations (e.g., clinical and nonclinical populations). Finally, the current study moves beyond the examination of simple associations between depressive symptoms and relationship outcomes to examine a potential cognitive mechanism (i.e., perception of emotional expressions) responsible for the relationship. Moreover, this mechanism is one that is likely malleable through cognitive therapy protocols that address negative biases within depression.

We recommend that future research be designed to replicate and build upon the current study in a number of ways. Because the current results cannot speak to emotion recognition skills among individuals with severe depression and common comorbid disorders, generalizability to such a population should be tested. Generalizability to different age groups and more ethnically and racially diverse samples should also be tested. In addition, because we did not directly measure participants' perception of their partners' emotions, partner-specific emotional expression stimuli should be developed and used to test the current model. Most importantly, because our results are based on cross-sectional data, experimental and longitudinal work should be initiated to test for the causal directionality that is assumed in the current study. Several alternative models may exist. For example, biased emotion perception may lead to elevated depressive symptoms and may lead one to perceive and report on one's use of psychological aggression in an altered fashion. It is also possible that engagement in psychological aggression may lead one to become more depressed and may alter the perception of emotional expressions. Because participants in the current study reported on their use of psychological aggression during the past year, rather than prospectively reporting on such behavior, it is especially important to rule out the possibility that engagement in psychological aggression is a predictor rather than an outcome variable. Particular laboratory methods, such as mood induction techniques and laboratory aggression paradigms, may be used to rule out these alternative explanations.[2] We hope that with the completion of additional research, the results of this study and future studies can be applied to the development of interventions to alleviate the negative social and relationship consequences of depression.

NOTES

1. To examine alternative directional paths, we also tested two reverse mediation models. First, we examined depressive symptoms as a mediator of the link between ratings of negative emotional expressions and psychological aggression perpetration. The indirect path for this model was not statistically significant ($M = -0.21$, $SE = 0.23$; 95% $CI = -0.776$–0.133). Second, we examined psychological aggression perpetration as a mediator of the link between depressive symptoms and ratings of negative emotional expressions. The indirect path for this model also was not statistically significant ($M = -0.02$, $SE = 0.01$; 95% $CI = -0.046$–0.003).

2. We thank an anonymous reviewer for these suggestions.

REFERENCES

Babcock, J. C., Green, C. E., & Webb, S. A. (2008). Decoding deficits of different types of batterers during presentation of facial affect slides. *Journal of Family Violence, 23,* 295–302. doi:10.1007/s10896-008-9151-1

Babcock, J. C., & LaTaillade, J. J. (2000). Evaluating interventions for men who batter. In J. P. Vincent & E. N. Jouriles (Eds.), *Domestic violence: Guidelines for research-informed practice* (pp. 37–77). Philadelphia: Jessica Kingsley Publishers.

Beck, A. T. (1967). *Depression: Clinical, experimental, and theoretical aspects.* New York: Harper and Row.

Beck, A. T., Steer, R. A., & Brown, G. K. (1996). *Beck Depression Inventory: Second edition manual.* San Antonio, TX: Psychological Corporation.

Beck, A. T., Steer, R. A., & Garbin, M. G. (1988). Psychometric properties of the Beck Depression Inventory: Twenty-five years of evaluation. *Clinical Psychology Review, 8,* 77–100. doi:10.1016/0272-7358(88)90050-5

Bower, G. H. (1981). Mood and memory. *American Psychologist, 39,* 129–148. doi:10.1037/0003-066X.36.2.129

Bylsma, L. M., Morris, B. H., & Rottenberg, J. (2008). A meta-analysis of emotional reactivity in major depressive disorder. *Clinical Psychology Review, 28,* 676–691. doi:10.1016/j.cpr.2007.10.001

Calvo, M. G., & Lundqvist, D. (2008). Facial expressions of emotion (KDEF): Identification under different display-duration conditions. *Behavior Research Methods, 40,* 109–115. doi:10.3758/BRM.40.1.109

Cavanagh, J., & Geisler, M. W. (2006). Mood effects on the ERP processing of emotional intensity in faces: A P3 investigation with depressed students. *International Journal of Psychophysiology, 60,* 27–33. doi:10.1016/j.ijpsycho.2005.04.005

Coker, A. L., Smith, P. H., McKeown, R. E., & King, M. J. (2000). Frequency and correlates of intimate partner violence by type: Physical, sexual, and psychological battering. *American Journal of Public Health, 90,* 1015–1023. doi:10.2105/AJPH.90.4.553

Connelly, C. D., Newton, R. R., & Aarons, G. A. (2005). A psychometric examination of English and Spanish versions of the Revised Conflict Tactics Scales. *Journal of Interpersonal Violence, 20,* 1560–1579. doi: 10.1177/0886260505280341

Dunn, B., Dalgleish, T., Lawrence, A. D., Cusack, R., & Ogilvie, A. D. (2004). Categorical and dimensional reports of experienced affect to emotion-inducing pictures. *Journal of Abnormal Psychology, 113,* 654–660. doi:10.1037/0021-843X.113.4.654

Ekman, P., & Friesen, W. V. (1978). *Facial Affect Coding System: A technique for the measurement of facial movement.* Palo Alto, CA: Consulting Psychologists Press.

Greenberg, P., Kessler, R., Nells, T., Finkelstein, S. N., & Berndt, E. R. (1996). Depression in the workplace: An economic perspective. In J. P. Feighner & W. F. Boyer (Eds.), *Selective serotonin reuptake inhibitors: Advances in basic research and clinical practice* (pp. 327–363). New York: Wiley.

Gotlib, I. H., & Beach, S. R. H. (1995). A marital/family discord model of depression: Implications for therapeutic intervention. In N. Jacobson & A. S. Gurman (Eds.), *Clinical handbook of couple therapy* (pp. 411–436). New York: Guilford Press.

Gotlib, I. H., & Hooley, J. M. (1988). Depression and marital distress: Current status and future directions. In S. Duck, D. F. Hay, S. E. Hobfoll, W. Ickes, & B. M. Montgomery (Eds.), *Handbook of personal relationships* (pp. 543–570). New York: Wiley.

Gotlib, I. H., & Whiffen, V. E. (1989). Depression and marital functioning: An examination of specificity and gender differences. *Journal of Abnormal Psychology, 98,* 23–30. doi:10.1037/0021-843X.98.1.23

Gur, R. C., Erwin, R. J., Gur, R. E., Zwil, A. S., Heimberg, C., & Kraemer, H. C. (1992). Facial emotion discrimination: II. Behavioral findings in depression. *Psychiatry Research, 42,* 241–251. doi:10.1016/0165-1781(92)90116-K

Hale, W. W., Jansen, J. H. C., Bouhuys, A. L., & van den Hoofdakker, R. H. (1998). The judgment of facial expressions by depressed patients, their partners, and controls. *Journal of Affective Disorders, 47,* 63–70. doi:10.1016/S0165-0327(97)00112-2

Joiner, T. E. (2002). Depression in its interpersonal context. In I. H. Gotlib & C. L. Hammen (Eds.), *Handbook of depression* (pp. 295–313). New York: Guilford Press.

Kellough, J. L., Beevers, C. G., Ellis, A. J., & Wells, T. (2008). Time course of selective attention in clinically depressed young adults: An eye tracking study. *Behavior Research and Therapy, 46,* 1238–1243. doi:10.1016/j.brat.2008.07.004

Kessler, R. C., Avenevoli, S., & Merikangas, S. K. (2001). Mood disorders in children and adolescents: An epidemiological perspective. *Biological Psychiatry, 49,* 1002–1014. doi:10.1016/S0006-3223(01)01129-5

Kessler, R. C., Berglund, P., Demler, O., Jin, R., Koretz, D., Merikangas, K. R., et al. (2003). The epidemiology of major depressive disorder: Results from the National Comorbidity Survey Replication (NCS-R). *Journal of the American Medical Association*, *289*, 3095–3105. doi:10.1001/jama.289.23.3095

Kim, H. K., & Capaldi, D. M. (2004). The association of antisocial behavior and depressive symptoms between partners and risk for aggression in romantic relationships. *Journal of Family Psychology*, *18*, 82–96. doi:10.1037/0893-3200.18.1.82

Krompinger, J. W., & Simons, R. F. (2009). Electrophysiological indicators of emotion processing biases in depressed undergraduates. *Biological Psychiatry*, *81*, 153–163. doi:10.1016/j.biopsycho.2009.03.007

Lederman, S. J., Klatzky, R. L., Abramowicz, A., Salsman, K., Kitada, R., & Hamilton, C. (2007). Haptic recognition of static and dynamic expressions of emotion in the live face. *Psychological Science*, *18*, 158–164. doi: 10.1111/j.1467-9280.2007.01866.x

LeDoux, J. (1996). *The emotional brain*. New York: Touchstone.

Marshall, A. D., & Holtworth-Munroe, A. (2010). Recognition of wives' emotional expressions: A mechanism in the relationship between psychopathology and intimate partner violence perpetration. *Journal of Family Psychology*, *24*, 21–30. doi:10.1037/a0017952

McCabe, S. B., & Gotlib, I. H. (1993). Interactions of couples with and without a depressed spouse: Self-report and observations of problem solving situations. *Journal of Social and Personal Relationships*, *10*, 589–599. doi:10.1177/0265407593104007

McFall, R. M. (1982). A review and reformulation of the concept of social skills. *Behavioral Assessment*, *4*, 1–33. doi:10.1007/BF01321377

Moffitt, T. E., Caspi, A., Krueger, R. F., Magdol, L., Margolin, G., Silva, P. A., & Sydney, R. (1997). Do partners agree about abuse in their relationship? A psychometric evaluation of interpartner agreement. *Psychological Assessment*, *9*, 47–56. doi:10.1037/1040-3590.9.1.47

Murphy, C. M., & Cascardi, M. (1999). Psychological abuse in marriage and dating relationships. In R. L. Hampton (Ed.), *Family violence* (2nd ed.; pp. 198–226). Thousand Oaks, CA: Sage.

Murphy, C. M., & O'Leary, K. D. (1989). Psychological aggression predicts physical aggression in early marriage. *Journal of Consulting and Clinical Psychology*, *57*, 579–582. doi:10.1037/0022-006X.57.5.579

Murray, C. J. L., & Lopez, A. D. (1996). *The global burden of disease: A comprehensive assessment to 2020*. Cambridge, MA: Harvard University Press.

O'Leary K., & Williams, M. C. (2006). Agreement about acts of aggression in marriage. *Journal of Family Psychology*, *20*, 656–662. doi:10.1037/0893-3200.20.4.656

Osman, A., Barrios, F. X., Gutierrez, P. M., Williams, J. E., & Bailey, J. (2008). Psychometric properties of the Beck Depression Inventory-II in nonclinical adolescent samples. *Journal of Clinical Psychology*, *64*, 83–102. doi:10.1002/jclp.20433

Parke, F. I., & Waters, K. (1996). *Computer facial animation*. Wellesley, MA: A. K. Peters.

Preacher, K. J., & Hayes, A. F. (2004). SPSS and SAS procedures for estimating indirect effects in simple mediation models. *Behavior Research Methods, Instruments, & Computers*, *36*, 717–731. doi:10.3758/BF03206553

Ruscio, J., & Ruscio, A. M. (2000). Informing the continuity controversy: A taxometric analysis of depression. *Journal of Abnormal Psychology*, *109*, 473–487. doi:10.1037/0021-843X.109.3.473

Russell, J. A. (2003). Core affect and the psychological construction of emotion. *Psychological Review*, *110*, 145–172. doi:10.1037/0033-295X.110.1.145

Schumacher, J. A., Slep, A. M. S., & Heyman, R. E. (2001). Risk factors for male-to-female partner psychological abuse. *Aggression and Violent Behavior*, *6*, 255–268. doi: 10.1016/S1359-1789(00)00025-2

Straight, E. S., Harper, W. K., & Arias, I. (2003). The impact of partner psychological abuse on health behaviors and health status in college women. *Journal of Interpersonal Violence, 18*, 1035–1054. doi:10.1177/0886260503254512

Straus, M. A. (2004). Cross-cultural reliability and validity of the Revised Conflict Tactics Scales: A study of university student dating couples in 17 nations. *Cross-Cultural Research, 38*, 407–432. doi:10.1177/1069397104269543

Straus, M. A., Hamby, S. L., & Boney-McCoy, S. (1996). The Revised Conflict Tactics Scales (CTS2): Development and preliminary psychometric data. *Journal of Family Issues, 17*, 283–316. doi:10.1177/019251396017003001

Straus, M. A., & Sweet, S. (1992). Verbal/symbolic aggression in couples: Incidence rates and relationships to personal characteristics. *Journal of Marriage and Family, 54*, 346–357. doi:10.2307/353066

Sullivan, M. D., La Croix, A. Z., & Russo, J. E. (2001). Depression and self-reported physical health in patients with coronary disease: Mediating and moderating factors. *Psychosomatic Medicine, 63*, 248–256. Retrieved from http://www.psychosomaticmedicine.org/

Vega, E. M., & O'Leary, D. K. (2007). Test-retest reliability of the Revised Conflict Tactics Scale (CTS2). *Journal of Family Violence, 22*, 703–708. doi:10.1007/s10896-007-9118-7

Wade, T. J., & Cairney, J. (2000). Major depressive disorder and marital transition among mothers: Results from a national panel study. *Journal of Nervous and Mental Disease, 188*, 741–750. doi:10.1097/00005053-200011000-00004

Youngren, M. A., & Lewinsohn, P. M. (1980). The functional relation between depression and problematic interpersonal behavior. *Journal of Abnormal Psychology, 89*, 333–341. doi:10.1037/0021-843X.89.3.333

Index